THE
MOUND-BUILDERS

A RECONSTRUCTION OF THE LIFE OF A PREHISTORIC AMERICAN
RACE, THROUGH EXPLORATION AND INTERPRETATION OF THEIR
EARTH MOUNDS, THEIR BURIALS, AND THEIR CULTURAL REMAINS

BY

HENRY CLYDE SHETRONE

THE UNIVERSITY OF ALABAMA PRESS

Tuscaloosa

Originally published by D. Appleton and Company, 1930

∞

The paper on which this book is printed meets the minimum requirements of
American National Standard for Information Science–Permanence of Paper for
Printed Library Materials, ANSI Z39.48–1984.

Library of Congress Cataloging-in-Publication Data

Shetrone, H. C.
The mound-builders / Henry Clyde Shetrone.
p. cm. — (Classics in southeastern archaeology) "Originally published by D.
Appleton and Company, 1930." Includes bibliographical references and index.
ISBN 0-8173-5086-1 (pbk. : alk. paper)
1. Mound-builders—United States.   2. Mounds—United States.   3. Burial—
United States.   4. Grave goods—United States.   5. United States—Antiquities.
I. Title.   II. Series. E73.S55 2004 977'.01—dc22
2003018557

DANVILLE
PUBLIC
LIBRARY

A gift in memory
of
Oscar McClain

PREFACE

T HE MOUND-BUILDERS" is dedicated to the average man and woman who, although fully awake to the human interest in their story, lack time and opportunity for digesting the rather extensive but often unavailable literature on the subject. This volume is intended to afford a belated answer to the oft-heard query, "Where can I find a book that will give me the important facts regarding the Moundbuilders?" If the professional prehistorian also finds the book a handy compendium of the archæology of the general mound area, its publication will be more than justified.

In a sense, the preparation of *The Mound-Builders* has been a pioneer undertaking, in that it attempts to combine scientific accuracy and popular presentation. Difficulties admittedly have been numerous; but the recent gratifying tendency to popularize science and the encouragement and assistance tendered by the author's coworkers in the field have removed all cause for hesitation.

Planning the book with the idea of obtaining something of order and sequence and of sustaining human interest was not the least of the problems involved. Considerable license admittedly has been taken in attempting to effect the desired result. Outside of a few restricted areas the mound-building complex has been only partly analyzed, and therefore it is difficult to compass as a whole. Technical archæological method, with its emphasis on culture groups and areas, with their present lack of definition, proved to be impractical for popular use. "Cultures," so-called, and "culture areas" are adaptable as working bases, but they defy specific application in a presentation of this character.

The scheme of "mound areas" herein employed is the author's method of meeting the difficulties which impose themselves. While these assumed areas have considerable basis of justification, they are not ultimately satisfactory—an admission which emphasizes the need for concerted and exhaustive exploration of the mound area as a whole and the coördination of resultant findings.

The author bespeaks the tolerance of his readers, particularly those who, through training and experience, are in a position to note his errors. The scant attention accorded the non-mound-building peoples of the area under consideration may at first thought appear regrettable; but since there is little or nothing in the culture of these which does not appear in that of the so-called Mound-builders, there appears to be no reason for their inclusion in the volume.

While the Ohio area is perhaps the best known of the several considered and thus furnishes the nucleus for the book, it would have been impossible of realization without the aid of authorities in the remaining areas and states. The author takes this opportunity of extending grateful acknowledgment and recognition to the following for photographs, data, mound locations, and permission to reproduce illustrations from publications:

Miss Margaret E. Ashley, Phillips Academy, Andover, Mass.
Dr. S. A. Barrett, Public Museum of the City of Milwaukee
Mr. Peter A. Brannon, Alabama Anthropological Society
Mr. Calvin A. Brown, University of Mississippi
Mr. Charles E. Brown, State Historical Society of Wisconsin
    Bureau of American Ethnology, Washington
Dr. Amos W. Butler, Indianapolis
Hon. P. E. Cox, State Archæologist of Tennesssee
Dr. Don L. Dickson, Lewistown, Illinois
Messrs. E. L. and M. H. Dickson, Lewistown, Illinois
Dr. Carl E. Guthe, University of Michigan
Dr. W. B. Hinsdale, University of Michigan
Dr. Charles R. Keyes, State Historical Society of Iowa
Mr. Stewart Kidd, Cincinnati
Dr. Wilton M. Krogman, University of Chicago
Mr. George Langford, Joliet, Illinois
Mr. J. Arthur MacLean, Toledo Museum of Art
Mr. W. C. McKern, Public Museum of the City of Milwaukee
Mr. Clarence B. Moore, Philadelphia
Dr. Warren K. Moorhead, Phillips Academy, Andover, Mass.

Prof. William H. Over, University of South Dakota
Dr. Arthur C. Parker, Rochester Municipal Museum
Mr. F. M. Setzler, Indiana Archæological Survey
Dr. John M. Swanton, Bureau of American Ethnology
Prof. William S. Webb, University of Kentucky
Dr. C. C. Willoughby, Peabody Museum, Harvard University
Dr. W. J. Wintemberg, National Museum of Canada

Members of the Ohio State Museum staff have been uniformly helpful; special mention is due the following: Miss Alice Senseney Davis, assistant librarian, for preparing the index; Mr. Howard R. Goodwin, staff artist, for drawings; Dr. Emerson F. Greenman, curator of archæology, for aid in compilation, and Mr. H. R. McPherson, business agent, for assistance in compiling data.

Mr. Arthur C. Johnson, Sr., president of the Ohio State Archæological and Historical Society, as well as members of its Board of Trustees, have rendered invaluable assistance and encouragement in the preparation of *The Mound-Builders*.

H. C. S.

CONTENTS

CHAPTER I

EARLY THEORIES AS TO ORIGIN AND IDENTITY

CHAPTER II

DISTRIBUTION AND CLASSIFICATION OF THE MOUNDS

CHAPTER III

ARCHITECTURE AND ENGINEERING

CHAPTER IV

AGRICULTURE, COMMERCE, AND INDUSTRY

CONTENTS

CONTENTS

ILLUSTRATIONS

INTRODUCTION TO THE 2004 EDITION

HENRY CLYDE SHETRONE AND THE MOUND-BUILDERS

Bradley T. Lepper

Rude effigies of by-gone savage hearts,
    Wrought from the silent everlasting rocks;
What varied store of long-forgotten arts
    And mystic rites, within themselves they lock!

Mute voices from the ages they span,
    Once vibrant—in a moment's hurried flight—
"Come be the guest of Death" their message ran:
    Thus ruled the primal law when might was right.

Footprints—last records of the fading van
    Of stealthy hosts, along the trail well worn;
Memorial of primeval bronze-browed man,
    His silent passing to an unknown bourne.

                                          H. C. Shetrone (1907)

HENRY CLYDE SHETRONE

Henry Clyde Shetrone (1876–1954) was born in Millersport, Ohio, a small town twenty miles due west of Columbus and barely ten miles south of the remarkable Newark Earthworks. Frank Setzler (1956:296), in his obituary of Shetrone published in *American Antiquity*, speculated that growing up in the vicinity of these remarkable monuments of antiquity may have had something to do with Shetrone's eventual decision to seek his fame and fortune as an archaeologist of the Mound Builders. Setzler (1956:296) and others have repeated the claim that he attended, but did not graduate from, Denison University in Granville, Ohio. There are, however, no records in the university's archives to substantiate this assertion. Certainly, Denison awarded him an honorary doctorate in 1944, acknowledging his achievements regardless of whether he was ever formally enrolled at the university.

Shetrone was a slightly built man, five feet, seven inches tall, with gray eyes and fine, almost effeminate, features. He married Lillie Mae Klinger of Columbus in 1905, but beyond that, we know little of his private life. Upon his death in 1954, his obituaries indicate that he was survived by a cousin and a brother-in-law, both of whom were living with him at the time. The cause of his death is not mentioned.

Shetrone served in the U.S. Volunteer Signal Corps during the Spanish-American War in 1898. He was stationed in Cuba and had attained the rank of corporal by the time he was discharged. After the war, he stayed on as the provincial superintendent of telegraphy for the Cuban government. Upon his return to the United States in 1902, he was employed as a commercial telegrapher in New York City. In 1903, he came back to Ohio and worked as a telegrapher for various newspapers in Columbus. Over the next decade, he worked his way up from press telegrapher to telegraph editor to financial editor to feature writer for the American Press Association.

Shetrone was passionately interested in archaeology and enjoyed writing stories about William C. Mills's excavations at the Adena, Gartner, Harness, and the smaller, conjoined, Seip mounds (Setzler 1956:297). Mills was, at that time, curator of archaeology for the Ohio State Archaeological and Historical Society, and he and Shetrone soon became good friends. In a letter Mills wrote to a Prof. Talkington of Lewiston, Idaho, in response to a request to purchase "specimens of the mound builders," Mills referred Talkington to Shetrone: "Mr. Shetrone is a very estimable gentleman, and . . . is one of our foremost collectors in Ohio." He "has one of the largest private collections in the State, and he may be able to furnish you with duplicates from his collection" (Mills 1910).

In 1913, Mills offered Shetrone a job as his assistant. Shetrone was 37 years old and had no formal education or training in archaeology, but Mills was impressed with his passion and, doubt-

Photograph of Henry Clyde Shetrone. The image is undated, but is clearly an early photograph. It may have been taken around the time of his appointment as Curator of Archaeology for the Ohio State Archaeological and Historical Society in 1921. Ohio Historical Society archives, Negative number OHS 11819. Used with permission.

less, with the extensive contacts Shetrone had established across the state through his collecting activities and his newspaper work.

SHETRONE AND OHIO ARCHAEOLOGY

Shetrone began his professional archaeological career by conducting archaeological surveys around the state (e.g., Swauger 1984:145–148). In addition to identifying sites for the *Archaeological Atlas of Ohio* (Mills 1914), he also aggressively sought to acquire private artifact collections for the state museum. In the William C. Mills Papers in the Ohio Historical Society's archives, there are several letters from Shetrone detailing his adventures in the field. Unfortunately, most of these are undated and include only a heading identifying the day of the week and where Shetrone happened to be on that day. He seems to have done most of his traveling by motorcycle, usually over "nasty" roads (Shetrone 1913a).

After spending a stormy night in Thornville, Ohio, in an "excecrable" "parody on a hotel," Shetrone left the next morning "via the B. & W. railway track. Not aboard one of their sumptuous trains, however, but as a foot passenger, pushing a motorcycle" (Shetrone 1913a, 1913b). The roads had become quagmires of "mud and water" and the railroad tracks were the only seminavigable routes available in this part of rural Ohio. He arrived "ragged and dirty" at an elderly woman's home late one evening to examine a collection and expressed surprise that she let him into her house (1913d).

In Meigs County alone, Shetrone recorded 25 sites, including "a number of mounds, an important shell heap, stone graves, . . . pictographs, village sites etc." (Shetrone 1913c). One of the petroglyphs he recorded is shown in Figure 151 (p. 235). Shetrone chiseled it from its rock face and brought it back to the museum. It is now on display, with two other petroglyphs from the same locality, at the small exhibit facility at the Newark Earthworks State Memorial. Shetrone continued to write articles for newspapers during this period, but he was now documenting his own archaeological endeavors (e.g., Shetrone 1914).

In 1918, Shetrone worked with Mills at Flint Ridge (Mills 1921) in Licking County, near the Newark Earthworks. They excavated workshops and quarries (see Figure 27, p. 67 and Figure 173, p. 265) along with Hazlett Mound, a large Hopewellian burial mound located at the western periphery of the ridge. At the base of this mound, they found the remains of an extraordinary structure built from blocks of flint (Figure 15, p. 45). In that same year, Shetrone published his first scholarly monograph for the Ohio State Archaeological and Historical Society: "The Indian in Ohio." This lengthy monograph primarily was concerned with the historic Native American tribes and their years of often violent contact with European Americans in the Ohio Country. There was, however, a substantial section on prehistoric Ohio, some of which Shetrone later copied verbatim into *The Mound-Builders.*

Shetrone's next paper, published in 1920, was "The Culture Problem in Ohio Archaeology." This was an important contribution in which he attempted to place the archaeological cultures he and Mills, and Mills's predecessor at the Ohio State Archaeological and Historical Society, Warren K. Moorehead, had defined into a more systematic cultural-historical framework. Bruce Trigger (1980:668) acknowledged Shetrone's work as the foundation upon which William C. McKern and others would build the Midwestern Taxonomic Method (McKern 1939), one of the earliest formal attempts to systematize the comparison of regional sequences based on similarities in artifact assemblages.

Shetrone identified seven prehistoric "groups" based on traits such as projectile point morphology, use of bone and antler, use of exotic raw materials, ceramic forms and decorations, burial practices, and mounds. These were the "Fort Ancient; the Hopewell; the Adena subgroup; the Stone Grave culture; the Iroquoian; the Glacial Kame, and the Algonquian group" (Shetrone 1920:152). He wondered whether the groups defined on the basis of these traits represented "a few broad and well-defined social divisions" or if they were not "almost synonymous with the terms tribe or nation, as of historic use" (1920:159). Ultimately, Shetrone decided that these taxonomic units represented the same sort of "cultural divisions" for which "frequent changes of habit" were as characteristic as they had been for the "historically observed" Native American tribes (1920:168).

He offered the following "chronological scheme" as a "tentative working hypothesis" (1920:169). The Algonquian group was "the earliest, the most persistent and widely distributed, and the last to disappear" (1920:169). The Fort Ancient, Hopewell, and Stone Grave groups were contemporaneous, and although Mills had speculated that the Adena subgroup represented an early phase of the Hopewell group, Shetrone decided that there was insufficient evidence to determine their chronological position (1920:169). Finally, the Iroquoian group arrived "in late prehistoric times" and departed Ohio by the middle of the seventeenth century (1920:169). The testing and substantive refinement of this model did not occur until the introduction of radiocarbon dating in the 1950s.

In 1921, Mills became the director of the Ohio State Archaeological and Historical Society and Shetrone took his place as curator. Over the next two years, they conducted extensive excavations at Mound City in Chillicothe (Figures 130–135, pp. 207–214).

Today, this remarkable concentration of Hopewellian burial mounds is part of Hopewell Culture National Historical Park. Mills published a detailed final report of their extensive explorations in 1922 (Mills 1922). Completing the process of cleaning and cataloging the many artifacts and human remains recovered during two seasons of work, analyzing the data, and producing a report within months of completing the excavation was a remarkable achievement reflecting hard work and a peerless dedication to Michael Faraday's dictum to "work, finish, publish."

After 1922, Shetrone took over complete responsibility for the museum's archaeological explorations. Between 1922 and 1926, Shetrone directed the excavation of Campbell Island village (p. 171), the Hine Mound and village site, Wright Mounds, Ginther Mound, Miesse Mound, the Hopewell Mound Group (Figure 120, p. 196), and the large Seip Mound (Figure 136, p. 215). Following the precedent established by his mentor Mills, Shetrone published the results of these excavations with phenomenal speed, although most of these reports were short monographs rather than comprehensive site reports (Shetrone 1923a, 1924, 1925, 1926; Shetrone and Greenman 1931).

Shetrone's field techniques were, for their time, exemplary. According to Clark Wissler, one of America's foremost early anthropologists, affiliated with both the American Museum of Natural History and Yale University, "Shetrone does not dig a mound, he dissects it as carefully and intelligently as a surgeon approaches a complicated internal structure" (1930:671). Shetrone's description of the excavation of a hypothetical mound is instructive in this regard:

> A party of workmen with picks and shovels step to the edge of the Mound and begin to dig, throwing the loose earth well behind them. . . . The entire mound . . . will be sliced off, as a cake might be, in five-foot sections, as deep as there is any evidence of artificial construction or disturbance. Surveying instruments, cameras, note-books, everything in readiness [Shetrone 1930d:301].

For all of his thoroughness and rigor, however, there is evidence that at least some of his excavation photographs were staged re-creations of what had been found when, one presumes, a camera was not in readiness. And, unfortunately, the re-creations did not always slavishly adhere to the facts of the original discovery. For example, Shetrone apparently altered the positions of some arti-facts when he reassembled the so-called grave of a master artisan for the photograph that appears in this book (Figure 125, p. 202; see Cowan and Greber 2003:7–8).

W. C. Mills died in 1928, and Shetrone, still following in Mills's footsteps, became the director of the Ohio State Archaeological and Historical Society. Shetrone had begun to work on a book-length synthesis of the archaeology of the "mound region" early in 1927. He set the project aside, however, when he became director of the society, and much of his time and energy in 1928 was con-sumed by "a rather pretentious [by which, I presume, he meant ambitious] program of Museum activities" (Shetrone 1930b). Ad-ministrative responsibilities increasingly would pull Shetrone away from archaeological fieldwork, but, like his mentor, he never wa-vered in his support for archaeological research, public education, and preservation. He took up the challenge of his Mound Builders book again in 1929 and within the year had finished the manu-script. He also wrote a lengthy two-part article on the Mound Builders for the American Museum of Natural History's maga-zine *Natural History*, effectively summarizing the data and argu-ments he presented in the 489 pages of *The Mound-Builders*. Shetrone even wrote a brief introduction to a popular novel por-traying the life of the Mound Builders:

We have been too prone to attribute treachery and unjustified cruelty to so-called uncivilized peoples; and while undoubt-edly the Mound-builders and the prehistoric Indians pos-sessed their share of these, beyond question they also had their share of the virtues. 'Mog, the Mound Builder,' depicts its characters as human beings which, of course, they were. Its effect on prospective young readers should be to furnish an interesting and a logical idea of these primitive peoples, and to inspire in them a desire to know more of their fascinating and romantic story through reading and study of the literature on the subject [Shetrone 1931: ix–x].

Shetrone presented a series of lectures on the subject of the Mound Builders for a local radio program (*Museum Echoes* 1930), and he announced at the Ohio State Archaeological and Historical Society Annual meeting in March 1930 "a project which will mark the culmination of the Society's archaeological explorations. This is nothing less than a moving-picture film, and probably a talking film, of the actual exploration of an important Ohio mound" (Shetrone 1930e:626). Unfortunately, this project was never completed.

From the spectacular museum exhibits displayed at the society's museum at the Ohio State University to his many and varied literary efforts to his forays into radio and film, Shetrone used every available means and media to present archaeology to a general audience. He perceived that a public museum could not function as an academic ivory tower, and he devoted his considerable energies to educating the public about the intrinsic value of prehistoric sites (especially mounds) as well as the importance of archaeological research as a means for unlocking the mysteries of the past.

THE MOUND-BUILDERS

The Mound-Builders. A reconstruction of the life of a prehistoric American race, through exploration and interpretation of their earth mounds, their burials, and their cultural remains was published by D. Appleton of New York in 1930. Shetrone dedicated the book to "the average man and woman who, . . .lack the time and opportunity for digesting the rather extensive but often unavailable literature on the subject" (p. v). He also hoped the book would be "a handy compendium of the archaeology of the general mound area" for the professional prehistorian as well (p. v). The book succeeded admirably as a descriptive compendium of mound-builder archaeology. The many photographs and illustrations vividly conveyed the art

and architecture of the mound-building peoples in all their regional and temporal diversity.

One limitation of the book for modern readers is the lack of an
accurate chronological framework. Shetrone worked before the
discovery of radiocarbon dating. And, since none of the known
sites in eastern North America had revealed a consistent strati-
graphic succession of mound-building cultures, he had no certain
way to determine their chronological sequence. He had presented
his ideas on how the "culture problem in Ohio archaeology" might
be resolved in his 1920 paper published in the *American Anthropologist*. It is in his popular writings, however, that Shetrone revealed the naïve evolutionary perspective that formed the basis for
his interpretations of culture history. In his earlier work on "The
Indian in Ohio," Shetrone summarized his views as follows:

> The growth and development of the human race has been
> likened to the changes through which the individual passes
> in his progress from infancy to adult life. The savage state
> corresponds to the infant, the barbarian stage to youth, and
> civilization to adult life [1918:288].

For Shetrone, "the province of archaeology [was] to consider
the material relics strewn along the pathway of prehistoric human
progress" (1918:459). In *The Mound-Builders*, Shetrone identified
the mechanism driving people along this upward path. It was a
"cosmic urge toward cultural improvement" (p. 36). From this point
of view, the unspectacular Fort Ancient culture, now known to
date from A.D. 1000 to 1550, could not be the inheritor of the
Hopewellian legacy (ca. 100 B.C.–A.D. 400). It either must have
preceded, or been a contemporary poor cousin to, the more preco-
cious Hopewell culture, which represented "the maximum cultural
attainment of the Mound area" (1930d:300). Although wrong in
several particulars, Shetrone was ahead of his time in overcoming
what historian of archaeology Bruce Trigger has called "the most
important single factor that has shaped the long-term development of American archaeology," i.e., "the traditional Euroamerican
stereotype which portrayed America's native peoples as being in-

herently unprogressive" (1980:662). In spite of Shetrone's more
enlightened view of Native Americans, he occasionally demonstrated a lack of sensitivity that can be jarring for modern readers.
The caption of one photograph of skeletons from a Fort Ancient
burial refers to their "jocular expressions" (p. 183). The religious
rituals of these villagers are referred to as "superstitious rites" (p.
184). And the modern descendants of the Mound Builders living
in the Great Lakes region are described rather coldly as fitting
subjects for "study and observation" (p. 268).

Shetrone was, for the most part, highly respectful of the ancient
peoples whose story he was attempting to uncover, as well as their
modern descendants (see, for example, the quotation from his introduction to *Mog, the Mound Builder,* quoted earlier). He observed
that "contrary to widespread popular belief, most of the historic
tribes of native American Indians were agricultural in varying degrees, and to corresponding degrees sedentary in their manner of
life" (p. 54). He took note of American Indian traditions related to
mound building (see, for example, p. 307), but ultimately decided
that "Indian tradition has little value as historical evidence" (p.
475). It is worth noting in this context that a much more recent
review of the contributions Native American oral traditions can
make to archaeology came to an equally pessimistic conclusion
(Mason 2000:264).

Trigger has observed that "the refutation of the Mound Builder
myth tended to involve the wholesale rejection not only of the
inflated claims that had been made about them. . .but also of many
genuine accomplishments of the various Indian groups who had
built mounds" (1980:666). Shetrone made a nearly identical observation in 1930: "In their zeal to correct the fanciful imaginings
of pioneer writers, more recent investigators have felt themselves
called upon to strip the Mound-builders of every vestige of interest and importance" (p. 471).

Shetrone intended *The Mound-Builders* as a tribute to

those mysterious people now known to have flourished in
undiscovered America while Europe was still in the Dark
Ages; who, while their fellow humans in the Old World were

laying the foundations of modern nations, languages and institutions, were developing a civilization which in many respects is unique and highly important [Ohio State Archaeological and Historical Society 1930].

Shetrone succeeded in preserving the wonder of the Mound Builders' achievements while rejecting the extravagant fantasies that had grown over the mounds like so many tenacious weeds (see Williams 1991:77–79).

The Mound-Builders was well received by its intended audience of general readers. A second printing was being planned within a few months of its release. The scholarly response was equally enthusiastic. Wissler reviewed it for his museum's popular magazine *Natural History*. He declared that "a good book on the Mound Builders has been wanting until now" (1930:670). In a form letter Shetrone had circulated to "Co-workers in the Archaeology of the 'Mound Region'" to solicit information for the book, he modestly stated that he had "no reason to assume that he is better fitted for this undertaking than another, unless perhaps the archaeological wealth of his local field and its exhaustive exploration, with the resulting great mass of data may afford him unusual advantage" (Shetrone 1930b). Wissler, at least, disagreed with such a modest assessment: "certain it is, that the only person to write such a book is the author of this volume" (1930:670).

Carl Guthe, an archaeologist at the University of Michigan, wrote that *The Mound-Builders,* "although designed primarily for the general public, may serve as a reference book for the archaeologist and a source of illuminating information for students in allied fields" (1931:603–604). William McKern, curator of archaeology with the Milwaukee Public Museum, expressed similar sentiments in a congratulatory letter to Shetrone: "I feel that the book fills a too long empty space on the shelves of our general libraries" (McKern 1930).

It was generally conceded that Shetrone placed too much emphasis on Ohio (Babcock 1931:75; Guthe 1931:603; Moorehead 1931:425), but Wissler regarded this as a strength of the volume: "The plan of the book is good, treating the Ohio mound area in full and from this as a point of regard reviewing the Great Lakes area, the Upper and Lower Mississippi areas, as well as certain marginal areas, like the Tennessee-Cumberland and Pennsylvania area" (1930:671).

More than one reviewer commented upon the prematurity of Shetrone's bold assertion that the Mound Builders had come to the Mississippi and Ohio valleys "from Mexico after the initial development of Middle American civilizations" (Wissler 1930:671; Guthe 1931:603), but most seemed to regard it as an acceptable extrapolation for a popular audience. Indeed, variations on this theme became the standard model for explaining the origins of Mound Builder culture for the next 25 years and more (see, for example, Webb and Baby 1957:60; Webb and Snow 1945:328–332; Griffin 1952:361, 1967:180). Actually, however, Shetrone's speculations in this regard were rather behind the times, William Henry Harrison having proposed a similar idea in 1839 (Harrison 1839:224, 226). Subsequent archaeologists, building on the work of Shetrone, Griffin, and others, would demonstrate that the pro-digious earthworks at North American sites such as Newark, Moundville, and Cahokia were not the products of transplanted Toltecans but were local developments.

The only overwhelmingly negative review was David Bushnell, Jr.'s lengthy dissection in the *American Anthropologist*. Bushnell was an anthropologist with the Bureau of American Ethnology who had authored an important monograph on "Native Cemeteries and Forms of Burial East of the Mississippi" (Bushnell 1920). After cataloging a number of more or less significant errors of fact in Shetrone's book, Bushnell concluded with the astonishing claim that Shetrone himself was promulgating the same old mound-builder myth: "many readers will reach the erroneous conclusion that the Mound Builders were mysterious tribes which lived in the distant past and long ago became extinct" (1931:424).

Many of Bushnell's particular criticisms were fair enough. In-deed, Shetrone should have known that Jefferson first published his *Notes on the State of Virginia* in 1785, not 1801, and that the "genesis of the white man's dominion of the Western World" be-gan with the Spanish settlements in Florida rather than with the

Jamestown colony (Bushnell 1931:421–422). Nevertheless, it would take a determined and mean-spirited effort to twist Shetrone's words into the views imputed to him by Bushnell. Certainly, Shetrone deliberately evoked the mystery of the mounds; mysteries sell books. And if no one bought and read the books, then this effort to educate the public was a vain expenditure of time and money. Shetrone's final answer to the question as to the identity of the Mound Builders was, for all of his tantalizing references to mystery, unequivocal: "they were cultural groups of the native American race" and "in many cases they were the racial ancestors of the Indian tribes of historic times" (p. 478).

AFTER THE MOUND-BUILDERS

In the years following the publication of *The Mound-Builders*, Shetrone increasingly and necessarily devoted himself to his administrative duties. The Great Depression led to a "drastic reorganization and modification of activities" at the Ohio Archaeological and Historical Society ("State" was officially dropped from the society's name in 1931), including the virtual elimination of major field projects (Shetrone 1932:552). By 1933, six staff positions had been eliminated and those who were retained suffered "deep salary cuts" (Shetrone 1933:352).

In spite of the Depression, it was in this period that the society was most aggressively acquiring significant archaeological sites for preservation. Between 1931 and 1935, the society added the following properties to the list of sites it managed: Inscription Rock, Leo Petroglyph, Fort Hill, Newark's Great Circle and Octagon earthworks, Flint Ridge, Wright Earthworks, and Tarlton Cross Mound. Indeed, the preservation of these sites for future generations may stand as Shetrone's most enduring legacy.

Shetrone addressed the problem of the earliest human presence in North America with his review of the "Folsom Phenomena as Seen from Ohio" in 1936. This important but little known paper did three things. First, it brought about an increased awareness of the significance of these distinctive projectile points to researchers in eastern North America. At this time, all fluted points were being referred to as "Folsom" or "Folsomoid." Most of the points Shetrone described would now be called Clovis, or Eastern fluted points. Second, Shetrone documented a surprisingly large number of these points from Ohio. Clearly, Ohio, in particular, and eastern North America, in general, could no longer be regarded as peripheral to this earliest chapter of America's prehistory. Third, he presented the first distributional analysis of Paleoindian points. This became a popular method for gaining insights into the chronology and lifeways of Paleoindians in the East, and usually Mason (1958) and Quimby (1958) are given credit for its development.

One of Shetrone's last major contributions to archaeology was the establishment in 1937 of the Lithic Laboratory for the Eastern United States. Its purpose was "to study the lithic materials. . .pertinent to the material culture of the American aborigines, and of methods and techniques employed in their utilization" (Shetrone 1938a:1). It was a short-lived venture but highly successful. Shetrone went to England to study and film the flintknappers of Brandon. He brought home-grown flintknappers (such as a young Don Crabtree) to Columbus for collaborative study. Under his direction the laboratory amassed a reference collection of lithic materials from across the United States, and H. Holmes Ellis, a research associate at the Lithic Laboratory, produced his "Flint-working Techniques of the American Indians: An Experimental Study" as a 1939 master's thesis for the Ohio State University (Ellis 1965).

Shetrone retired in 1947 and was appointed director emeritus of the Ohio Archaeological and Historical Society. He held that position until his death on 23 November 1954. He was still publishing scholarly articles and left unfinished a major synthesis of Ohio archaeology (Shetrone 1949).

SHETRONE'S LEGACY

James Griffin has written that in the 1920s, "the Ohio State Museum was the dominant center for archaeology west of the Appalachians and east of the Rocky Mountains" (1985:268). By the 1930s, however, that reputation already was diminishing. Some might argue, therefore, that Shetrone was responsible for the decline of the Ohio Archaeological and Historical Society's aggressive program of archaeological research.

Richard Morgan, the Ohio Archaeological and Historical Society's curator of archaeology from 1938 until 1947, and James Rodabaugh, Morgan's research associate, attributed the decline in perceived preeminence to a shift in priorities. After 1930, the society emphasized "the correlation and systematization" of the data obtained in its previous decades of excavation with the purpose of solving "problems in cultural classification, chronology, and the relation of Ohio cultures to those of other parts of the country" (Morgan and Rodabaugh 1947:9–10). In addition, as director, Shetrone made a deliberate decision to commit the diminishing resources of the society to preserving archaeological sites and "to interpret Ohio archaeology for the general public" (Morgan and Rodabaugh 1947:10).

We are still debating the relative merits of giving priority to research versus public education about that research, but Shetrone's decision, however well founded, turned out to be singularly ill timed. It left Ohio out of "the tremendous stimulus" provided by one of the most important factors to shape the archaeology of the eastern United States in this century (Guthe 1952:3): the large sums of money made available to states by a succession of federal government relief agencies, including the Federal Emergency Relief Administration, the Civil Works Administration, the Civilian Conservation Corps, the Works Progress Administration, as well as funds distributed by the National Park Service.

While Shetrone devoted these federal dollars to expanding park facilities at Ohio Archaeological and Historical Society sites and organizing artifact and archival collections, Ohio's neighbors, most especially Kentucky and Indiana, used this federal largess to pay for large-scale excavations (Kardulias 1989:119). As a result, the Ohio Archaeological and Historical Society gave up its preeminence in eastern North American archaeology.

According to Kardulias, the diminished importance of fieldwork began a trend in which archaeological research became less central to the mission of the Ohio Archaeological and Historical Society (1989:120). The trend was "difficult to reverse," and in 1954, perhaps not coincidentally the year of Shetrone's death, the society dropped "Archaeological" from its name and became simply the Ohio Historical Society (Kardulias 1989:120). The name change was not intended to "imply a change in the functions of the society," and its "archaeological work" was to continue to be "an important phase of its activities" (*Museum Echoes* 1954:39). But, with the best will in the world, the abbreviation of the name cannot really be construed as anything but a reflection of the society's declining interest in archaeology. As Griffin perceived, Ohio's golden age of archaeology, heralded by Moorehead and presided over by Mills and Shetrone, had come to an end. Shetrone's *The Mound-Builders* represents its crowning achievement, but it was also, in some ways, its swan song.

The Mound-Builders is a testament to Shetrone's success at working toward "correlation and systematization" of data, as well as public education. It was a comprehensive synthesis of Ohio's mound-building cultures in relation to what was then known about the archaeology of eastern North America, and it was intended for a general, as well as a scholarly, audience (see p. v). Yet Shetrone was no armchair popularizer. His work was based on years of excavation and firsthand familiarity with much of the data. His popularizations echoed with the ring of the shovel and trowel in gravelly soil. He wrote as one of the most experienced excavators in American archaeology, and he had not just excavated mounds—he had been buried in one. (His own laconic account of this adventure, worthy of an Indiana Jones, appears on page 219, although Setzler gives a rather more complete narrative of the incident in his tribute to Shetrone [1956:297–298].)

Shetrone's vivid prose had been polished by his years of newspaper reporting, and while some passages may seem excessively florid to modern sensibilities, his work was immensely popular. The popularity of the work may have been partially responsible for Bushnell's unfairly harsh review of it (or, perhaps Bushnell was simply miffed that Shetrone had not seen fit to cite his monograph on Native American burial practices in eastern North America). Sadly, even today, scientists who write successfully for a popular audience often are regarded with disdain by their more elitist colleagues. There is an unfortunate presumption that "real scientists" do science; that is, they do research and write up the results for their colleagues. They do not deign to write for the uninitiated masses. Shetrone, by doing just that, and doing it quite successfully, drew increased attention to his nonacademic background, allowing self-conscious (and self-righteous) "professionals" like Bushnell to dismiss his real contributions to the field.

And Shetrone's contributions were considerable. He helped to build the largest state-administered system of archaeological and historic sites in the United States, totaling, as of 2002, 62 sites in 39 of Ohio's 88 counties. According to David Hurst Thomas, curator of archaeology for the American Museum of Natural History, the Ohio Historical Society's museum "contains arguably the best collection of pre-contact American Indian objects from eastern North America" (Thomas 1994:278–279). The bulk of this collection was assembled by Moorehead, Mills, and Shetrone.

Carl Guthe observed that by 1929, the "monolithic concept of the Mound Builders was disintegrating because of the diversified nature and more critical examination of recently acquired archaeological information" (1967:434). It was the data Shetrone gleaned from his years of exploration in Ohio, combined with the works of others he collected and summarized, that finally undermined any notion that the builders of mounds in eastern North America could be encompassed by a single, monolithic mound-builder culture.

Meltzer has written that by 1934, when the Society for American Archaeology was organized, "the field of archaeology had changed dramatically. . . . It was no longer possible to become an archaeologist simply by declaration and without some sort of formal training" (Meltzer 1985:258). Henry Clyde Shetrone may have been the last of the great, nonacademically trained archaeologists. He was not the last such archaeologist to make a significant contribution to the field, for that still is happening across North America today, but the last to hold a leadership position in a major state-sponsored institution. Shetrone played a pivotal role in shaping the direction of archaeological research, preservation, and public education in eastern North America for the generation between Frederic Ward Putnam and James Bennet Griffin. *The Mound-*

Builders was his magnum opus, and it stands as the most influential archaeological synthesis written in this period.

When the book was published, an old acquaintance whom Shetrone had not seen since his days of working in the newspaper business, sent him a short letter of congratulations:

> It's a far cry from punching a telegrapher's key on a morning paper and draining a long beer to the dregs in Whiskey Alley, to doing a book on "The Mound Builders," but it would seem, without knowing anything of the subject, that you did a good job of it.
>
> I congratulate you [Leu 1930].

This letter is not just a personal tribute; it is a testimonial to Shetrone's success at conveying the wonder of archaeology and the story of the Mound Builders to a wide audience of folks who knew little of the subject. It also is a touching reminder of Shetrone's roots. He had, indeed, come a long way—from Whiskey Alley to the directorship of the Ohio Archaeological and Historical Society—and his rise was mirrored in the remarkable advancements in our understanding of the rich and varied cultures of the Mound Builders.

Although the golden age of archaeology at the Ohio Historical Society may have ended with Shetrone, the solid efforts of subsequent directors and curators of archaeology continued—and continue—to make important contributions to archaeological research, preservation, and public education. I extend my heartfelt thanks to the director emeritus, Gary Ness, for his general support and for his particular permission to consult the closed files of former directors William C. Mills's and Henry C. Shetrone's papers. I am grateful to Martha Potter Otto, current curator of archaeology, for her support and encouragement. I also thank Donald Gehlbach for providing me with some useful leads to information about Shetrone's early years at the Ohio Historical Society.

I express my sincere appreciation to Stephen Williams, Terry Barnhart, Neal Hitch, and Jeff Gill for their helpful comments on an earlier draft of this manuscript. Any errors of fact or interpretation remaining are solely my responsibility. I either failed to heed their advice or introduced new mistakes after they reviewed the paper.

Finally, I offer my thanks to Steve Williams for recommending me to write this introduction.

REFERENCES CITED

Babcock, W. M.
  1931   Review of *The Mound-Builders*. Minnesota History 12(1):75–76.
Bushnell, D. I., Jr.
  1920   Native Cemeteries and Forms of Burial East of the Mississippi. *Bulletin* No. 71, Bureau of American Ethnology, Smithsonian Institution, Washington, D.C.
  1931   Review of *The Mound-Builders*. American Anthropologist 33:421–424.
Cowan, F. L., and N. B. Greber
  2003   Hopewell Mound 11: Yet Another Look at an Old Collection. *Hopewell Archeology* 5(2):7–11.
Ellis, H. H.
  1965   *Flint-working Techniques of the American Indians: An Experimental Study*. Rev. ed. Ohio Historical Society, Columbus.
Griffin, J. B.
  1952   Culture Periods in Eastern United States Archeology. In *Archeology of Eastern North America*, edited by J. B. Griffin, pp. 352–364. University of Chicago Press, Chicago.
  1967   Eastern North American Archaeology: A Summary. *Science* 156:175–191.
  1985   The Formation of the Society for American Archaeology. *American Antiquity* 50:261–271.
Guthe, C. E.
  1931   Review of *The Mound Builders*. Mississippi Valley Historical Review 17(4):603–604.
  1952   Twenty-five Years of Archeology in the Eastern United States. In *Archeology of Eastern North America*, edited by J. B. Griffin,

pp. 1–12. University of Chicago Press, Chicago.

1967 Reflections on the Founding of the Society for American Archaeology. *American Antiquity* 32:433–440.

Harrison, W. H.

1839 A Discourse on the Aborigines of the Valley of Ohio. *Transactions of the Historical and Philosophical Society of Ohio* 1, Pt. 2. Geo. W. Bradbury & Co., Cincinnati.

Kardulias, P. N.

1989 A History of Public Archaeology in Ohio. *Ohio History* 98:101–130.

Leu, F. W.

1930 Letter to H. C. Shetrone, ca. 1930. On file, Ohio Historical Society, Archaeology Collections Facility, Columbus, Ohio.

Mason, R. J.

1958 Late Pleistocene Geochronology and the Paleo-Indian Penetration into the Lower Michigan Peninsula. *Anthropological Papers No. 11*, Museum of Anthropology, University of Michigan, Ann Arbor.

2000 Archaeology and Native North American Oral Traditions. *American Antiquity* 65:239–266.

McKern, W. C.

1930 Letter to Shetrone, 10 October 1930. On file, Ohio Historical Society, Archaeology Collections Facility, Correspondence files. Columbus.

1939 The Midwestern Taxonomic Method as an Aid to Archaeological Culture Study. *American Antiquity* 4:301–313.

Meltzer, D. J.

1985 North American Archaeology and Archaeologists, 1879–1934. *American Antiquity* 50(2):249–260.

Mills, W. C.

1910 Letter to Prof. H. Talkington, 3 February 1910. W. C. Mills Papers, Ohio Historical Society, Archives Library, Columbus.

1914 *Archaeological Atlas of Ohio*. Ohio State Archaeological and Historical Society, Columbus.

1921 Flint Ridge. *Ohio State Archaeological and Historical Quarterly* 30:90–161.

1922 Exploration of the Mound City Group. *Ohio State Archaeologi-*

cal and Historical Quarterly 31:423–584.

Moorehead, W. K.

    1931   Review of *The Mound Builders.* American Anthropologist
          33:424–426.

Morgan, R. G., and J. H. Rodabaugh

    1947   *Bibliography of Ohio Archaeology.* Ohio State Archaeological and
          Historical Society, Columbus.

Museum Echoes

    1930   Museum Radio Program. *Museum Echoes* 3(3):21.

    1937   The Lithic Laboratory. *Museum Echoes* 10(5):1.

    1954   Annual Meeting Highlights. *Museum Echoes* 27(5):39–40.

Ohio State Archaeological and Historical Society

    1930   Christmas Gifts Brochure advertising the release of The Mound
          Builders. Ohio State Archaeological and Historical Society, Co-
          lumbus.

Quimby, G. I.

    1958   Fluted Points and Geochronology of the Lake Michigan Ba-
          sin. *American Antiquity* 23:247–254.

Setzler, F. M.

    1956   Henry Clyde Shetrone, 1876–1954. *American Antiquity* 21:296–
          299.

Swauger, J. L.

    1984   *Petroglyphs of Ohio.* Ohio University Press, Athens.

Thomas, D. H.

    1994   *Exploring Ancient Native America: An Archaeological Guide.*
          Macmillan, New York.

Trigger, B. G.

    1980   Archaeology and the Image of the American Indian. *American
          Antiquity* 45:662–676.

Webb, W. S., and R. S. Baby

    1957   *The Adena People, No. 2.* Ohio Historical Society, Columbus.

Webb, W. S., and C. E. Snow

    1945   The Adena People. *University of Kentucky, Reports in Anthro-
          pology and Archaeology* 6.

Williams, S.

    1991   *Fantastic Archaeology: The Wild Side of North American Prehis-
          tory.* University of Pennsylvania Press, Philadelphia.

Wissler, C.
1930   Review of *The Mound Builders*. Natural History 30(6):670–671.

WORKS BY H. C. SHETRONE

1907   ArrowHeads. Poem. *Ohio Magazine* 3:244.
1913a Letter to W. C. Mills, Sunday, 31 May 1913[?]. W. C. Mills Papers, Ohio Historical Society, Archives Library, Columbus.
1913b Letter to W. C. Mills, 3 June 1913[?]. W. C. Mills Papers, Ohio Historical Society, Archives Library, Columbus.
1913c Letter to W. C. Mills, 22 August 1913. On file, Ohio Historical Society, Archaeology Collections Facility, Columbus. [Excerpts of this letter, along with other letters from Shetrone to Mills, are published in Swauger (1984:145–146).]
1913d Letter to W. C. Mills, 15 September 1913. W. C. Mills Papers, Ohio Historical Society, Archives Library, Columbus.
1914   Records of Primitive Men Found at Great Bend in Ohio River. *Youngstown Vindicator*, 19 February:20.
1918   The Indian in Ohio, with a Map of the Ohio Country. *Ohio State Archaeological and Historical Society Quarterly* 27:274–510.
1920   The Culture Problem in Ohio Archaeology. *American Anthropologist* 22(2):144–172.
1923a Explorations of the Campbell Island Village Site and the Hine Mound and Village Site. *Ohio State Archaeological and Historical Society Quarterly* 32:434–467.
1923b The Spetnagle Cache of Flint Spear Points. *Ohio State Archaeological and Historical Society Quarterly* 32:638–640.
1924   Explorations of the Wright Group of Pre-historic Earthworks. *Ohio State Archaeological and Historical Society Quarterly* 33:341–358.
1925   Exploration of the Ginther Mound: The Miesse Mound. *Ohio State Archaeological and Historical Society Quarterly* 34:154–168.
1926   Explorations of the Hopewell Group of Prehistoric Earthworks. *Ohio State Archaeological and Historical Society Quarterly* 35:1–227.
1927   [with A. C. Spetnagel] Report on the Work of Restoring the Mound City Group, in Camp Sherman, Ross County, Ohio.

Ohio State Archaeological and Historical Quarterly 35:643–645.

1928 Some Ohio Caves and Rock Shelters Bearing Evidences of Human Occupancy. *Ohio State Archaeological and Historical Society Quarterly* 37:1–34.

1930a Archaeological Field Work in North America during 1929: Ohio. *American Anthropologist* 32:366–367.

1930b "To the writer's Co-workers in the Archaeology of the `Mound Region.'" Letter. Facsimile on file, Henry C. Shetrone Papers, Ohio Historical Society Archives, Columbus.

1930c *The Mound-Builders. A Reconstruction of the Life of a Prehistoric American Race, through Exploration and Interpretation of Their Earth Mounds, Their Burials, and Their Cultural Remains.* D. Appleton, New York. Reprinted in 1941.

1930d The Mound Builders. *Natural History* 30:293–304, 402–408.

1930e Director's Report. *Ohio State Archaeological and Historical Society Quarterly* 39:620–629.

1931a [with E. F. Greenman] Explorations of the Seip Group of Prehistoric Earthworks. *Ohio State Archaeological and Historical Society Quarterly* 40:343–509.

1931b Introduction to *Mog, the Mound Builder*, by Irving Crump, pp. ix–x. Dodd Mead & Co., New York.

1932 Report of Director. *Ohio State Archaeological and Historical Society Quarterly* 41:552–558.

1933 Director's Report. *Ohio State Archaeological and Historical Society Quarterly* 42:349–353.

1936 The Folsom Phenomena as Seen from Ohio. *Ohio State Archaeological and Historical Society Quarterly* 45:240–526.

1937a Nicotiana: An Ethnologic, Historic and Literary Novelty. *Ohio State Archaeological and Historical Society Quarterly* 46:81–102.

1937b Anent the Newark Earthworks. *Museum Echoes* 10(1):1.

1938a Lithic Laboratory Now a Reality. *Museum Echoes* 11(1):1.

1938b The Society: A Quarter Century of Progress. *Ohio State Archaeological and Historical Society Quarterly* 47:206–211.

1938c *Primer of Ohio Archaeology: The Mound Builders and the Indians.* Ohio State Archaeological and Historical Society, Columbus.

1941a West Virginia Archaeology. *West Virginia History* 2(2):99–101.

1941b The Ohio Aborigines. In *The Foundations of Ohio*, by B. W.

Bond, Jr., pp. 34–59. The History of the State of Ohio, vol. 1, edited by C. Wittke, Ohio State Archaeological and Historical Society, Columbus.

1944a A Unique Prehistoric Irrigation Project. *Ohio Journal of Science* 44(5):203–212.

1944b Trailing Adam's Ancestors. *Ohio State Archaeological and Historical Society Quarterly* 53:83–105.

1945 Caleb Atwater: Versatile Pioneer, a Re-appraisal. *Ohio State Archaeological and Historical Society Quarterly* 54:79–88.

1948a Aboriginal Art of the Eastern United States. *Art Quarterly* 11(4):307–323.

1948b Fauna of the Mound Builders. *Fauna* 10:46–47.

1949 Ohio Archaeology and Archaeologists. Manuscript on file, Ohio Historical Society, Columbus.

1953 Biographic Sketch of Harry Raymond McPherson. *Ohio Archaeologist* 3(3):27–30.

1953 Marine Shells from Ohio Pre-Columbian Burial Mounds. *Nautilus* 68:11–14.

THE
MOUND-BUILDERS

THE
MOUND – BUILDERS

INTRODUCTION

No sign of habitation meets the eye;
Only some ancient furrows I discern
And verdant mounds, and from them sadly learn
That hereabout men used to live and die.
                                        —WILTON.

MOUND-BUILDERS! What magic in the very word;
what an epitome of all that is romantic and mysterious in human experience! Mere mention of the
name suffices to conjure visions of a shadowy race dimly viewed
across the ages—come from no one knows whence, gone no one
knows whither, or when. Giants in physical stature and legion
in numbers; weird rites and long-lost magic arts; populous
cities and impressive temples; haughty priests and human
sacrifice!

Who of the older generation does not recall the thrill imparted by the all too brief references in early textbooks and
historical literature to those mysterious denizens of the primeval forest and their no less mysterious mounds? Who of the
younger generation, thumbing these musty tomes, is not cap-
tivated by the romance lurking in the mellowed woodcut
illustrations supplementing the meager text? An intriguing bit
of landscape, hill and vale; above, great birds wheeling silently
through the azure sky; a ruminative cow, grateful for the noon-
day shade of the giant elms; a lazily speculative pedestrian,
pondering the mysteries of the nearby ancient mound, while
"all the air a solemn stillness holds." Fairyland!

Who were the Mound-builders? Whence came they, and
when? Why did they build mounds? What of their fate?

I

But do we really wish to know? Isn't fiction, after all, stranger than truth? If the archæologist can translate fancy into fact, should he attempt to do so, knowing full well that only in the unknown and the unexplored are romance and mystery at their best and that the known all too readily becomes the commonplace? The writer has hesitated to assume the task. You may wonder why.

From the very dawn days of human intelligence man has been concerned with two sets of phenomena, natural and supernatural. The first he has accepted as a matter of course for the reason that he could see, feel, and understand them—could measure them by the yardstick of ordinary human experience. They were everyday business. The phenomena that would not conform to such analysis were another matter.

Man's striving after explanation and understanding of these (to him) supernatural phenomena, particularly as affecting his origin, past life, and future destiny, has resulted in an impressive complex of activities and accomplishments which, taken together, constitute an important part of his ethical culture. As a whole, they may be considered as significant gestures of the finite human mind groping for understanding of the infinite —a declaration that man cannot, or will not, live by bread alone.

Those elements of this ingenious complex which have survived to become a part of present-day civilization, through their acceptance as fact, are components of history and religion; in so far as they apply to primitive man, we think of them under the term "mythology."

By the time that our Aryan forbears began their migrations from the ancestral home to spread themselves over Europe and the western world, a body of tradition, legend, myth, and ballad had grown up in answer to the age-old queries regarding things unobvious and unknown—the supernatural. Reading the pages of classical Greek and Roman history, we meet with heroes, Harpies, and Hydras; divinities and dryads; Centaurs and Cyclops; Graces and Furies; nymphs and naiads; we consult the Oracle and read the future through divination. Proceeding, we find our immediate ancestors, in the British Isles and on the Continent, reveling in witches, goblins, and gnomes; fairies, spirits, and sprites; while not a few giants lurk in the dark places. And along with the colonists came most of these to American shores. They are with us today; but we have taken a forward step, and with more courage than our ancestors we have retained only those which are friendly and helpful and have discarded, for the most part, those which are unfriendly and harmful. Witches are no longer in vogue.

And although we continue to associate mythology only with the infancy of the race, we find that just beneath the veneer which is civilization it is still very much in evidence. We realize that this intangible part of our culture complex, although it cannot be measured or weighed, still plays an indispensable part in our lives. We must have fairies, good spirits, Santa Claus. We must have romance, mystery, magic—let's-pretend and make-believe. And now that science and exploration have pushed back the frontiers of Fairyland so far that there remains hardly an unexplored corner for the little people of our imagination, we may possibly, and perhaps rightly, feel that our cherished conceptions of the Mound-builders should be retained, with all their pleasant illusions, as a last sanctuary for our romantic fancies.

Archæologists have noticed the difficulty of replacing in the popular mind the often erroneous early ideas regarding the Mound-builders with the newly acquired truths. Some have intimated that the public prefers to retain its cherished illusions and should be permitted to do so. But in the end, the writer has decided that his readers have reached a plane where they are ready to believe, with him, that while truth may not be stranger than fiction, fact may be, and is, more interesting, more worth while, and just as romantic as fancy. Moreover, when all that is likely to be learned of the Mound-builders is told, there will remain an abundance of mystery and uncertainty to feed our imaginations.

It is not strange that one branch of the human family should be interested in the mute remains of another, even though forgotten ages have intervened since the two parted company at the threshold of the common ancestral home—the one to pass without leaving a purposeful record, and the other to make and to write history. The Mound-builder left no intentional record of his activities; but because he was human and therefore one of us, we gladly assume the task of interpreting the fortuitous fingerprints that he left on earth and stone and of translating them into terms of written history.

CHAPTER I

EARLY THEORIES AS TO ORIGIN AND IDENTITY

Speculations of the pioneers—Early literature—Thomas Jefferson, pioneer archæologist—William Henry Harrison and Caleb Atwater—The classical contribution of Squier and Davis—Activities of the Bureau of American Ethnology—Recent contributors.

WHEN European colonists shouldered their way westward from the Atlantic Coast to take up their abodes in the country of the Mound-builders, their attention naturally was attracted to the numerous old mounds and interesting minor relics, mute evidences of former human occupancy. Discovery that the mounds contained human remains dispelled any tendency toward belief that they might be of natural origin. Here, then, was romance and mystery indeed. True, the task of gaining a foothold in the inhospitable wilderness and of conquering the forbidding forest was one to tax the indomitable energy and courage of the early settlers. Nevertheless, there must be an outlet for their mental and spiritual needs, and as means for recreational activities were scant, the mounds and their unknown builders fitted nicely into the pattern of pioneer life. Then and there originated the basic queries as to who, when, whence, why, where, what, and whither. A puzzle worthy of their best mental efforts and a stimulus to their imaginations was ready provided for the pioneers in the newly discovered territory which was henceforth to be their home land.

SPECULATIONS OF THE PIONEERS

A complex of romantic and fanciful theories regarding the vanished hosts who had been their predecessors in the land was inevitable. From the first the human tendency to exaggerate and embellish the unknown was manifest; and it was just as inevitable that much of the theory formulated without precedent and in the absence of even a nucleus of fact should prove eventually to be erroneous. Viewed from the present and softened by time, the experiences of the pioneers in taming the wilderness constitute an epic romance in themselves; but those engaged in the actual project were too close to reality to see it as other than commonplace. So it was that the American Mound-builder became for them, and has remained for many of their successors, the great American epic.

An early composite word picture of the Mound-builders, not yet entirely faded, may be restored by slightly paraphrasing the words of the late J. W. Powell, the noted anthropologist:

For more than a century the ghosts of a vanished nation . . . ambuscaded in the vast solitudes of the continent, and the forest-covered mounds [were] usually regarded as the mysterious sepulchres of its kings and nobles. It was an alluring conjecture that a powerful people, superior to the Indians, once occupied the valley of the Ohio and the Appalachian ranges, their empire stretching from the Hudson Bay to the Gulf, with its flanks on the western prairies and the eastern ocean; a people with a confederated government, a chief ruler, a great central capitol, a highly developed religion, with homes and husbandry, and advanced textile, fictile and ductile arts; with a language, perhaps with letters—all swept away by an invasion of copper-hued Huns from some unknown region of the earth, prior to the landing of Columbus.

And now that science, in its own good time, is able to supply definite answers to some (not all) of the queries regarding the Mound-builders and their culture, who shall say that the traditional story of our pioneers, with all its fanciful imaginings, has not served a justifiable end? Like our Old World forbears, we have taken the unknown and have woven it into the fabric of the larger human story. To the writer, the Mound-builder epic, as developed by the American pioneers, is in itself a most interesting and worth-while phenomenon—a present day, or rather an historic, illustration of human tradition in the making.

As is generally true, the reaction from the traditional to the historic, the definitely proven, has been to the other extreme. Some modern writers are too much inclined to discredit altogether the earlier theories and beliefs and to strip the Mound-builders entirely of the interest and cultural importance which really are theirs. In all such reactions the truth is usually to be found in the middle ground; and in presenting the latest findings in the matter, the writer will assume what he feels to be true, namely, that the Mound-builders, while not the fancifully freakish race formerly supposed, were, all in all, a most interesting and important branch of the human family.

Inevitably, speculation as to the origin and racial affinities of the Mound-builders was in evidence from the first. The belief held by some that they were native or indigenous to America was an early and a natural one. It was noted that the buffalo, the beaver, maize and tobacco, and many others of the fauna and flora were, so far as known, native to America, and it seemed quite logical to suppose that the Mound-builders, and the Indians as well, originated on the continent and, like Topsy, "jest growed." Aside from the theory of native origin, the Mound-builders were traced variously, through some apparent or fancied resemblance, to practically every known people of the world. From the ancient Chinese, Phœnicians, and Egyptians at the one end to the Welsh and the Irish at the other is but a suggestion of the range of supposed sources of origin. The Ten Lost Tribes of Israel seem to have been an alluring subject of consideration for those who saw an opportunity of clearing up two major mysteries in the simplest possible manner. Even mythical isles and lost continents were evoked to aid in solving the perplexing problem.

All this early speculation and theorizing furnished good "copy" for pioneer newspapers and periodicals; and ere long articles, pamphlets, and books began to make their appearance, presenting the views of their authors and discussing those of others. Some few writers admitted that they did not know; but most of them assumed very definite and confident attitudes

FIG. 1. THE MARIETTA GROUP OF PREHISTORIC EARTHWORKS

After the painting by C. R. Sullivan, 1832. This venerable picture, itself almost an archæological item, depicts the important group of earthworks at the junction of the Muskingum with the Ohio River. General Rufus Putnam, recognizing, as did the "first Ohioans," the strategic importance and scenic beauty of the spot, preempted it as the site of the first settlement of the Ohio Company and capital of the great Northwest Territory (1788). Note the old fortification, Campus Martius, and the first log cabin of the Ohio Company.

and were assiduous in marshaling evidence in support of their theories. One thing, at least, was certain: since the mounds were indisputably the work of human hands and thus of the greatest possible human interest, no stone, and no mound, was to be left unturned in the effort to solve the mystery.

EARLY LITERATURE

Casual reference to the mounds of the southeastern states, where exploration and settlement were comparatively early, and particularly to those of Florida, are found in the writings of the chroniclers of De Soto; in Adair's *Account of American Indians* (1775); in Bernard Romans' *History of Florida* (1776); and in William Bartram's *Travels in Florida* (1779). As early as 1772 the Rev. David Jones, of Freehold, New Jersey, after a sojourn among the western Indians, submitted a plan and description of the imposing works at Circleville, Ohio.

With the opening of the Ohio country and the establishment of Fort Harmar and the town of Marietta, at the mouth of the Muskingum, came numerous reports of the now famous Marietta earthworks. These included descriptions of the Marietta Group and the Grave Creek Mound, on the (West) Virginia side of the river, sent by General Samuel H. Parsons in 1786 to President Willard of Harvard College and to President Stiles of Yale College; plans and descriptions of the Marietta works, attributed to Captain Jonathan Heart, transmitted by General Harmar to General Thomas Mifflin of Philadelphia in 1787; and in the same year a similar contribution by Colonel Winthrop Sargent. Shortly after the turn of the century came the well-known descriptions of this great group by Bishop James Madison and the Rev. Thaddeus M. Harris.

Of by far the greatest interest and importance among the early reports, however, is the rare old map of the Marietta works prepared by General Rufus Putnam for the Ohio Company in 1788. This venerable document, carefully preserved in the library of Marietta College, may be regarded as the

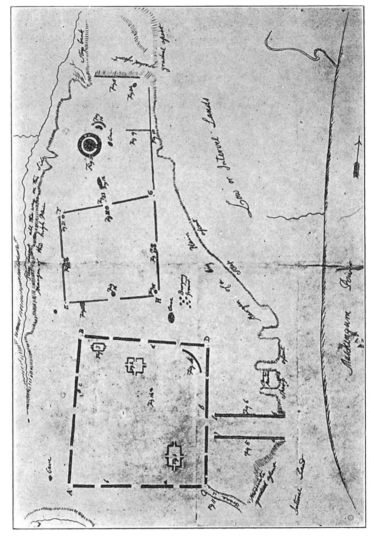

FIG. 2. MAP OF THE MARIETTA WORKS BY GENERAL RUFUS PUTNAM, 1788

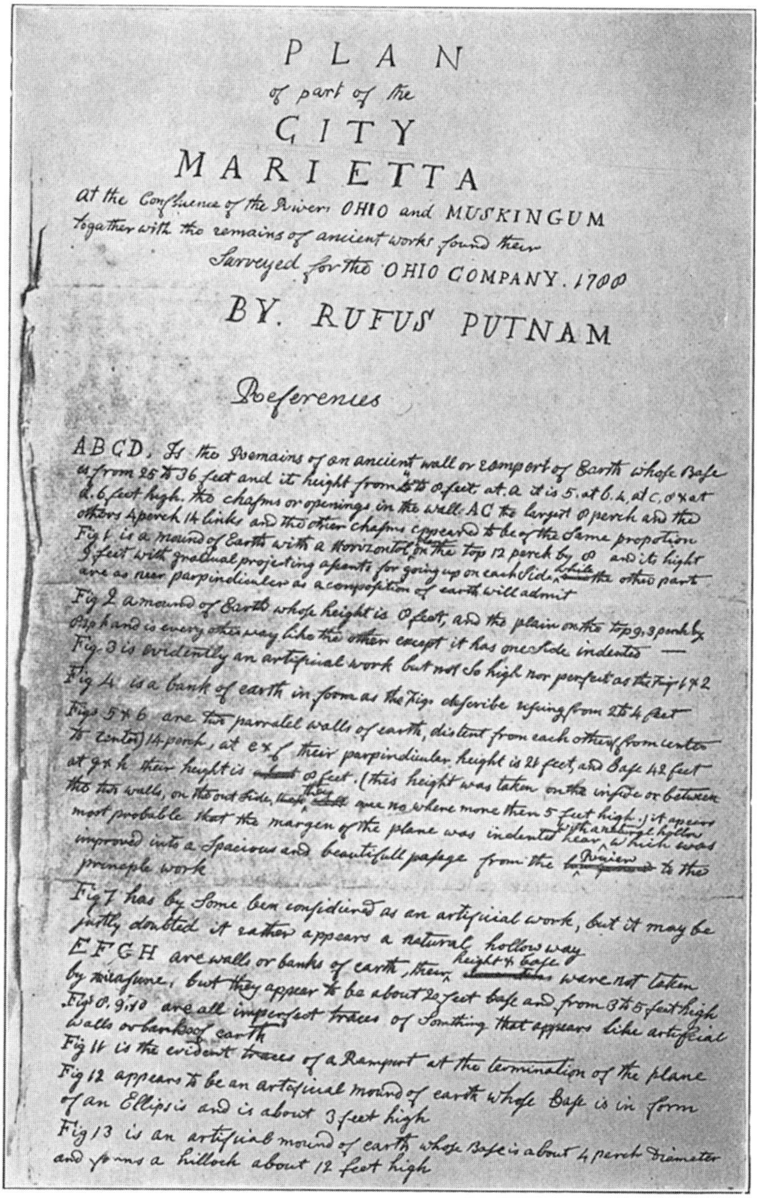

PLAN
of part of the
CITY
MARIETTA
At the Confluence of the Rivers OHIO *and* MUSKINGUM
together with the remains of ancient works found their
Surveyed for the OHIO COMPANY. 1788

BY. RUFUS PUTNAM

References

ABCD, Is the Remains of an ancient wall or rampart of Earth whose Base is from 25 to 36 feet and it height from 5 to 6 feet at. A it is 5. at C. &. at C. &. at b. 6 feet high. the chasms or openings in the wall AC the largest 8 perch and the others 4 perch 14 links and the other chasms appeared to be of the same propotion

Fig 1. is a mound of Earth with a Horizontol on the top 12 perch by 8 and it hight is 9 feet with gradual projecting afents for going up on each side while the other part are as near parpindiculer as a composition of earth will admit

Fig 2 a mound of Earth whose height is 8 feet, and the plain on the top 9, 3 perch by 8 up h and is every other way like the other except it has one side indented

Fig 3 is evidently an artificial work but not so high nor perfect as the Fig 1 & 2

Fig 4 is a bank of earth in form as the Figs describe rising from 2 to 4 feet

Figs 5 & 6 are two parralel walls of earth, distant from each other from center to center 14 perch, at C & f their parpindiculer height is 2 feet, and Base 42 feet at 9 & h their height is about 8 feet. (this height was taken on the inside or between the two walls, on the out side, they are no where more then 5 feet high. It appears most probable that the margin of the plane was indented hear, which was improved into a spacious and beautifull pasage from the — Rivier — to the principle work

Fig 7 has by some been considerd as an artificial work, but it may be justly doubted it rather appears a natural hollow way

EFGH are walls or banks of earth, their height & base were not taken by measure, but they appear to be about 20 feet base and, from 3 to 5 feet high

Figs 8, 9, 10 are all imperfect traces of something that appears like artificial walls or banks of earth

Fig 11 is the evident traces of a Rampart at the termination of the plane

Fig 12 appears to be an artificial mound of earth whose Base is in form of an Ellipsis and is about 3 feet high

Fig 13 is an artificial mound of earth whose Base is about 4 perch diameter and forms a hillock about 12 feet high

FIG. 3. FIRST PAGE OF "REFERENCES" ACCOMPANYING THE RUFUS PUTNAM MAP OF THE MARIETTA WORKS, 1788

11

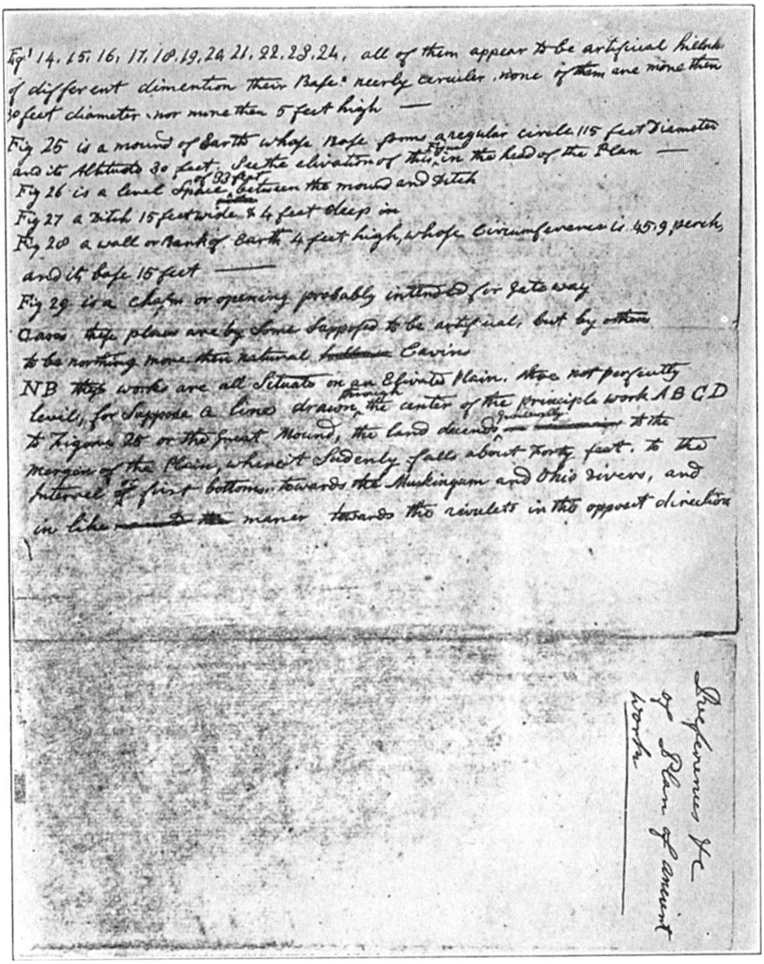

Figs 14. 15. 16. 17. 18. 19. 20. 21. 22. 23. 24. all of them appear to be artificial hillock of different dimention their Base nearly circular, none of them are more then 30 feet diameter, nor more then 5 feet high —

Fig 25 is a mound of Earth whose Base forms a regular circle 115 feet Diameter and its Altitude 30 feet. See the elevation of this Figure in the head of the Plan —

Fig 26 is a level Space of 33 feet between the mound and Ditch

Fig 27 a Ditch 15 feet wide & 4 feet deep in

Fig 28 a wall or Bank of Earth 4 feet high, whose Circumference is 45.9 perch, and its base 15 feet —

Fig 29 is a chasm or opening probably intended for Gate way

Caves these places are by Some Supposed to be artificial, but by others to be nothing more then natural ~~hollows~~ Cavin

NB ~~these~~ works are all Situate on an Elevated Plain. tho not perfectly levil, for Suppose a line drawn through the center of the principle work A B C D to Figure 25 or the great Mound, the land decends gradually ~~[illegible]~~ to the margin of the Plain, where it Sudenly falls about Forty feet. to the Interval or first bottoms. towards the Muskingum and Ohio rivers, and in like ~~[illegible]~~ maner towards the rivulets in the opposit direction

References &c of Plan of Ancient Works

Fig. 4. Second page of "References" accompanying the Rufus Putnam map of the Marietta works

genesis of the science of archæology in the United States. General Putnam, it will be recalled, made an enviable record as an officer in the War of Independence under General Washington. As surveyor and military engineer, he selected the site for West Point and constructed the fortifications there. He was a leader in the Ohio Company, which opened the great Northwest Territory to white settlement, and is credited with preventing the introduction of slavery in the country north and west of the Ohio River.

The Rufus Putnam map has come to be an archæological treasure; and although it has been reproduced at least once with its original appearance restored by photographic methods, it is thought fitting here to present this time-stained document (Figure 2) and its accompanying "References" (Figures 3 and 4) in the handwriting of General Putnam, only slightly retouched in the interest of legibility. Few readers may care to take the trouble to decipher the "References" in this reduced reproduction, but the purpose of this volume is served by the mere presentation of the earliest important document of the now highly developed science of American archæology.

In what may be termed the speculative period, the literature on the mounds and their builders, though not voluminous, was varied and interesting. An entire volume might be devoted to a compilation and consideration of these early contributions, but a few selected references, as typical of the whole, will suffice for our present purpose. The list of early writers on the subject contains such notables as the versatile Benjamin Franklin and Noah Webster; Ezra Stiles, president of Yale College; Thomas Jefferson and Bishop James Madison of Virginia; Caleb Atwater and William Henry Harrison of Ohio; DeWitt Clinton of New York; and others.

Because of the lack of information and precedent it was inevitable that there should be divergent theories among these early thinkers as to the origin of the mounds and the identity of their builders. But few of the ancient tumuli had been observed, and perhaps none of them examined, when Franklin and Webster first took cognizance of them. Their early belief was that the mounds toward the south were erected by De Soto and other Spanish explorers, although later Webster came to believe that they were attributable to the ancestors of the native Indian tribesmen.

When, in 1797, Dr. Benjamin S. Barton published a work entitled *New Views on the Origin of the Tribes of America,* he materially strengthened the already widely held theory that the mounds had been built by an extinct and superior race of people. Rev. Thaddeus M. Harris, of Massachusetts, a few years later reiterated the belief in the "lost-race" theory in his *Tour into the Territory Northwest of the Alleghany Mountains* (1805). Opposed to this school of writers and scholars were those who believed that the earlier representatives of the native Indian tribes were the actual builders of the mounds. Among the first to voice this theory was the Rt. Rev. James Madison, first Protestant Episcopal bishop of Virginia and one-time president of William and Mary College. In 1803, in the *Journal of the American Philosophical Society,* Bishop Madison discussed the mooted question and strongly upheld the view that the American Indians were the authors of the mounds.

THOMAS JEFFERSON, PIONEER ARCHÆOLOGIST

In the galaxy of notables who at this early date were finding time to devote attention to the Mound-builder puzzle was Thomas Jefferson of Virginia. With the War of Independence just concluded, he perhaps found welcome diversion from the strenuous part he had played therein through indulgence of a natural interest in the mysterious and unknown. At any rate he not only has the distinction of being among the earlier writers on the mounds, but has established himself as one of the very earliest real explorers of them. In his quaint volume, *Notes on Virginia,* written, as set forth in the "Advertisement," in 1781-82, and published in 1801, Jefferson discusses the mounds of his native state and describes his examination thereof. The fact that his explorations were among the earliest recorded, together with the importance and standing of their author, is sufficient justification for transcribing here portions of his notes; moreover, they are timely for the reason that they are sufficiently early and primitive to be regarded as archæological in themselves; and again, they afford an interesting comparison with the now highly developed technique of archæological exploration.

Jefferson, speaking of the mounds as "barrows," goes on to say:

That they were repositories of the dead, has been obvious to all; but on what particular occasion constructed, was a matter of doubt. Some have thought that they covered the bones of those who have fallen in battles fought on the spot of interment. Some ascribed them to the custom, said to prevail among the Indians, of collecting, at certain periods, the bones of all their dead, wheresoever deposited at the time of death. Others again supposed them the general sepulchres for towns, conjectured to have been on or near these grounds; and this opinion is supported by the quality of the lands in which they are found . . . and by a tradition, said to be handed down from the aboriginal Indians, that, when they settled in a town, the first person who died was placed erect, and earth put about him, so as to cover and support him; that when another died, a narrow passage was dug to the first, the second reclined against him, and the cover of earth replaced, and so on.

There being one of these [barrows or mounds] in my neighborhood I wished to satisfy myself whether any, and which of these opinions were just. For this purpose I determined to open and examine it thoroughly. It was situated on the low grounds of the Rivanna, about two miles above its principal fork, and opposite to some hills, on which had been an Indian town. It was of a spheroidical form, of about 40 feet diameter at the base, and had been of about 12 feet altitude. . . .

I first dug superficially in several parts of it, and came to collections of human bones, at different depths, from six inches to three feet below the surface. These were lying in the utmost confusion. . . Bones of the most distant parts were found together, as, for instance, the small bones of the foot in the hollow of the skull. . . . I proceeded then to make a perpendicular cut through the body of the barrow, that I might examine its internal structure. . . . At the bottom . . . I found bones; above these, a few stones, brought from the cliff a quarter of a mile off, and from the river, one-eighth of a mile off; then a large interval of earth, then a stratum of bones, and so on. At one end of the section were four strata of bones, plainly distinguishable; at the other, three; the strata in one part not ranging with those in another. . . . I conjectured that in this barrow might have been a thousand skeletons.

Every one will readily seize the circumstances above related, which militate against the opinion, that it covered only the bones of persons fallen in battle; and against the tradition also, which would make it the common sepulchre of a town, in which the bodies were placed upright, and touching each other. Appearances certainly indicate that it has derived both origin and growth from the accustomary collection of bones, and deposition of them together; . . .

The reader will gather that Jefferson, considering only the sparse occurrence of simple, unpretentious mounds in Virginia and unacquainted with the more striking and complex mound groups and earthworks farther west, readily attributed them to the native Indian tribesmen. In this vein he proceeds to speculate on the origin of the Indians thus: "Great question has arisen from whence came those aboriginals of America?" He discusses the possibilities of America being peopled from Europe by way of Iceland, Greenland, and Labrador, and from Asia by way of Kamchatka or Behring Strait, finding the second theory more tenable. Comparing and contrasting the languages of the native Americans and the "red men" of Asia, he notes the striking linguistic diversity of America as compared with the latter. Assuming a common origin for the two and supposing diversity in the form of numerous language groups and dialects to be dependent on the lapse of time, he naïvely concludes that "a greater number of these radical changes of language having taken place among the red men of America, proves them of greater antiquity than those of Asia."

Additional mound locations are recorded farther along in the *Notes*, as follows:

There is another barrow, much resembling this, in the low grounds of the south branch of the Shenandoah where it is crossed by the road leading from the Rockfish gap to Staunton. . . . There is another on a hill in the Blue Ridge of mountains, a few miles north of Wood's gap, which is made up of small stones thrown together. . . . There are also many others in other parts of the country."

Although Jefferson's explorations failed to solve the problem of the mounds and their builders or to produce much in the way of "relics," his estimate of a thousand burials for his tumulus probably has not been equaled in any single mound. Nevertheless, his archæological activities and his quaint account thereof may well be taken as the classical inception of the science of archæology in America.

WILLIAM HENRY HARRISON AND CALEB ATWATER

By first exploring mounds and then becoming president of the United States, Jefferson set a worthy mark for ambitious archæologists. He was, however, but one of several of our presidents who were interested in the mounds and their builders. It is recorded that as early as 1788 General Washington, in a letter to General Baker, expressed the wish that the ancient mounds be made to give up their secret. As governor of Ohio, President Rutherford B. Hayes indicated his interest in the subject, as did President Harding while chief executive of the state.

William Henry Harrison, the president of log-cabin fame, early turned his attention to the numerous mounds adjacent to his home in southwestern Ohio and wrote and lectured concerning them. And although President Harrison's interest in the subject was, in point of time, more recent than that of Thomas Jefferson, it centered in the very heart of the mound region proper and affords the most typical and representative example of the speculative period of Mound-builder literature. Not only is Harrison's *Discourse on the Aborigines of the Valley of the Ohio* a classical literary contribution of its time, but it affords a glimpse of unsuspected sentiment in the rugged character of this warrior, statesman, and president. It is believed that the reader may find, as does the author, in the quaintness and charm of Harrison's *Discourse* justification for the following excerpts.

Commenting on what a traveler descending the Ohio River in presettlement days might have seen, he observes:

His eye might have rested on some stupendous mound, or lengthened line of ramparts . . . which proved that the country had once been possessed by a numerous and laborious people. But he would have seen, also, indubitable evidences that centuries had passed away since these remains had been occupied by those for whose use they had been reared. . . . He would not fail to arrive at the conclusion that their departure . . . must have been a matter of necessity. For no people in any stage of civilization, would willingly have abandoned such a country; endeared to them, as it must have been, by long residence and the labor they had bestowed upon it. . . . If they had been made to yield to a more numerous or more gallant people, what country had received the fugitives? And what has become of the conquerors? . . .

To aid us in coming to anything like a satisfactory conclusion in answer to those questions, we possess only a solitary recorded fact. For everything else, we must search amidst the remains which are still before us, for all that we wish to know of the history and character of this nameless people. And although the result of such an examination may be far from satisfactory, it will not be entirely barren of information. We learn first, from the extensive country covered by their remains, that they were a numerous people. Secondly, that they were congregated in considerable cities. . . . Thirdly, that they were essentially an agricultural people; because, collected as they were in great numbers, they could have depended on the chase but for a small portion of their subsistence. . . . The impossibility of assigning any other purpose to which the greater number, and many of the largest of their remains could be applied, . . . confirm the fact that they had a national religion; in the celebration of which, all that was pompous, gorgeous, and imposing, that a semi-barbarous nation could devise was brought into occasional display. That there were a numerous priesthood, and altars often smoking with hecatombs of victims. . . .

This much do these ancient remains furnish us, as to the condition and character of the people who erected them. I have persuaded myself that I have gleaned from them, also, some interesting facts in their history. It may, however, be proper first to remark, that the solitary recorded fact to which I have alluded, to enable us to determine their ultimate fate, is that which has been furnished to us by the historians of Mexico.

The pictural records of that nation, ascribe their origin to the Astecks, a people who are said to have arrived first in Mexico about the middle of the Seventh century. An American author, the Rt. Rev. Bishop Madison, of Virginia, having with much labor investi-

gated this subject, declares his conviction that these Astecks are
one and the same people with those who once inhabited the valley
of the Ohio. The probabilities are certainly in favor of this opinion.
Adopting it, therefore . . . we refer again to the works they have
left us, to gain what knowledge we can of the cause and manner
of their leaving the Ohio valley. For the reasons formerly stated,
I assume the fact that they were compelled to fly from a more
numerous or a more gallant people. No doubt the contest was long

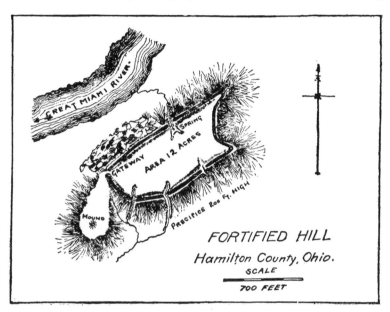

FIG. 5.   MAP OF MIAMI FORT

Prehistoric fortification near the mouth of the Great Miami River, examined
and described by William Henry Harrison.

and bloody, and that the country, so long their residence, was not
abandoned to their rivals until their numbers were too much reduced to continue the contest. Taking into consideration all the
circumstances, . . . I have come to the conclusion that these people
were assailed both from their northern and their southern frontier;
made to recede from both directions, and that their last effort at
resistance was made on the banks of the Ohio.

I have adopted this opinion, from the different character of their
works, which are there found, from those in the interior. Great as
some of the latter are, . . . I am persuaded they never were intended for military defenses. On the contrary, those upon the Ohio

river were evidently designed for that purpose. The three that I have examined, those of Marietta, Cincinnati and the mouth of the Great Miami, particularly the latter, have a military character stamped upon them which cannot be mistaken. The engineers . . . who directed the execution of the Miami works [Figure 5], appear to have known the importance of flank defenses. And if their bastions are not as perfect, as to form, as those which are in use in modern engineering, their position, as well as that of the long line of curtains, are precisely as they should be.

This position then, . . . strong by nature, and improved by the expenditure of great labor, . . . would be the scene of their last efforts to retain possession of the country they had so long inhabited. The interest which everyone feels, who visits this beautiful and commanding spot, would be greatly heightened, if he could persuade himself of the reasonableness of my deductions, from the facts I have stated. That this elevated ridge, from which are now to be seen flourishing villages, and plains of unrivaled fertility, possessed by a people in the full enjoyment of peace and liberty, and all that peace and liberty can give; whose matrons, like those of Sparta, have never seen the smoke of an enemy's fire, once presented a scene of war, and war in its most horrid form, where blood is the object, and the deficiencies of the field made up by the slaughter of innocence and imbecility. That it was here that a feeble band was collected, "remnant of mighty battles fought in vain," to make a last effort for the country of their birth, the ashes of their ancestors, and the altars of their gods. That the crisis was met with fortitude, and sustained with valor, need not be doubted. . . . But their efforts were vain, and flight or death were the sad alternatives. . . . But there is every reason to believe, that they were the founders of a great empire, and that ages before they assumed the more modern and distinguished name of Mexicans, the Astecks had lost in the more mild and uniform climate of Anhuac, all remembrance of the banks of the Ohio. . . .

In relation to their conquerors, I have little to say, and perhaps, that little not very satisfactory. Although I deny the occupation of the banks of the Ohio, for centuries before its discovery by Europeans, I think that there are indubitable marks of its being thickly inhabited by a race of men, inferior to the authors of the great works we have been considering, after the departure of the latter. Upon many places, remains of pottery, pipes, stone hatchets and other articles, are found in great abundance, which are evidently of inferior workmanship to those of the former people. But I have one other fact to offer, which furnishes still better evidence of my opinion. I have before mentioned Cincinnati as one of the positions occupied by the more civilized people. When I first saw the upper plain on which that city stands, it was literally covered with low lines of embankments. I had the honor to attend General Wayne, two years afterward, in an excursion to examine them (1793). . . . The number and variety of figures in which these lines were drawn, was almost endless, and as I have said, almost covered the plain. . . . Now, if these lines were ever of the height of the others made by the same people . . . or unless their erection was ages anterior to the others, there must have been some other cause than the attrition of the rain (for it is a dead level) to bring them down to their then state. That cause I take to have been continued cultivation . . . of another people, and the probability is, that people were the conquerors of the original possessors.

To the question of the former, and the cause of no recent vestige of settlements being found on the Ohio, I can offer only a conjecture; but one which appears to me to be far from improbable.

The *Discourse* at this point reviews the records of numerous disastrous floods of the Ohio River and postulates one greater than any of historic record.

The occurrence of such a flood, when the banks of the Ohio were occupied by numerous Indian towns and villages, nearly all of which must have been swept off, was well calculated to determine them to a removal, not only from actual suffering, but from the suggestions of superstition; an occurrence so unusual, being construed into a warning from heaven, to seek a residence on the smaller streams.

These quotations from two illustrious presidents-to-be furnish typical examples of the range of early theory regarding the Mound-builders: Jefferson, cool, matter-of-fact, seeking only for information justified by the evidence at hand and inclined to consider the mounds as the work of the Indians; Harrison, warm, romantic, and imaginative, construing the evidence as indicative of the existence of mighty hosts of a superior vanished race. One cannot but feel an apparent contradiction between the literary productions quoted and the characters of the two authors as they are popularly conceived: the effusive writing of William Henry Harrison would seem better suited to the Virginia statesman than to the warrior of the western frontier, and vice versa, until it is remembered that Harrison, too, was a Virginian and a classical scholar. While it is apparent that Jefferson would have made a better, or at least a safer, archæologist, literature would have been the loser had not Harrison given us his *Discourse*.

Of a somewhat different character and a decade earlier than the picturesque Harrison *Discourse* were the contributions of Caleb Atwater, Ohio's first historian. To Atwater may be attributed the earliest systematic examinations and descriptions of mounds and earthworks. Under the classic title of *Archæologia Americana,* published by the American Antiquarian Society in 1820, he described and figured the Circleville Group of earthworks and mounds, as well as others of the state, and embellished his text with engravings of artifacts found in his explorations. Atwater's contribution, considering the almost total lack of precedent, was a most creditable one.

During the two or three decades following the appearance of *Archæologia Americana* a number of writers mentioned and described mounds and earthworks. Their writings, however, were mostly local in character, speculative in some instances, and mainly based upon previous discussions, including that of Atwater.

THE CLASSICAL CONTRIBUTION OF SQUIER AND DAVIS

In the year 1848 the world awoke to find on its doorstep what has come to be considered the great classic of American archæology, *Ancient Monuments of the Mississippi Valley,* by E. G. Squier and E. H. Davis. Through this monumental production, issued as the first volume of the now long series of publications of the Smithsonian Institution, public interest for the first time was definitely and sharply focused on the subject of the Mound-builders and their works. Like the minor publications preceding it, Squier and Davis' great monograph is often in error in the light of present-day knowledge; yet it contains invaluable finely executed maps, detailed measurements, and descriptions which otherwise would be lost to history. *Ancient Monuments* is now a rare and highly sought literary and scientific treasure, the pride of any student of American archæology who is so fortunate as to possess a copy of the book.

Squier and Davis described and figured the major works of the Ohio area and the lower Mississippi region, as well as many of the less important ones. Considerable attention was accorded the so-called effigy mounds of the Wisconsin region

FIG. 6. AN EARLY ILLUSTRATION OF THE ANCIENT BURIAL MOUNDS

This old wood-cut from Squier and Davis' *Ancient Monuments* is typical of the early literature on the Mound-builders; it illustrates the facility with which the artists of the period succeeded in portraying the mystery and romance which enshrouded these prehistoric remains in pioneer days.

and other remains of the country to the north and west. Their maps and drawings were from their own surveys and from those of others, including Colonel Charles Whittlesey, James McBride, and Lucas Sullivant of Ohio.

Incidental to their explorations, Squier and Davis accumulated an excellent collection of specimens from the mounds, together with many rare artifacts found on the surface. Despite their efforts to arouse sufficient interest in the United States to take this collection off their hands at a price which would reimburse them for their financial outlay, they were unsuccessful. The collection was taken abroad, and it is now owned by the Blackmore Museum of Salisbury, England.

With the awakening of interest in American archæology through Squier and Davis' volume and the realization of its

FIG. 7. THE LATE DR. WILLIAM C. MILLS

At the time of his death, in 1928, Director of the Ohio State Museum, and for many years recognized as the foremost exponent of mound exploration.

importance in the story of mankind, individuals and institutions began the inauguration of more careful methods of exploration and study of the Mound-builders. From this beginning, in keeping with the growth of the science, the mound area has received marked and effective consideration, with the result that many of the perplexing queries have been answered and much light has been thrown on others.

ACTIVITIES OF THE BUREAU OF AMERICAN ETHNOLOGY

The first important move under the new régime was taken by no less an agency than the Bureau of American Ethnology of the Smithsonian Institution. Under the direction of Dr. Cyrus Thomas, of the Bureau, an extensive survey of the mound area, accompanied by explorations of numerous tumuli, was carried through the decade from 1880 to 1890. Practically every state in which mounds exist was accorded a partial examination, from which far-reaching results were obtained. From the accumulated evidence published in the Twelfth Annual Report (1890-91) of the Bureau, Thomas deduced that the mounds and earthworks were attributable to tribes of the native race—the American Indians; that their builders, for the most part, were the ancestors of the historic Indian tribes; and that while some of the mounds doubtless were of substantial antiquity, some few at least had been built subsequent to the discovery of America. This was the first institutional expression on the moot question of the identity of the builders of the mounds, and as such it carried much weight.

The mound survey conducted by the Bureau of American Ethnology may be said to have marked the end of speculative exploration and the beginning of scientific examination of the prehistoric remains. From that time to the present, explorations based upon the precedents set by Thomas and the data accumulated by him and earlier explorers have been almost continuously contributing to the total of knowledge concerning the past.

RECENT CONTRIBUTORS

At about the same time as the Bureau's survey Professor Frederick W. Putnam of Harvard University began a series of explorations in Ohio and adjacent territory. At the time of his death Professor Putnam was the acknowledged dean of

American archæologists, and by many he is regarded as the originator of scientific mound exploration. His outstanding explorations were conducted in Tennessee and at the Turner Group of mounds and the Madisonville prehistoric village site, both in Hamilton County, Ohio. The rich material taken from these sites is to be seen in the Peabody Museum of Harvard University, and reports of the explorations were published by that institution.

Perhaps the man most closely identified with mound exploration, and one who contributed most to placing the science of American archæology on its present high plane, was Dr. William C. Mills, until his death in 1928 director of the Ohio State Museum. Dr. Mills, called by a contemporary "the foremost exponent of scientific mound exploration," confined his labors to the rich Ohio field, and the material therefrom, displayed in the Ohio State Museum at Columbus, constitutes the best collection of mound artifacts in existence. Reports of his official explorations were published by the Ohio Archæological and Historical Society.

The part which other explorers of the past, as well as those of today, have played in the science will be noted in the following pages. Since the time of Squier and Davis the literature on the mounds, their builders, and their exploration has been voluminous. It takes the form, for the most part, of reports of explorations; and although numerous general treatises have made their appearance, few of them are of outstanding importance. A list of the more important contributions and of their authors may be found in the appended bibliography.

CHAPTER II

DISTRIBUTION AND CLASSIFICATION OF THE MOUNDS

Diffusion of the mound-building trait—The general mound area of the United States—Cultural divisions of the general mound area—Varieties and purposes of mounds: burial, effigy, and domiciliary—Earthworks and enclosures: defensive, ceremonial, and anomalous.

THE accompanying map [1] of the "general mound area" (Figure 8) shows, first of all, that the Mound-builders were by no means confined to a limited territory. The mounds and earthworks, monuments to their spectacular march through the centuries, are distributed quite generally along the Mississippi and the Ohio, with important subareas in the Tennessee-Cumberland district and in the Gulf states, and minor ones in Florida, western New York, and southern Michigan. It will be noted, however, that the coastal states northward from North Carolina are practically devoid of mounds, an indication that the Alleghany Mountains served as a prehistoric boundary line. For this reason the Mound-builders' remains did not come to the attention, to any appreciable extent, of the New England and the Virginia colonists, and therefore they play but little part in our Colonial history.

DIFFUSION OF THE MOUND-BUILDING TRAIT

Ancient mounds, however, are not confined to the comparatively large area corresponding to the eastern United States— the so-called "general mound area." In a sense, mounds are

---

[1] This map, based on that published by the Bureau of American Ethnology, Twelfth Annual Report, is only tentative in its presentation of the tumuli; it attempts to indicate the distribution, rather than individual mounds, which on a map of so small scale manifestly would be impossible. The Bureau of American Ethnology map is the only one ever published showing the distribution of the mounds of the entire area, and at the time of its compilation (1890) mound locations, except in a few favored localities, had not been recorded. An idea of the actual number of mounds really in existence, or rather of record, may be had from the fact that the State of Ohio or of Wisconsin contains more mounds than are recorded on the entire area of this early map.

almost world-wide in their occurrence and distribution, and wherever primitive peoples have lived, in any age, they may have possessed the trait of building mounds in some form, mostly as monuments to their dead.

FIG. 9.   A TYPICAL CONICAL MOUND

The Kilvert Mound, Ross County, Ohio. Mounds of this type are scattered generally over the Middle Western states; almost invariably they were constructed for mortuary purposes.

The extent of the mound-building trait has been aptly summarized by the noted archæologist Gerard Fowke, as follows:

Mounds are among the earliest and most widely distributed memorials of the dead. Savages could pile up earth and stone before they could carve a rock or hew a piece of wood. Barbarians would feel that they were showing greater honor to the memory of a leader whose loss bore upon all alike, by the erection of a monument to which every individual might contribute a share of time and labor. Nothing is more enduring; and when settled into compactness and covered with sod, a heap of earth will remain unchanged through vicissitudes that reduce to ruins any other product of human industry. It is expected, then, that such tumuli would be of world-wide occurrence; and belong not only to primitive ages when men were debarred by limited resources from constructing more elaborate tombs, but continue to be built as tokens of general esteem or affection long after architectural skill had made magnificent structures possible.

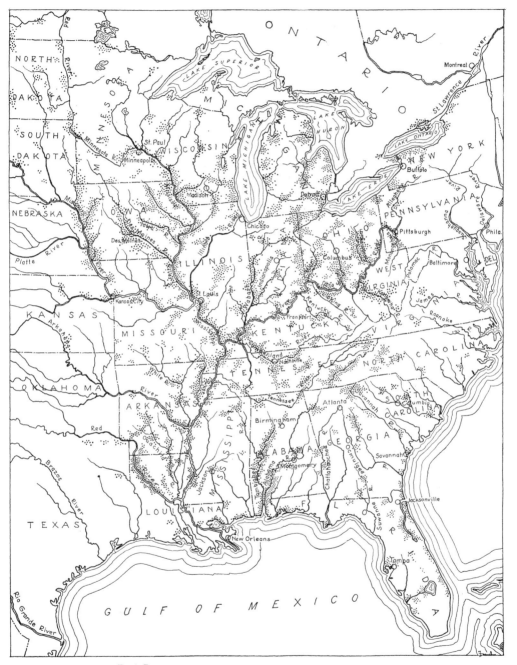

Fig. 8. Distribution of mounds and earthworks in the eastern United States
Red dots indicate relative occurrence and comparative distribution rather than individual major remains.

If one wishes to trace the custom of mound-building in other parts of the world, he will find, in addition to numerous tumuli in Mexico and South America, that mounds occur in great numbers over Europe from the Atlantic Ocean to the Ural Mountains; almost entirely across the great continent of Asia, particularly on the extensive steppes and plains; and to some extent in northern Africa. In the British Isles, in the Orkneys, and in Denmark they occur by the thousand. In Denmark it is of record that King Gorm and his queen, who died about the middle of the Tenth Century, were buried in mounds. The custom of mound burial obtained in England until about the same time. A mound at Cogstad, Norway, is said to cover the remains of a Norwegian king, buried in a Viking war vessel.

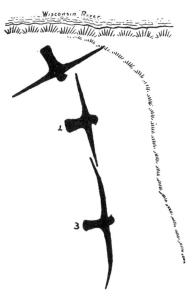

FIG. 10. A TYPICAL EFFIGY
MOUND GROUP

The Lower Dells Group, in Sauk County, Wisconsin. The lower of the three birds, which are represented as flying in unison, has a wing spread of 240 feet.

The burial place of the Roman emperor Julian, who died in conflict with the Persians at Samara, on the Tigris, in the year 363, is marked by a "huge tumulus."

Travelers in Asia Minor, Syria, and Mesopotamia are astonished at the numbers and great size of the tumuli. The great mound on the site of Nineveh, not primarily a burial mound, is said to cover upward of 100 acres, with a maximum height of 90 feet.

According to Sir John Lubbock, in his *Prehistoric Times*, several heroes of the Trojan War were buried under mounds. The valiant Achilles erected a mound over the remains of his friend Patroclus; Hector, slayer of Patroclus and in turn victim of Achilles' wrath, enjoys a similar resting place. And if these examples, selected at random, are not sufficient to attest the antiquity and popularity of mounds as monuments to the dead, it may be added that Alexander the Great heaped a tumulus over his friend Hephæstion at a cost of more than the equivalent of one million dollars.

Although not all prehistoric mounds are burial tumuli, the great majority may be classed as such, for usually they are found either to cover the remains of the dead or to commemorate their passing. To draw an analogy perhaps hardly permissible from an ethnological standpoint, such monumental works as the Egyptian pyramids and the hardly less imposing pyramids of Middle America are in a sense but highly evolved forms of burial and memorial mounds; and, continuing the evolution, the highly ornate and artistic marble and granite shafts in present-day cemeteries are but modern expressions of the primitive earthen tumulus—tombstones, monuments to the dead.

THE GENERAL MOUND AREA OF THE UNITED STATES

In considering that portion of the United States designated as the general mound area, we find that the trait of building mounds was inordinately developed, so much so, in fact, as to be an outstanding trait and as such setting apart the peoples responsible for their erection as sharply distinctive from any other primitive people.

If all the mounds of the general area were alike physically and as to contents, the task of describing them would be greatly simplified. If the accumulated evidence of exploration disclosed basic similarities, with only the slight deviations to be expected in the culture of any primitive people, however homogeneous, scattered over a great expanse of territory, then it logically might be assumed that the mounds throughout the entire area were the product of a specific people. Evidences of cultural evolution, normally from a lower to a higher plane and to an extent corresponding with the length of time of occupancy, might be confidently looked for. To the reader it may come as something of a surprise to learn that there are in the general mound area numerous kinds of mounds, representing an equal number of kinds, or cultures, of Mound-builders. To the archæologist this means simply that various branches or tribes of our prehistoric inhabitants, racially akin but culturally differing, possessed the common trait of building mounds. The logical belief is that the trait, or the germ of it, had been developed before the several divisions dispersed from a common nucleus; or, what seems more likely, that it originated with some of them and through diffusion or borrowing became common to all.

In classifying the several varieties of mounds, the tendency, from the archæological point of view, is to separate them into "cultures." This clearly is the logical and the ideal procedure. But the archæology of the mound region is yet in its infancy, and its development is not sufficient to admit of such a classification being carried out in its entirety. Few of the recognized cultures are exhaustively known, and many of them are hardly known at all; moreover, their geographical extent is undetermined, and in many instances they intrude and overlap one another. For these reasons the cultural classification appears inadequate or impracticable for a popular consideration such as this, and the reader will have to be content, for the present, with the scheme here used, tentative and unsatisfactory as it admittedly is.

CULTURAL DIVISIONS OF THE GENERAL MOUND AREA

Reference to the map of the mound area shows a striking tendency for these major remains to group themselves geographically or topographically. Primarily, none or few would be expected in territory that is, or was, mountainous or swampy and therefore unfit for human occupancy. Again, they would be expected to be most in evidence in close proximity to water supplies and waterways. That these surmises are correct is attested by the mound distribution. Waterways clearly were the determining factor in occupancy, and the several groups or subareas correspond to and were determined by water systems. Not only is water a requisite of life, but in the instance of the Mound-builders the lakes, rivers, and streams served as highways for travel, supplementing or even supplanting the land trails.

The classification here adopted recognizes six archæological subareas—areas we shall term them from this time on. The apparent grouping, geographically, may be in part accidental, but to a greater degree it is clearly determined by the location of waterways. At the same time the scheme contains much of the element of cultural distinction; thus the adopted classification is further justified in that it is a composite one, based on geographical as well as cultural considerations.

The recognized areas, as outlined on the map, are the Ohio area; the Upper Mississippi area; the Lower Mississippi area; the Great Lakes area; the Tennessee-Cumberland area; and the Peninsular area. The geographical affinities of each are apparent; the cultural characteristics will be noted presently.

VARIETIES AND PURPOSES OF MOUNDS: BURIAL, EFFIGY, AND DOMICILIARY

Hitherto we have employed the term "mound" in a broad sense, to comprise artificial works of earth and stone of every kind; but since not all such works had their origin in a common impulse, it is necessary, in the interest of understanding and appreciation, to differentiate the several classes of prehistoric remains. By far the greater number of the tumuli (practically all those of conical form) were constructed for mortuary purposes, and these are known as "burial" or "sepulchral" mounds. Formerly some of this type were termed "lookout" or "signal" mounds, but it is now believed that such comparatively low structures, under primitive conditions of uncleared forests, would have been of little advantage for such purposes. Ceremonially they may have served as such at times; but the prehistoric scout wishing to transmit signals to his tribe or to

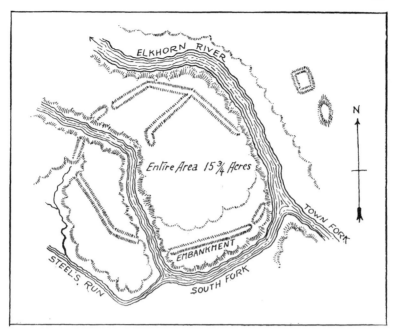

FIG. 11. A TYPICAL FORTIFICATION ERECTED FOR PURPOSES OF DEFENSE
A work near Lexington, Kentucky. Redrawn from Squier and Davis.

spy upon the enemy doubtless was sufficiently practical to select an outstanding elevation or a tall tree as more effective for his purpose.

A modification of the conical mound known as the "truncated," "flat-topped," or "platform" mound, occurring freely in the lower Mississippi valley, served as bases for domiciliary and ceremonial structures and the houses of chiefs and sachems. They are sometimes known as "house" mounds and "temple" mounds.

The so-called "effigy" or "image" mounds were constructed in the forms of birds, animals, serpents, and humans. They occur mostly in southern Wisconsin and adjacent areas. Two or three notable examples are found in Ohio, to be described presently. The effigy mounds are believed to have had their origin in sacred or religious observances and appear to be totemic in character. They sometimes contain human burials.

EARTHWORKS AND ENCLOSURES: DEFENSIVE, CEREMONIAL,
AND ANOMALOUS

Of the earthworks, so-called, two principal types occur. The prehistoric fortifications are embankments of earth or stone, or the two in combination, enclosing the tops of hills and other strategic locations, and appear to have been purely defensive in character. They are distributed rather widely throughout the mound area but are more common in Ohio and adjacent portions of other states, examples being the formidable works known as Fort Ancient and Fort Hill, in Ohio (see Chapter X). A second class of earthworks are the striking geometric enclosures in connection with mounds and sites of the highly developed Hopewell culture of Mound-builders centering in southern Ohio. These enclosures represent geometric figures—squares, circles, octagons, crescents, and so forth,

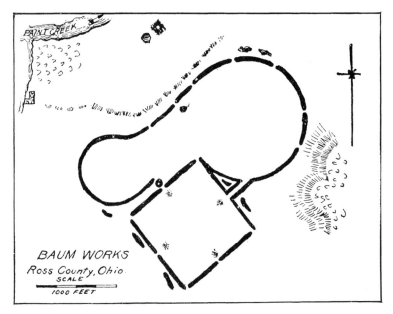

FIG. 12. A GEOMETRIC EARTHWORK

Representing a square and circles in combination; peculiar to the Hopewell culture of Mound-builders centering in Ohio.

and at times they so nearly approach true geometric forms that early writers believed their builders to have had a working knowledge of geometry. The purpose of the geometric earthworks was a sacred or a social one, or perhaps a combination of the two.

In addition to the principal types of mounds and earthworks so far mentioned, there occur occasional anomalous structures the use and purpose of which is problematical. The extensive shell heaps occurring along the seaboard and adjacent to certain rivers and streams, as well as the numerous old village sites, cemeteries, and other evidences of human occupancy, also have their place in the story of the Mound-builders and other prehistoric peoples of the eastern United States.

We have seen that mounds are widely distributed through both time and space, and that they are attributable to peoples ranging from a low degree of culture to comparatively high attainment. In considering our own mound area, where the mound-building trait attained its greatest development, we shall see for ourselves what manner of men they were; if we do not expect too much of them, or too little, we shall find them a most interesting and worth-while people. Subsequent chapters, under the several areas in which the mounds are grouped, attempt to tell what has been learned concerning the mounds and their builders through the medium of the archæologist's spade and trowel.

CHAPTER III

ARCHITECTURE AND ENGINEERING

Primitive architecture of native American tribes—Structural achievements of the Mound-builders—Magnitude of mound-building operations—Construction and purpose of the mounds—Use of stone in building of mounds—Stone burial vaults and stone graves—Timber structures—Primitive engineering in the mound area—Geometric earthworks and their construction.

THE origin and development of architecture furnishes a fascinating chapter to the student of human culture. In the so-called civilized countries of today the landscape is literally dotted with structures and edifices reflecting the high development of architecture and engineering. But it is a far cry back to the days of savagery, when human beings were content with the natural shelter afforded by trees, overhanging rocks, and caves. Gradually, as the cosmic urge toward cultural improvement asserted itself, rude shelters of sticks, brush, bark, and stones were constructed. These in turn were supplanted by lodges and tipis of poles, mats, and skins, often of a portable nature to suit the convenience of nomadic peoples. The character of these shelters improved with the cultural status of their builders, and both advances were decidedly dependent upon available supplies of suitable building materials—stone, clay, and timber. At first, artificial structures were intended as dwellings or domiciles solely for the convenience of the living; but as religious, social, technical, and æsthetic traits developed, there arose a corresponding differentiation in the uses to which artificial structures were devoted. In addition to dwellings, there came into existence structures for defense and protection, buildings for social and religious observances, tombs for the remains of the dead, and so forth.

Within the territory embraced by the present United States there were several distinct stages of primitive architectural development, corresponding to the culture status of the primitive inhabitants and influenced largely by the natural environment imposed by climate, rainfall, topography, and other factors.

The reader is more or less familiar with the unique snow and ice igloos of the Eskimo, within the Arctic regions; with the elaborate and highly developed houses, of wood construction, erected by the tribes of the northwest coast; and with the striking cliff dwellings and adobe communal houses of the Pueblo peoples of the southwestern arid region. Intermediate in development between the first-named and the Pueblo are the tipis of skins and matting of the Plains Indians; the bark long houses of the Iroquois; the grass lodges of the Wichita; and the mat houses of the southern tribes.

Our interest for the moment, however, is with the architecture of the Mound-builders. Viewed from the standpoint of present-day interpretation of the terms architecture and engineering, it would appear at first glance that neither of these arts plays an important part in the archæology of the mound region. Although it is true that the builders of the mounds had made no particularly significant strides in the building arts, nevertheless many initial steps in the evolution of architecture and engineering are to be found in their surviving major remains. Few of the recognized essentials of architecture, as the offset span and the keystone arch, were known to the Mound-builders, yet they had advanced far beyond the status of the savage, who contents himself with nature's canopy and natural shelters for protection from the elements and from his enemies.

STRUCTURAL ACHIEVEMENTS OF THE MOUND-BUILDERS

Of the several outstanding prehistoric culture groups within the United States, only two have left behind them major evidences of their existence. These are the Pueblo peoples, with their cliff dwellings and great communal houses, and the so-called Mound-builders, whose impressive earthworks are a very part of the physical geography of the Mississippi valley and the country to the east and south. The Pueblos built of stone and clay, so largely and so well that their edifices afford an unintentional record of their lives. The Mound-builders, while utilizing mostly clay and earth, operated on a scale so extensive as to leave an almost equally distinct record. Comparing the architecture of the two, a striking distinction is evident. The Pueblos built almost exclusively for the living— for shelter and protection. Their dead were accorded but scant attention and often were buried in the rubbish heaps adjacent to their domiciles. The Mound-builders, on the other hand, built mostly for the dead, and always with the idea of the hereafter in mind. The abodes of the living, mere shelters of poles, bark, matting, and skins, long since have disappeared. The Pueblo peoples survived and witnessed the coming of the Europeans; the Mound-builders, so far as their distinctive culture is concerned, lie within the prehistoric past. Had the mound-building peoples possessed adequate supplies of available stone for building purposes, who shall say that they might not have survived to become an outstanding, perhaps a dominant, element of the native American race?

Anthropologists have indicated the importance of available building materials not only in the development of architecture, but in the unfolding of human culture in general. While wood and clay were serviceable building materials, neither was sufficiently durable to sustain cumulative growth and thus to encourage cumulative effort. Structures built of wood or clay were short-lived in usefulness and must needs be frequently rebuilt or replaced. An abundant supply of accessible stone, however, furnished building material of a lasting character, through which the structural arts became more permanent, better established, and cumulative as to results. Without stone, it is pointed out, the development of architecture, and the entire range of human activities, would have been immeasurably retarded. This quite obvious inference is forcefully corroborated in archæological explorations: the structures erected by peoples utilizing stone in their building arts survive in recognizable form, while buildings of wood or clay construction either have entirely disappeared or at best are mere heaps or ruins.

In considering the architecture of the mound area it is convenient to observe (1) structures of earth, comprising the so-called mounds (burial, effigy, platform, and so forth), fortifications (for defense), and enclosures (of social and religious import); (2) structures of stone, comprising rooms or compartments within the mounds, the so-called stone graves, and stone used in the same manner as earth, though to a lesser extent, in constructing mounds, fortifications, and earthworks; and (3) structures of wood, including houses or dwellings, sacred structures, and log tombs or burial vaults within the burial mounds.

MAGNITUDE OF MOUND-BUILDING OPERATIONS

The use of earth far exceeds that of all other materials in the major remains of the Mound-builders. As noted in the preceding chapter, the mounds and earthworks, scattered over twenty or more states and numbering perhaps 100,000 in the aggregate, are the outstanding feature of the archæological area. The simple forms represented in the several types already noted impose no architectural problems, with the possible exception of the geometric enclosures, found principally in the State of Ohio. Aside from these, the primary conical tumuli, the elongate or linear mounds, and the irregular structures represent little more than the elementary labor involved.

Although a smaller burial mound or a simple wall of earth thrown up across an exposed sector of a defensive site indicates a comparatively small amount of labor, the erection of the larger mounds and earthworks represents the expenditure of a surprising amount of energy. This is particularly apparent when it is remembered that the work was done, not with the advantages of modern engineering devices, but under strictly primitive conditions. Yet in the reaction which followed earlier attempts to picture the Mound-builders as prodigies in every conceivable way, some modern writers have gone to extremes in minimizing the accomplishments of the authors of the mounds.

Keeping in mind the approximate total of mounds and earthworks in the general mound area, some idea of the great expenditure of labor in their construction under primitive conditions may be gained from consideration of a single mound.

FIG. 13. THE MOST COMMON TYPE OF MOUND-BUILDER CONSTRUCTION

The many thousands of burial tumuli, of earth and stone, scattered throughout the general mound area, represent the bulk of architectural activity of the Mound-builders.

In the examination of the Seip Mound, in Ross County, Ohio, the Ohio State Museum's archæological survey spent three entire summers—the equivalent of nine months of intensive labor. This mound was 250 feet long, 150 feet wide, and 30 feet in height, its cubic content being something over 20,000 cubic yards, or, expressed in more familiar terms, full-sized wagonloads of earth. Owing to the fact that in mounds of this culture all burials and other intentional inclusions rest upon the base line or floor level, the removal of 90 per cent of the structure was little more than a question of how most quickly and easily to effect the task. An average force of fifteen laborers, with picks and shovels, was employed in undercutting the exposed face of the mound, taking advantage of gravity in detaching masses of earth, and in keeping the working trench clear. Teams and scrapers were employed continually in supplementing the efforts of the workmen after the detached earth had been inspected for possible inclusions.

Although the work of razing the Seip Mound, aided as it was by gravity, proved to be a major undertaking, its restoration was and continues to be a problem difficult of solution. Despite the fact that not more than 40 per cent of the total amount of earth need be handled in effecting the restoration and that all of this amount lies in close proximity to the tumulus site, the task of replacing the detached earth in its original position is a puzzling one. The use of teams and scrapers for conveying earth to a height of 30 feet has proved a difficult, but in the end the best available, method. The Seip Mound admittedly is much larger than the average and involves construction problems foreign to the smaller tumuli. However, compared with the great Cahokia Mound, which is 100 feet in height and covers 16 acres of ground, or even with several of the eighty-five minor tumuli comprising the Cahokia Group, it appears very modest. At any rate, the problems arising from its exploration and restoration are indicative of the labor expended in erecting the many thousands of artificial earthen structures within the general mound area.

This expenditure of labor not only has been a matter of wonder and speculation, but has received rather serious consideration, for the most part by those who have recognized, quite properly, the importance of correcting early imaginative theories regarding the mound-building peoples. An example is the estimate of a prominent archæologist who, by careful mathematical calculations, showed that a conical mound 20 feet high, 100 feet in diameter at the base, and containing a trifle less than 2,000 cubic yards could be constructed by fifty laborers under primitive conditions in slightly more than 100 days. These calculations assume that the primitive workman would carry an average of one-half a cubic foot per load, equivalent to 45 pounds in weight, and that the distance traveled to obtain the earth should permit him to contribute at least twenty such loads per day. In the case of larger mounds, particularly as the growing structure increased in height, the individual laborer's daily contribution would be decreased. The writer's observations in connection with mound exploration, checked by careful measurement and weighing of individual

FIG. 14.   STONE WALL OF A PREHISTORIC FORTIFICATION

Flint Ridge, Licking County, Ohio. The occurrence of easily accessible stone in many sections of the mound area encouraged its use in structural activities.

loads of earth composing the tumuli, led to the belief that the primitive workman seldom carried loads above 20 or 25 pounds in weight, presumably for the reason that the primitive carrying baskets were not adapted to greater strain.

Computing the time required for the construction of earthworks under primitive conditions, however, is much like figuring an extended automobile trip on paper. In practice the estimates usually fall short of actuality. If it could be assumed that each individual worker engaged in erecting a mound was 100 per cent efficient; that he expended the full eight or ten hours each day for the entire period; and that weather and other factors remained constantly favorable, then such calculations would be much more dependable. Assuming, however, that the figures cited are reasonably accurate, and that fifty workmen would construct a mound containing 2,000 cubic yards of earth within a period of approximately 100 working days, then we find that the Seip Mound, with a cubic content of 20,000 yards, should be built by fifty workmen in 1,000 days. By varying the number of workmen, guessing the number of days in each year on which they could or would work, and making allowances for other factors entering into the primitive human equation, some idea of the time required for mound construction may be gained. In a mound 30 feet in height, like the Seip Mound, the labor naturally would become more arduous as the prospective mound increased in height, and the requisite time would be much longer.

The same authority, computing the cubic contents of all the mounds and earthworks in the state of Ohio to be 30,000,000 cubic yards, finds that a thousand men working 300 days in the year, each contributing the equivalent of one wagonload of earth daily, would accomplish the task of building them within a century. No small labor this, if the estimate is accepted as reasonable; and when it is applied to the probable 100,000 artificial earthworks of the entire mound area, the aggregate of labor, energy, and industry becomes surprising to contemplate.

CONSTRUCTION AND PURPOSE OF THE MOUNDS

The manner in which the mounds and earthworks were erected is entirely obvious, since it is known that no beasts of burden or mechanical aids of advanced type were in use by their builders. Each individual worker constituted himself a sort of porter or stevedore. Armed with a carrying basket or similar receptacle, he repaired to the nearest spot where the required earth could be procured. Digging sticks, stone hoes, clamshells, and shoulder blades of deer and elk served as implements for loosening the earth. The individual offerings then were carried to the mound and added to the growing heap.

The erection of a large mound was not the work of a day or of a year. Exploration discloses the fact that tumuli of exceptional size were the products of several years of activity. What are termed seasonal lines are plainly visible in cross sections of large mounds, showing just where the work of construction had ceased with the approach of winter and where it had been resumed later. The earth composing the mounds was not brought from a distance, as has been so often reported; rather it was obtained from the most convenient nearby sources.

There has been much speculation as to the motive behind mound-building, entailing as it did such strenuous and prolonged purposeful labor. Early writers were inclined to believe that a highly organized system of government based on despotic control of the masses, amounting to actual slavery, existed among the Mound-builders. This theory has little or nothing to support it, however. It is probable that the common impulse of respect and veneration for the dead, particularly for those of high standing, was sufficient to engage the energies of all who were physically able to contribute to the erection of the earthen memorials. The common desire for protection from wild animals and human enemies would engender sufficient coöperation to produce the earthworks for defense.

If the reader still finds it difficult to credit so vast an expenditure of labor under other than conditions of force, citation of a present-day people, the Chinese, may be convincing. With their striking veneration for the dead, amounting almost to worship, the Chinese continue to make almost unbelievable sacrifices, often to the point of impoverishment, in order to contribute to their honor. While Chinese of the better class erect pretentious tombs over their departed, vast areas of valuable land are encumbered by countless small mounds marking the resting places of the humble dead.

USE OF STONE IN BUILDING OF MOUNDS

As indicated on an earlier page, the use of stone by the Mound-builders for construction purposes was of secondary

FIG. 15. STONE WALL OF A BURIAL ROOM

From a mound on Flint Ridge, Licking County, Ohio. The use of stone for burial vaults and graves was quite general in the mound area.

importance as compared with earth. The reason for this is obvious. Although stone, in a sense, is almost universal in its distribution, the occurrence of available supplies of qualities suitable for major structural purposes is restricted to definite localities. While there was an abundance of stone of many varieties within the general mound area, it seems not to have been of a nature to encourage liberal use in building construction, such as that developed in the Pueblo–Cliff-dweller region.

FIG. 16. A TYPICAL STONE GRAVE

Illustrating one of the principal uses of stone by the Mound-builders. The flat stones which covered the top are laid to one side in their original positions. This grave, from the Seip Mound, Ross County, Ohio, contained a cremated burial.

In the construction of their mounds and earthworks the Mound-builders frequently made use of stone in much the same way as they used earth. Mounds and cairns constructed wholly or in part of stone are not uncommon, particularly in the Upper Mississippi, the Ohio, and the Tennessee areas. Many of the more impressive defensive earthworks in the same general regions are built of stone or of stone and earth intermingled, no distinction being made between the two materials for such construction. On the whole, employment of stone, either as bulk structural material or in more specialized uses, appears to have been dependent on its ready availability.

In the sense of actual building, only incipient forms of stone construction are found in the mound area. No examples of actual dressing of stone or laying up of masonry walls, as practiced by the Pueblo peoples, are known in the mound

Fig. 17. Imprints of logs forming a timbered structure in a Wisconsin mound
Courtesy of the Milwaukee Public Museum.

area. The nearest approach to actual masonry is found in certain mounds of southern Missouri, where explorations by Gerard Fowke and others revealed rectangular stone walls, outlining rooms or compartments, laid up to a height of several feet with selected flat stones (see Chapter XVI). The same practice is noted in adjacent regions of the Mississippi valley and occasionally elsewhere, notably in a mound located on Flint Ridge, in Licking County, Ohio (Figure 15), and in a group situated in southeastern Iowa explored by the Davenport Academy of Science. An interesting and widely distributed use of stone in supplementing earth construction is that at the base of mounds and earthworks, bastionlike, to avert erosion and washing away of the earth. This use is strikingly illustrated at the great Fort Ancient, in Warren County, Ohio, and at the base of the Seip Mound, in Ross County, to which further reference will be made.

Perhaps the best-known use of stone in the mound area was its employment in the so-called stone graves. Throughout a wide area, embracing southern Missouri, parts of Kentucky, Tennessee, and adjacent regions, many thousands of stone graves have been discovered. These are boxlike cists, or rather dug graves lined with rough flat stones, either with or without bottom platforms and top coverings of similar stones (Figure 16). In a sub-floor burial within the Tremper Mound, in Scioto County, Ohio, the walls of the grave were carefully lined with selected small flat stones laid up after the fashion of masonry but without mortar.

TIMBER STRUCTURES

The employment of timber for structural purposes by the Mound-builders doubtless was much more extensive than can be proved by direct evidence. The material, being perishable, would leave no very obvious indications of its use. Within the mounds of several of the cultures of the general area, however, there appear evidences of timber structures, in the form of post holes, log and timber molds, and even partly preserved timbers themselves. In the Lower Mississippi area, in connection with the flat-topped house and temple mounds, these evidences are particularly striking. Outlines of circular and rectangular rooms, singly or conjoined, are of frequent occurrence, while the remains of wattled walls, constructed of reeds, matting, and poles, the interstices chinked with clay, are much in evidence. The preservation of such remains was due to the fact that dwellings and ceremonial structures burned or fallen into decay were covered with earth in order that the site might again be utilized for dwelling purposes.

In the highly developed Hopewell culture of southern Ohio, western Illinois, and adjacent portions of Iowa, the remains of prestructures of timbers are characteristic of the mounds. These may take the form, as in the noted Tremper Mound, of large ceremonial structures divided into rooms or compartments, or they may be simple log cists or charnel houses for the inhumation of the dead. In the Ogden Mound, of the same culture, near Lewistown, Illinois, tunneling operations have revealed remarkable structural phenomena in the form of dome-shaped structures of timbers and poles with what appear to be the remains of reed walls, probably wattled (see Chapter XV). The explanation of the occurrences within these mounds is that the sites of the tumuli originally were occupied by these wooden structures, which, following their occupancy or ceremonial use, were covered by the protecting mounds of earth and thus partially preserved. Mounds of the lower cultures present but few evidences of the use of wood.

FIG. 18. PREHISTORIC
WATTLE-WORK

A reconstruction of the wall of a Mound-builder dwelling. Remains of wattled walls occur freely in the house mounds of the southern areas. After Thomas.

PRIMITIVE ENGINEERING IN THE MOUND AREA

An interesting primitive experiment in structural engineering was disclosed in the Seip Mound (Figure 19). On the site of this large tumulus there had been erected a rectangular log structure serving as a burial vault or charnel house for six individuals. This number, in contrast with the usual one or two bodies placed within the log chambers, necessitated a structure of unaccustomed size, its measurements being approximately 8 feet wide by 11 feet long, with a height of 8 feet. After the multiple burial had been made in the charnel house, the customary primary mound was erected over it. Unfortunately the primitive engineer failed properly to figure the

FIG. 19. A PREHISTORIC EXPERIMENT IN STRUCTURAL ENGINEERING

The caved-in primary mound of the Seip Mound, Ross County, Ohio, in which a log charnel house of unusual size collapsed under the weight of the covering earth. Later the primitive workmen rebuilt the apex. The man in the picture is standing upon the caved-in structure; the restored apex is immediately behind his shoulders.

strength of his timbers, with the result that the superincumbent earth of the protecting mound proved too heavy for the wooden structure; after a time it collapsed, permitting the upper portion of the mound to cave in and partially fill the interior chamber. Undaunted, however, the primitive workmen carried earth and carefully rebuilt the upper portions of the mound, restoring its apex to the original form.

In the great mound proper, which later came to enclose this primary mound and several similar ones, a clever bit of engineering was disclosed. Anticipating the erosion which naturally would attack an earthen structure 30 feet in height, with slopes so steep as to tax the physical endurance of those ascending it, a trench had been carefully dug completely around the outer margin of the mound, more than 600 feet in circumference. Within this trench there had been placed a retaining wall of sandstone slabs, set on edge and inclining with the upward slope of the mound. Against this retaining wall there was carried a layer of heavy gravel and small boulders, thickest at the base of the mound and diminishing to the apex, which prevented the washing down of the underlying earth. Surveyor's instruments show an accumulation adjacent to the margin of the mound as a result of erosion of less than five inches, despite the fact that the elements for centuries have beaten upon it.

GEOMETRIC EARTHWORKS AND THEIR CONSTRUCTION

The engineering ingenuity of the builders of the mounds is perhaps best illustrated in the so-called geometric earthworks of southern Ohio. These, as has been mentioned, are earthen embankments of circular, square, octagonal, and other geometric forms, enclosing up to 100 or more acres of ground. Early writers expatiated on the geometric science of the Mound-builders, basing their theories on the supposed exactness of the squares, circles, and other figures in which their earthworks were designed. Even Squier and Davis, the pioneer archæologists in the mound area, insisted that the figures, or many of them, were geometrically exact and that they could be the result of nothing short of a considerable development of mathematical knowledge on the part of their builders.

It remained for Gerard Fowke to furnish an authoritative finding in this matter. Through a series of painstaking surveys, conducted at the great Newark works and elsewhere in the Ohio area, he showed that although none of the enclosures is an exact geometric figure, a number of them approximate very closely to such and that simple means for describing them were known to and used by their builders. The great "Fair-Ground Circle" of the Newark works (Figure 20) was found to measure 1,189 feet in its longest diameter and 1,163

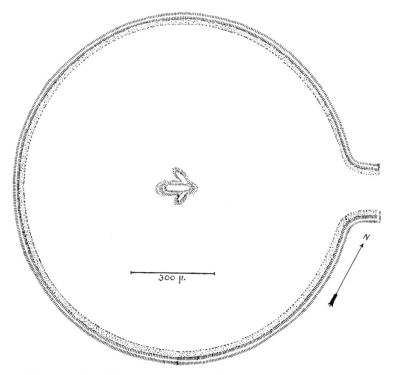

FIG. 20. THE "FAIR-GROUND CIRCLE" OF THE NEWARK WORKS

An example of the accuracy with which the builders of the Hopewell culture earthworks at times constructed their geometric enclosures. The "Fair-ground Circle" has a mean diameter of 1,175 feet, and the lines of a true circle would fall within the zone of its wall, which is from 35 to 55 feet wide.

feet in its shortest, the circumference of a true circle falling within the ring or zone occupied by the wall, which varies in width from 35 to 55 feet. The smaller circle of the group has a maximum diameter of 1,059 feet and a minimum of 1,050, the widest divergence between this figure and an exact circle of the mean diameter of 1,054.5 feet being only 4.5 feet. The square enclosure of the group likewise approximates closely a true geometric figure. Circular figures, it is pointed out, may be very easily described, even by primitive peoples, by means of stakes and thongs; square and octagonal figures, while more difficult, may be described by fairly simple methods. As a result of these observations it is clear that the Mound-builders knew and made use of the simple elements of geometry and surveying.

CHAPTER IV

AGRICULTURE, COMMERCE, AND INDUSTRY

The mound-building peoples as agriculturists—Corn, beans, squash, and other food plants—Tobacco and its cultivation—Agricultural implements and methods—Prehistoric cornfields and garden beds—Commercial activities: trade, barter, and exchange—Character and extent of Mound-builder commerce—Primitive industry of the mound area—The quarrying of flint and other materials—The mining of copper, iron ore, and other minerals—The quest for fresh-water pearls—Minor raw materials—The art of flint-chipping—Use of copper and other metals—Utilization of stone, bone, shell, and wood—Pottery and pottery-making—The textile arts: spinning and weaving.

THE fact that agriculture, commerce, and industry were extensive and diversified activities in the economy of the Mound-builders, as evidenced by exploration of the ancient mounds and village sites, is indicative of the comparatively high status to which several of the prehistoric cultures had attained. The reconstruction of these activities, from the mute evidences of exploration and through comparison with customs of historic representatives of the native American race, constitutes a most interesting phase of archæological procedure.

THE MOUND-BUILDING PEOPLES AS AGRICULTURISTS

It is customary to think of agriculture as pertaining only to civilized peoples, or at least to peoples who have emerged from so-called barbarism into the realm of what we are pleased to term civilization. As a matter of fact, the beginnings of agriculture can be traced back to very primitive times and primitive peoples, and the artificial fostering of food plants seems to be almost instinctive with the human race. Contrary to widespread popular belief, most of the historic tribes of native American Indians were agricultural in varying degrees, and to corresponding degrees sedentary in their manner of life.

54

Agricultural development in the United States in prehistoric times ranged from those occasional tribes which were purely nomadic and without apparent agriculture to those which, like the Pueblos of the Southwest, had developed artificial propagation of food plants to a high degree.

Second only to the Pueblos with their intensive agriculture aided by irrigation were the peoples of the general mound area. As in all the more advanced areas of North and Central America, maize, or Indian corn, was the staple agricultural product with the builders of the mounds. The giant cereal was supplemented by other cultivated products, such as beans, squash, pumpkins, melons, sunflowers, and probably a number of other plants of real or fancied value for food and medicinal purposes. And though maize was the staple food product throughout the mound area, the indispensable tobacco seems to have commanded almost equal attention from the mound-building peoples.

The manner in which the archæologist proceeds to determine the extent to which the Mound-builders had developed the science of agriculture and to identify the plants they cultivated is of exceptional interest. The process consists principally in discovering, in the mounds and village sites, the actual plant materials which served as food, both cultivated and uncultivated; in finding, under the same conditions, the implements and utensils used in planting, cultivating, harvesting, and preparing such products for food purposes; in observing the material evidences of cultivation of the soil, such as extensive and systematic irregularities of the surface, usually designated as "cornfields" and "garden beds"; and in studying for purposes of comparison the methods of agriculture practiced by the historic tribes of the native American race at the time of discovery and colonization.

CORN, BEANS, SQUASH, AND OTHER FOOD PLANTS

In addition to all the native wild fruits, nuts, seeds, and other edible plant elements, there occur freely in the mounds and village sites of the general mound area remains of such cultivated products as corn, beans, squash, tobacco, and some minor products. Corn, being the most important and of widest distribution, naturally is most in evidence. Not only do grains of corn and corn-cobs occur separately and a b u n d a n t l y , either in a charred condition, or as impressions in the ground, but actual ears of the cereal occasionally are found.

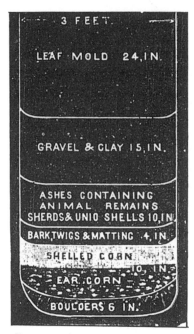

FIG. 21. A STORAGE REFUSE PIT

The archæologist is indebted for many important finds to the practice of certain mound-building peoples of utilizing pits for the storage of grain and seeds and later using the same pits for disposing of household refuse. The illustration shows a cross-section of a storage pit at the Madisonville site, Hamilton County, Ohio, explored by Professor Frederick W. Putnam.

Maize, or Indian corn, is perhaps America's greatest single gift to the world. When Columbus and the discoverers who followed him came in contact with the native Americans, civilized peoples for the first time made the acquaintance of Indian corn. The story of the spread of corn to all parts of the world where it can be grown, and of the part it played in the colonization and settlement of America by Europeans, constitutes romance unique in human interest. Most of the early explorers, including De Soto, Cartier, Champlain, La Salle, and others, record the importance of maize cultivation among the Indian tribes eastward from the great plains. From Massachusetts to Florida; in the St. Lawrence valley and adjacent to the Great Lakes; in the valleys of the Ohio and the Mississippi; in fact, wherever there were native tribesmen, there were corn and cornfields. It has been pointed out that but for maize the peopling of America by Europeans would have been delayed at least a century. Captain John Smith and his Jamestown colony as well as the New England colonists depended for subsistence in great part on the corn obtained from the Indians during the early struggles to establish a foothold in the New World. Furthermore, the planting, cultivation, and storage of corn were learned by the white men from the Indian tribesmen. Hominy, succotash, corn-bread, and other corn foods came from the same source.

The exact origin of Indian corn is not known. Botanists are inclined to believe that it may have been derived from a native seed-bearing grass of southern Mexico and Guatemala known locally as *teocentli* and belonging to the botanical family *Euchlœna*. The assumption is that the native Americans, finding the seeds of the *teocentli* edible, began to select the choicer plants and seeds for cultivation and thus in time evolved the plant as known at the time of the European discovery. Taking the sev-

FIG. 22. MOUND-BUILDER CORN

Baum village site, Ross County, Ohio.

eral varieties of native maize as evolved by the Indians, modern agriculture has improved them in several directions, with the result that we have the standard varieties of today.

In the storage and refuse pits dug in the ground in connection with the prehistoric village sites in Ohio and other sections of the mound area, there are often found considerable quantities of corn, beans, and other food products, which owe their preservation to the fact that fire had accidentally reached the stored supplies and partially consumed them. Such accidents, of frequent occurrence in the villages of the Mound-builders, were, of course, disasters to the inhabitants; but since the charring of vegetable substances often results in their indefinite preservation, in form and outline at least, the archæologist is gratefully inclined to paraphrase the old adage as to the "ill wind that blows nobody good" by declaring that "it's an ill fire that burns nobody good." In a storage pit at the Baum prehistoric village site, in Ross County, Ohio, there was found upward of a bushel of mixed corn and beans, rendered unfit for food by accidental burning but perfectly preserved in carbonized form. Neither the corn nor any other of the cultivated food plants of the Mound-builders and others of the native Americans were as highly perfected as those of today, but the fact that these products had been greatly improved in comparison with the native wild varieties is significant.

TOBACCO AND ITS CULTIVATION

Tobacco, for which the world is also indebted to the native American peoples, until recently might have been classed as a gift of somewhat doubtful merit. With its spread throughout the world and its present almost universal use, however, it may be assumed that the odium formerly attaching to the weed in some quarters has practically disappeared and that it is accepted as a contribution of value. Deferring for a later chapter any detailed comment on the use of tobacco by the Mound-builders, it may be recalled here that Columbus and subsequent explorers were astonished to find the American natives using the plant not only for smoking but as the nucleus of a complex of ceremonial and ritual observances so intricate as to be entirely beyond their comprehension.

Some forty varieties of the tobacco plant have been identified by botanists, not all of which were or are used economically. *Nicotiana tabacum,* the original Virginia tobacco, and two or three species of *Solanaceæ* are the principal ones valued as narcotics. Everyone is familiar with the story of Sir Walter Raleigh and his naïve experience when, on his return from America to England, he essayed to smoke a pipe of tobacco; an attendant, so the story goes, thinking him to be on fire, with rare presence of mind dashed a pitcher of water over his honor's head. Although it required a century or more following its discovery among the American natives for Europeans to adopt the use of tobacco, its popularity thereafter increased rapidly. Perhaps no other plant affords so striking an example of diffusion, from the ethnological point of view. The colonies of Virginia and Maryland, it may be recalled, at one time cultivated the plant almost to the exclusion of food crops, with the result that they were at times threatened with famine.

Although tobacco itself, owing to its perishable nature, has seldom been discovered in the mounds and village sites, it has been found in some of the dry caves of the mound region, associated with human remains of considerable antiquity. That it played an important part in the economy and ceremonial activities of the Mound-builders, however, is evidenced by the finding of many tobacco pipes of varied types and patterns. A single exception to the absence of tobacco from the ancient sites was the finding of a pipe in the ashes of a fireplace in the Feurt prehistoric village site in which the partly burned tobacco still remained.

It may logically be assumed that much of the tobacco smoked by the Mound-builders was decidedly "rank," judged by present-day standards, and that its flavor and strength were modified by blending with other herbs, after the manner of the historic Indians and pioneer whites in preparing "kinnikinick."

AGRICULTURAL IMPLEMENTS AND METHODS

Of the variety of implements and utensils found in the ancient sites, certain types were obviously adapted to use in connection with agriculture and the storage and preparation of agricultural products. These types include such implements as the digging stick and the hoe made by lashing to a wooden handle a blade of stone, a mussel shell (Figure 23), or the shoulder blade of the deer or the elk. Clearly these were the implements used in the cultivation of crops, and since the

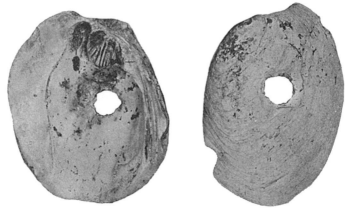

FIG. 23. HOES MADE FROM MUSSEL SHELLS

Lashed to a stick as a handle, these primitive implements were used in cultivating the soil. Scale, 2/3.

primitive agriculturists might select the loose, fertile soil of the bottom lands for cultivation, they sufficed for the purpose. Over a large area corresponding to the middle Mississippi valley, and particularly in southern Illinois and eastern Missouri, highly specialized hoes and spades of flint are found. These, made mostly from light-colored flint quarried in Union County, Illinois, are designated as agricultural implements. In Florida and the region adjacent to the southeastern seaboard and the Gulf of Mexico, marine conch shells, with sticks for handles, were freely used. Potteryware, particularly pottery vessels of large size, was used for storing grain and seeds and as containers for meal, while other pottery vessels were used in cooking. Stone mortars (Figure 24) and pestles for grinding grain and seeds are adjuncts of every village site which, with other more generalized artifacts of domestic use, add their contribution to the evidence of agriculture.

PREHISTORIC CORNFIELDS AND GARDEN BEDS

Besides the evidence afforded by the finding of actual plant products and the implements used in their cultivation, there remain for mention the scant but important evidences left in

FIG. 24. STONE MORTAR

Used for grinding corn, nuts, and seeds; the primitive type of grist-mill. From the Feurt village site, Scioto County, Ohio. Scale, 1/4.

the soil itself as a result of prehistoric agricultural activities. From the records of early observers it is known that very definite practices obtained among the native tribesmen with respect to agriculture, and these may safely be used as a basis for interpreting the prehistoric evidences. Among these practices was that of the Huron tribes and others of using prepared "hills," circular and about two feet apart, where, year after year, they planted their maize. The occurrence in some sections of the mound area, particularly in Michigan and Wisconsin, of the so-called "cornfields" (Figure 25) and "garden beds" (Figure 26) suggests similar agricultural practices. These corn-

FIG. 25.   A PREHISTORIC CORNFIELD ON THE CAMPUS OF CARROLL COL-
LEGE, WAUKESHA, WISCONSIN
Courtesy of the Wisconsin Archæological Society.

fields and garden beds, prehistoric as to origin, consist of considerable areas of uniformly spaced hills and ridges of soil.
There is little or no doubt that they represent the cultivated
fields of the prehistoric peoples who occupied these regions
prior to the coming of the white men.

COMMERCIAL ACTIVITIES: TRADE, BARTER, AND EXCHANGE

Certain activities of primitive peoples may be grouped under
the term commerce, which may be understood to include trade,
barter, and exchange as means of securing raw materials or
finished goods from sources other than those of the immediate
environment. In advanced economic society such factors as
means of travel and transportation and a medium of exchange
are regarded as essentials to commerce. In primitive commerce,
such as obtained in the general mound area, either among the

cognate peoples or between them and outside areas, these factors were the basic or rudimentary ones represented by travel on foot or by canoe and, in lieu of the modern medium known as money, the tender of materials or goods in exchange.

Commercial enterprise, as represented by exchange, trade, and barter, was well developed among the native American tribes, but the greater part of it naturally had to do with goods of a perishable nature; and since only materials resistant to decay are preserved to archæology, the record obviously is incomplete. Trade in foodstuffs and other perishable commodities must have exceeded in the aggregate the objects and materials found preserved, in whole or in part, in the mounds, graves, and village sites.

No definite medium of exchange corresponding to the wampum of the Iroquois and other historic tribes has been identified in the prehistoric sites. As is generally true among primitive peoples, the exchange of goods, value for value, obviated the need for money as it is known today. Pearls, pearl beads, and other raw materials and manufactured goods were traded freely among the several cultures and areas, the basis of exchange being, as at present, the law of supply and demand.

FIG. 26. PREHISTORIC GARDEN BEDS NEAR OSHKOSH, WISCONSIN

-The melting snow accentuates the irregularity of the surface due to the presence of the ancient furrows.

CHARACTER AND EXTENT OF MOUND-BUILDER COMMERCE

By far the greater bulk of the trading of which the mounds afford direct evidence centered about the mineral products in the form of raw materials. Those tribes living in regions where mineral products generally desirable for the manufacture of implements, utensils, and ornaments occurred, found ready market for them among other tribes. Thus the peoples living adjacent to Lake Superior found that the abundant native copper of that region was a commodity in constant demand from those sections of the mound area where it did not occur. Although the mound-building peoples never emerged from the so-called Stone Age, they had discovered that copper, treated as a malleable stone and worked by similar methods, was superior to stone for many purposes. Adjacent to the source of supply, the metal was in general use, not only for ornamental purposes, but for the manufacture of implements as well. Outside of the region of immediate occurrence the use of the metal decreased until at a distance of a few hundred miles it came to be looked upon as a rare and valued commodity, to be used only for objects of personal adornment and artistic execution. In the regions far removed from the copper deposits, the metal came to be a precious metal among peoples to whom all was gold that glittered.

The peoples of the Gulf Coast and the southeastern seaboard possessed for purposes of trade and barter unlimited supplies of marine shells, shark teeth, tortoise-shell, and other marine products; those of the lower Alleghany region had mica, steatite, quartz, and other minerals; those of the interior valleys offered stores of fresh-water pearls; and the tribes of the Far West supplied obsidian, grizzly-bear teeth, and other commodities. The peoples of the several regions derived their particular varieties of flint from local deposits, often in demand by those of adjacent regions where the mineral was lacking or of poor quality, and the trade in this necessity was more important than might be supposed. The tribes living in the glaciated areas possessed inexhaustible supplies of glacial boulders, highly desirable for the making of stone implements, and these durable materials were in demand in localities where they did not occur.

In addition to the exchange of commodities, the evidences of exploration indicate that certain tribes of mound-building peoples, particularly the more highly developed ones, made pilgrimages or sent out expeditions to distant sources of supply for desired raw materials. The presence of obsidian and grizzly-bear canine teeth in the mounds of the Hopewell culture of Ohio, Illinois, Iowa, and Wisconsin strengthens this inference. The nearest and the most likely source of each of these commodities is the Rocky Mountain region in the Yellowstone Park district, and since there is little or no evidence of their presence or use in intervening territory, their abundant and widespread use in the Hopewell area appears to indicate special expeditions for securing them.

PRIMITIVE INDUSTRY OF THE MOUND AREA

The building of mounds and earthworks and the practice of agriculture, both major industrial activities, have been sufficiently discussed in earlier pages, while those activities which were intertribal have been dealt with under the head of commerce in the foregoing paragraphs. Such æsthetic concepts as art and social, religious, and burial practices will be considered in succeeding chapters. Thus there remain for consideration under the head of industry only those local activities, mostly utilitarian in character, which have to do with the procuring of materials and supplies and the utilization of these, together with materials obtained from outside sources, in local domestic economy. The primary requisites, food, clothing, and shelter, and their procurement and, to a lesser extent, recreation and warfare, the principal objectives of these activities, are pictured in more detail in Chapter VIII. In the discussion of primitive activities as practiced by the Mound-builders, in the pages immediately following, the reader will find the genesis of many present-day industries.

THE QUARRYING OF FLINT AND OTHER MATERIALS

A leading industry of the Mound-builders and other prehistoric peoples was the quarrying and working of flint. The fact that flint and flinty rocks were used by aboriginal peoples in manufacturing tools and implements serving practically the same basic purposes for which metal tools are used today makes it readily apparent that flint was of the utmost importance. What metals mean to present-day civilization, flint meant to the aborigines.

It would be difficult indeed to conceive of any trait or custom of primitive man that holds more of human interest or upon which his advancement was more dependent than the utilization of flint. The flint-chipping concept made its appearance very early in human culture and is regarded by anthropologists as the greatest single factor in cultural development. Probably the discovery of flint and its peculiar adaptation to human needs was accidental. It is assumed that man's first use of a tool—in fact, the first mechanical act of man—was to pick up a convenient water-worn stone for use as a weapon or for pounding or breaking something. Sooner or later some aborigine made such use of a stone that happened to be of a flinty nature and, accidentally breaking it, discovered that the broken fragments were possessed of sharp cutting edges. In the classical legend the boy, extracting the remains of a pet pig from the embers of the burned dwelling, scorched his fingers; placing them instinctively in his mouth for cooling, he discovered, quite accidentally, the delectable qualities of roast pig. Primitive man in breaking his flinty hammerstone may have cut his fingers and thus discovered the cutting qualities of flint, just as many a boy playing with glass (an artificially produced silicious or flinty substance) has made similar discovery.

Having found a material from which implements for cutting, piercing, drilling, and sawing could be produced, primitive man looked about him for available supplies of flint of good quality. These discovered, quarrying began and soon became a major industry. Thousands, even millions, of chipped flint arrow-

Fig. 27.   A prehistoric flint quarry, flint ridge, licking county, OHIO

The battered boulder above was found within the quarry, near the blade of the shovel, just where the primitive quarryman had discontinued work.

points, spearheads, knives, scrapers, drills, and other implements, scattered throughout the mound area and everywhere else that primitive peoples have lived, attest the importance of flint and flint quarrying. Within the general mound area there are hundreds of localities where flint occurs and where it was quarried in prehistoric times.

The more important flint deposits are the great Flint Ridge, in Licking and Muskingum counties, Ohio; those near Hot Springs, Arkansas; and the Mill Creek deposits in Union County, Illinois. Other deposits and quarry sites occur in New York State, Michigan, southern Indiana, West Virginia, Kentucky, Tennessee, and in practically every other state in which mounds are located. The deposit of flint at Flint Ridge extends along the crest of a series of connected hills or elevations which have survived the leveling process of glaciation. The old pits and quarries cover an area of hundreds of acres, and nearby are the workshops where the raw flint was chipped into rough blank forms for transportation to nearby and distant camps and villages. The flint here is of massive formation, as is that in the vicinity of Hot Springs and many other localities. The deposit at Mill Creek, Illinois, and that in the Wyandot cave region of southern Indiana are of the so-called nodular variety. Digging sticks, stone hoes, and stone picks were utilized in removing the earth covering of the flint deposits, the material then being worked out or detached by means of stone mauls, wooden pries, and wedges, sometimes supplemented by fire for detaching portions of the mass.

Important prehistoric quarries where a flinty rock known as quartzite was obtained are located on Piney Branch of Rock Creek in the suburbs of Washington, D. C. The quartzite occurs in the form of boulders embedded in the Cretaceous bluffs of the region. Quartzite, although inferior in workability to so-called flint, was extensively quarried and utilized for making chipped implements. Other varieties of flinty rocks similarly used were argillite, rhyolite, and jasper. Quarries of these materials have been noted in several sections of Pennsylvania and elsewhere.

The quarrying of steatite or soapstone for the manufacture of utensils, pipes, and ornaments was likewise an important prehistoric industry. Old quarry sites have been found extensively along the eastern slopes of the Appalachian Mountains, and objects made from the material are found frequently in mounds and graves over a wide area. Mica was extensively quarried in Virginia and North Carolina and was widely used by the mound-building peoples, particularly in Ohio and throughout the southern regions.

The quarrying processes were obviously the simplest possible methods for procuring the desired materials, and the tools employed were the rudimentary ones available to the primitive quarrymen. Stone of other varieties, as sandstone, limestone, granite and argillite, for use in making tools, implements and ornaments was obtained either by quarrying or by the simpler methods of detaching fragments from exposed masses or merely picking them from the drift or stream beds.

THE MINING OF COPPER, IRON ORE, AND OTHER MINERALS

While flint was without a rival in the earlier stages of human development, primitive man instinctively sought for substitutes which would better serve his needs. Such a substitute the Mound-builders found in copper, which occurs freely native in northern Michigan and on Isle Royale in Lake Superior and in lesser abundance in some other sections of the general mound area. The native metal occurs embedded in a rock matrix in masses of various size. The primitive miners procured it by clearing away the covering of earth, breaking away the enclosing rock, and freeing the small nuggets or detaching portions of the larger masses. Adjacent to the copper deposits glacial action has carried nuggets and masses for some distance to the southward. Much of the copper used by the aborigines of the mound area was obtained from this glacial drift, particularly in Michigan, Wisconsin, and Minnesota.

In the copper region of northern Michigan and the Lake Superior district numerous and striking evidences of the mining of the metal in prehistoric times are to be found. Great numbers of stone mauls or sledges, by means of which the rock enclosing the copper was broken away, are found adjacent to the primitive mines. Within the mine pits and shafts occasionally are found large masses of copper which because of their size and weight defied the efforts of the aborigines to raise them. In one such instance a mass of copper weighing three tons, lying 16 feet below the surface, had been removed from its bed and transported for some distance by means of poles and pries. A similar mass of six tons had been similarly detached and was found resting on a supporting platform of logs. Within the copper area the marks of stone tools are often observed on large masses where fragments of the metal have been cut away. Along the trails leading from the copper mines to the distant villages of the Mound-builders in Ohio and other states, nuggets and small masses of copper are found where they had been dropped or lost by the "commercial travelers" of primitive times. This copper of primitive commerce is found scattered in greater or less abundance throughout the territory east of the great plains.

Another metallic substance much used by both the mound-building and the non-mound-building aborigines was the variety of iron ore known as hematite. This mineral, which varies greatly in physical properties, especially in color and hardness, was used not only for the manufacture of implements and ornaments, but for producing paints and pigments of red, brown, and yellow tints. In some localities, as in the coal measures of southeastern Ohio and in West Virginia, hematite was available as a surface or subsurface deposit. Elsewhere, as in the Iron Mountain district of Missouri and in the vicinity of Marquette, Michigan, the aborigines conducted mining operations, as in the case of copper, to obtain the mineral. The most noted prehistoric hematite mines are located in Franklin County, Missouri, where tortuous drifts were driven to considerable depths into the deposits of hematite and allied iron oxides.

Other metallic substances of restricted primitive use were

silver, found associated with the copper; gold, occurring sparingly, the source unidentified; galena or lead ore, obtained in Illinois and Kentucky; meteoric iron, probably from local meteorites or possibly from the Cañon Diablo deposits in Wyoming; and hematite, found in West Virginia and southern Ohio.

The subject of fresh-water pearls may very properly be introduced at this point since the quest for pearls constituted a major industry among the builders of the mounds. Although entirely æsthetic in their relationship to aboriginal culture, as will be shown in connection with the discussion of their use for personal adornment (Chapter VI), the quest for fresh-water pearls and their utilization assumed an inordinately important place in the culture of the Mound-builders and others of the native American tribesmen. Whereas wampum or shell disks served the later historic tribesmen as a medium of exchange, pearls beyond question represented the most valuable asset of the trader in the days when the mounds were being built. Not only were pearls sought and used by the Mound-builders throughout practically the entire area, but they continued to be highly prized until and even after the arrival of Europeans on the continent. Early white explorers in Florida, Virginia, and the southern states found these gems in lavish use by the natives and naturally themselves quickly contracted "pearl fever." Stories of fabulous pearls of great size and beauty were circulated, and Indian settlements, as well as Indian burial grounds, were plundered in the wild quest for the gems. One of the chroniclers of De Soto's expedition records that the great explorer obtained from a burial place on the Savannah River, just below the present city of Augusta, some 350 pounds of the gems.

Pearls are obtained from two quite distinct sources. Oriental pearls are the product of certain marine bivalve mollusks belonging to the *Margaritifera* family, while fresh-water pearls are produced by the *Unionidæ*, the fresh-water clams or mussels. A number of species of both the marine and the fresh-water mollusks produce the gem. A pearl is the result of a pathological condition of the individual mollusk which secretes it. A grain of sand, bacteria, or other irritating particle finds lodgment within its folds or mantle; unable to expel the irritant, the mollusk envelops it in a nacreous secretion which hardens, and smooths its rough surface and in time, through the depositing of successive layers of nacre, produces the pearls. The Mississippi and the Ohio and their tributaries and many streams of the southern states are the favored homes of the fresh-water clam, and therefore the source of fresh-water pearls. The countless thousands of the gems found in mounds and graves of prehistoric times are indicative of the importance among the Mound-builders of the quest for pearls.

MINOR RAW MATERIALS

The principal sources of raw materials used by the mound-building peoples and the manner in which they were obtained have been discussed at some length. In addition they utilized many other materials of more obvious origin, as clay for pottery-making; bast and fibers of various wild plants for the weaving of fabrics; timber and wood for construction purposes and for the manufacture of wooden implements and utensils; animal products, such as furs, feathers, skins, sinews, bone, and shell; and, as a matter of course, everything of an edible nature, whether plant or animal, as food. The more obvious details of primitive domestic economy, which readily present themselves to the mind, need not be discussed in this connection.

The primitive utilization of raw materials in the fabrication and manufacture of implements, ornaments, and utensils, the construction of dwellings, and the making of clothing is a fascinating and profitable study. In a later chapter dealing with the Ohio archæological area an attempt is made to reconstruct the life and activities of a specific Mound-builder village; but since this particular site is of rather low cultural level and not altogether representative of the Mound-builder culture complex, a few of the outstanding traits of common usage will be considered at this point.

The art of chipping flint may be characterized as the most widespread, as well as the essential, element of early human culture. So general was its distribution among primitive peoples that it may be fancied that nature, recognizing it as indispensable, made the practice instinctive with human beings in the savage and barbarian stages of development.

The mound-building peoples had developed the flint-chipping technique to a high degree, and the non-mound-building tribesmen were proficient in the art. Throughout the general mound area flint or flinty rocks, and minerals such as chert, chalcedony, rhyolite, novaculite, argillite,

FIG. 28. THE PENETRATION OF A FLINT ARROWPOINT

This shows a human dorsal vertebra in which is embedded to a depth of 3/4 inch a flint arrowpoint which, from its position, must have passed entirely through the chest of the victim, from front to rear. Scale, 2/3.

quartz, and quartzite, were utilized in the making of chipped implements. Beginning with simple flakes, used as scrapers and cutting tools, the series of types includes such forms as arrow-points and spearheads, knives, drills and perforators, chisels, saws, and problematical forms. Perhaps the most difficult accomplishment of the prehistoric flint-chipper was the striking off from pieces of selected flint of the long slender flakes known as "flake knives." The culmination of the art is found in the graceful ceremonial spearpoints and curved knives of obsidian taken from the Hopewell culture mounds, and the ceremonial blades, daggers, and swords found in the Etowah Group of Georgia and elsewhere throughout the South. Some of these are pictured in Chapter VI.

In principle the chipping of flint is a simple matter, but in practice it is much more difficult. Although it is not, as so frequently has been asserted, a lost art, yet no person of today, so far as is known, has been able to equal the best efforts of the prehistoric craftsman. The instinctive ability of the bar-

FIG. 29. THE MANUFACTURE OF FLINT ARROWPOINTS

A rough blank was first chipped from a fragment of suitable flint; this blank then was carefully worked into a leaf-shaped blade, and from this, by chipping notches to form the stem, the completed arrowpoint was fashioned. Scale, full size.

barian plus generations of cumulative effort resulted in a degree of perfection not otherwise readily attainable. Many theories have been advanced in explanation of how flint was chipped. A widespread but erroneous belief is that the prehistoric artisans heated the flint and then by means of drops of water detached the flakes. Records of early observers among the Indian tribesmen while they were still in possession of their original culture furnish conclusive evidence of the actual methods employed, and this evidence has been confirmed by the experiments of modern students and scientists.

Theoretically the art of flint-chipping consists in detaching flakes from a piece of suitable material by means of pressure or by percussion. Flinty minerals have the property of breaking with a conchoidal fracture, the detached chips or flakes displaying sharp cutting edges. Glass, which is a silicious or flinty material artificially produced, exhibits these properties in a degree modified only by its brittleness. While the broken surfaces may not be flat, they are, as contrasted with granite, sandstone, or any non-flinty rock, always smooth. Taking

FIG. 30. OBSIDIAN FLAKE AND ARROWPOINT MADE FROM IT
After Fowke. Scale, full size.

advantage of these properties, the primitive flint-chipper selected the most suitable material at hand. With a stone hammer or merely a convenient pebble he struck off the corners and superfluous parts of the nucleus, thus effecting the primary chipping by the percussion method. For the secondary and finishing stages of the work the pressure method was the more practical. With a chipping tool of bone or antler, shaped somewhat like a common pencil and varying in size in accordance with the work to be done, the artisan quickly and neatly shaped the specimen to suit his needs. Supporting the piece of flint on the palm of his hand, protected by a pad of leather or buckskin, or placing it upon a more substantial support if the specimen were large and required the exertion of greater force, he applied the end of the chipping tool to the edge of the flint and by properly directed pressure was able to detach one flake after another.

It is an easy matter to attain sufficient skill to produce ordinary small arrowpoints, but the making of larger specimens, particularly if they are thin and broad, requiring the detaching of long flakes, is an art acquired only after long experiment and practice. The writer has spent considerable time in such experimentation and has been able to produce such creditable results as those shown in Figure 29. The conclusion is inescapable, however, that even with the master chippers of prehistoric times the production of an exceptionally large and fine flint blade required not only skill but the good fortune of securing a piece of flint that would lend itself to the undertaking. Such exceptional specimens, rarely found, were doubtless prized tribal possessions or a part of the medicine kit of the shaman or medicine man. The impressive ceremonial obsidian blades from the Hopewell mounds, some of which measure 18 inches in length and more than six inches in width, must have been the cherished possessions of the chiefs or priests, possibly used and displayed only on the occasions of important ceremonies.

USE OF COPPER AND OTHER METALS

Although the highly developed Mayas, Aztecs, and Incas of Middle and South America had learned the secret of smelting metals and therefore had passed over into the so-called Age of Metals, the mound-building peoples remained altogether in the Stone Age. In using copper and other metals they treated them as malleable stone, hammering them into form and finishing prospective artifacts by grinding and polishing. By constantly annealing copper they were able to pound it into thin sheets from which their remarkable artistic scroll and repoussé ornaments were made. Annealing, it may be explained, consists in heating a metal and allowing it to cool slowly, by which process it is softened. Under the hammer, copper tends to harden and split apart, and experiment has shown that the native metal cannot be pounded into thin sheets without this repeated heating and gradual cooling.

Since the Mound-builders had not learned to melt any metal,

FIG. 31. COPPER AXE AND HATCHET

These characteristic implements of the Mound-builders closely resemble in form the modern types, but instead of having perforations to accommodate handles, they either were secured in grooves cut into the handles or were lashed to them by means of thongs. Scale, 1/2.

it is clear that the old and widespread belief that they possessed a long-lost secret process of hardening copper is unwarranted. Unconsciously, perhaps, they did effect a certain degree of hardening, but only such as hammering of the metal would produce. It may seem odd, in view of the extensive use of fire as an adjunct to burial, cremation, and sacred ritual, that the builders of the mounds should not have learned that copper and other metals could be worked by melting or extracted by smelting. However, when it is remembered that heat of an intensity of 2,000 degrees Fahrenheit is required to melt copper and that silver and even iron would not be much softened in an ordinary open fire, it is not so strange after all. Yet it is probable that the more advanced cultures were on the verge of this discovery. The peoples of Middle America, with their much higher civilization and their manufacture of bronze, used this metal mainly for ornament and almost not at all for implements, practically all their admirable architecture being effected with stone tools.

Near the source of copper supplies, as in the Hopewell culture of Ohio and the upper middle Mississippi region, the mound peoples utilized copper both for implements and for ornament. Further to the south, in the Cumberland-Tennessee

FIG. 32.   CHISELS MADE FROM METEORIC IRON

Note how the specimens at the top and right correspond in shape to the beaver-tooth chisel shown below and taken from the same mound.   Scale, 2/3.

area and in the area bordering the Gulf, the metal was too precious to be used for utility purposes and was treasured solely for ornament. The utility forms made from copper comprise adze and axe blades, spuds, knives, spearpoints, mauls used in quarrying operations, and some minor artifacts. The range of ornamental forms is varied, as will be seen when we come to consider the artistic accomplishments of the Mound-builders in Chapter VI.

Meteoric iron, used sparingly both for implements and for ornaments, and silver, serving the latter purpose, were worked in the same manner as copper. The same is true of gold, which has been found in a few instances in the southern mounds and notably in the Turner Group of southern Ohio.

UTILIZATION OF STONE, BONE, SHELL, AND WOOD

In addition to flint and copper, practically all other native materials suitable for construction and manufacture entered into the domestic economy of the Mound-builders. Timber, worked by means of fire, cutting, scraping, and drilling, was employed in house construction and in erecting charnel houses and log tombs, as well as for bows, arrows, spears, and a great variety of useful implements, utensils, and ornaments. Stone, the metal of the Mound-builders, served a variety of purposes where a hard, durable substance was required. The material was worked by the primitive processes of breaking, pecking or crumbling, abrading or grinding, sawing, polishing, drilling, and so forth. Granite, diorite, syenite, quartzite, and other hard varieties served for making the blades of axes, hatchets, tomahawks, celts, chisels, and pestles; sandstone was useful for abrading implements and for mortars for grinding corn, seeds, and nuts. The softer and showier varieties, as pipestone, argillite, banded slate,

FIG. 33. THE MANUFACTURE OF A STONE TOBACCO PIPE

At the top is shown an unworked piece of pipestone, as it came from the quarry; from this, by pecking and polishing, the finished pipe at the bottom was fashioned, after passing through the intermediate stages shown. Scale, 2/3.

steatite, and chlorite, served for making pipes, beads, and ornaments.

POTTERY AND POTTERY-MAKING

The earliest forms of containers used by primitive man were shells, hollow stones, gourds, and other natural products. Con-

FIG. 34. A MOUND-BUILDER POTTERY VESSEL

Typical of the highly developed Hopewell culture. Scale, 1/3.

tainers of bark, skin, and so forth were probably the earliest artificial forms, and these were followed by vessels of bark and wood and by rude basketry. Pottery-ware was a comparatively late invention, and many of the native American tribes did not reach the plane of development where pottery-making appears. The foremost pottery-makers of the area within the United States were the ancient Pueblo tribesmen of the Southwest, especially the Zuni and the Hopi, who had developed the fictile arts to a high degree. Next in importance within the continental area were the mound-building peoples of the Mississippi and Ohio valleys and the Gulf states. The Hopewell peoples of the middle Mississippi valley and of southern Ohio had attained to the making of artistic pottery-ware, particularly in the so-called ceremonial varieties. Their development of the art, however, was not comparable with that of the tribes farther south, as in Tennessee, Arkansas, Alabama, and Mississippi. Within this area there have been found hundreds, even thousands, of vessels of diversified form, and decorative treatment. The modeling of vessels in life forms, such as birds, animals, and the human head, is a feature of this area. In some instances exceptionally pleasing color decorations were applied to the clay vessels, and the use of incised and stamped designs, either conventional or realistic, was quite general. Especially prepared paddles, with carved designs or wrapped with cord, were used for decorating the exteriors of vessels, while the use of woven fabric as a means of impressing decorations on the vessels while yet in the plastic state is much in evidence. The vessels of the mound area correspond in form to bowls, vases, bottles, cups, and dishes, and many of them are quite pleasing even from the modern point of view, as examples to be pictured later will show. Perhaps no other primitive industry is more fascinating than the fictile art.

Selected varieties of clay were used in the making of pottery-ware, and the quality of the product depended greatly on the available supplies of basic material. The clay was tempered by the addition of granulated stone, shell, and potsherds to avert undue shrinking and cracking in the firing process, which was done simply in an open fire or, among the more advanced tribes, in rudely prepared ovens. No particular mechanical devices for shaping the vessels were employed, such as the potter's wheel, the work being done entirely by hand and with the use of such simple aids as paddles and smoothing tools. Starting with a disk of clay as a base, the primitive potter added coils or bits of clay to form the walls, allowing the prospective vessel to dry sufficiently as the work progressed that it might retain its form until burned. The use of a shallow basket or the base of a broken pot as an aid in starting the vessel prevailed in some sections.

In Florida and adjacent regions the modeling of life forms in the round, often of grotesque appearance, was practiced. Several of these forms are pictured later. Tobacco pipes and some other minor objects were made from clay, particularly in the Iroquois region of New York and the St. Lawrence valley.

THE TEXTILE ARTS: SPINNING AND WEAVING

Spinning and weaving, like pottery-making, are somewhat belated developments of human culture, and the fact that

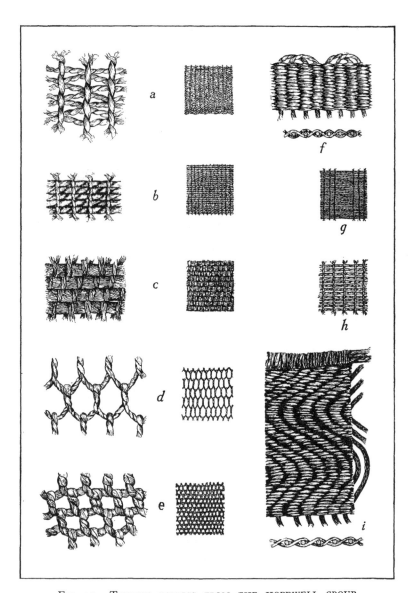

FIG. 35. TEXTILE FABRICS FROM THE HOPEWELL GROUP

a–c, g–i, twined weaving; *f,* in-and-out weaving; *d, c,* netting. Scale *a e,* enlarged; all others about 2/3. Courtesy of C. C. Willoughby.

the more advanced peoples of the mound area wove serviceable and ofttimes artistic fabrics is indicative of their high culture status.

Primitive weaving had its beginning in the simple twining of fibers into cord and the plaiting of bark and reeds into a rude sort of matting. Then followed basketry, and eventually the making of cloth or woven fabric. Only in the Pueblo region of the area within the present United States is anything ap-

FIG. 36. WOVEN FABRIC FROM THE SEIP MOUND

Cloth of various weaves, preserved by contact with copper, is of frequent occurrence in the burial tumuli. Scale, 2/3.

proximating a loom known to have been used, and there it attained only to the dignity of the false loom or half loom, utilizing in the simplest way the initial principles of the modern loom. The comparatively well-made fabrics of the Hopewell mounds and the Etowah Group of Georgia indicate that some convenient adaptation of the loom was in use in these areas.

Bast, the inner bark and fibers of certain trees, and the fibers of a number of wild plants, as nettle, swamp milkweed, and a grasslike plant occurring in Georgia and Florida known as nolina, were utilized for spinning and weaving by the Mound-builders. Bird feathers, fur, and hair were used either alone or intertwined with vegetable fibers in weaving cloth, as is demonstrated by the finding of imprints of such fabrics preserved on copper objects from the mounds.

The simplest form of Mound-builder fabric is a sort of matting, woven or plaited from rushes, grass, or the outer splint of the southern cane. The primary forms of cloth proper are woven from coarse plant fibers and resemble the well-known burlap of the present day. Several varieties or variations of weaving were practiced, as is shown in Figure 35. Woven fabrics with colored designs, usually in black, tan, and maroon, are found occasionally in the Hopewell mounds of Ohio (Figure 53). The designs are purely conventional and typical of the art of the Mound-builders. Similar cloth with colored designs has recently been found by Moorehead in the Etowah Group of mounds near Cartersville, Georgia. A fine variety of cloth, closely resembling both in texture and in color, the homespun linen of pioneer days, was recently found in the Seip Mound, of Ross County, Ohio. Several thicknesses of this interesting fabric had been deposited in a ceremonial or votive offering between large rectangular copper breastplates, and through the preservative action of the decomposing copper the cloth was remarkably well preserved (Figure 36). Fine examples of cloth with colored designs were found in the same mound. The fragments recovered, preserved beneath large copper plates, represented corresponding portions of a ceremonial burial shroud upon and beneath which had been placed the bodies of four adults and two children.

In addition to woven fabrics, quantities of tanned skin, constituting leather of the finest and thinnest grade, have been found in the Hopewell, Etowah, and other southern mounds.

CHAPTER V

THE MOUND-BUILDER BURIAL COMPLEX

The concept of a hereafter—Modes of disposing of the dead—Burial in ordinary graves and cemeteries—Mound interment and its accompanying rites—The practice of cremation—Sacrifices to the dead and to deities—Human interest recorded in burials—Human skulls as burial trophies.

LIFE, death, and the hereafter constitute a mighty trinity in human affairs, regardless of culture status, æsthetic or material. The complex embraces and influences every human concept, from beginning to end; hence the vast body of associated ritualism is no more than in keeping with its importance. Life—or rather birth, as the inception of life—continues to be a miracle, as death is the greatest human calamity, to be compensated for only in a hereafter.

THE CONCEPT OF A HEREAFTER

The nature of the ceremonies attending birth among the Mound-builders, we can only surmise through study of the rites observed by the historic Indians and other peoples of comparable attainment. The awe of death, however, and its inseparably associated concept of a hereafter find material expression in burials of the ancient mounds and cemeteries and in the minor artifacts interred with the dead. Zealous observance of funeral rites, linked with ceremonial procedures which can only be interpreted as having to do with belief in a future existence, are strikingly in evidence in the archæology of the mound region. That these rites and observances for the dead and the hereafter predominated over concern for the living clearly appears when we contrast the imposing tombs and the burials they cover with the scant remains of domiciliary structures.

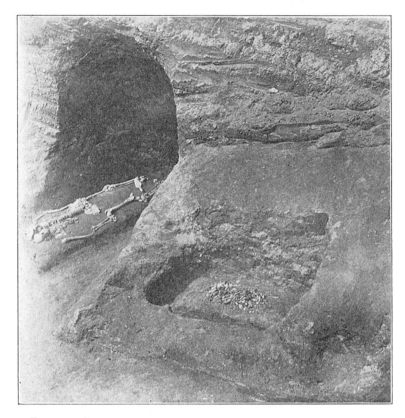

FIG. 37. A CREMATED AND AN UNCREMATED BURIAL SIDE BY SIDE
From the Seip Mound, Ross County, Ohio.

The countless burial mounds, and to a less extent the
ceremonial earthworks, constitute the major evidence of this
solicitude for the dead. The amazing expenditure of energy and
labor in erecting these structures is not to be fully accounted
for by the sentiment of respect and reverence for the departed;
the concept that all does not end with death is clearly indicated. The erection of earth coverings over carefully prepared
graves is almost instinctive, but the placing with the dead of
personal ornaments, implements, and utensils, and with important personages of ceremonial artifacts, indicates anticipated
needs in an after-life. Study and interpretation of the burial

mounds and cemeteries has revealed burial customs which bring the Mound-builders very close to us in human interest.

MODES OF DISPOSING OF THE DEAD

Classification of the modes of disposing of the dead in the mound area is somewhat difficult. To begin with the corpse itself, archæological evidence shows that prior to disposal the remains might or might not be cremated, depending upon local custom. In either case it is assumed that burial of some sort was accorded, although it is conceivable that burial of cremated bodies might at times be considered superfluous and the ashes or charred bones might be "scattered to the four winds," analogous to a somewhat rare present-day custom. From the abundant cremated burials within the mounds, however, it does not appear that any particular distinction was made between cremated and noncremated remains in burial observances or in the form of the grave provided.

Besides these alternative modes of preparing bodies for burial, a third was the widespread practice of removing the

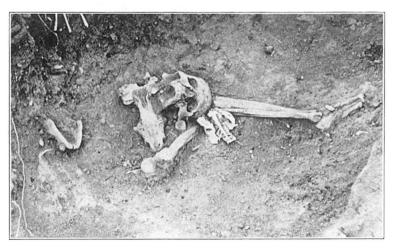

FIG. 38.   A REBURIAL OR BUNDLE BURIAL

Only a portion of the skeleton was present in this grave. Note the bear skull alongside the human skull. From the Feurt village site, Scioto County, Ohio.

flesh from the bones before interment. This practice may have been largely due to the exigencies of transporting the remains of those who died at a distance from their homes to their final burial places; sanitary considerations and the difficulties of transport would be factors influencing such a custom. Not infrequently the bones of skeletons that were denuded of flesh before burial are found painted or covered with ocher, hematite, or other mineral pigment as a ceremonial or funerary

FIG. 39.   A GROUP BURIAL

In the Dickson Mound, Lewistown, Illinois. More than three hundred skeletons were buried here. Courtesy of Dr. Don F. Dickson.

rite. Closely analogous are the so-called "bundle" burials, likewise of frequent occurrence, in which the bones, often only the longer ones and the skull, are disarticulated and arranged as though they had been tied in bundles for convenience in carrying. This type of burial indicates transportation of the body from a distance, where the individual may have died or been killed in war; on the other hand, it may reflect the common practice of temporary burial, surface or aerial, and later inhumation in the final resting place. An apt illustration of reburial is found in a custom of the historic Indians of the Great Lakes region, where periodic transfers of temporary burials to permanent resting places were accompanied by appropriate ceremonies, sometimes known as the Feast of the Dead.

On the basis of place of interment, the burial customs of the Mound-builders may be classified as (1) burial in graves dug into the surface, in the present-day fashion, and occurring either singly or collectively as in cemeteries; and (2) burial within or beneath mounds. The distinction between these two forms of burial is not as great as it may appear to the

FIG. 40. A DRY CAVE BURIAL

Kettle Hill Cave, Fairfield County, Ohio. A body wrapped in woven fabric is unintentionally mummified as a result of the dust-dry condition of the cave.

casual observer. The objective in each case is to deposit the remains beneath the soil as a protective covering, and this purpose is as well served in the one way as in the other. Ordinary inhumation within a grave excavated in the ground results in placing the remains below the normal surface; whereas in mound burial the process is reversed, and the surface of the ground over a limited area is raised above the remains. Regarded in this way, a mound might be termed an inverted grave.

BURIAL IN ORDINARY GRAVES AND CEMETERIES

The simple dug grave, occurring singly, in groups, or in cemeteries, is characteristic of the entire mound area. Usually grave burials are found adjacent to mounds and earthworks, as features of the camp and village sites of the aboriginal inhabitants of the vicinity. The graves may be rectangular, circular, or irregular in form; usually they are comparatively shallow. Not infrequently exploration discloses that graves were lined with wood, bark, or stone. Throughout the so-called stone-grave area, comprising southern Illinois, parts of Kentucky, and Tennessee and contiguous territory to the south and east, the use of flat stones for lining and covering boxlike cists of the type illustrated in Figure 16 is an outstanding trait. A variation of the simple dug grave, which was usually intended for a single individual, are the bone pits and ossuaries occurring in the Great Lakes region and elsewhere, in which reburials and bundle burials were interred promiscuously and often in great numbers. Although no definite attempt to provide coffins for the dead has been noted in burials of the mound area, quite frequently bodies were wrapped in matting, woven fabric, or skins, and they usually were laid upon a bed of bark

FIG. 41. AN UNCOMMON FORM OF SKELETON BURIAL

Superimposed on this skeleton were the cremated remains of another, extending from the head to the knees. From the Miesse Mound, Ross County, Ohio.

FIG. 42. A FLEXED SKELETAL BURIAL
From the Feurt Mound, Scioto County, Ohio.

covering the bottom of the grave. An interesting modification of stone-grave burial, and one which may be considered an important evolutionary step in burial customs, is found in the so-called stone-vault burial mounds of central and southern Missouri, already referred to and to be further described in Chapter XVI. The stone vaults are roughly circular or rectangular pens or enclosures, constructed of flat stones; burials, both cremated and skeletal, were placed in them in numbers, and the vaults were then covered with sufficient earth to create small and medium-sized mounds.

Ordinary interment, that is, inhumation of the body in the flesh, assumed various positions in different areas or according to the customs or whim of the individual tribes or cultures. Burial with the body reposing on the back with legs and arms extended was common, as in the Hopewell culture of the Ohio and Illinois-Iowa-Wisconsin areas. Flexed burial, in which the body lay upon the side with knees drawn up toward the face, was widespread, particularly in the less advanced cultures. Burial in a sitting or squatting position has often been reported and has been verified in North Carolina, Georgia, and Florida (see Chapter XVIII), but it was rare in the area as a whole. Bundle burial and scattered or reburial, as above noted, were common forms of interment.

In the Lower Mississippi area, and to a less extent elsewhere, burial of the dead upon and beneath the floors of dwellings was practiced. This was notably frequent in Alabama, where dwellings appear to have been burned following interment. In a number of instances exploration has disclosed that after such a burial beneath the floor of a dwelling erected on the characteristic flat-topped house mound, earth was carried and laid down to a depth of a foot or more and habitation resumed thereon. As many as three and even four successive occupations of a given site have been noted.

Fig. 43.—A stone cairn over a burial

The flat stones of this cairn are in the form of an arch. Near Ripley, Ohio. After Fowke.

Stone cairns, which are merely miniature mounds or piles of stone erected over graves, may be considered as intermediate between graves proper and burial mounds. These cairns are found in various parts of the mound area, notably along the Ohio River in southern Ohio and Indiana. As a rule the culture represented by cairn burial was comparatively low in development.

Contrary to popular belief, the Mound-builders paid but little attention to the points of the compass in arranging their burials. This is true even in mounds and cemeteries of the higher cultures. Yet occasional instances are recorded of intentional orientation, as in a mound in Bradley County, Louisiana, where Clarence B. Moore found all the skeletons with heads pointing directly to the south. An interesting arrangement of skeletons noted infrequently in several sections of the mound area is illustrated in the accompanying floor plan of the Kiefer Mound, in Miami County, Ohio (Figure 44). The twelve skeletons contained in this tumulus lay in a circle with their heads toward the center of the mound which was occupied by a pretentious fireplace. All the skeletons were disposed on their backs, extended, but the skulls of three of them had been detached and placed between the knees.

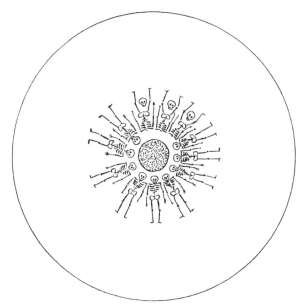

FIG. 44. FLOOR PLAN OF THE KIEFER MOUND, MIAMI COUNTY, OHIO

Twelve skeletons were found arranged in a circle, with their heads toward the center of the mound which was occupied by a fireplace. The skulls of three adjoining skeletons rested between their knees.

MOUND INTERMENT AND ITS ACCOMPANYING RITES

In mound burial proper most of the forms of graves and mortuary customs encountered in non-mound burial occur. Burials within mounds may be in graves dug beneath the floor or base line, or they may be placed directly upon the floor, or they may occur at any place from beneath the floor to the top of the mound. In the lower cultures burials usually occur indiscriminately within the mound, the structure having had

FIG. 45. A LOG TOMB BURIAL

The molds of the logs forming the rectangular sepulcher over the cremated burial are clearly seen. The burial was unusual in that it comprised a stone grave as well as a log sepulcher. From the Seip Mound, Ross County, Ohio.

its origin in the custom of placing a burial without much preliminary preparation on the surface and piling earth above it, the process being repeated from time to time as need arose for burial facilities. In the mounds of the higher cultures where prestructures of timbers to be described later were in vogue, as in the Hopewell and some of the southern tumuli, vaults or pens of logs or stones were often built and burials placed within

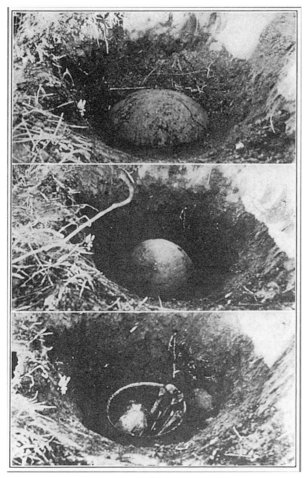

FIG. 46.   URN BURIAL

The upper picture shows a large inverted burial urn in process of excavation; in the second is seen a similar vessel partly exposed; and in the third a mortuary vessel containing skull and long bones. From the explorations of the Alabama Anthropological Society, near Montgomery, Alabama.

them before construction of the mound proper was begun. An interesting custom of the Lower Mississippi region, and one which prevailed to some extent in Alabama, Georgia, northern Florida, and elsewhere, was the so-called urn burial. This mode of disposing of the dead is particularly prominent along the Alabama River in Alabama and was much in evidence at the great Moundville Group (Chapter XVII). Recently the explorations of the Alabama Anthropological Society have yielded numerous examples of the trait and have shown it to be much more extensive than was formerly supposed. Urn burial consisted in depositing either skeletal parts or cremated remains in specially constructed mortuary vessels of burned clay and interring them in the mounds or in adjoining cemeteries. The openings of the mortuary vessels were often covered with other smaller vessels made especially for the purpose. Urn burial or corresponding forms of interment have been found in most other parts of the United States where primitive peoples have lived, though to a less extent than in the mound region.

Scientific exploration of mounds and accompanying burial sites has not been prosecuted in many parts of the mound area, and much of the early exploration took little heed of burial customs. For these reasons there are many blanks in our knowledge of the subject. Recently several of the more important states, archæologically speaking, have inaugurated programs of exploration which will throw much light on obscure phases of the burial complex. Nevertheless, from the results of exploration, chiefly of mounds of the Hopewell culture in Ohio, it is possible to afford the reader an idea of the main features of mound burial, particularly as it was practiced by the more highly developed cultures of the general area.

In a later chapter dealing with the Hopewell culture will be found a description of the prestructures of timber which occupied the sites of the tumuli prior to their erection. Exploration shows that these structures were ceremonial in purpose and that funeral rites and disposal of the dead were among their principal uses. That these mortuary observances were ceremonious and pretentious in the extreme is indicated by the fact that a portion of each structure seems to have been set apart as a chapel or audience room for the assembled congregation. There is also evidence that a space within the structure was used for preparing feasts in connection with the funeral rites; and it appears quite certain that something akin

FIG. 47. A TYPICAL CREMATORY BASIN

In these receptacles, constructed of puddled clay and built into the floors of the
mounds, the Hopewell peoples are believed to have cremated their dead.

to the sacred perpetual fires of the Cherokee and other historic
tribes of the southern region was a trait of the Hopewell peoples. In this connection it is interesting to note that the Cherokee, Natchez, and others believed that perpetual fire burned
beneath some of the mounds, while the ceremony of creating
or kindling "new fire" at certain intervals was practiced by
numerous and widely separated historic tribes.

THE PRACTICE OF CREMATION

Disposal of the dead by the Hopewell, and by some others
of the mound-building peoples, was in either of two ways.
The body might be deposited on a slightly elevated earthen
platform on the floor of the sacred structure, or it might be
cremated and the incinerated remains similarly disposed of.
In either case the remains usually were covered with a cabin-
like structure of logs, and this, in turn, with a small primary
mound of earth with a ceremonial outer covering of sand or
gravel (see Figure 10).

The crematories or basins in which it is supposed that cremation was effected are almost invariable accompaniments of Hopewell mounds. They are rectangular shallow basins depressed in the floor level, constructed of puddled clay carefully troweled into form, with sides and ends sloping inward and downward to a flat base or bottom. Burning, either intentional or as an incident of cremation, imparted to the clay basins the color and hardness of soft brick. Rarely incinerated human remains are found in a basin, but as a rule they are empty. Whereas at the present time cremation of the dead is generally looked upon as an innovation affected mostly by the well-to-do and the æsthetically minded, with the Hopewell and other cultures of the Mound-builders it was the rule rather than the exception. Of the total number of Hopewell burials exhumed by the Ohio State Museum's surveys fully 75 per cent have been cremated. And whereas today it is generally the exceptional person who is accorded cremation, with the Hopewell peoples apparently the reverse held: the average individual was cremated and the important personage was buried in the flesh. An interesting historic analogy is found

FIG. 48. A TYPICAL CREMATED BURIAL OF THE HOPEWELL CULTURE
With the incinerated remains are copper breastplates and a copper crescent.

FIG. 49.   A CREMATORY BASIN AND A GROUP OF FIVE CREMATED BURIALS
From the Mound City Group, Ross County, Ohio.

among the Indian tribes of the Northwest Coast, where formerly cremation was generally practiced except in the case of
shamans and other important persons whose remains were
deposited uncremated in specially constructed houses for the
dead.

SACRIFICES TO THE DEAD AND TO DEITIES

The idea of sacrifice, in some form or other, is found quite
generally as a part of the culture complex of primitive peoples. It may take the form of an offering to the dead or to
deities, and it may range from a few grains of meal or a pinch
of tobacco strewn on the wind to the sacrifice of human life
itself. Strangely enough, human sacrifice makes its appearance
as a rite only in rather advanced stages of culture and is regarded as a "symptom of incipient civilization." In primitive
America, only in the highly developed civilizations of Mexico
and Peru did culture reach a point where human sacrifice was
practiced. An isolated exception is found among Pawnee Indians

of our Southwest, who formerly sacrificed a young captive female on the occasion of a certain yearly ceremony.

Despite the fact that early writers attributed human sacrifice to the Hopewell and other highly evolved mound-building peoples, there is no real evidence and scant probability that it was practiced among them. Minor sacrifices, principally of cherished personal and tribal possessions, both to the dead and to their divinities, are indicated by the evidences of ex-

FIG. 50.   CEREMONIAL OFFERING OF FLINT DISKS

More than eight thousand of these disks comprised a votive or sacrificial offering, taken by W. K. Moorehead and later explorers from a mound of the Hopewell Group, Ross County, Ohio.

ploration. Just which was the intended recipient of any given sacrifice or offering it is usually difficult or impossible to determine.

The interesting and often intricate sacrificial or ceremonial offerings of the Hopewell peoples may be found at almost any point in a mound, either on the floor of the structure or within the body of the tumulus itself. The more pretentious offerings seldom are placed immediately with the dead; often they are located upon or adjacent to what appear to be shrines or altars.

Objects accompanying interred remains are usually of a personal nature, mostly articles of personal adornment or individual implements and utensils, and clearly are personal tributes as distinguished from offerings to the gods. Exceptions occur in the case of highly important individuals, with whose remains tribal or ceremonial objects may be deposited.

The choicest and most cherished possessions, personal and tribal, constitute the Hopewell sacrificial offerings, and it is due in great measure to this rite of sacrifice that many of their artistic productions and ceremonial objects are recovered in exploration. Since the sacred and purifying fires were an inevitable part of these observances, most perishable objects were consumed; sufficient remains, in some instances, however, to show that on occasion birds and animals, or parts thereof, were complements of sacrifice. A number of examples of the finding of ceremonial or sacrificial offerings in the Hopewell mounds are cited in the later chapter dealing with that culture in Ohio. Most striking of all, perhaps, is the offering taken from a mound of the Hopewell Group proper, which comprised thousands of flint implements, aggregating several tons in weight, fashioned of material which had been transported from a far distant source (Figure 50).

The length of time a sacred structure or mortuary of the Hopewell would serve depended on the size of the building and the rate of mortality. When the available burial space was exhausted, it might be extended by means of additions to the main structure; but usually it was abandoned and another structure erected. In case of abandonment, the prestructure was intentionally burned, in accordance with the concept of the sacred fire with its powers of purification, and perhaps of its release of the spirit essence from the material bodies deposited within.

HUMAN INTEREST RECORDED IN BURIALS

In the descriptions of important individual burials in the chapter on the Hopewell culture in Ohio, the reader will obtain many glimpses of human interest revealed in burial customs. A few additional references to interesting burials of the culture at this point may help to further a more complete appreciation of the Mound-builder burial complex.

Love for offspring is, of course, universal with the human race; hence it is not surprising to find that the Mound-builders lavished affection on their children. This is evidenced in numerous burials throughout the area, particularly in the

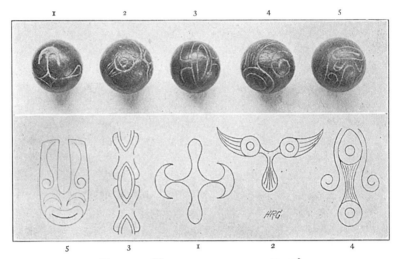

FIG. 51.   MARBLES AN ANCIENT GAME?

These interesting specimens, exactly resembling the marbles of present-day juvenile pastime, are engraved with interesting conventional designs. The symbols, as numbered to indicate the relation of the developments to the originals, represent (1) a cosmic design, (2) a bird, (3) a beetle (repeated), (4) an unidentified figure, and (5) a human face mask. The "marbles" were found with the remains of a youth of eight or nine years of age, in the Seip Mound, Ross County, Ohio. Scale, about 4/5.

Lower Mississippi region and in the Hopewell culture districts. The placing of miniature ornaments, implements, and utensils with burials of children was a common practice, not alone in the more highly developed cultures but in the less advanced ones as well. In a grave of the central Seip Mound were the remains of a woman, presumably the mother, and a child. With the bones of the mother there were the usual copper breast-plate, ear spools, and shell drinking cup or food container; with the child there reposed similar ornaments and utensils but of strikingly diminutive size.

In another grave of the same mound were found the remains of a youth of nine or ten years. The skeleton was accompanied by the usual diminutive personal possessions and in addition by a number of stone spheres, of handsome chlorite, in shape and size exactly resembling present-day marbles (Figure 51). These objects were engraved with pleasing conventional designs, each different from the others, one being a representation of the human face. Although the game of marbles is known to have been an ancient pastime, it does not appear in the complex list of games of the native Americans of historic record. Nevertheless, from the evidence it would be plausible to surmise that a similar game may have been enjoyed by the builders of the mounds. It was impossible to determine the sex of the youth in this burial because of the immaturity and poor state of preservation of the skeletal remains, but the interpretation of the unusual burial offered by a laborer on the mound may not be far wrong. It was, he facetiously declared, the burial of the champion boy marble player of the community; when his promising career was cut short by death, his favorite marbles were buried along with him.

HUMAN SKULLS AS BURIAL TROPHIES

Another interesting burial, briefly referred to and pictured in Chapter IX, was unearthed in a small mound of the Hopewell Group proper. In a carefully prepared grave there reposed the remains of an old man. In years he must have realized the allotted three score and ten, for he was utterly toothless. That he was a person of high rank, perhaps a chief, a shaman, or a medicine man, was attested by the many implements and ornaments buried with him. Alongside his skull there reposed another human skull, that of a young male. On it are numerous marks of the flint knife used in carefully removing the scalp and tissues. A helmet-shaped copper headplate and vestiges of a cap or bonnet of woven fabric to which the headplate had been attached surmounted the skull. It may reasonably be surmised that the old man was a war chief and the separate skull that of a vanquished enemy, placed in the grave as a trophy of his prowess; or perhaps it was that of a cherished relative, preserved as a personal or family relic.

Trophy skulls, so called, and separate jaws, both upper and lower, frequently are found with Hopewell-culture burials. Usually they are pierced with holes for suspension, and some-

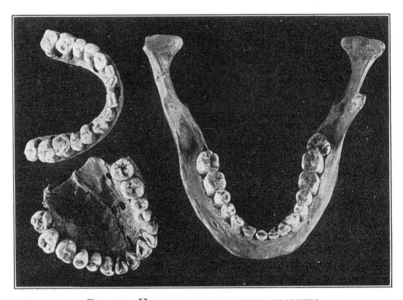

FIG. 52. HUMAN JAWS AS BURIAL TROPHIES

A lower jaw (right) and two upper jaws, cut away from the skulls, perforated for attachment. From the Hopewell Group, Ross County, Ohio.

times portions of them are cut or ground away. Anthropologists find that primitive peoples not infrequently retain as trophies the heads and skulls of vanquished enemies. They likewise preserve as family relics the heads and skulls of friends and relatives. In which class the trophy skulls and jaws of the Hopewell peoples belong remains to be determined.

Despite the fact that thousands of mounds and cemeteries with their tens of thousands of burials are scattered over the general mound region, it is probable that not all the aboriginal denizens of the area found their last resting places therein. Perhaps, like the ancient Egyptians, many of them failed to pass the judgment of the dead and the ordeal of crossing the Stygian lake, thus forfeiting the honor of mound burial. The widespread practice of cremation gives rise to the thought that burial may not have been deemed essential in all instances.

CHAPTER VI

THE MOUND-BUILDER AS ARTIST

The significance of native American art—Distinctive phases of Mound-builder art—Personal adornment and decoration—Pearls and pearl necklaces—Art as a measure of culture status—Depiction of the human face and figure—Sculpture of bird and animal forms—Realistic, symbolic, and conventional designs—Engraving on bone—Ceramic art—Pottery of the Lower Mississippi area—Ceremonial and problematical artifacts.

STUDY and appreciation of native American art have assumed very decided importance within the past few years. The collections of interesting objects from the highly developed civilizations of Mexico and Middle and South America in the larger museums are attracting marked attention from students of art; steps are being taken to revive and perpetuate the arts of the Pueblo tribesmen of the southwestern United States, particularly the crafts of basketry and weaving; and students in public schools and colleges, as well as artists and students of art, are frequenting the museums where objects from the ancient mounds are displayed. Recently an exhibition of native American art was held at the Toledo Museum of Art in which the æsthetic creations of the native peoples of both continents, historic and prehistoric, were featured exclusively. At the Ohio State Museum at Columbus the study of the art of the Mound-builders has been made a part of the public school curriculum and a feature of the Department of Fine Arts of the Ohio State University. Artists are finding in the artistic expression of aboriginal culture a wealth of ideas and motives which can be adapted to modern use. Numerous prehistoric designs are being utilized in the designing of modern fabrics and in the decoration of modern products of an artistic nature. It is natural, perhaps, to conceive of primitive art as being amateurish, and therefore it is surprising to find that often it is quite the reverse.

FIG. 53. WOVEN FABRIC IN COLORED DESIGNS

With three skeletons in the central Seip Mound, Ross County, Ohio, there were found, preserved by the chemical action of large copper breastplates, corresponding portions of burial robes bearing designs in color. The photograph above was taken *in situ*. The background of the fabric is maroon in color, with tan designs, outlined in black. The designs are not woven into the cloth, but are effected by staining or dyeing with mineral colors, possibly by the use of stamps or dies. Scale, 1/2.

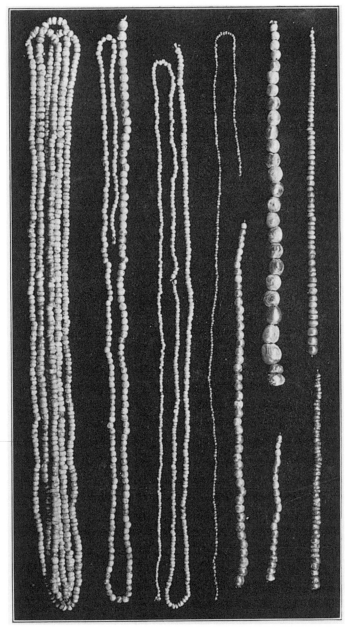

FIG. 54. STRANDS OF PEARLS FROM MOUND BURIALS

The mound-building peoples were excessively fond of pearls, the search for which was an important industry. The photograph shows pearls ranging from tiny seed pearls to specimens as large as a small marble. Scale, 2/5.

108

THE SIGNIFICANCE OF NATIVE AMERICAN ART

So fascinating and so intricate and complex is the subject of native American art, even when the study is confined to the Mound-builder area, that volumes would be required to do it justice. The difficulty of presenting the art of the Mound-builders intelligibly in so brief a space as is here available will

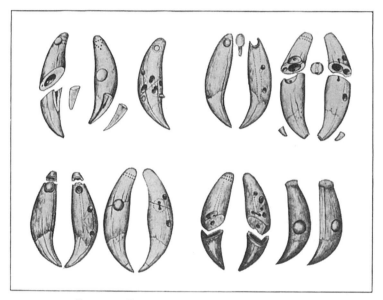

FIG. 55.   PENDANTS MADE FROM BEAR TEETH

Not content with the product of the native brown or black bear, the Hopewell peoples went, or sent, to the far-distant Rocky Mountain district for canine teeth of the grizzly bear. These they drilled for suspension from the neck or for attachment to clothing, cut them into fanciful forms, and often set them with fresh-water pearls. Scale, 1/4.

be readily apparent. No more than a hurried outline is possible, but it is hoped that this may suffice to induce the reader to pursue the subject further in its interesting ramifications. A number of partial general studies of mound art have been made, and numerous special or local monographs are to be had. Among the former may be mentioned *The Art of the Great Earthwork Builders of Ohio* by Dr. C. C. Willoughby and *Aboriginal Pottery of the Eastern United States* by Dr.

FIG. 56. SPOOL-SHAPED COPPER EAR ORNAMENTS

The copper ear spool is one of the commonest objects of adornment of the Hopewell culture of Mound-builders. Usually they are made of copper, but those in the illustration are fashioned from copper with one side faced with silver foil and the other with thin-pounded meteoric iron. From the Hopewell Group, Ross County, Ohio. Scale, full size.

W. H. Holmes; and among the latter, the reports of mound explorations in the southern states by Clarence B. Moore. These, with many other references, will be found listed in the bibliography at the end of this volume.

Not only may the artist discover among the patterns and designs of the art of the mound areas motives suitable for present-day use, either in their original or in modified form,

FIG. 57. EAR RINGS OF CHLORITE

Ear ornaments of stone are sometimes found. These interesting specimens are perfect circles and indicate that the mound-building peoples possessed some mechanical device for describing and executing true circles. From the Hopewell Group, Ross County, Ohio. Scale, 3/4.

but the student may also find in these ancient productions a wealth of information bearing upon the development of art as an element of human culture. Study of an extended series of objects from the mounds discloses many initial and developmental stages in the growth of art, demonstrating that natural objects may generate æsthetic appreciation in primitive man resulting in their adaptation to ornamental use; that such natural objects or effects come later to be artificially produced; and that through successive copying and variation these reproductions become in time entirely distinct from the originating motives. The origin and development of conventional and symbolic design and of sculpture and the graphic arts are particularly well illustrated, or at least strikingly suggested, in the old mound art, as are also such interesting other aspects of art history as the influence of available materials on æsthetic expression and the relation between utility and artistic treatment.

The art complex of the Mound-builders is complicated, in keeping with the generalization of art which goes with primitive culture and the consequent overlapping of the utility, ceremonial, symbolic, religious, and what may be considered the purely artistic concepts. Furthermore, the limited study so far accorded the subject leaves much to be desired in the way of exact knowledge. These difficulties, together with lack of space, seriously hamper the attempt to present here a reasonably orderly and systematic survey.

DISTINCTIVE PHASES OF MOUND-BUILDER ART

At the outset it may be said that practically all the basic forms of art are found within the range of Mound-builder remains. While the term art, employed in a broad sense, may include the entire range of human cultural activities, in the present chapter it is used to designate only those which have their origin and development mainly in the realm of taste—the innate liking of humankind for symmetry and beauty. Because of the generalization of primitive art it is not always practicable to consider its æsthetic elements apart from the utility aspects because of their close affinity; the reader, however, will readily distinguish between the two, even when both are present in the same objective specimen.

In dealing with the art of a primitive people it is customary to classify its various phases under a few rather specific headings, and we may conveniently follow this practice in indicating the range of the art of the Mound-builders.

1. The building arts, as exercised in the construction of dwellings, ceremonial and religious structures, and so forth, in which certain æsthetic and symbolic elements may be in evidence, claim the primary place. These artistic elements may or may not appear as essentials in construction, although architectural style very naturally had its beginnings in primitive

FIG. 58.   COPPER FINGER RINGS

Some of the Mound-builders, especially those of the Adena culture in Ohio, made and used finger rings like these. Scale, nearly full size.

building activities. In the matter of embellishment, however, particularly in the contributions of the sculptor and the painter, art does become a definite adjunct to the building arts. This is evidenced in the elaborate paintings of animals and conventional figures on the walls of the Pueblo kivas and in the sand paintings on their floors; in the decorations applied to the walls of the skin tipis of the Plains tribes of Indians; in the carved and painted pillars and totem poles of the Northwest Coast tribes; and in the somewhat obscure but unmistakable evidences of similar practices, nonessential to construction, in the ruins of ceremonial structures within the ancient burial mounds.

2. Sculptural art, including carving, having its origin in the fashioning of implements, ornaments, and utensils from

stone and other hard materials, at first was purely utilitarian but in time assumed artistic functions in the form of embellishment and decoration. In the highly evolved cultures of Middle America sculpture was an integral part of building construction; to the northward the elaborately carved totem poles of the tribes of the Northwest Coast and the ivory carvings of the Eskimo are notable, as are also the wood carvings of the early pile-dwelling peoples of Florida. Within the mound area the highly artistic carvings, both in relief and in the

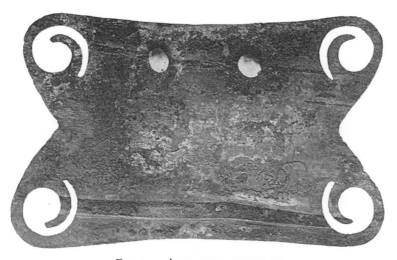

FIG. 59.   A COPPER BREASTPLATE

Copper breastplates probably were worn primarily for ornament and secondarily as protection from arrows. The specimen shown, more than a foot in length, bears a pleasing scroll design. The breastplates were suspended by a thong or cord from the neck, the cord being passed through two perforations and tied through large drilled pearls. Scale, 1/3.

round, executed in stone and other materials are outstanding among the products of Stone Age peoples of the world. These include ornaments, images, and ceremonial objects, and particularly the effigies of animals, birds, and the human head imposed upon stone tobacco pipes.

3. The plastic art is exemplified in pottery vessels and pipes and in certain terra-cotta images of animals, birds, and the human form, apparently symbolic or religious in their

nature. The high development of the fictile art in the Pueblo region is well known. Although not so highly evolved within the mound area, pottery-making was nevertheless one of the more important activities, particularly in the regions south of the Ohio River. The motives used in the plastic art were mostly animistic, including animals, birds, and the human form, with inanimate natural elements also much in evidence, such as the sun, clouds, lightning, and other natural phenomena. Not only for the purpose of embellishment but in the very forms of pottery vessels, were these elements utilized and imitated.

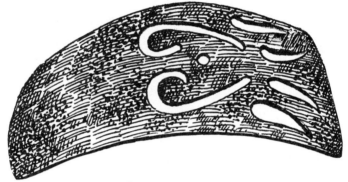

FIG. 60.   CURVED HEADDRESS OF COPPER
Found with a burial in the Hopewell Group, Ross County, Ohio. Scale, 1/2.

4. The metallurgic art in the regions north of Mexico, confined principally to the mound area, found its expression in the extensive use of copper and to a less extent of silver, meteoric iron, and gold. The many implements, ornaments, and symbolic or ceremonial objects of copper, particularly those from the mounds of the Hopewell culture and of the Etowah and allied cultures of the region to the south, are strikingly impressive, from the viewpoints both of industrial activity and of artistic achievement. Varied ways of handling copper and other metals are in evidence, such as silhouette and outline, cut-out or excising, and repoussé, all of them, however, being effected without the melting or smelting of the basic materials.

5. The textile art, including the making of cloth or woven fabric, basketry, needlework, beadwork, and quillwork, is the art which affords the primitive artist his greatest opportunity for detailed and ingenious application. The weaving and blanket-making of the tribes of the Southwest and of the Pacific Coast region are well known, as are the beadwork and the feather and quill products of the Plains tribes. Archæological evidences within the mounds indicate a remarkable development of the textile art among the Mound-builders, but since

FIG. 61.   AN ELABORATE HEADDRESS

Copper, mica, and pearls contribute to the make-up of this headdress, taken from a burial of the Hopewell Group. The curved portion was designed to fit the contour of the head, while the wing-like appendages dropped along the sides of the face. The design probably was intended to represent a bird or a butterfly. The headdress had been sewed to a bonnet-like appurtenance which covered the head and fell to the shoulders at the rear. Scale, 1/3.

the materials of the craft are mostly of a perishable nature, the extent to which it was developed can only be conjectured. Woven fabric of good quality, some of it with colored designs, has been recovered from the ancient tumuli.

6. The art of painting, with its subordinates, engraving, tattooing, and so forth, was an important factor in native American culture. Paints and colors were used almost universally for decorating potteryware, ornaments, and the human body, their use in the fictile art being most prominent

in the Pueblo region of the Southwest. Within the mound area extensive use of pigments for many purposes is disclosed in the mound burials, particularly those of the Hopewell and the Lower Mississippi regions. Engraving, incising, and stamping were favorite methods of decorating potteryware over a wide area.

PERSONAL ADORNMENT AND DECORATION

As we view the instinctive egotism of humankind, increasingly in evidence as observation descends the scale of human cultural development, it may be assumed that art had its inception in personal adornment. While objects of utility are of frequent occurrence in mound burials, articles of a personal nature are much more common.

Primitive man, like his civilized descendants, preferred to occupy his last resting place bedecked with his favorite jewels rather than accompanied by an axe or a hoe, the symbols of hard labor. Among the earliest articles of personal adornment were beads, and the Mound-builders had them in great numbers and of many varieties. There are beads of shell and of bone; beads of copper; beads made from teeth and claws of animals and birds; and beads—strands and necklaces of them—made from pearls, the jewel preëminent of the Mound-builder. The countless numbers of these "solidified drops of dew" found in the high-culture mounds of Ohio and to a less extent in the tumuli of the southern districts indicate that the pearl complex of the mound-building peoples amounted almost to a mania. In the category of beads, since they were used in a similar manner, are the many animal teeth and jaws, particularly the large canine teeth of the bear (Figure 55), which were drilled for suspension or attachment and often set with large fresh-water pearls. Human jaws, and even skulls, were similarly treated but perhaps served a different purpose, to be noted presently.

Next in order of abundant occurrence in the mounds are the so-called ear spools or ear ornaments (Figure 56). These,

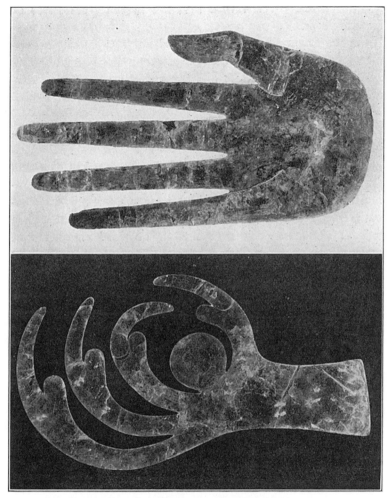

FIG. 62. DESIGNS CUT FROM MICA

Hand and eagle's foot, from mounds of the Ohio Hopewell culture. The hand symbol, with realistic thumb and conventionalized fingers, is suggestive of the human-hand design so prevalent in the art of the southern mound area. Such designs in mica were sewed to clothing or robes for ornamentation or as ceremonial insignia. Scale, about 2/5.

resembling in size and shape the small wooden spools on which milady's embroidery floss is wound, are usually made of copper, although in the southern districts they may be made of stone. Not infrequently one or both ends or faces of these ornaments are covered with thin foil beaten from silver or meteoric iron.

Copper finger-rings, bracelets, and anklets; copper breast-plates (worn presumably partly for protection against arrows and partly as ornaments); and buttons of wood or stone covered with copper foil are other common adjuncts of mound burials. Pretentious copper headplates, sometimes embellished with pearls, mica, and feathers, are among the most striking of the personal ornaments. These were worn attached to bonnetlike appurtenances of woven fabric, the ensemble forming an impressive headdress. A burial unearthed by W. K. Moorehead in the Hopewell Group, of Ross County, Ohio, was accompanied by a copper headdress which was embellished with a pair of imitation deer antlers made of wood covered with copper (see Chapter IX). A similar headdress was found by the Dickson brothers in a mound of the Liverpool Group near Liverpool, Illinois. Designs cut from silvery mica, representing the human form and hand as well as symbolic designs, are characteristic of the Hopewell culture mounds. In addition to objects of imperishable materials, there are found the remains of various ornaments made of wood, shell, fabric, and feathers. Conventional designs and effigies of birds made from marine tortoise-shell, seemingly used as articles of personal adornment, occasionally are found with burials.

PEARLS AND PEARL NECKLACES

Judging from the evidence of mound explorations and comparison with their kinsmen, the historic tribes of Indians, the Mound-builders must have possessed an elaborate complex of personal adornment and ceremonial costume. But perhaps no other of their traits carries with it so much sentiment and romance as does their use of pearls. In the interior mound region the use of pearls was extensive. This is particularly true of the Hopewell area, where the quest for pearls must have constituted a major activity. In a mound of the Turner Group, in Hamilton County, Ohio, Professor Putnam discovered some 60,000 of the gems, ranging from seed pearls to specimens of great size. These, a part of a ceremonial or sacrificial offering, were both drilled and undrilled. In the central mound of the Hopewell Group Moorehead found many thousands of pearls, while the writer, from the same group and from the Seip Group, recently explored, removed thousands

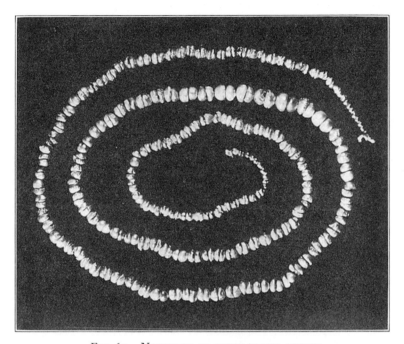

FIG. 63.   NECKLACE OF FRESH-WATER PEARLS

The pearls comprising this prehistoric necklace, while mostly of the type known as baroque, are exceptionally well preserved. The discovery of the necklace in a mound of the Hopewell Group, Ross County, Ohio, is described in Chapter IX. One-third natural size.

of pearls of every form and size. In the major groups of the Hopewell culture, throughout their range, many burials yield at least a few pearls, while the ceremonial offerings not infrequently contain many thousands. For the most part they are so badly damaged through long exposure to moisture and the acidity of the soil, or through the fires of cremation, as to be worthless as gems. Yet, even when soft and crumbly, many

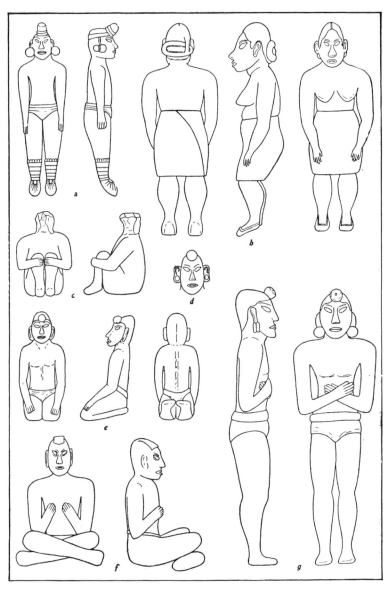

FIG. 64.   RESTORATIONS OF TERRA-COTTA FIGURINES FROM THE TURNER
GROUP, HAMILTON COUNTY, OHIO

After drawings by Dr. C. C. Willoughby, director of the Peabody Museum of
Harvard University. Scale, 1/3.

FIG. 65. Two of the terra-cotta figurines from the Turner
GROUP

The female and the male figures are respectively *b* and *g* in the restorations
illustrated in Figure 64. Courtesy of the Peabody Museum of Harvard University.
Scale, about 2/3.

of the pearls retain their brilliant luster and pleasing appearance.

An exception to the general rule of deterioration in the pearls from the mounds is a necklace of the gems found with a skeleton in a small mound of the Hopewell Group by the writer in 1925. This, the finest American prehistoric pearl necklace known (Figure 63), is remarkable for its preservation rather than for the form or size of the pearls. Apart from slight discoloration due to infiltration of metallic salts, the gems are in almost fresh condition so far as hardness and solidity are concerned. This unusual condition was due to the fact that the skeleton on which the necklace was found had been covered with several thicknesses of woven fabric and bark; besides, a large copper breastplate, through the chemical action of the metal, had further protected the strand of beads lying beneath it. In fresh condition the thousands of fine pearls taken from the Ohio mounds would represent many times over the proverbial king's ransom.

FIG. 66. SCULPTURE OF A HUMAN HEAD

This human head, carved on a stone tobacco-pipe, is one of the finest bits of Mound-builder sculpture extant. Note the haughty dignity of the face and the bonnet-like headdress. A chaplet of pearls encircles the forehead, and incised lines probably represent facial painting or tattooing. Taken from the Mound City Group, Ross County, Ohio, by Squier and Davis in 1846. Scale, full size.

Few, perhaps, realize the important part that pearls played in the Spanish conquest of Middle America. So great was the wealth of gems taken by the Spanish invaders from the natives or obtained in various other ways that for upwards of a century their value exceeded that of all other exports to Europe. It is recorded that more than 700 pounds of pearls were sent to Seville alone in a single year, and the courts of Spain and other

European countries for a time lived in what may well be styled the Pearl Age. At the time of discovery, pearls were temptingly in evidence among the peoples of Mexico and Peru. The palace of Montezuma is said to have been studded with pearls, while the Aztecs used them not only for personal adornment but to bedeck their gods and temples. The pearl fisheries of the Middle American aborigines were mainly on the coasts of Venezuela, Panama, and Mexico.

ART AS A MEASURE OF CULTURE STATUS

Ranked solely on their artistic development, the general status of the Hopewell peoples and of certain highly advanced groups of the southern districts would be placed too high in the scale of human culture. This inordinate development, comprising the geometric earthworks of the Hopewell peoples and the minor objects of art occurring throughout the general mound area, is responsible for the world-wide interest in the Moundbuilders and their culture. It indicates, moreover, such advanced concepts as division of labor and individual specialization in the arts and industries, thus giving these interesting peoples a further claim to be regarded as having advanced to a rather high cultural plane. Certain small sculptured productions, as the effigies of birds, animals, and the human form, and conventional designs engraved on bone and other materials, found in the mounds of the Hopewell and the more southerly cultures, have been pronounced the artistic equals of any similar objects produced by Stone Age peoples at any other time or place, not excepting the highly evolved cultures of Middle America or even those of ancient Egypt. Nevertheless, it must be admitted that in more material things the achievements of the Mound-builders did not equal their æsthetic development.

DEPICTIONS OF THE HUMAN FACE AND FIGURE

Sculptures of the human form, or what might be termed self-portraiture, while not of abundant occurrence in the mound

FIG. 67. SCULPTURE
OF THE HUMAN
FIGURE

One of the finest of
the full-length human-
figure effigies of the
mound culture; found
by Dr. William C. Mills
in the Adena Mound,
Ross County, Ohio. Note
the headdress, the ear
spools, and the loin cloth
tied in an interesting
manner in the rear. This
specimen is a tobacco
pipe of the tubular form,
the headdress being the
mouth-piece, while the
bowl is beneath the
feet. Scale, 1/2.

area, are of paramount interest and importance. To be able to see the Mound-
builder as he saw himself is intriguing;
and although the prehistoric artist probably had not reached a point where individual portraiture was attempted, the human images and figurines left with their
burials and in their tombs afford at least
a composite or generalized likeness of the
builders of the mounds.

Perhaps the most striking of these human sculptures are a series of terra-cotta
figurines taken by Professor Putnam from
the Turner Group of mounds, belonging
to the Hopewell culture. Although these
images were more or less mutilated, presumably in keeping with the custom of
"killing" or sacrificing artifacts either in
honor of the departed or as a tribute to
Mound-builder deities, they have been
most effectively reassembled, studied,
figured, and described by C. C. Willoughby, director of the Peabody Museum
of Harvard University. The figurines, as
will be noted in the illustrations (Figures
64 and 65), include both male and female
individuals, cleverly and artistically executed. Mongoloid features, with slanting
eyes and other characteristics, are unquestionably portrayed. Details of costumes, including the loin cloths of the
males and the short skirts of the females,
together with such personal ornaments as
headdresses, hair ornaments, and ear
spools are plainly indicated.

An admirable sculpture of the human head is that forming
the bowl of a tobacco pipe found by Squier and Davis in the

Mound City Group of Ohio (Figure 66). The features are boldly and strikingly executed, and the face is adorned with incised lines, probably intended to represent tattooing. A typical Hopewell headdress, with incipient antlers, covers the head, while encircling the forehead and face is a row of small freshwater pearls set into shallow cavities drilled into the pipestone from which the specimen is made.

FIG. 68.   A SCULPTURED SACRED IMAGE

This stone image of a human being, probably intended to serve as an idol, was found by Professor Warren K. Moorehead in a mound of the great Etowah Group, on Etowah River, Cartersville, Georgia. The image, which is the size of a five-year-old boy, was buried in a stone grave, exactly as though it were the burial of a human being. Courtesy of Phillips Academy, Andover, Massachusetts.

An unusual example of full-length human sculpture is found in a tubular tobacco pipe representing the human form found in the Adena Mound, near Chillicothe, Ohio, by Dr. Mills. In this fine specimen (Figure 67) there should be noted the headdress, the ear spools, and the scant attire covering the loins.

An interesting human image probably intended to serve as an idol was taken from the Etowah Group of Georgia by Professor Moorehead. The image, as shown in Figure 68, occupied a stone grave, boxlike in form, in which it had been interred exactly as though it were a human being. While these "graven images" are by no means rare in the southern area, the Etowah specimen is unique in size and in being interred in a grave.

FIG. 69. PIPES THAT ARE WORKS OF ART

These are four of upwards of two hundred similar tobacco pipes constituting a ceremonial or sacrificial offering in the Tremper Mound, Scioto County, Ohio. They represent the hawk, or eagle; the dog, the only domestic animal of the Mound-builders; the raccoon; and the quail, or Bob-White. Scale 2/3.

SCULPTURES OF BIRD AND ANIMAL FORMS

The so-called effigy tobacco pipes of the Hopewell mound-building culture are among the finest examples of Stone Age art. They are executed in the images of animals, birds, and the human head. Many of them are exquisitely fashioned and so realistic that the particular species of bird or animal is readily recognizable. Some of the image pipes have the eyes set with points of copper or with pearls. In the bird pipes the overlapping feather effect is so carefully done and the minute incised lines are drawn with such confidence and accuracy that they compare favorably with the work of the modern skilled engraver.

Close observation on the part of the prehistoric sculptor is evidenced in these effigy pipes, as in other phases of Mound-builder art. That he was a student of nature is strikingly manifest in numerous instances. Among the many effigy pipes obtained from the Tremper Mound in Scioto County, Ohio, there occur such interesting specimens as the owl with head turned looking to the rear; the raccoon with its front paw inserted in a crawfish hole, fishing for its favorite tidbit; the otter, premier fisherman of the animal world, is shown in several instances with a captured fish; the sandhill crane bearing the crest of red feathers, indicated in red pigment; the bear displaying its characteristic snarl with bared teeth. More detailed attention will be given the important subject of tobacco pipes and smoking customs in the following chapter.

REALISTIC, SYMBOLIC, AND CONVENTIONAL DESIGNS

Both realistic and conventional designs, the latter mostly symbolic in their significance, are found executed in copper pounded into thin sheets. They may be merely plain, undecorated designs or patterns cut from the sheet copper, or they may be further elaborated by means of excised or cut-out patterns or repoussé figures, as shown in the accompanying illustrations. The best-known discovery of copper patterns and de-

signs was that of Moorehead in the great central mound of the
Hopewell Group of Ross County, Ohio. Among these are the
well-known and widely distributed swastika, the emblem of
friendship; cosmic designs representing the cardinal points or
the four winds; conventionalized serpent heads with forked
tongues; and the trefoil, quatrefoil, and other geometric figures. Similar specimens have been found by Professor Putnam
in the Turner Group; by Moorehead in the Etowah mounds;
by Moore at Moundville, Alabama; by Mills in the Mound
City and Tremper groups; and by the writer in the Hopewell
and Seip groups.

The series of three copper designs from the Mound City
Group, shown in Figure 71, affords a striking suggestion as to
the origin and development of conventional design, so widely
in use at the present time. In the first of the series, all of which
are from a single grave and presumably the work of a single
artist, the primitive craftsman has depicted the flying eagle
as realistically as lay within his power; in the second specimen
the eagle motive has become a conventionalized design; while
in the third the eagle has become so highly conventionalized
that but for its association it would hardly be recognizable
by any but the student of conventionalized art forms.

A remarkable art development is disclosed in certain
repoussé designs in copper from the Etowah Group of Georgia; from Moundville, Alabama; from Union County, Illinois;
and from certain other localities in the southern states. The
Etowah plates (Figure 73) depict rampant warriors, equipped
with all the paraphernalia of war and wearing antler headdresses, feather robes, and other ceremonial accoutrements.
A favorite motive is a warrior with the severed head of a
human victim held in one hand while in the other is the ceremonial axe or sword with which decapitation was effected.

Art of this character was not confined to copper. Other
materials serving as bases for pretentious designs were stone,
shell, and bone. At the Etowah Group Moorehead found numerous shell gorgets or breast ornaments, two of which, depicting
the "elk-man" warrior and the pileated woodpecker are illus-

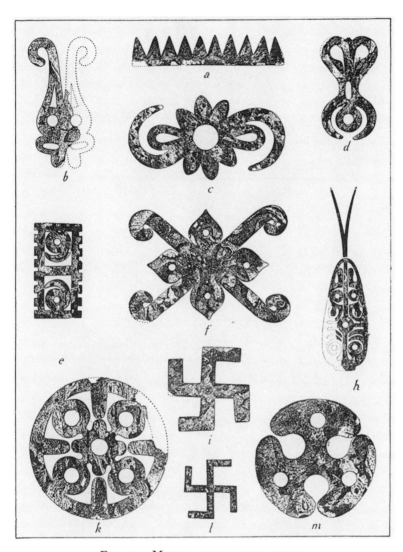

FIG. 70. MOUND ART IN SHEET COPPER

Ten remarkable art forms, illustrative of the interesting symbolism of the Hopewell culture of Mound-builders, are shown in the above drawings by Dr. C. C. Willoughby, director of the Peabody Museum of Harvard University. All these were found by Professor Moorehead in the Hopewell Group, with the exception of *c*, which is from the Turner Group. The interesting swastika, in its usual angular form, is shown as *i–l*; *h* is a highly conventionalized serpent's head; while the quatrefoil, *k*, is probably a cosmic or world symbol. Scale, 1/5. Courtesy of Dr. C. C. Willoughby.

FIG. 71. THE DEVELOPMENT OF CONVENTIONAL DESIGNS

These three large copper ornaments, found in a grave of the Mound City Group, Ross County, Ohio, afford a striking illustration of the development from life forms of conventional design. In the first the primitive artist has depicted the flying eagle as realistically as he could; in the second the eagle motive has become a conventional design; while in the third of the series the eagle is so highly conventionalized that but for its association it would hardly be recognizable by any but the student of conventionalized design. Scale, 1/4.

trated in Figure 75. Similar objects have been found by Moore and other explorers in the mounds and stone graves of Tennessee, Alabama, and adjacent territory. An engraving of intertwined plumed rattlesnakes on a large stone disk from a mound in Mississippi is shown in Figure 76.

FIG. 72.   DOUBLE-HEADED EAGLE DESIGN IN COPPER

These specimens are from a mound of the Mound City Group, Ross County, Ohio. They show that the use of the double-headed eagle was by no means confined to the old Austrian and Russian monarchies. The design has a long and interesting history in the Old World, being traced from its supposed origin in Egypt to Asia Minor and thence to Europe as a result of the Crusades. From Spain it was carried to Mexico, where it was adopted by the native tribesmen. Its appearance in a prehistoric American mound, however, is a novelty indeed, and is of interest to the student of the diffusion and the independent origin of culture traits. Scale, 2/3.

ENGRAVING ON BONE

Most remarkable of all the mound art are the intricate conventionalized engravings on human bones found in the Hopewell and Turner groups by Moorehead and Putnam. Two examples of this striking art form are shown in Figure 77. The upper specimen, from a mound of the Hopewell culture formerly located on the site of Cincinnati, was engraved on a portion of a human arm bone. This design, which is executed with much nicety and precision, represents, in the opinion of

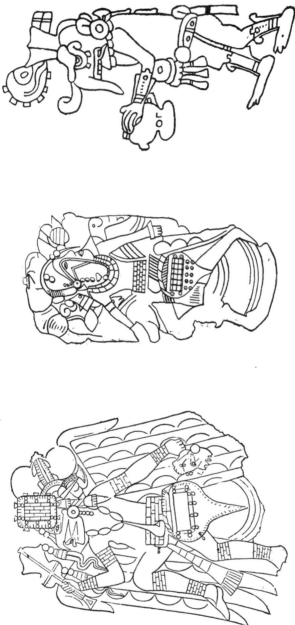

FIG. 73. REPOUSSÉ DESIGNS OF HUMAN FIGURES IN COPPER

The two drawings at the left are from two unusual repoussé plates from the Etowah Group of Georgia. The specimen to the left (scale, 3/8), from the explorations of the Bureau of American Ethnology, represents a warrior equipped with wings and wearing an elaborate headdress and many ceremonial ornaments. In the left hand he holds a severed human head and in the right a ceremonial axe with which presumably the head has been cut off. The middle figure (scale, 1/2), found by Professor Moorehead in the same group, is of a more benign expression of countenance and less belligerent, but elaborately costumed. For comparison there is shown at the right a design from the Mayan Codex to indicate the similarity of Southern Mound art to that of Mexico.

Dr. C. C. Willoughby, a highly conventionalized carnivorous animal. The lower specimen, from the Hopewell Group, engraved on a portion of a human femur, represents the conventionalized foot and claws of the bear. Various other examples of mound art, on stone tobacco pipes and in sheet mica, are shown in Figure 78.

The symbolic and totemic designs of the Hopewell peoples and of the highly developed cultures farther south offer a fascinating subject for study. Dr. William H. Holmes, director

FIG. 74. COPPER PLATE BEARING DANCING FIGURES
From Union County, Illinois, Scale, 1/2

of the National Gallery of Art of the Smithsonian Institution, and Dr. Charles C. Willoughby, director of the Peabody Museum of Harvard University, have paid particular attention to this branch of American archæology and are the recognized authorities thereon. Both have written extensively on the subject, the former in the publications of the Bureau of American Ethnology and the latter in the *Memoirs* of the Peabody Museum and in the Holmes Anniversary Volume. H. R. Goodwin, staff artist of the Ohio State Museum, a designer of long

FIG. 75. MOUND-BUILDER ART IN SHELL

These two shell gorgets, worn suspended at the neck for ornament, are from the Etowah Group, Georgia, explorations of Professor Moorehead. The specimen at the left represents a warrior equipped with an elaborate headdress bearing deer antlers and with various ornaments and weapons. In the right hand the figure holds a severed human head and in the left a ceremonial knife or weapon. The figure at the right shows a common decorative motive of the Etowah culture peoples—the pileated woodpecker, the design being repeated. Scale, full size. Courtesy of Phillips Academy, Andover, Massachusetts.

FIG. 76. AN ENGRAVED STONE DISK

The plumed intertwined rattlesnake is the decorative motive on this remarkable ceremonial stone disk from a mound in Alabama; the original is in the
Ohio State Museum. The serpent figures prominently in the art of the prehistoric
cultures of Mexico and Central America and is found in mounds and graves of
our southern states. Scale, 2/5.

experience, has created numerous designs in color for use in
textiles, taking his motives entirely and directly from the art
objects of the mounds.

CERAMIC ART

So important a medium of artistic expression is potteryware, the product of the fictile arts, that it calls for rather full
consideration. Although potteryware is common to all parts of
the general mound area, in the lower cultures it is mostly of a
utility sort, decorated, if at all, with simple cord and fabric

markings and with primary designs. This is particularly true of the districts lying north and west of the Ohio River; yet a rather striking development of the potter's art is to be noted in the Iroquois region of New York State and the St. Lawrence valley, where the ware is distinctive and well made, as are the elaborate tobacco pipes of burned clay (see Chapter XIII). Descending the Mississippi valley, a higher development of potteryware, apparently influenced by the southern area, comes to notice a short distance above St. Louis and is present in both the Mississippi and the Illinois River valleys. In this region a varied offering of potteryware, sometimes in effigy form, increases in importance as it reaches and merges with the Tennessee-Cumberland and the Lower Mississippi areas.

The outstanding pottery development of the northern districts is that of the Hopewell culture, centering in southern Ohio but well represented in western Illinois, eastern Iowa and southern Wisconsin. The utility ware of the culture is not impressive; the so-called ceremonial ware, however, was an important medium of art expression, though not equaling the ware of the regions south of the Ohio. Hopewell ceremonial vessels are distinctive in the entire area in being often equipped with flattened bases and with feet (Figure 79). The latter, four in number, are merely mammary-like projections equally spaced to correspond to the four oval or flattened faces or sides of the vessels. The rim in this form naturally assumes a square or rectangular aspect. Handles are never present in this type, and the probability that the vessels were suspended or carried by means of a cord or thong around the constricted neck is strengthened by the almost invariable presence around the short neck of a circle of punctuate depressions parallel to and below which is a solid encircling incised line. Vessels of this type often bear upon each of the four flattened surfaces conventionalized designs, such as the roseate spoonbill and the shoveler duck, indicated by incised outline, the interspaces being filled by crosshatching and roulette patterns, as shown in Figure 79.

FIG. 77. ENGRAVINGS ON HUMAN BONE

Most surprising of the artistic products of the Hopewell peoples are the designs engraved on human bones. The upper specimen of the two shown above depicts a conventionalized carnivorous animal on a portion of a human arm bone. It is from the Cincinnati, Ohio, Group, and the developments of the design are by Dr. G. B. Gordon. The lower specimen, from the Hopewell Group, is a portion of a human femur bearing a design representing the foot and claws of a bear. Scale, about 1/3. Courtesy of Dr. C. C. Willoughby.

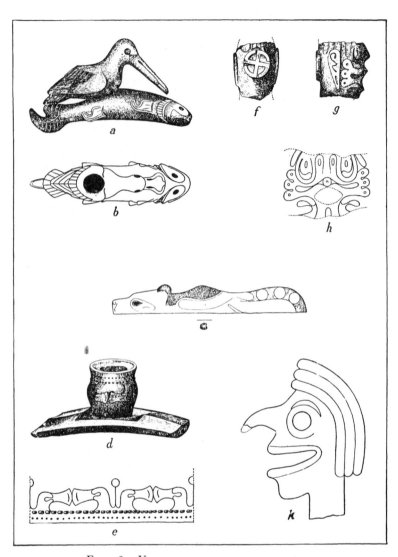

FIG. 78. VARIED EXAMPLES OF MOUND ART

After drawings by Dr. C. C. Willoughby. *a, b,* an unusual tobacco pipe, representing the roseate spoonbill with a fish (from the Hopewell Group) ; *c,* effigy of the bear, in sheet mica, the facial and body markings in colored pigment (Turner Group) ; *d, e,* pipe, bearing incised conventionalized heads of the roseate spoonbill (Hopewell Group) ; *f, g,* pipe bowl with elaborate facial markings and a swastika-like cosmic symbol (Harness Group, Ross County, Ohio) ; *k,* a grotesque life-size human mask cut from mica (Turner Group). Scale, about 1/4. Courtesy of Dr. C. C. Willoughby.

POTTERY OF THE LOWER MISSISSIPPI AREA

The pottery of the Lower Mississippi area will be rather fully described in the chapter dealing with that province; nevertheless its importance in Mound-builder art is sufficient to justify more than passing mention at this time, even at the risk of repetition.

The design motives on the southern potteryware consist mainly of the following forms: the swastika and various modifications thereof, almost invariably curvilinear; concentric circles and curved figures made of parallel lines; combinations of curved and diagonal straight lines; the cross-

FIG. 79. A TYPICAL CEREMONIAL VESSEL OF THE HOPEWELL CULTURE

The conventionalized design of the roseate spoon-bill or perhaps of the shoveler duck is characteristic of the Hopewell culture potteryware, as are the feet with which the vessel is equipped. Scale, 1/3.

hatch pattern, usually in the interspaces between distinct patterns enclosed in circular lines, dots or elliptical punch marks occasionally replacing the crosshatch; the sun pattern, consisting of a series of points in a circle. Single motives consisting of scrolls or circles are often repeated either three or four times to form a complete design. Many of the four-sided figures made in this way appear to have been derived from the swastika. The true spiral seems to be absent from the art of the Lower Mississippi area. Quite characteristic of the region are patterns made of single motives three or four times repeated, accompanied by small circles tangent to one another or to the main figure, the space between these designs being generally cross-hatched and the whole pattern divided at intervals by three or four diagonal lines, the central line having incised, pointed dots at intervals (Figure 82). Apparently the artists of the region did not copy botanical forms. Foliate patterns and shapes de-

FIG. 80. DESIGNS OCCURRING ON POTTERYWARE OF THE UPPER AND
MIDDLE PORTIONS OF THE LOWER MISSISSIPPI AREA

In addition to these geometric and symbolic designs, life motives were freely
used. After Holmes, Bureau of American Ethnology.

FIG. 81.   TYPICAL POTTERY FORMS AND DECORATIONS FROM SOUTHERN
ALABAMA MOUNDS
Scale, 1/10. Bureau of American Ethnology.

rived from vegetable forms such as the gourd are extremely
rare.

Life forms, animal, reptile, and human, are found modeled
in the round in clay and stone and incised on clay, stone,
copper, and shell. A form of vessel with the head and tail

of a bird sculptured on opposite sides of the rim, sometimes realistically and sometimes highly conventionalized, is quite common in the region, usually in clay but sometimes in stone. The effigy forms and many others are often symbolic rather than æsthetic. Pure fancy, no doubt, had a place in the creation of unusual forms.

At Moundville, Alabama, where incised bird effigies are abundant, composite birds are common. Often a bird incised on a pot has the head and neck of the heron and the tongue

FIG. 82.   SCROLL AND CIRCLE DESIGN ON POTTERYWARE

From Glendora Plantation, Louisiana. Cross hatching usually completes such designs. Scale, 1/2. After Clarence B. Moore.

and fanlike tail of the woodpecker. These incised bird patterns generally show both the head and body in profile, but at least one representation of the woodpecker from the front, with the head in profile and the wings spread, was found at Moundville. Usually these birds are two-headed, one head inverted, both arising from a common body with a single pair of wings. The eagle is another common form. The rattlesnake, horned and feathered as in Mexico, is incised on Moundville pots, and certain scroll motives are probably highly conventionalized serpents. Perhaps the greater number of vessels found with burials are culinary and without decoration. The highly decorated forms may have been made purposely as ceremonial vessels or mortuary tributes. Certain vessels found

FIG. 83. BIRD AND SERPENT DESIGNS ON POTTERYWARE

Both from Moundville, Alabama. In the upper design the conventionalized eagle heads are arranged to form a swastika. The serpent is plumed and winged, as in Mexico. Scale, 3/8. After Moore.

both in Arkansas and in Alabama, however, were made for this latter purpose alone, as they are decorated either in relief or incised with the human skull (slightly conventionalized), bones of the forearm, and the hand and eye, the two latter as in life. The hand and eye are often found, separately or together, apart from the skull and long-bone pattern, and when together the eye is usually on the palm of the hand. Very often but three or four fingers, with or without finger nails, represent the whole hand. Six sets of fingers making up a single pattern have been regarded as symbolic of the "six world quarters," that is, east, west, north, south, up, and down, a

FIG. 84. EARTHENWARE BOTTLE WITH SUN PATTERN AND SWASTIKA IN PIGMENT

From Miller County, Arkansas. The swastika-like figure within the sun pattern is supposed to be a cosmic symbol. Height, 7 1/2 inches. Courtesy of Clarence B. Moore.

concept possessed by certain Mexican stocks. In fact, most, if not all, of these Lower Mississippi designs are symbolic. Further reference to them is made in Chapter XVII.

Patterns or designs derived from life forms are rarely, if at all, found applied in pigment. The sun pattern and various modifications of the swastika are done in paint, incised on vessels and on shell and excised or in repoussé on copper. The sun pattern has been found forming the outline of a vessel at the rim.

An interesting development of the fictile art is found in southeastern Missouri and northeastern Arkansas adjacent to the Mississippi River. In this restricted region there occurs a form of pottery vessel fashioned in the image of the human head and face, with characteristic and detailed facial markings and of particularly expert workmanship (Figure 85). These vessels may be taken as among the best examples of human portrayal in the mound region.

FIG. 85.   POTTERY VESSEL IN EFFIGY OF THE HUMAN HEAD

From the Riggs Mound, on St. Francis River, Arkansas. Scale, 1/4. After Thruston, *Antiquities of Tennessee*. Courtesy of Stewart Kidd, Cincinnati.

An effective example of art development appears in the "teapot" form of vessels occurring in Arkansas and adjacent territory. Here is seen a type of vessel, originally made in the effigy of an animal, the head and tail of which, at first purely ornamental, have evolved into utility spout and decorative knob. This development, in the opinion of students of the evolution of decorative design, is one of the most striking in native American art.

Many individual pottery vessels of the Lower Mississippi region not only represent the maximum artistic attainment of primitive America, but, despite the present-day artistic traditions, are entitled to a place with the best ceramic productions of all time. Examples of exceptional specimens are those found at Greer, Arkansas, and Glendora Plantation and Foster Place, Louisiana, described in the chapter dealing with those states. An earthenware pipe found on Red River, in Louisiana, is remarkable in that it depicts a kneeling human figure holding a tobacco pipe. A smoke passage extends from the pipe to the

FIG. 86. COLOR WARE OF VASE OR BOTTLE FORM

The design is incised and painted in yellow on an olive-green ground. From Crittenden County, Arkansas. Height, 9 inches. Courtesy of Clarence B. Moore.

mouth of the figure ostensibly to permit the tobacco smoke to exhale therefrom, thus suggesting an analogous practice in modern fountains. While not fashioned from clay, the noted stone vessel made in the image of a duck found at Moundville, Alabama, illustrated in connection with the Moundville

Group in Chapter XVII, is plainly in imitation of the effigy pottery forms. It is admittedly one of the finest known specimens of native American art.

CEREMONIAL AND PROBLEMATICAL ARTIFACTS

The more subtle phases of prehistoric culture do not yield so readily to interpretation through the evidences of exploration as do the more obvious and material activities. Moreover, in primitive society the social, political, religious, and artistic concepts, with their complex of ceremony and ritualism, are likely to be closely interwoven and even among living peoples difficult to interpret in terms of civilized understanding and appreciation. Again, they are less likely to afford to archæological exploration substantial material remains, so that only by careful translation of the fragmentary evidences of the mounds and through comparison with similar concepts of living or historic peoples may even a partial understanding be had.

Although perhaps not more appropriate in this chapter than in another, it seems logical to include here certain types of ceremonial artifacts along with the consideration of art, since both are æsthetic in their sphere.

Numerous objects, mostly of stone, bone, and shell, are found with burials and sacrificial offerings, the purpose of which is difficult to explain. To the student of anthropology these so-called ceremonial objects, taken as a whole, are intelligible in an abstract manner, but they are not of particular interest to the layman. It is known that in a broad sense they served as talismans, charms, fetishes, and amulets, in the same manner that any primitive people of today makes use of similar objects, the exact purpose of which the owners cannot always explain.

More obvious as to usage are certain ceremonial weapons, usually gigantic in size and clearly too large for utility purposes. These were the property of shamans and medicine men and the insignia of chiefs—tribal possessions, perhaps, which were brought forth and exhibited to the proletariat only on

Fig. 87. Ceremonial blades of obsidian and quartz

Probably unique as to number, size, and the skill required in their production
are the ceremonial blades in the form of spearpoints and knives, taken from the
great central mound of the Hopewell Group by Moorehead in 1891. Over one
hundred of these ceremonial specimens, part of a ceremonial or sacrificial offering, comprised the find, the specimens ranging in size from 6 inches to 18 inches
in length. The specimen shown at the left, of obsidian, is over 17 inches long;
that at the right, of quartz, from the Seip Mounds, is 13 inches in length.
Scale, 1/3.

special occasions, "big medicine," as with our historic Indian tribes. Outstanding among these ceremonial objects are certain extremely rare and beautifully made ceremonial spearpoints, knives, and daggers chipped from flint and obsidian. Many of these rare objects were found by Moorehead in the central

FIG. 88.   CEREMONIAL AXES OF COPPER

These immense specimens, like the huge ceremonial blades of obsidian, were not intended for utility purposes but were probably used in the ceremonial proceedings of the Hopewell peoples, being part of the paraphernalia of the priests and medicine men and displayed only on state occasions. They weigh 38 and 27 pounds respectively, the smaller one being from the Seip Group, Ross County, Ohio, while the larger specimen was found by Moorehead in the Hopewell Group. Scale, 1/8.

mound of the Hopewell Group (Figure 87), by the writer in another mound of the same group, by Mills in the Mound City Group, and by McKern in the Wisconsin Hopewell mounds. Some of the longest of these measure as much as 18 inches, with a width of six inches or more. In the same classification are certain long slender "swords," chipped from flint, found by Moorehead in the Etowah Group of Georgia (see Chapter XVIII); and a series of flint maces, batons, and so forth discovered some years ago in Tennessee and now in the Historical Society's Museum at St. Louis. Gigantic copper axes (Figure 88), several of which were found in the Hopewell and the Seip groups, ranging in weight up to 38 pounds, are similar in purpose to the above.

Some appreciation of the purpose served by these ceremonial artifacts may be had from comparison with similar objects of historic use by the American Indians. One example is the sacred Palladium pipe of the Arapaho described in the next chapter. Other noted objects of a similar nature are the sacred medicine arrows of the Cheyenne, which have been in charge of a special priest from the earliest traditional period of the nation and which are brought forth only on rare occasions; the sacred metal plates of the Creeks, exhibited only on the occasion of the annual Green Corn Dance, which they believe to have been given them by a supernatural being at the very beginning of their existence; the sacred box of the Cherokee, formerly guarded constantly by an armed sentinel who with drawn bow prevented strangers from too close approach; and the sacred stone image in the form of the head and bust of a human still zealously guarded by the Kiowa Indians and not exhibited even to their own tribesmen of the present generation.

Of the doubtless impressive body of religious, social, and political ritual of the Mound-builders only slight traces are to be found in the material remains within the mounds. The student of the Mound-builder culture, however, possessed of a knowledge of the culture of the historic highly developed peoples of the Southwest and of Middle America, may reach a fairly accurate estimate of the culture complex of prehistoric peoples through methods of comparison and analogy.

The handiwork of the Mound-builder peoples is, in a very true sense, real art. Although the rule is not general for the entire mound area, in the several centers of high artistic development there is to be noted what may be termed a finished art rather than the amateurish art which usually is associated with primitive culture. A surprising feature is that little evidence of progressive evolution exists within the area, with the resulting archæological query as to where the development took place. The artists of the Mound-builders presumably had little in the way of precedent to guide or to hamper them. For the most part they went directly to nature for their inspiration.

CHAPTER VII

TOBACCO PIPES AND SMOKING CUSTOMS

Primitive smoking a ceremonial procedure—Smoking customs of the American Indians—Calumets and the calumet ceremony—The Mound-builder smoking complex—Distribution and types of tobacco pipes—Pipes as votive and sacrificial offerings.

TOBACCO pipes, in common with most artifacts of the Mound-builders, present both utility and æsthetic aspects. The æsthetic interest, however, both artistic and ceremonial, greatly exceeds the utility, and is so important as to justify extended discussion in this special chapter, notwithstanding the attention already given to pipe design and manufacture as a Mound-builder art and industry.

PRIMITIVE SMOKING A CEREMONIAL PROCEDURE

While in a sense the highly ornate pipes of the mound-building peoples served a utility purpose, it is probable that the everyday pipe of the confirmed smoker is to be found in the plainer, less pretentious stone pipes of rather frequent occurrence and that other ordinary pipes were made of wood or even from the prosaic corncob. The abundant occurrence of pipes and the occasional finding of tobacco itself within the ancient mounds and habitation sites are conclusive evidences that their builders were strongly addicted to the use of the weed. As is so often true of archæological evidence, however, the interpretation of these pipes and other items entering into the tobacco-using complex of the Mound-builders is dependent in great part on comparison and analogy with historic peoples—in this instance with their relatives the American Indians. It is well known that tobacco-smoking as practiced by the American Indians under normal conditions partakes strongly of the ceremonial, and analogy doubtless may extend the concept to the mound-building peoples of prehistoric times.

The use of tobacco has been alternately lauded and condemned, and it is not yet accepted in every quarter as an unalloyed blessing notwithstanding the recent great extension of sentiment in its favor. Nevertheless no other trait of the American aborigines has evoked more human interest or figured more prominently in literature. As a result, the use of the plant by the native Americans, from the days of discovery to the present, is well known and fully recorded in studies and reports of ethnologists and other observers. In the interest of understanding and appreciation of tobacco and its use by the mound-building peoples a brief digest of this information is essential.

Present-day use of tobacco, particularly in America, is very largely a utility trait. It is true that a certain amount of sentiment and social amenity attaches to smoking, and tobacco pipes and other media for using tobacco afford something of an opportunity for artistic expression; but in the main the trait finds its justification in the quest for enjoyment and in the stimulation or sedative effect accruing to the smoker. With the American Indian, however, though these utility considerations were factors in the use of tobacco, they were overshadowed by its ceremonial significance and the artistic development which invariably accompanies the ceremonial. Keeping in mind the characteristic phlegmatic temperament of the native American race, it would be difficult to picture either the historic Indian or the prehistoric builder of mounds as voicing the sensuous utterance of Kingsley's character in *Westward Ho!* or enthusing over the more delicate tribute to tobacco contained in Ingersoll's *Christmas Sermon*.

SMOKING CUSTOMS OF THE AMERICAN INDIANS

Among the native American tribes of historic record tobacco-smoking was practiced as a medicinal agency and was supposed to be endowed with most potent curative powers. It was in ceremonial proceedings, however, such as councils and treaty-making, whether with other tribes or with whites, that the practice was of greatest significance. No important undertaking could be launched and no peace effected without the smoking of the calumet. The ceremonial burning or smoking of tobacco was a sacrifice to idols after the manner of offering incense; priests smoked tobacco and inhaled the fumes in

FIG. 89. CONICAL AND ELBOW TYPES OF PIPES

These simple forms are characteristic of a wide area of the mound region, particularly with the simpler cultures of aborigines. Scale, 3/4.

preparation for receiving oracles and messages from the spirit world; and the narcotic properties of the weed were made use of for inducing sleep. Socially, the burning or smoking of tobacco and the offering of facilities for so doing were regarded as the highest compliment that could be paid to visiting guests or to notables of other tribes or white men of importance. The chroniclers of De Soto record that the great explorer was

FIG. 90. AN UNUSUAL TYPE OF PIPE

This form, with incipient wings, suggests a highly conventionalized bird.
Found near Chillicothe, Ohio. Scale, 2/5.

received by the Indians as though he and his men were deities
and that tobacco was burned as incense to celebrate their
advent among the tribesmen. The following brief extract from
the writings of J. D. McGuire, a foremost authority on the
American aborigines, is illustrative of the importance of the
tobacco ceremony among the native Indian tribes:

The Hopi, in their ceremonies, offer smoke to their sacred images,
and the ceremonies of the pipe are observed with great decorum;
the head chief is attended by an assistant of nearly equal rank, who
ceremoniously lights the pipe, and with certain formalities and set
words hands it to the chief, who blows the smoke to the world
quarters and over the altar as a preliminary to his invocation. In
religious ceremonies in general, the priest usually blows the smoke
over the altar to the world quarters. In the councils of some tribes
the pipe was handed to the head chief by the official pipe-keeper;
after lighting it he handed it on; and it was passed around in the

FIG. 91. AN ANIMAL EFFIGY PIPE
Found in Ross County, Ohio. Scale, 1/4.

council house, usually from left to right, until each one had smoked and thus fitted himself for serious deliberation. In some tribes the pipe, in being passed from one individual to another during a ceremony, is differently grasped and held, according to the nature of the ceremony or to the taboo obligation of the individual. Among other tribes the decoration of pipes, and especially of the pipe-stems, has great ceremonial and ethnic significance; even the attachment holding the pipe to the stem is fixed with special care, and the early death of an individual, or other calamity, it was believed, would ensue were the pipe dropped from the stem during a ceremony. Every individual engaging in war, hunting, fishing or husbandry, and every clan and phratry made supplication to the gods, by means of smoke, which was believed to bring good and to arrest evil, to give protection from enemies, to bring game or fish, allay storms, and to protect one while journeying.

In the ceremonial use of tobacco the pipe bowl was regarded as a miniature altar, on which was effected the burning of the tobacco as incense, either as an offering to the gods or in honor of important personages. It was but natural that so important a ceremonial object as the tobacco pipe should become identified with another of equal importance, the so-called calumet.

CALUMETS AND THE CALUMET CEREMONY

The calumet, as originally employed, consisted of two highly symbolic reeds or wooden stems, painted or decorated with symbolic colors and patterns, the one representing the male procreative power and signifying the fatherhood of nature, and the other the female reproductive power or the motherhood of nature. Each was perforated to permit the passage of the breath or spirit of life. Originally the calumet shafts (usually the male and the female shafts united) were independent of the pipe bowl as such. The combining of the two resulted in what has been termed the most profoundly sacred object in the possession of the native American tribesmen. Since the adornments on the calumet shafts were symbolic representations of the dominant gods or deities of the Indians, the combination came to be "a veritable executive council of the gods." So sacred indeed was the calumet pipe that a special chant and dance in its honor were widely observed. The combination has been described as a "highly complex synthetic symbol of the source, reproduction, and conservation of life."

The calumet, popularly known as the war pipe and the peace pipe, was employed as a general talisman for averting evil and for insuring good; for assuring favorable weather, particularly in bringing rain in time of drought; as a protection and passport to travelers and emissaries; in the conciliation of ene-

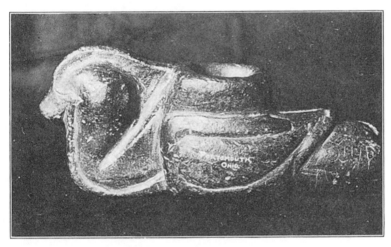

FIG. 92. BIRD EFFIGY PIPE

This massive specimen, found near Portsmouth, Ohio, is suggestive of the Lower Mississippi area. Scale, 3/5.

mies; in the binding of contracts and treaties; in perfecting alliances between or among tribes and nations; and in concluding peace negotiations. Calumets were in general use among the Indians, but more notably among the tribes of the West, where the Pawnee and some others believed the calumet to be a gift from the sun. It was generally believed that violations of obligations incurred under the calumet ceremony could not escape punishment; hence the fact that but few instances of failure to abide by such agreements are recorded.

FIG. 93. HUMAN AND BIRD EFFIGY PIPES

These three specimens, found in central Tennessee, are typical of the region south of the Ohio River. Scale, 1/3.

FIG. 94. AN UNUSUAL EFFIGY PIPE

This specimen, from the Hopewell Group, is made to represent the heads and intertwined necks of wild ducks or geese and is an exceptionally fine example of mound art. Scale, 2/3.

The veneration accorded the ceremonial pipes and calumets by certain Indian tribes is illustrated in the protection accorded the so-called Palladium pipe of the Arapaho Nation, which has been so zealously guarded that only one white man ever has seen it. The Palladium or seicha pipe is kept under constant guard and brought forth only on special occasions. The Arapaho believe that they have possessed this relic from the beginning of the world.

An outstanding historic example of the calumet ceremony was the smoking of the peace pipe in connection with the

FIG. 95. A TYPICAL PLATFORM PIPE

Pipes of the Hopewell mounds are almost exclusively of this platform type, one end of the base serving as a handhold while the other end is the mouthpiece and is drilled with a perforation connecting with the bowl. Scale, 3/4.

making of the Greenville Treaty, in 1795, at Fort Greenville in what is now western Ohio. On this solemn occasion General "Mad Anthony" Wayne, representing the white contingent in the negotiations, united with ninety-odd chiefs of the Indian tribes in smoking the pipe of peace, thus effecting a virtual seal to this important American cession. Through the Treaty of Greenville, thus affirmed, the vast Northwest Territory, out of which were subsequently carved the present great states of Ohio, Indiana, Illinois, Michigan, and Wisconsin, was transferred effectively from Indian to white control and its fertile acres, after years of bloody fighting, were opened to white settlement. The famous Greenville Treaty calumet, together with other relics of the event and of General Wayne, are now cherished possessions of the Ohio State Museum. The peace pipe was the Indians' pledge of loyal allegiance to the Treaty.

THE MOUND-BUILDER SMOKING COMPLEX

Equipped with this brief sketch of tobacco and smoking customs among the historic Indian tribes, the student of archæology will readily recognize the existence of a similar and even more elaborate complex in the culture of the Moundbuilders. The abundant occurrence of tobacco pipes and minor indications of the use of the plant in smoking are unmistakable evidences of the importance of the trait among these aborigines. A single example of the many available ones illustrating the analogies between the prehistoric and the historic is shown in the pipe illustrated as Figure 94. This specimen is carved to represent the heads and necks of two wild ducks, the necks being intertwined about the bowl of the pipe. The Pawnee Indians, in a ceremony known as the hako, make and use a similar calumet by drawing over a hollow reed or tube the skins from the heads and necks of two ducks. To the Pawnee this bird represents much that is admirable: it is at home not only on land and water, but in the trackless paths of the air. It is logical to see in the effigy pipe from the ancient mound a very similar significance.

DISTRIBUTION AND TYPES OF TOBACCO PIPES

The distribution of native American tobacco pipes is very broad, but their frequency of occurrence rapidly declines toward the Southwest and the Mexican border. In the Pueblo region and southward the simple tubular pipe, resembling in form the modern cigar-holder, is typical, while in Middle and South America the smoking of tobacco, where it occurred, seems to have been in the form of cigarettes and cigars, the prototypes of the modern pipeless methods of smoking.

FIG. 96. BIRD EFFIGY PIPE

This unusual specimen may be intended to represent the Carolina paroquet now almost extinct but formerly quite abundant in Ohio. Scale, full size.

Pipes range in form and size from those of the simplest possible type and smallest dimensions to those of elaborate workmanship and liberal content, depending upon the location and the custom of their makers and users. They were not confined by any means to the mound-building peoples but were common alike to most of the native Indian nations. Stone of workable varieties and pleasing appearance was much used, as were clay, wood, bone, and other materials. The pottery pipes of the region formerly occupied by the Iroquois, in New

FIG. 97. SQUIRREL EFFIGY PIPE

A platform type from the Tremper Mound of the Hopewell culture, Scioto County, Ohio. Scale, full size.

York State, are striking in form and decoration and often occur in effigy shapes (see Chapter XIII). The flat-base monitor pipes of the middle Atlantic states and the effigy pipes of the lower mound area are interesting and highly developed forms, although not as artistic in conception and execution as the noted platform pipes of the Hopewell culture (Figure 95). In the region south of the Ohio River and including most of the southern states there have been found in mounds and on the surface great numbers of image pipes, usually of large size and made in the effigies of animals, birds, and the human form. An example of a form frequently found is shown in Figure 98.

PIPES AS VOTIVE AND SACRIFICIAL OFFERINGS

The tobacco pipes of the Hopewell culture have a distinctive form known archæologically as the platform type. A remarkable sacrificial or votive offering of these rare pipes, upward of two hundred in number, was taken from the Tremper Mound, in Scioto County, Ohio, by the late Dr. Mills and the writer, for the Ohio State Museum. Approximately one-half the number were of the typical plain form; the remainder were sculptured in the images of birds and animals native to the region. A similar and almost equally important find was made by Squier and Davis in the Mound City Group of Ohio in 1846, and numerous fine specimens now in the Davenport Public Museum were found in the Hopewell mounds of eastern Iowa and adjacent portions of Illinois. While most forms of tobacco pipes were fashioned either with an obvious stem as a part of the pipe proper or with a perforation intended to accommodate a separate stem of reed, wood, or bone, the Hopewell platform pipes were complete in themselves, as the specimen in Figure 96 shows. One end of the platform, it will be noted, is drilled with a hole which connects with the bowl;

FIG. 98. A VOTIVE OFFERING OF TOBACCO PIPES

Placed immediately above a multiple burial in the Seip Mound were five very large tobacco pipes in the images of animals and birds. Two of these pipes, which appear to have been placed above the burials as guardians thereof, are shown in place, about to be removed.

this drilled end served as the mouthpiece or stem, while the opposite end of the platform served as a handhold.

A decidedly interesting and perhaps unique employment of tobacco pipes in a ceremonial manner or as an adjunct of burial occurred in the great central tumulus of the Seip Group of mounds in Ross County, Ohio. Above the six burials occupying the charnel house of the mound there were placed five massive pipes, carved in the images of the wolf, the Indian dog, the owl, the bear, and the whippoorwill or nighthawk (Figure 98). From their position these images may have been intended to guard and keep watch over those who slept below. Strangely enough, these pipes were not typical of the builders of the mound but belonged to the culture of the lower Mississippi valley. All of them are exceptionally massive as contrasted with the delicate pipes of the Hopewell peoples, and all are typical in form and treatment of the culture to the south. Their presence in a Hopewell mound in Ohio is an instance of the liberality with which the Hopewell peoples drew upon the southland for supplies; moreover, they excite curiosity as to whether they may have been obtained in a peaceful manner through the ordinary channels of trade and barter or whether they were obtained in some more questionable manner. There comes to mind the overrunning of the territory of the Chaldeans by the Elamites and the carrying away of cherished household lares and penates.

CHAPTER VIII

THE OHIO AREA: I, THE ADENA AND FORT ANCIENT CULTURES

The various cultures of the Ohio area—The Adena culture and its characteristics—The Fort Ancient culture—Habitation sites of the Fort Ancient
culture—The Feurt mounds and village site—Reconstruction of the life
of a Fort Ancient village—Primitive industries—Cultivated and uncultivated food products—Recreation and amusement—A burial mound in the
making—Primitive methods of sanitation.

THE order in which the several archæological divisions
of the general mound area are here discussed is purely
arbitrary; it might be reversed or rearranged in any
manner without affecting the ultimate result. The placing of
the Ohio area at the head of the list is not due to discrimina-
tion, but rather to the facts that it is unquestionably the most
important and varied of the several areas and has received
more exhaustive exploration and therefore is better known than
any other. The high æsthetic development of the great Hopewell culture centering in south-central Ohio is known throughout the world, and Hopewell is a synonym for all that is most
striking and important in the literature of the mounds. As
a result of the publicity attending explorations of this culture,
Ohio has come to be generally regarded as the Mound-builder
state; and since the writer has been closely identified with
the Ohio explorations and hence is exceptionally familiar with
their disclosures, it is but natural that they should introduce
the series of sectional studies to follow.

THE VARIOUS CULTURES OF THE OHIO AREA

Since, as we have already shown, mound areas conform to
waterways and topography rather than to the bounds of political geography, the Ohio area is not coextensive with the

State of Ohio. The northern portion of the state, adjacent to Lake Erie, has its affinities with the assumed Great Lakes area, while to the south and west the Ohio area extends over

FIG. 99. ARCHÆOLOGICAL MAP OF OHIO
Showing the distribution and location of the mounds and earthworks of the state.

adjacent portions of Pennsylvania, West Virginia, Kentucky, and Indiana. The drainage of the state is divided fairly evenly between Lake Erie and the Ohio River by a watershed crossing the state from east to west. The northern drainage area is characterized by scattering mounds, by small enclosures of indeterminate origin, and by habitation sites and minor remains of Iroquoian peoples, mainly Erie. Thus it is mainly with the southern portion, approximately two-thirds, of the state that the description of the Ohio mound area is concerned.

Within this area three outstanding cultures of Mound-builders are identified, and while all of them are represented by remains in territory immediately contiguous to the state proper, the nuclei and greatest development of the three are to be found within the boundaries of Ohio. It has been estimated that more than five thousand mounds and earthworks exist, or have existed, within the confines of the state. These three cultures are now to be discussed in the order of their importance, beginning with that least in evidence, the so-called Adena culture, and passing in order to the Fort Ancient and and the Hopewell cultures.

THE ADENA CULTURE AND ITS CHARACTERISTICS

The Adena culture of Mound-builders is most in evidence in the valleys of the Scioto and Miami rivers, from the latitude of Columbus southward to the Ohio. Their mounds are found also south of the Ohio River in Kentucky and West Virginia, particularly in the lower course of the Kanawha valley; and recent explorations in southeastern Indiana demonstrate their existence in the Whitewater valley of that state.

Burial mounds, singly or in small groups, often of three in triangular arrangement, constitute the major evidences of the Adena occupancy. No earthworks and no very obvious village sites of their builders have been recorded, possibly owing to the scant attention so far accorded the culture. Their mounds, however, are noted for their symmetry of form and careful construction and often are of great size. Like the Hopewell mounds, those of the Adena occur in close proximity to streams.

The Adena culture takes its name from historic "Adena," near Chillicothe, Ohio, the pretentious estate of Thomas Worth-

ington, early governor of Ohio. Here was located the Adena
Mound so-called, which was explored by the Ohio Archæological and Historical Society through its then curator, Dr. William C. Mills, in 1901. The Adena Mound was the first of its
class to be scientifically examined and reported and thus became the type mound of what has come to be known as the
Adena culture. In the Adena Mound Dr. Mills found uncremated burials enclosed in log cists, bracelets and other orna-

FIG. 100.   THE MIAMISBURG MOUND

This tumulus, situated in Montgomery County, Ohio, is typical of the Adena
culture. It is slightly under 70 feet in height, is the largest conical mound in
Ohio, and with the exception of the Grave Creek Mound at Moundsville, West
Virginia, is the largest of all the conical burial mounds.

ments of copper, objects of mica, and the artistic human effigy
pipe illustrated in Figure 67.

The two most striking mounds of the culture so far identified are the Miamisburg Mound, near the town of that name
in Montgomery County, Ohio, and the great Grave Creek
Mound in Marshall County, West Virginia. The Miamisburg
Mound, the largest in Ohio, is approximately 68 feet in height
with a diameter at the base of more than 250 feet and is
exceptionally symmetrical in form; it has not been explored.

The Grave Creek Mound is slightly higher and somewhat greater in diameter than the Miamisburg tumulus. We shall refer again in Chapter XI to the results of its partial exploration by tunneling by Schoolcraft, recorded in Volume I of the *Transactions of the American Ethnological Society*. The log sepulchers and the objects found with burials were similar to those characterizing the Adena Mound, thus indicating close cultural affinity.

From the examination of the Adena Mound, the Westenhaver Mound in Pickaway County, Ohio, and other subsequent explorations, the Adena culture is known to have the following characteristics: shapely conical mounds, located singly or in groups; uncremated burials, in log cists, placed either below, above, or on the original surface; use of copper, mainly for ornaments; use of mica; admirable artistic ability in sculpturing small objects in the round; use of tubular tobacco pipes. Far too little is known of the Adena type of mounds, and further exploration promises to enhance the importance of the culture.

THE FORT ANCIENT CULTURE

The second of the outstanding cultures of the Ohio area takes its name from the great prehistoric fortification known as Fort Ancient, situated in Warren County, Ohio, to be later described in Chapter X. Although in the early stages of archæological exploration a common origin was assumed and accepted for the imposing old Fort and the mounds and village sites occurring nearby, there has developed some doubt as to whether this identification is justifiable. Within and immediately adjacent to the Fort and extending for some distance up and down the Miami River on which it is located there are numerous habitation sites of a populous Moundbuilder culture. Earliest exploration of the culture centered in these sites, and it was assumed, naturally, that they were attributable to the builders of the Fort; hence the name, the Fort Ancient culture. Later there arose the question as to whether the occupants of the village sites really were the builders of the Fort, or whether their occupancy of the region was at a later date. If the latter is true, it is assumed that another and an earlier people or culture was the author of the great Fort Ancient. The question may later be answered by further exploration of the Fort site.

The Fort Ancient peoples left behind them, in addition to mounds, extensive village sites containing minute evidences of their everyday life, and through extensive exploration of these

FIG. 101.   EXCAVATION OF ONE OF THE FEURT MOUNDS, SCIOTO COUNTY, OHIO

This tumulus, typical of the Fort Ancient culture, contained burials below and on the base line as well as in the body of the mound proper.

the culture is perhaps better known than any other of the general mound area. From these examinations it is known that the Fort Ancient peoples were widely spread throughout central and southern Ohio and down the Ohio River and its tributaries, particularly in Indiana and Kentucky. They were much less advanced culturally than the Hopewell, or even in some respects the Adena, but obviously were a most practical and self-sufficient group—in a sense the most representative of the

Ohio area. The habitation sites of the Fort Ancient peoples are of preëminent interest; they constitute, in fact, the major material evidences of their existence, the development of the mound-building trait having been comparatively weak among them.

HABITATION SITES OF THE FORT ANCIENT CULTURE

The outstanding site of Fort Ancient culture habitation (with Fort Ancient proper, for the time at least, uncertain as to origin) is the great Madisonville site, near the city of Cincinnati. This site, covering an area of many acres, comprises one of the most extensive aboriginal cemeteries and habitations in the mound area, and in connection with it there were several burial mounds. Through its then director, Professor Frederick W. Putnam, the Peabody Museum of Harvard University conducted explorations of the site throughout a period of nearly thirty years, from 1882 to 1911. A wealth of potteryware, implements, and ornaments and much skeletal material were secured.

Several other important sites of the Fort Ancient culture have been explored by the Ohio State Museum, under Dr. William C. Mills, its former director, and the writer. Of the many outstanding sites in Ohio there may be mentioned the Baum and the Gartner sites, in Ross County; the Campbell Island site, in Butler County; and the Feurt mounds and village site, in Scioto County, all of which have been examined by the Museum. Sites of the culture are known to exist in territory immediately contiguous to Ohio, on the south and southwest, but the only one of them that has been carefully explored and reported is the Fox Farm site, in Mason County, Kentucky. This site, it may be said, was found to correspond in all essential characteristics with those above enumerated, allowing, of course, for minor local differentiations, always to be expected. An extensive village site near Lawrenceburg, Indiana, adjacent to the Ohio River and not far distant from Fort Miami, appears to be of Fort Ancient culture.

Since the purpose of archæological exploration is to gather

information regarding the life history of vanished peoples, it is appropriate to offer the reader at this point an example of the tentative reconstruction of the life of a prehistoric village from the evidence resulting from examination of a specific site.

THE FEURT MOUNDS AND VILLAGE SITE

The Feurt mounds and prehistoric village, in Scioto County, Ohio, may be taken as a typical habitation site of the Fort

FIG. 102.   CIRCULAR FIREPLACE OF PUDDLED CLAY

Found adjacent to a house site in the Feurt prehistoric village site of the Fort Ancient culture. Scale, 1/10.

Ancient culture. This site was explored for the Ohio State Museum in 1916 by Dr. Mills, assisted by the writer. It is situated five miles north of the city of Portsmouth, on the east side of the Scioto River, and occupies a picturesque and strategic location on the second terrace projecting promontory-wise into the low ground constituting the river bottom. The Scioto bottoms at this point are very broad, and the second terrace, extremely narrow, is terminated immediately on the east by the high hills characteristic of the county.

The site of this prehistoric village, comprising s o m e four acres, had long been under cultivation. From its soil, of apparently inexhaustible fertility from the accumulated d é b r i s of human occupation, were turned up by the plow numerous b o n e s of animals, occasional h u m a n skeletons, b r o k e n potteryware, a n d implements, utensils,

FIG. 103. STONE CELTS OR HATCHET BLADES

These wedge-shaped implements, mounted in wooden handles and secured by thongs, served as axes, hatchets, and tomahawks. Scale, 1/3.

and ornaments of flint, stone, bone, and shell. Little did the plowman dream that beneath the few inches of soil disturbed in the yearly routine of cultivation there reposed the life story of a prehistoric people. But to the trained explorer a certain primitive custom, to be referred to presently, encouraged the hope that this perfunctory disturbance of the surface had not obliterated the records of the human drama as enacted in this aboriginal Ohio community.

The work of uncovering, step by step, the site of this once populous village, afforded repeated glimpses of the intimate, everyday life of its prehistoric inhabitants and

FIG. 104. STONE HAND HAMMER

A natural water-worn stone, of convenient size and shape to fit the hand, was primitive man's first and most useful implement. Scale, 1/2.

made possible a very accurate and detailed understanding of their customs, arts, and industries. A force of workmen, with picks, shovels, and trowels, was employed for several weeks in cutting down the accumulated soil, from the surface to the original level of the ground, or until all trace of human habitation disappeared. As this soil was removed, it was closely examined, and everything of artificial origin was carefully scrutinized for any possible information it might disclose.

A detailed account of this process might prove somewhat tiresome, although every step thereof, to the explorers at least, was fascinating and instructive. As of possibly greater interest it is proposed to invite the reader to pay a visit to the village and its inhabitants as they were at the time of their greatest prosperity, viewing through the eyes of the explorer and his interpretation of the evidence the various activities of the inhabitants as influenced by the several seasons of the year. The Fort Ancient aboriginal culture, besides being the most extensive and representative of the several which occupied the Ohio area, is also the best known, and an adequate impression of the Feurt village and its inhabitants will afford an understanding of the culture as a whole.

RECONSTRUCTION OF THE LIFE OF A FORT ANCIENT VILLAGE

Approaching the village, by way of the trail which flanks the high hills along the eastern side of the narrow second river terrace on which it is located, we first note that it comprises a community of several hundred persons. These—men, women, and children—are seen to be of average size and physique and in physical characteristics similar to the Indians of historic times. Before giving attention to their costumes and other personal details, we are impatient to satisfy our curiosity as to the village itself. It appears to be rather carelessly and unevenly laid out, yet with a semblance of streets or passageways. On either side of these are ranged tipis, of skins and bark, and rude huts, built of poles and bark, apparently in some instances "chinked" with clay and grass, form-

ing a sort of wattlework. Within these domiciles, or immediately adjacent to them, are the family fireplaces, made
basin-shaped, of puddled clay; they serve both for cooking
and for supplying warmth. Everywhere, in and about these
rude homes, are the residents of the village, variously occupied in their respective pursuits.

The clothes of the inhabitants are made from skins of wild
animals, feathers, and coarse fabric or cloth woven from
vegetable fiber, grass, and hair. The amount of clothing worn
varies from practically nothing in hot weather to heavy garments, made principally from the furs of native wild animals,
in the colder seasons. Men, women, and children alike are
profusely adorned with necklaces, bracelets, and armbands
of beads made from shell, bone, or stone.

FIG. 105. "DISCOIDALS" OR GAME STONES

These were used in games somewhat resembling the modern quoits. From the
Feurt Site. Scale, 2/3.

As with other primitive peoples, we find that the arts and
industries of the inhabitants of the Feurt village center about
three primary purposes, namely, the securing and preparation
of food, the providing of clothing and shelter, and amusement
or recreation. As we turn to observe how these purposes are
achieved under such primitive conditions, we are quickly impressed with the fact that with these people the three most
serviceable materials in the manufacture of implements, utensils, and ornaments are wood, stone, and bone. The first serves
a wide range of usefulness, from the maintenance of fires for
warmth and cooking to the construction of tipis and the

manufacture of bows and arrows, spears and innumerable other objects. In various kinds of stone our primitive friends find their nearest approach to metal for the manufacture of cutting, scraping, pounding, and perforating implements, and in its disintegrated product, clay, the material for their potteryware. Bone of different kinds (including antler and shell) is employed in making fishhooks, awls, perforators, needles, arrow- and spearpoints, scrapers, hoes, chisels, and ornaments such as beads, pendants, and so forth.

PRIMITIVE INDUSTRIES

We are not surprised to note the extensive use of wood, but the employment of stone and bone draws our attention to the work of certain individuals who appear to be especially engaged in the manufacture of articles from these materials. First we pause to observe a workman who is fashioning various tools and implements from granite, sandstone, and other hard stones. The most abundant type of implement from the workshop of this particular artisan is a wedge-shaped, or thick chisel-like, tool shaped something like an axe blade. These tools, mounted in wooden handles, are used as axes, hatchets, or tomahawks, serving the purposes of those implements not only in the chase and domestic routine, but also in warfare; or held in the hand like a chisel, they serve for skinning game and dressing hides. Other implements are the hand hammer, usually a natural water-worn stone of convenient size and shape to be held readily in the hand though sometimes modified to conform to that purpose, used in cracking nuts, in pounding grain, in breaking bones, and in the multiplicity of purposes which the hammer serves in civilized communities; mortars or metates, made from a convenient slab of sandstone, one face of which is ground out, basin-shaped, to be used in grinding corn into meal; and gaming stones, made usually of sandstone, fashioned in disks from the size of a silver dollar to that of a biscuit. These latter, which often bear designs graved upon their surfaces, are used in a pitching game, somewhat resembling our game of horseshoes or quoits, and also in gambling or gaming after the fashion of our modern dominoes and chess.

While all the materials used in the manufacture of the objects so far described are obtained on the site or from the nearby river banks, we discover that for the manufacture of certain articles the inhabitants find it necessary to resort to a distant source of supply. This is true of flint, which is obtained to some extent locally but mostly from the flint deposits across the Ohio River in Kentucky and from Flint Ridge, in Licking and Muskingum counties, Ohio. As we turn our attention

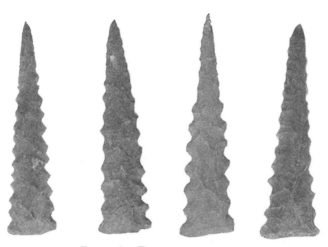

FIG. 106. FLINT ARROWPOINTS

The peoples of the Fort Ancient culture were expert chippers of flint. Scale, full size.

to the flint-chipper, we see that his is one of the most highly developed arts of the village. We find him seated on the ground beside a supply of flint, in rough blocks, secured through special journeys to the source of supply at considerable cost of time and labor. With a stone hammer the workman fractures his block of flint in such a way as to obtain large and comparatively thin and regular flakes. Then with simple pencil-shaped implements of bone or antler, he skillfully forces off secondary flakes or chips by means of concentrated pressure applied at the edges of the flake in such a way as to take

advantage of the cleavage of the flint. Among his finished products are beautifully wrought arrow- and spearpoints, triangular in outline; blades used as knives and scrapers; and drills for b o r i n g

FIG. 107.   FLINT KNIFE BLADES
From the Feurt village site. Scale, 2/3.

wood, stone, bone, and other materials.

Nearby sits the pipe-maker of the community, likewise supplied with material suitable for his craft. Much of this is a variety of pipestone, of very fine grain and texture, varying in color from almost white, through the various subdued grays, tans, and browns, to flesh, pink, and even red. This material is procured on the crest of the high hills to the east of the village. The workman, using first his stone hammer, then a tough stone or flint for pecking, and finally the ever-present whetstone of gritty sandstone for rubbing and polish-ing, fashions his fin-ished products in vari-ous designs. These are usually plain oval in shape but sometimes L-shaped or of other forms, and they are not infrequently decorated with pleasing conven-tional carvings or the i m a g e s of animals, birds, or the human face.

FIG. 108.   STONE TOBACCO PIPES
Many such pipes have been found at the Feurt village site.

Perhaps as important as any other of the village industries is that of pottery-making. Selecting a supply of clean, tough clay, the potter first tempers it by liberal admixture with powdered mussel shells. It is then deftly shaped into vessels, often decorated with incised designs, and finished by baking in fireplaces. The vessels are used for containing water, for storing food, and in cooking.

We note at a glance that the inhabitants of the Feurt village are in the so-called Stone Age of human development; and yet, from the extensive use of bone as a material for fashioning implements and ornaments, the designation of a bone-age people would not be far amiss. At various places throughout the village, workmen are engaged in the manufacture of objects of bone in g r e a t numbers. Principal of these are awl-like implements or per- f o r a t o r s , made mostly from the leg bones of the deer and wild turkey, although s u i t a b l e bones of other animals and birds are not slighted. These leg bones are first cut or broken in two at the middle; the inner end of each

FIG. 109. A TYPICAL POTTERY VESSEL

Hundreds of broken pottery vessels and a number of perfect specimens were found at the Feurt site. Scale, 1/3.

half is then ground to a sharp point by rubbing with a grinding stone of gritty sandstone. The awls thus fashioned are used for perforating hides and leather in making clothing and moccasins and for other similar purposes. They likewise play an important part in eating, by serving as forks for removing meat and other foods from the clay cooking pot and for extracting marrow from bones.

Besides the perforating tools, the artisans in bone are producing implements resembling the carpenter's drawing knife, by beveling and sharpening one face of the leg bones of the deer and the elk; chisel-like implements, used in cutting and scraping; and long bodkin-shaped objects, sometimes decorated with incised designs, worn in the hair as ornaments or hair-pins. From deer antler they fashion small cylindrical implements for chipping flint, and from the hollow wing bones of the eagle, the owl, and other birds they cut tubular sections to be worn as beads. Certain close-grained sections of bone are selected and made into fishhooks, much the same in size and shape as those with which we are acquainted except that their makers have not learned the importance of the barb.

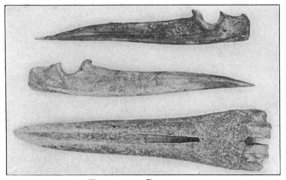

FIG. 110.   BONE AWLS
Awls and perforators were among the most useful of all implements to prehistoric man. From the Feurt village site. Scale, 2/3.

In working bone the artisan resorts to numerous expedients, such as breaking, by means of his hand hammer; cutting, with a flint knife; burning, until the action of the fire has so weakened the material that it can be broken; and finally, grinding and polishing with the whetstones or grindstones of gritty rock.

CULTIVATED AND UNCULTIVATED FOOD PRODUCTS

Below the terrace on which the village stands is a busy group of workers, mostly women and girls. They are "tending" their gardens or truck patches, in which have been planted their staple cereal, Indian corn or maize. Besides corn, there is a variety of bean, a sort of squash or pumpkin, and perhaps a few other vegetables. Second only in importance to corn is the crop of tobacco, a very important adjunct to the life of the village. The loose, rich soil selected for the growing crops needs but little cultivation. Rude hoes, made from mussel shells or shoulder blades of the deer fitted w i t h w o o d e n handles, and sharpened sticks are the tools used in working the soil. The products of the garden are consumed as they become available, and any surplus is dried and preserved for winter use. For the storage of these supplies of corn and other food products, pits are dug in the ground and lined with bark.

Having satisfied our curiosity as to the manner in which food supplies are obtained by artificial propagation or cultivation, we are glad to have the opportunity of observing how the natural or spontaneous products of nature are utilized. A party of hunters has just returned from the chase. They are armed with bows and arrows, spears, and various traps and snares. They bring with them a bear, a deer, wild turkey, and numerous smaller animals and birds, as well as fish and mussels taken from the river. Wild fruits and nuts, in season, are also a part of the bounty.

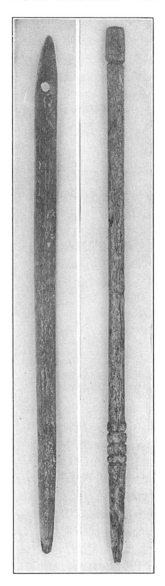

FIG. 111. BONE NEEDLE
AND BODKIN

It is interesting to compare these primitive forms, from the Feurt site, with their modern successors. Scale, full-size.

The successful hunters turn over their supplies to the women, who dress and prepare the game for food. The repast ready, the hungry hunters and their families squat upon the ground around the common kettle in which has been cooked a mixture of whatever may have been available. With their bone forks, used spearlike, they help themselves to its contents.

RECREATION AND AMUSEMENT

After the feast there is much smoking of tobacco, and although the weed, as produced in the village gardens and smoked in the rude pipes of wood or stone, would hardly meet the requirements of cultivated taste, evidently it quite satisfies our hosts. Recreation is provided in the form of games in which the stone disks we have seen manufactured are used. Some engage in pitching these, quoits-like, while others are engrossed in a game of chance, in which the disks, bearing marks signifying their relative importance or value, are used as counters.

A BURIAL MOUND IN THE MAKING

We are, of course, properly sympathetic when we learn that a member of the community has died, but we are not averse to learning the use of the heaps of earth or mounds adjoining the village which we already have guessed hold some relationship to burial. After the usual ceremonies incident to such occasions, which among uncivilized peoples are ritualistic and pretentious, the body of the deceased is conveyed to one of the mounds. There it is laid on the ground and hurriedly covered with bark, grass, and roughly woven fabric; then earth, obtained from any convenient place in the neighborhood, is carried and heaped over it. No regard is paid to direction in placing the body, which is deposited in the posture it assumed when life became extinct.

On inquiry we learn that others have already been similarly buried in or on the mound and that still others will find their last resting places there. While burials are sometimes made in ordinary graves throughout the village, not infrequently within the very tipis where the dead had lived, the mounds are the preferred and usual places of burial, and their sole function consists in providing a resting place for and a monument to the departed. From the modern or civilized point of view, we are inclined to wonderment that our familiar mode of burial in graves dug beneath the surface is not generally practiced, especially since we learn that the Feurt inhabitants

FIG. 112. A DOUBLE BURIAL, FEURT VILLAGE SITE

The jocular expressions of the skulls of this burial, often noted in prehistoric interments, are the result of the dropping of the lower jaw.

knew and used this method to a considerable extent. But upon further reflection we conclude that, after all, the mound burial has its advantages, since it not only results in interring the bodies beneath the ground, but at the same time provides for them a fitting and a lasting monument. The mound burial, apparently so different from the grave burial but really very similar, reverses the operation of excavating a receptacle beneath the surface level by heaping the covering of earth above the surface. Thus the mound burial of the Feurt village, we conclude, may be termed an "inverted" grave.

SOCIAL AND RELIGIOUS CONCEPTS

Although the residents of the village are loath to acquaint us with the details of their social and religious customs and rites, we are able to gather sufficient evidence to convince us that they bear out the rule of marked similarity as among diverse uncivilized peoples of a similar degree of cultural advancement. This indicates a considerable degree of social order, in which the family and the tribe exert a restraining influence; a conception of right and wrong, and therefore a morality; and government of the limited sort necessary for so primitive a community. Their religion consists mainly in reverence for, or fear of, natural objects and phenomena, in which they vest magic powers for good and evil, and in propitiating which they observe myriad ceremonies and superstitious rites.

PRIMITIVE METHODS OF SANITATION

A feature of the life of these primitive villagers which perhaps is the least pleasing of any we have observed is the method employed in maintaining a semblance of public sanitation. While the accumulation in and around their domiciles of débris and garbage from the chase, the kitchen, and other domestic activities is to be expected in an uncivilized people, it would seem that the Feurt villagers are determined to outdo all others in this respect. Instead of collecting and removing the garbage, they prefer the much more laborious method, when the accumulation becomes so great as to be unbearably obnoxious, of carrying earth and burying the débris where it lies scattered about. As a result of this practice it is apparent that the level of the village already has been raised at some points as much as several feet above the original surface of the ground. The only justification that occurs to us as we contemplate this peculiar proceeding is that, should the archæologist at some distant date chance upon the site where this village once had stood and choose to explore its ruins, what a gratifying record of its erstwhile activities he would find.

CHAPTER IX

THE OHIO AREA: II, THE HOPEWELL CULTURE

Extent of the Hopewell culture—Geometric earthworks of the culture—Characteristics of the Hopewell mounds—The Tremper Mound—The Hopewell Group—The Mound City Group—The Edwin Harness Group—The Seip Group—The Turner Group.

THE third of the three outstanding cultures of the Ohio area, the Hopewell, is now to be described; and while no very intimate understanding of their everyday life can be promised, because of the non-discovery of distinctive habitation sites, their remarkable æsthetic development and their striking geometric earthworks will more than compensate for the lack of the homely detail we are able to reconstruct for the Fort Ancient peoples.

EXTENT OF THE HOPEWELL CULTURE

The Hopewell peoples, unlike those of other centers of advanced cultural attainment in America, lived wholly within the prehistoric period and had disappeared from the theater of action before Europeans came upon the scene. The Incas of Peru, or their descendants; the Aztecs of Mexico, and the Pueblos of our Southwest were extant peoples at the time of European discovery and exploration. The story of the Hopewell peoples must be written in its entirety from archæological exploration and interpretation.

The term "Hopewell," it may be explained at the outset, is the name given to a particular group of mounds and earthworks and, in a broader sense, to all other groups built by the same culture or kind of aborigines. The Hopewell Group proper is situated near Chillicothe, in Ross County, Ohio, on land belonging to the late Captain M. C. Hopewell, in whose

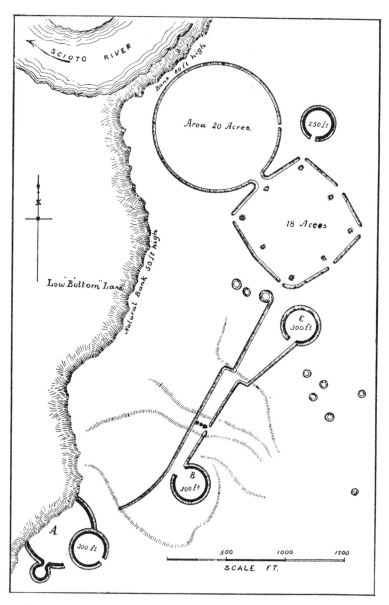

FIG. 113.   MAP OF THE HIGH BANK WORKS, ROSS COUNTY, OHIO
A typical example of the geometric enclosures of the Hopewell culture.

honor it was named. The Hopewell Group was the first of its kind to be examined, and when other mounds and groups in various parts of the state were explored and found to be similar to it, all these were designated as belonging to the Hopewell culture. Thus the term "Hopewell" has come to serve as a generic name for all remains of its class, wherever found.

The Hopewell peoples were responsible for the erection of a score or more of imposing geometric earthworks and accompanying mounds scattered throughout southern Ohio and

FIG. 114. A CIRCULAR ENCLOSURE OF THE HOPEWELL CULTURE

The moat on the inside of this small earthwork in Franklin County, Ohio, is still sufficiently deep to hold water the greater part of the year.

contiguous territory. A lateral extension of the culture trends westward across Indiana, culminating in rather important sub-areas in Illinois and southeastern Iowa. Scattered remains of the culture have been noted in southern Michigan, and quite recently one or more mounds, probably a group of them, have been identified in southern Wisconsin. Further reference will be made to these marginal mounds in describing the areas in which they occur. Whether this extension westward indicates migration into Ohio from the west and northwest, or whether it is merely a lateral or marginal outthrust from the parent nucleus in Ohio, may be determined when adequate additional exploration has been made.

The most striking external features of the Hopewell remains are the great geometric enclosures or earthworks. These are circular, oval, crescent, square, and octagonal figures, singly or in combination, the earthen walls of which enclose from an acre or less to as much as 100 acres. Although these enclosures often approximate true geometric figures, they are not, as was formerly supposed, the result of precise mathematics but merely of careful application of the rule-of-thumb ingenuity of their builders. They vary in height from almost imperceptible embankments to elevations of 20 feet or higher. So arresting are the enclosures of the Hopewell peoples that Dr. Charles C. Willoughby has designated them as the "Great Earthwork Builders of Ohio." Although in several instances major earthwork groups are devoid of accompanying mounds, tumuli are usually found associated with the enclosures, the number varying from a single mound to as many as thirty. It may be noted that in the marginal subareas of Illinois, Wisconsin, Michigan, and Iowa the Hopewell mounds, with one possible exception, are unaccompanied by earthworks.

Of the more than twenty major groups of Hopewell works in the Ohio area, several are of outstanding interest and importance. Some of these are described in the following pages; of others, more details will be found in Chapter XII. The Marietta Group and that formerly on the site of the present city of Cincinnati are of historic interest from the fact that their sites were chosen for the two earliest settlements and successive capitals of the Northwest Territory. The Marietta works and the Newark works are remarkable for their great size and impressiveness; while the Mound City, the Hopewell, the Harness, and the Seip groups, in Ross County; the Turner Group, in Hamilton County; and the Tremper Mound,

FIG. 115. A TYPICAL HOPEWELL BURIAL

The arched opening above the grave is the result of the decay and collapse of the cabin-like structure of logs surrounding and enclosing the burial. The skeleton is accompanied by many relics of copper, mica, shell, and pearls and doubtless was that of a person of affluence and importance. From the Central mound of the Hopewell Group.

in Scioto County, are noted for the liberality with which they have rewarded the pick and shovel of the archæologist. The locations of several of these groups are indicative of the mutual taste with which both Mound-builder and white man selected the sites of their towns—Marietta, Portsmouth, Cincinnati, Newark, Chillicothe, Circleville, the last named taking its appellation from the great circular earthwork which occupied the site and determined the layout of the town.

CHARACTERISTICS OF THE HOPEWELL MOUNDS

The mounds of the Hopewell culture, with their contained phenomena, are not less impressive than the geometric earthworks, and the custom which prompted their builders to sacrifice their most cherished material possessions as accompaniments of their interments and as offerings to their gods assured to the archæologist a wealth of evidence bearing upon their cultural attainments.

Because of the surprisingly high level of these attainments, particularly as regards artistic accomplishment, the mounds of the culture properly merit reasonably detailed attention. Of the six outstanding groups that have been explored, as mentioned above, five were examined by the Ohio State Museum and the remaining one, the Turner Group, by Professor Frederick W. Putnam for Harvard University.

The burial mounds of the Hopewell peoples are complex in their structure and fascinating as to contents. Exploration reveals, in large measure, the manner of their construction and the purposes they served. As a rule the mounds are found to have covered the sites of buildings or structures of a ceremonial or sacred character. These buildings are identified as the temples wherein were celebrated the sacred rites and ceremonies attending burial of the dead, of an elaborateness characteristic of peoples in the primitive stages of civilization. To the archæologist, equipped with the experience resulting from extensive exploration and a knowledge of the ways of primitive folk, the story unfolded through examination of a Hopewell mound and its prestructure is vivid and realistic. He sees the characters in the human drama as though projected on a screen—speechless, not sharply defined, it is true, but none the less distinct. Religious and social functions, chiefs and councils, priests and portents, medicine men and magic, all these, and more, pass over the screen and are transferred graphically and pictorially to his records.

The story exhumed from the average Hopewell mound briefly is this:

Having selected a suitable location for a settlement, the Hopewell band or tribe set aside an appropriate area as a sacred place. The surface was cleared of trees, underbrush, and other impediments, the loose top soil was removed, and

FIG. 116. AN INDIVIDUAL LOAD OF EARTH

In a mound of the Hopewell culture was found this basketful of soil where the weary or careless worker had dropped it on the common heap, basket and all. The outline of the load, about 30 pounds in weight, and the imprint of the basket will be noted.

the firm subsurface was carefully plastered over with tough clay. On this was strewn an inch or more of sand or fine gravel, and the floor of the prospective structure was complete. En-closing this area, usually circular or oval in form, upright

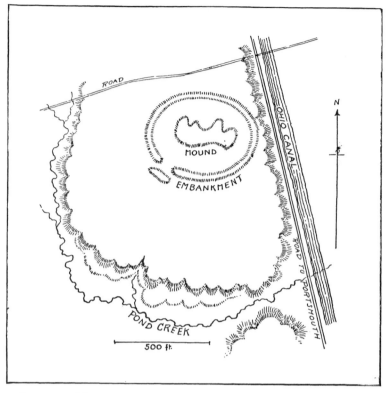

FIG. 117. MAP OF THE TREMPER MOUND AND EARTHWORK, SCIOTO
COUNTY, OHIO

This interesting tumulus, resembling the effigy of an animal, has yielded many
fine relics of the Hopewell culture. Redrawn from Squier and Davis.

timbers or posts were set into the ground at close intervals,
forming the outer walls of the structure. In some instances
posts were set to form partitions, which divided the enclosed
space into compartments or rooms. These enclosing walls of
posts appear to have been supplemented by wattlework of
twigs and clay, and at least portions of the structure were
provided with rooflike coverings of thatch. An alternative of
this plan was the delimiting of the floor space by means of a
circumvallation or wall of earth and stones, corral-like, on
which palisades were erected. Within this enclosure smaller
structures of upright posts were sometimes constructed.

Into the resulting enclosure the Hopewell peoples brought their dead for the elaborate funeral ceremonies and disposal of the remains, as already described in detail in Chapter V.

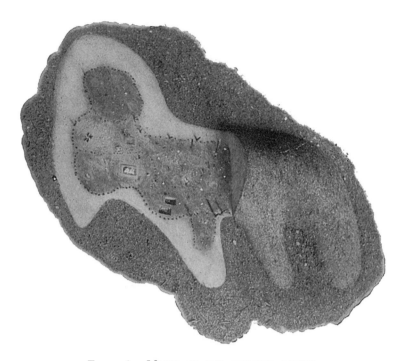

FIG. 118. MODEL OF THE TREMPER MOUND

The tumulus is shown slightly more than half explored, revealing the floor of the sacred structure which occupied the site previous to its erection. Note the post-molds which outline the outer walls and inner partitions. The three compartments at the left, in the order of their occurrence from left to right, are the crematory "room"; the shrine room where, alongside the basinlike shrine, numerous fine relics were deposited as a sacrificial offering to the dead and to their deities; and the burial chamber where, in the large rectangular repository, the cremated remains were deposited. In the large audience chamber at center there may be seen two graves, dug into and beneath the floor.

When a particular sacred structure had served its purpose, it was intentionally destroyed by fire as a part of the ceremonial ritual attending funeral rites.

With the burning of the structure, erection of the superimposed mound was begun, sometimes while the embers were still glowing, as is shown by the evidences of exploration. Each individual of the community probably contributed to the task, by no means a slight undertaking in the case of a large tumulus. Earth was carried in any convenient manner—in detached clods, in carrying baskets, and doubtless even in buckskin aprons, each individual load being dumped upon the growing heap to add its little to the whole. The size, and often the form, of these individual loads are frequently readily discernible as exploration proceeds, owing to the fact that individual workers obtained their earth from various places, so that there appears a dumping of black soil here, a load of yellow clay there, and adjacent to either a basketful of another kind or color. In two instances the writer has found individual loads intact, where the weary or careless worker had dropped them on the common heap "basket and all."

THE TREMPER MOUND

Rather typical of the Hopewell mounds as a class was the Tremper Mound, situated just across the Scioto River from the Feurt mounds and site, of the Fort Ancient culture, in Scioto County. This mound was explored by the Ohio State Museum in 1915, under the direction of Dr. William C. Mills and the writer. Although less than one mile apart and probably coexistent as to time, the contrast between the culture of the Tremper Mound and that of the Feurt site is most striking, as the reader will readily see.

Because of its peculiar form the Tremper Mound for many years was regarded as an effigy mound and was supposed to represent some animal—an elephant, a tapir, or whatever individual imagination dictated. Squier and Davis, who first described the mound and its accompanying works classed the tumulus with the effigy mounds, found mostly in Wisconsin. After careful consideration on the part of Dr. Mills it was decided that the Tremper Mound was not an effigy but a complex burial mound of the Hopewell class, an impression which proved to be correct.

As is characteristic of mounds of its culture, the Tremper

Mound was found to cover the site of a building or structure
of a ceremonial nature, devoted to the purposes already described. In a way these structures suggest the council houses
and the long houses of the historic Iroquois. But they were
much more. In addition to staging the religious and probably
the social functions of the community, the Tremper structure
served as a place for cremation of the dead, disposal of their
ashes in prepared receptacles or depositories, and observance

FIG. 119.   EXPLORING THE TREMPER MOUND

of the obsequies incident thereto. In this latter respect it might
be likened to the church and its accompanying burial ground
of present-day or pioneer rural communities. With the disposal
of the dead and the holding of the accompanying ceremonies
common to both, the Tremper culture differs mainly in disposal
by cremation instead of burial in conventional graves.

The prestructure of the Tremper Mound had been erected
in the manner described on an earlier page of this chapter.
The main portion of the structure, an oval approximately 200
feet long and 100 feet wide, corresponded to the body of the

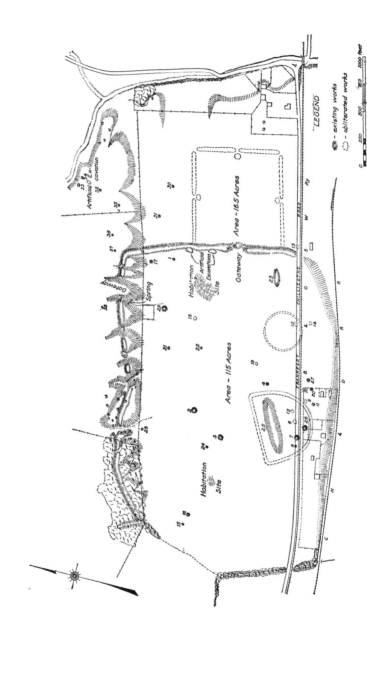

FIG. 120. MAP OF THE HOPEWELL GROUP OF EARTHWORKS, ROSS COUNTY, OHIO

From the survey by F. R. Jones during the explorations of the writer for the Ohio State Museum, 1922-25.

FIG. 121. THE ANTLERED KING

This skeleton of a Mound-builder, found in the great central mound of the Hopewell Group by Professor Warren K. Moorehead, wore an elaborate head-dress of copper and imitation deer antlers and was bedecked with pearl beads, copper breastplates, and other ornaments. After Moorehead.

supposed "elephant" (see Figure 48). Exploration disclosed that several additions had been made to the original building, thus supplying the head, legs, and tail of the animal. Several doorways gave entrance and exit to and from the structure and its added compartments. It will readily be seen how, in covering the site of the compound structure with a minimum of labor, the completed mound would come to have resemblance to a quadruped.

In addition to the post molds and charred remains of posts and timbers by which the walls of the structure and its compartments were traced, there were found the mutely eloquent evidences of the human drama of its builders. These consisted of basins of burned clay, set into the floor, in which cremation is supposed to have been effected; troughlike receptacles or depositories containing the ashes of the cremated dead; an extensive ceremonial or votive offering of rare ob-

FIG. 122. A STONE GRAVE BURIAL OF THE HOPEWELL GROUP

The skeleton in the background occupies a pretentious stone grave and is accompanied by numerous implements and ornaments. With the skeleton in the foreground was a large shell container, a copper breastplate, and numerous beads on the chest.

jects placed on and about a shrine, in honor of the dead or their deities; and other minor evidences of the activities of its authors scattered throughout the structure and the covering mound.

The arrangement and position of the several compartments of the structure and their accompanying phenomena suggest order and purpose. From its great size the principal compartment might be designated as the audience room, and it was here, judging from the number of crematory basins, that the rite of cremation was carried out. In a smaller compartment, which may be designated as the vault or crypt, was located the

great communal depository, and here were the ashes of numerous cremated bodies. A third compartment, the shrine room,
contained the remarkable collection of objects comprising the
votive offering—exquisitely carved stone tobacco pipes in the
images of native birds and animals and ornaments, implements, and utensils of stone, flint, bone, copper, mica, pearl,
and other materials, all showing the same high development of
the artistic instinct. Still another compartment plainly had

FIG. 123.   A HOPEWELL BURIAL ACCOMPANIED BY A TROPHY SKULL

With the skeleton of a venerable male, accompanied by many implements and
ornaments, there was found the separate skull of a young male wearing a copper
headplate. The latter probably was a trophy skull, either that of an enemy
captured in battle or that of a relative retained as a family relic.

served as a kitchen and workroom. The bones of various animals and birds used for food and fragments of pottery vessels
used in preparing it were strewn upon the floor, while the
presence of mica, flint, and other materials suggested the manufacture of implements and ornaments.

Within the compartments dedicated as the depositories for
human ashes and the votive offering were located highly specialized fireplaces, built basin-shaped upon the floor from
carefully puddled and troweled clay. These contained the cold
remains of wood fires and showed that they had been used

long and perhaps continuously, the earth beneath them being burned red to a comparatively great depth. Their location and condition suggest their use for sacred or ceremonial fires such as among some primitive peoples are kept burning perpetually.

Examination of the Tremper Mound showed that the pre-structure, like others of its kind, had been used for a long period of time and that when it was abandoned it was intentionally burned and the mound heaped over the site as a monument thereto.

THE HOPEWELL GROUP

The Hopewell Group of earthworks, the type station for remains of its culture, has the distinction of having submitted its hidden stores of information to three distinct explorations. First described and mapped by Caleb Atwater in 1820, it was again surveyed and partially examined by the pioneer archæologists Squier and Davis in 1846. Professor Warren K. Moorehead for the World's Columbian Exposition Commission conducted extensive explorations of the site in 1891-92. Its final and exhaustive examination was carried out by the writer, for the Ohio State Museum, beginning in 1922 and ending in 1925.

While it is evident to the most casual observer that the sites occupied by all important groups of the Hopewell culture were carefully selected by their builders, the location of the Hopewell Group is easily the most impressive. The region (Union Township, Ross County) is marked by the glacial moraine and presents the interesting phenomenon of rugged, unglaciated hills, bordering the North Fork of Paint Creek, in close proximity to glacial formations of almost equal size and impressiveness.

The accompanying map of the Hopewell Group (Figure 120), made at the time of the recent exploration, illustrates its size, form, and physical features and shows the locations of its more than thirty burial mounds. Circumstances at the time precluded the restoration of the mounds examined, but it is hoped that this may be effected at a later date. On the whole, the site is still well worth visiting, in view of its combined archæological and scenic interest. The earth composing most of the mounds remains practically where they originally stood, and the embankments of the enclosures, in part at least, are quite bold.

The examination by Squier and Davis was unpretentious and superficial; nevertheless, their modest efforts were richly rewarded. In Mound 1, one of the smallest of the group, measuring not over three feet in height, they obtained hundreds

FIG. 124. A DOUBLE BURIAL OF THE HOPEWELL GROUP

In this grave there reposed the skeletons of a male and a female, presumably husband and wife. Note the copper headplate on the skull of the male, the copper bracelets on the wrists of each, and the copper axe at the foot of the grave.

of specimens, among which were "coiled serpents carved in stone and enveloped in sheet mica and copper; pottery; carved fragments of ivory; fossil teeth; numerous fine sculptures in stone, etc." Of the four mounds into which they dug, that known as Mound 2 was the most important, in the light of subsequent explorations. Their report records that: "There are two layers of disks chipped out of hornstone, some nearly round, others in the form of spearheads. They are of various

FIG. 125. THE GRAVE OF A MASTER ARTISAN

In a small mound of the Hopewell group there reposed the cremated remains
of what is believed to have been the master flint-chipper of the community.
With him was placed a large quantity of obsidian or volcanic glass, from which
material many fine ceremonial spears and knives found in various mounds of the
group, had been fabricated.

sizes but are for the most part about six inches long by four
wide. They were placed side by side, a little reclining, and
one layer resting immediately on the other. Out of an excavation six feet long and four feet wide not far from six hundred
were thrown. The deposit extends beyond the limits of the
excavation on every side." From Mound 9 they obtained thin,
finely made obsidian blades, scrolls cut from mica, woven
fabric, bone needles, pearls, and so forth.

Much more exhaustive was the examination of the Hopewell
mounds by Professor Moorehead. The vast amount of interesting material obtained through his explorations was exhibited at the Columbian Exposition of 1893, and may now be
seen at the Field Museum of Natural History, Chicago. His
report described the group as he found it, detailed the work of
exploration, and illustrated the material therefrom.

Following Squier and Davis' comment on the great cache of

flint disks in Mound 2, archæologists naturally looked forward to its further examination. Moorehead had the pleasurable experience of recovering the greater number of those remaining—more than seven thousand, the equivalent of a "four-horse wagonload" (see Figure 50). The recent examination, to be noted presently, removed still others, in addition to several important burials.

From Mound 23 Moorehead exhumed more than fifty burials, with which were found human jaws, cut and perforated for ornaments or trophies; pipes, copper ornaments, pearl

FIG. 126. CEREMONIAL BLADES OF OBSIDIAN FROM THE HOPEWELL GROUP

These unique specimens, the longest of which measures 18 inches, were found during the explorations of W. K. Moorehead and of the author. They doubtless were ceremonial, rather than utilitarian, in their use.

beads; a copper spud or axe weighing 17 pounds; and a unique dish or bowl, of white limestone, 14 inches in diameter. This mound was 150 feet long, approximately 55 feet wide, and from 10 to 12 feet in height.

But it was in the great central mound of the group, measuring 500 feet in length, 180 feet in width, and originally 33 feet in height, that Moorehead made his greatest finds. A series of five trenches through the smaller diameter of the tumulus disclosed more than one hundred and fifty burials, some of which were richly supplied with artifacts, and in addition at least three impressive ceremonial or votive offerings. These were respectively a deposit of artistic designs and figures in copper, placed within the body of the mound; an offering of copper implements, including a copper axe of 38 pounds weight (Figure 88), placed with a double skeleton burial on the floor of the mound; and a cache of miscellaneous objects, found within a so-called "altar" or basin.

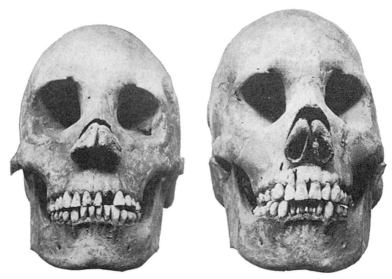

FIG. 127. A NOVELTY IN NOSES

In the double burial of a young male and female in the central mound of the Hopewell Group, each of the skulls was supplied with an artificial nose of copper.

The copper designs of the first-mentioned offering comprised circular, square, and diamond-shaped figures; conventional and cosmic designs in the form of trefoils, quatrefoils, and other patterns; effigies of the fish and the bird; conventionalized serpent heads, swastikas, and so forth. A number of these designs are illustrated in Figure 70 in Chapter VI. The offering of copper implements comprised, in addition to the axe already noted, sixty-six other axes of various sizes and twenty-three copper breastplates; with them were beads of shell and pearl and objects of bone and meteoric iron. The re-

FIG. 128. A DESIGN IN MICA FROM A HOPEWELL BURIAL

The workman is in the act of lifting from the skeleton a rare ceremonial or imitation spearhead wrought from silvery mica.

markable offering found in connection with the basin or "altar" comprised "mica ornaments, spool-shaped ear ornaments, copper balls, many other copper objects, large beads, bears' and panthers' teeth, carved bones, effigies carved out of stone, stone tablets, slate ornaments, beautiful stone and terra-cotta rings, quartz crystals worked into various forms, flint knives, and cloth." A striking burial was uncovered which, besides being accompanied by numerous unusual specimens, bore a headdress equipped with imitation deer antlers made of wood and covered with copper. With still other burials were found artistically engraved human bones, effigies of birds and animals, and ornaments of marine tortoise-shell.

The Ohio State Museum's examination of the Hopewell Group consumed the equivalent of three full summers' work. All existing mounds, including several small domiciliary mounds on the adjacent plateau, were exhaustively explored, regardless of whether they had been examined previously or not. A wealth of material, now displayed in the Museum, was the result.

Complete examination of Mound 2 showed it to be a burial mound, covering the site of a sacred structure, in which were important burials, a crematory basin, and, occupying the central area, the great cache or offering of chipped flint disks. One hundred or more of these were found, bringing the total for the deposit to more than eight thousand. One of the burials of this mound was enclosed in a stone grave (Figure 122);

FIG. 129. A HOPEWELL CREMATORY BASIN WITH CREMATED BURIAL

Very rarely the crematory basins contain human remains, but the one here shown, from a mound of the Hopewell Group, held the charred remains of a child with numerous shell beads and other objects.

another, the skeleton of an aged toothless male, was accompanied by a human skull equipped with a helmetlike copper headdress (Figure 123); while a third burial comprised the skeletons of a male and a female, reposing side by side (Figure 124). All the burials were richly supplied with ornaments and implements.

In Mound 11 the Museum survey found a unique deposit. Alongside a crematory basin reposed the charred remains of a skeleton, accompanied by ornaments of mica and pearls. Adjacent to the burial was a large deposit of several hundred pounds of obsidian or volcanic glass. Encircling the burial and its accompanying phenomena was a border of boulders. The obsidian was in fragments, chunks, and chips, clearly the raw material used in fashioning obsidian knives and ceremonial spear- and arrowpoints. Many of the latter, together with large ceremonial blades of a unique character and size, were found

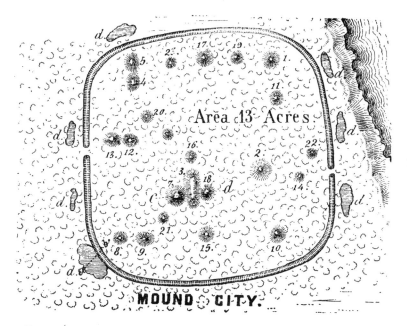

Fig. 130. Map of the Mound City Group, Ross County, Ohio

Situated just north of the city of Chillicothe, the Mound City Group is one of the more striking and important of the Hopewell culture remains. The site has been successively occupied by military camps, headquarters, and cantonments in all the wars in which Ohio has participated, the World War cantonment known as Camp Sherman being the most recent. Mound City has been converted into a free state park and all conveniences are provided for tourists and sightseers.

by Moorehead and the Museum survey in other mounds of the group. The nearest source of obsidian supply was known to be the Rocky Mountains, and the question had been mooted whether these artifacts had been manufactured by the Hopewell artisans, or had been procured ready-made from Far Western tribes. Here, at last, was the answer. Many of the fragments of the raw material displayed bruised and battered edges, the result of its being carried pickaback halfway across the continent from the far-distant source of supply. It seems logical to suppose that the burial in this mound was that of the master flint-chipper of the community and that the material of his craft had been buried with him as a tribute to his important office.

In a very small mound within the large enclosure (No. 17) the Museum survey found two separate ceremonial or votive offerings. These comprised hundreds of rare and interesting

FIG. 131. THE CENTER OF THE MOUND CITY GROUP

This picture, taken before the establishment of Camp Sherman, shows the three central mounds. The group comprises a total of twenty-three mounds, lying within a rectangular earthen enclosure having an area of 13 acres.

objects, such as plain and effigy types of stone tobacco pipes; effigies of the eagle and the crow; many gorgets and tablets of slate and handsome micaceous chlorite; ornaments ground from transparent quartz or crystals; ornaments and implements of copper, meteoric iron, stone, flint, bone, shell, silver, and so forth; upwards of one hundred stone celts, ungrooved axes, and digging tools; and quantities of raw materials, as graphite, micaceous hematite, chlorite, "gold stone," and galena. Other interesting objects were a human head in copper, in the round; cup-shaped and boat-shaped objects of quartz crystal; small saucer-shaped dishes of chlorite; and many cone-shaped specimens of pyrite. No burials were found in this mound; it appears to have been dedicated solely to the enclosed votive offerings.

In a small mound (No. 26) adjacent to the great central tumulus another important votive offering was found, while one of several skeletons was accompanied by the necklace of pearl beads of exceptional interest illustrated in Figure 63 in

FIG. 132. CROSS-SECTION OF A SMALL MOUND CITY TUMULUS

The barrack buildings of Camp Sherman, a World War cantonment, were erected over the smaller tumuli of the Mound City Group. In this picture there are shown two crematory basins on two distinct floors of the mound and the ceremonial strata of sand in the body of the structure.

Chapter VI. Owing to the fact that the body had been covered with several thicknesses of bark, it was unusually well preserved. In addition, an elaborate garment or burial robe of woven fabric covered the remains, which were accompanied by numerous artifacts. The necklace of pearls lay for the most part beneath a large copper breastplate, and it was owing to the preservative action of the salts of copper that the pearls were in such excellent condition. The necklace, probably the finest ever taken from a Stone Age burial, consists of 332

FIG. 133. THE MICA COVERING OF A PRETENTIOUS BURIAL

This rectangular arrangement of sheets of mica placed upon the floor of one of the Mound City tumuli proved to be the threshold to the elaborate burial shown in the lower picture. Upon a rectangular earthen platform were found three cremated burials and many ornaments.

pearls. While some of the individual pearls are of the desirable spherical and button-shaped forms, most of them are of the common baroque type, the principal significance of the necklace being its remarkable state of preservation. A human skull, perforated for suspension, lay near the head of the burial proper. It presumably was interred as a trophy or as a personal or family relic.

From the great central mound of the group the Museum survey exhumed a total of forty-seven burials. Many of these were of decided interest, but space will permit mention here of only a few. Perhaps the most important was the double burial found in Mound 25. Lying side by side in a common grave, extended upon their backs, were the skeletons of a male and a female, both of them comparatively young. That of the male indicated an individual of nearly six feet in height and of striking massiveness and muscularity. The accompanying skeleton indicated a comely young female of medium size. Both were richly bedecked with ornaments, the double burial being an imposing example of barbaric splendor. At the head, neck, hips, and knees of the female and completely encircling the skeleton were thousands of pearl beads and buttons of wood and stone covered with copper; extending the full length of the grave along one side was a row of copper ear ornaments; at the wrists of the female were copper bracelets; copper ear ornaments adorned the ears of both, and both wore necklaces

FIG. 134. A MICA-LINED GRAVE

This rectangular basin-like grave, in a mound of the Mound City Group, was completely lined with sheets of mica and contained four cremated burials.

FIG. 135. PANORAMA

Comprising the enclosure and mounds of the Mound City Group as restored

of grizzly-bear canines and copper breastplates on the chest. Lying across the collar-bone of each skeleton, from points beneath the ears to about the lower extremity of the breast-bone, were copper rods, about one foot long, on which apparently the hair had been secured. Strangest of all, each skull was equipped with an artificial nose of copper (Figure 127). The copper noses were doubtless post-mortem insertions, and a plausible explanation of them would be that the Hopewell builders, obviously familiar with human anatomy and realizing that the nasal appendage decomposes quickly after death, supplied this favored young couple with imperishable noses that they might not pass into the beyond lacking these useful and ornamental features.

Another burial of the central mound, besides being accompanied by numerous artifacts, bore an elaborate headdress of copper, mica, and pearls, fashioned to represent a bird; another was accompanied by ornaments made from marine tortoise-shell and jaws of the barracuda; and still another, by images and designs cut from silvery mica. In addition to the

OF MOUND CITY PARK
by the Ohio Archæological and Historical Society, Photograph by Hathaway.

burials and their contents, several crematory basins were disclosed in the mound.

THE MOUND CITY GROUP

The Mound City Group, incorporated in the site of Camp Sherman, a World War cantonment of importance situated at the northern edge of the town of Chillicothe, Ross County, is the most widely known of the Hopewell works. The group consists of twenty-three mounds lying within a rectangular enclosure of 13 acres. The embankment of the enclosure is low and unpretentious. The mounds range from slight elevations to the central mound of the group which measured approximately 18 feet in height.

Mound City became a noted site following its partial exploration by Squier and Davis in 1846 and publication of their report in *Ancient Monuments*. Their most important find comprised upwards of two hundred stone tobacco pipes, many of which were fashioned in the images of birds, animals, and the human head. In addition to its archæological importance, Mound City is extremely interesting from the scenic standpoint and has achieved an historic background from the fact that it has been the site of military camps, headquarters, and cantonments in practically all the wars in which Ohio has taken part.

At the beginning of the World War the tumuli of Mound City were threatened with destruction to make way for the barrack buildings of Camp Sherman. Intercession by the Ohio State Museum resulted in their rescue, but not until after several minor mounds had been demolished. The exploration of the group was carried out by the Museum in 1920 and 1921. Many interesting burials and innumerable artifacts, now displayed in the Museum, were exhumed, and in addition two remarkable ceremonial or sacrificial offerings were disclosed. One of these, located in Mound 13 of the group, occupied a basinlike shrine which was completely lined with large sheets of mica (Figure 134). Among the many objects with this votive offering were fine image tobacco pipes and implements and ornaments of copper and obsidian. A pretentious offering in the large central mound comprised among other things intricate conventional designs and figures in copper, the latter representing the human form, human hands, birds, turtles, and various animals.

After exploration the tract of 55 acres on which Mound City is located was turned over to the Ohio Archæological and Historical Society by the War Department and since then has been converted into a fine park. All the mounds and earthworks have been restored to their former condition, and the group is thus preserved for all time.

THE EDWIN HARNESS GROUP

The Edwin Harness Group, situated in the Scioto valley, 10 miles south of Mound City, was explored for the Ohio State Museum by Dr. William C. Mills in 1903-05. The earthworks consist of a combination of geometric enclosures—a square, a large circle, and a smaller circle (Figure 169). Within the large circle is the great burial mound of the group, while outside its embankment are several smaller tumuli. The central mound, 160 feet long and 16 feet high, at the time of its final exploration was the third largest of the Hopewell burial tumuli. Prior to Dr. Mills' examination it had been subjected to partial exploration by Squier and Davis; by Professor Putnam, for Harvard University, and by Professor Moorehead, for the Ohio State Museum.

FIG. 136. THE CENTRAL MOUND OF THE SEIP GROUP, ROSS COUNTY, OHIO
This huge tumulus, measuring 250 feet in length and 30 feet in height, has yielded one hundred burials and numerous artifacts as a result of its recent exploration by the Ohio State Museum. Note laborers at extreme right, beginning the work of exploration.

The Harness Group is remarkable for the number of burials it contained. In addition to 133 burials exhumed in the final examination, the previous partial explorations had disclosed a sufficient number to bring the total to 200 or more. Although fully 15,000 specimens were obtained in the several explorations, the mound contained no ceremonial offerings and therefore no specimens peculiarly outstanding.

A fine model of the large mound in process of exploration, showing the locations and character of its burials, is in the Ohio State Museum. Like most others of its culture, the Harness Mound was found to have covered the site of a sacred structure.

FIG. 137. CROSS-SECTION OF THE CENTRAL SEIP MOUND

This view shows stone grave burial; cremated burials with arch above, resulting from decay of log-cabin structure built over them; caving in of structure over charnel-house; and restoration of apex of primary mound with its covering of ceremonial gravel.

The Seip Group of mounds and earthworks, named for the owner of the land, is located in the valley of Paint Creek, in the southwestern part of Ross County. With respect to the area enclosed by its earthworks—a square enclosure, a large circle, and a smaller circle—it is the largest of the Hopewell works (see Figure 168 in Chapter XII). The walls of the enclosures, never bold, are now mostly obliterated. A large central mound, another of approximately half its size, both within the large circle, and several minor mounds outside the enclosure complete the group. The smaller of the two large mounds was explored by Dr. Mills early in the century. The largest tumulus of the group was examined by the writer in 1926-28.

The central mound of the Seip Group (Figure 136) is second in size of all known Hopewell tumuli, being exceeded only by the great central mound of the Hopewell Group proper. It measured 250 feet in length, 150 in width, and had a height of 30 feet. The cubic content of this great tumulus was approximately 20,000 cubic yards, the equivalent of as many ordinary wagonloads of earth. Three full summers were required for its examination.

The most striking feature of the examination was the finding of an interior sepulcher or vault, constructed of logs and timbers, in which reposed four adult skeletons, placed side by side and extended on their backs, while lying at their heads, transversely, were the skeletons of two infants (Figure 138). Whether or not this was a family tomb or a sepulcher devoted to the "royalty" of the community, it is indisputable that the occupants were of the elect. The burials were accompanied by a rich array of artifacts, some of which were unique. There were thousands of pearls, from which circumstance newspaper reports at the time designated the interments as the "great pearl burial." Implements and ornaments of copper, mica, tortoise-shell, and silver were found in profusion. A single individual, an adult male, wore the same type of artificial

FIG. 138. MULTIPLE BURIAL IN THE SEIP MOUND

The skeletons of four adults and two children, interred within a burial chamber of logs and timbers, doubtless were those of persons of unusual importance. Many thousands of pearl beads and numerous ornaments and implements of copper, marine tortoiseshell, and other materials accompanied the burials. Beneath large copper breastplates and preserved by the chemical action of the copper were found portions of burial shrouds of woven fabric with colored designs.

nose and the copper rodlike hair ornaments found in the double burial of the Hopewell Group. Imprints of an elaborate burial robe were apparent, and beneath and preserved by large copper breastplates accompanying three of the four adults portions of this shroud were well preserved. The burial robe or shroud, of woven fabric, proved to be a unique find in that it bore colored designs (Figure 53). These designs, conventional in character, were in tan, maroon, and black.

Two important votive offerings occurred in the central Seip Mound. In one of these reposed a huge ceremonial copper axe weighing 28 pounds (Figure 140). Over this were placed twelve large copper breastplates, overlapping one another, and between them were many thicknesses of woven fabric (Figure 36). This fabric, preserved by the chemical action of the copper, is very similar in weave, texture, and color to the

Fig. 139. A stone grave cremated burial of the Seip mound

This cremated burial was unusual for the culture, in that it occupied a boxlike structure of flat stones. With the cremated bones will be noted a stone axe, copper ear ornaments, and pendants made from wildcat jaws.

homespun linen of pioneer days. It is perhaps the only woven fabric preserved in its original color and practically unstained so far taken from a mound. The other votive offering was the five massive effigy pipes of the Lower Mississippi culture to which reference was made in Chapter VII.

It may interest the reader to know that in the exploration of this mound a serious accident occurred. In order to obtain frequent cross-section measurements and photographs, at intervals of 15 feet the face of the mound was cleared off to present a vertical exposure throughout its height. On one such occasion, when a vertical wall of earth 30 feet high had been exposed, a portion of the top caved off, dropped to the floor below, and buried the writer. When exhumed he was unconscious for an appreciable time and was taken to the hospital with numerous broken bones but ultimately made a complete recovery.

The great Seip Mound at the time of writing is being restored and converted into a charming park of ten acres extent. The specimens from both the mounds explored, together with a model of the group, are to be seen at the Ohio State Museum.

THE TURNER GROUP

The Turner Group of mounds and earthworks, situated in Anderson Township, Butler County, adjacent to the Little Miami River about eight miles above its junction with the Ohio, is in many respects one of the most remarkable of all the Hopewell culture groups. It was explored by the Peabody Museum of Harvard University, under Professor Frederick W. Putnam, beginning in 1882, with periodical renewals extending through a period of ten years or more. Not only is the Turner Group notable as a major work of complex character, but also because of the remarkable finds of minor relics discovered with its numerous burials and in the sacrificial or votive offerings contained in its mounds.

The Turner Group consisted of a circular enclosure, 480 feet in diameter, connected by a graded way 600 feet long with a large oval enclosure measuring 1,500 feet in length by 950 feet in width. The circular enclosure was situated on an elevation identified as a detached portion of the first, or upper, river terrace, from which the graded way descended to connect with the large enclosure, on the second or lower terrace some 30 feet below. To the south of the circle was a long, narrow enclosure, with low parallel walls, extending for upwards of half a mile, curved and joined at the ends. A total of fourteen mounds lay within the two enclosures, twelve of them being inside the large oval.

The story of the exploration of this great group is worthy of a volume to itself, but only casual comment can be given it here; the interested student is referred to the official report for details. Outstanding features of the explorations were the finding beneath the walls of the great enclosure of evidences of buildings and of intensive occupancy; the discovery, within the area of the oval enclosure, of extensive burial places, interment having been made in elaborate stone graves; and the presence beneath the floors of some of the mounds of intricate systems of connecting pits and tunnels, the purpose of which remains unexplained.

Of the fourteen mounds within the enclosures, one-half were comprised in a connected group arranged in a manner suggesting the figure of an animal. The bases of the mounds composing this group were outlined by low walls of stone. In the largest of these, occupying the position corresponding to the head of the suggested animal, there was found a central "altar" or basin, from which was taken one of the most remarkable sacrificial or votive offerings on record. Among the thousands of objects comprising this cache were numerous nuggets of copper, meteoric iron, and silver; small sheets of

FIG. 140. CEREMONIAL AXE OF COPPER FROM THE SEIP MOUND

The immense copper axes found with funerary offerings in the Hopewell culture mounds apparently were ceremonial possessions of chiefs and medicine men. The specimen shown is 20 inches long and weighs 28 pounds.

gold, hammered from nuggets; many symbols and ornaments wrought from copper; ear ornaments, bracelets, beads, and buttons of copper; beads and other ornaments of meteoric iron; large crystals; numerous effigy objects and designs cut from mica, some of which were painted in colors; containers made from large ocean shells; imitation canine teeth of the bear, of shell; more than 20,000 shell beads, of various types; 35,000 pearl beads; 12,000 pearls, unperforated; beads and pendants made from the teeth of the bear, alligator, and various other animals; many chipped blades of flint and obsidian; ornaments of terra cotta and tortoise-shell; and engraved disks of bone bearing conventional designs.

In the second largest mound of the group, corresponding to a segment of the suggested body of the effigy, was found a similar offering, from which were taken the following: nuggets of native copper and pieces of meteoric iron; many odd fossils, concretions, and peculiarly shaped stones; pearl beads; copper bracelets, beads, and cones; worked bone, shell, teeth and claws of animals; flint implements; effigy of a horned serpent, cut from mica; stone effigy of a horned serpent monster; and a remarkable series of terra-cotta human images or figurines of which illustrations will be found in Chapter VI (Figures 64 and 65). These last are the most remarkable examples of self-portraiture of the so-called Mound-builders so far discovered. They illustrate, from the viewpoint of their makers, not only physical characteristics, but details of costume, ornamentation, and methods of dressing the hair.

The interesting specimens taken from the Turner Group are displayed at the Peabody Museum, Cambridge. A fine model of the group may be seen at the Cincinnati Museum of Art. The Turner Group, as is true of the Camden works and the Milford works located a few miles to the north, is now practically obliterated.

CHAPTER X

The Great Fort Ancient—Other important fortifications—The Great Serpent Mound—Other effigy mounds.

IN addition to the three distinct cultures described in the preceding chapters, there are in the Ohio mound area two major classes of earthworks which demand attention. These are the so-called hilltop enclosures or fortifications, obviously intended for purposes of defense, and the effigy or image mounds. Despite the fact that considerable exploration has been done in and adjacent to remains of these two classes, the identity of their builders is not definitely known. It may be stated, however, that the cultural affinity of the former is with the Fort Ancient culture, and this is true also, though in somewhat less degree, of the effigy remains.

THE GREAT FORT ANCIENT

The outstanding example of the defensive works in the Ohio area—and in the entire mound area, if not in the world— is the noted Fort Ancient, situated on the east bank of the Little Miami River in Warren County, Ohio. Much has been written about Fort Ancient, and thousands of tourists and visitors, from all parts of the world, annually inspect this monument of a bygone people and linger to marvel at its majestic proportions and to revel in the beauty of the district.

The Fort occupies a peninsulalike headland of approximately 100 acres projecting from the adjacent plateau and overlooks the river from a height of approximately 270 feet. The location is eminently strategic, with precipitous declivities dropping to the river along the west side while the greater extent of the opposite side and both ends are flanked by deep

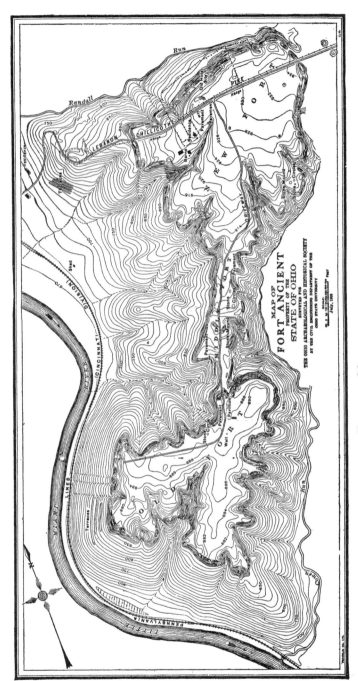

FIG. 141. MAP OF FORT ANCIENT

FIG. 142. FORT ANCIENT IN WINTER

Two views of the walls of the "old fort," looking toward the east, showing the numerous gateways interrupting the embankment.

ravines. The only level approach is at the northeast, where exceptionally high walls afforded protection from encroaching enemies. The form of the Fort has been likened to that of the Western continents, which it somewhat resembles. The narrow isthmus between the two larger divisions of the enclosure divides it into what are known as the "old fort," to the south, and the "new fort."

The walls of Fort Ancient, following the sinuous margin of the terrain on which it is located, measure slightly more than three and one-half miles in length and vary in height from six or seven feet to approximately twenty feet, the greatest altitude being at the level approach toward the northeast. These walls are composed mostly of earth and clay, taken from the moat or ditch paralleling them on their inner margin. At various places along their outer slopes they are underlaid with flat stones, apparently to prevent erosion and under-

FIG. 143. VIEW FROM FORT ANCIENT

Looking to the north up the Little Miami valley, from Point Lookout, elevated 275 feet above the bed of the river. Photograph by C. C. Anderson.

mining by rainfall. Just outside the gateway where the highway enters the Fort from the east are two conical mounds, from which extend low, parallel walls for a distance of upward of 1,000 feet to the northeast, where they unite and enclose a third conical mound. Within these parallel earthen walls was an area paved with rough slabs of stone, lying a foot or two below the present surface.

Several small burial mounds within the walls of the Fort and a habitation site located within the "old fort" yielded human remains and numerous artifacts similar to those found

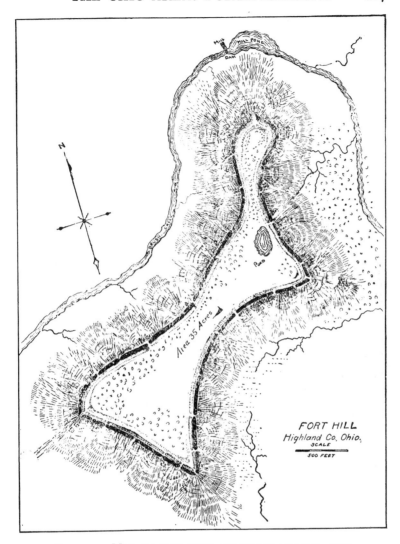

FIG. 144. MAP OF FORT HILL, HIGHLAND COUNTY, OHIO

Fort Hill is one of the most impressive and best preserved of the fortifications of the entire mound area. Its massive walls are constructed for the most part of stone.

in sites adjacent to the Fort in the nearby river valley which pertain to the Fort Ancient culture. Originally the relics found within the Fort were attributed to the peoples who constructed

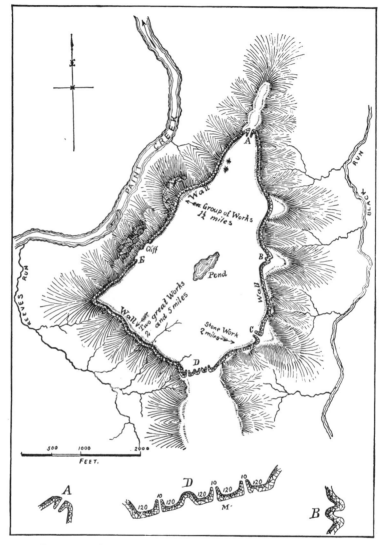

FIG. 145. MAP OF SPRUCE HILL FORT, ROSS COUNTY, OHIO

This noted prehistoric monument is typical of the hilltop fortifications of southern Ohio and adjacent portions of Kentucky and Indiana.

it, but recently this has been questioned and the possibility is recognized that they may belong to tribes who occupied the site subsequent to its primary occupation and the building of the Fort. Additional exploration will be required to determine the facts.

Fort Ancient and the land on which it is located is now one of Ohio's numerous state parks, in custody of the Ohio Archæological and Historical Society. The view from Point Lookout, at the northwest angle of the "old fort," overlooking the valley of the Miami to the northward, is one of the most inspiring in the Middle West.

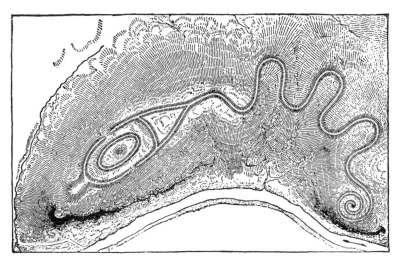

FIG. 146. MAP OF THE GREAT SERPENT MOUND

From a survey made by Professor W. H. Holmes for the Bureau of American Ethnology.

OTHER IMPORTANT FORTIFICATIONS

Other important examples of the hilltop enclosures or fortifications are Fort Hill, in Highland County; Spruce Hill Fort, in Ross County; Glenford Fort, in Perry County; and Fort Miami, near the mouth of the Great Miami River.

Fort Hill, located near the town of Sinking Springs, Highland County, is the best-preserved work of its kind in Ohio. The greater part of its area of 50 acres is covered with heavy forest. The site is a fairly level, detached elevation, isolated from adjacent highlands by Brush Creek and deep ravines,

This great effigy mound, supposed to have been erected as an adjunct to reli-
in length. It is the largest and most impressive prehistoric effigy known. The
for all time. Through the generosity of certain ladies of Boston, who supplied
the Peabody Museum of Harvard University and made repairs to the mound.
ological and Historical Society, to be maintained as a free state park. Photograph

the declivities being exceptionally abrupt and access to the summit exceedingly difficult. The form of the enclosure has been likened to that of a human lower leg and foot (Figure 144). The wall of the Fort, composed mostly of blocks and slabs of the sandstone which underlies the site, varies in height from five feet to twelve or more feet and is somewhat more than one mile in length.

A puzzling feature of Fort Hill, as of Fort Ancient and others of the defensive works, is the great number of gateways interrupting the walls, the purpose of which is not apparent from the standpoint of modern military engineering. The inaccessibility of the site of Fort Hill, "which has enabled it to withstand the siege of time and human demolition" better than any other similar earthwork, must have served equally well its original purpose of defense.

Spruce Hill Fort, near the town of Bourneville, Ross County, is almost as inaccessible as Fort Hill and nearly as impressive. Its walls also are composed principally of stone, as are those likewise of Glenford Fort, in Perry County. Not particularly different from others of its class is Fort Miami, near the mouth of the Great Miami, in Hamilton County (Figure 4). Its

THE GREAT SERPENT MOUND

gious or ceremonial observances of its builders, measures more than 1,300 feet
efforts of the late Professor Frederick W. Putnam have preserved the mound
funds for the purpose, Professor Putnam effected the purchase of the land for
In 1900 the Trustees of Harvard deeded the entire property to the Ohio Archæ-

location is exceptionally strategic, however, and the fact, already noted, that it was first described and surveyed by
William Henry Harrison adds to its interest. A few miles up the
river, near the city of Hamilton, in Butler County, is still
another of the hilltop fortifications. Other enclosures, smaller
as a rule and indeterminable as to purpose, are found throughout northern Ohio, particularly in Huron and Ashland counties and in the Cuyahoga valley.

THE GREAT SERPENT MOUND

The famous Great Serpent Mound is located on Brush
Creek, in Adams County in southern Ohio. It occupies a high
ridge, or rocky cliff, which thrusts itself into the peaceful
valley like a promontory into a calm sea and extends back
into a smiling land suggestive of happiness and prosperity.
The head of the serpent impinges upon a sheer precipice of
rock, 100 feet high, overlooking the waters of Brush Creek,
while the undulating body terminates in triple coils at the
tail, 1,000 feet to the southward. The length of the serpent,
following its sinuous coils, is 1,330 feet. The somewhat tri-

angular head gives the impression of an open mouth and
spread jaws, in front of which is an oval or egg-shaped figure
which the serpent seems about to swallow. The height of the
embankment of the effigy is from two feet to three and one-
half feet.

The Great Serpent Mound was saved from the fate that has
overtaken so many of our prehistoric monuments through the
efforts of Professor Frederick W. Putnam, who in 1887
effected its purchase for the Peabody Museum of Harvard

FIG. 148. SERPENT MOUND PARK

A view of the anterior portion of the great serpent, looking toward the head.
The men at the extreme right furnish a scale for judging the size of this, the
greatest of all effigy earthworks. Photograph by B. E. Kelley.

University. Later it was deeded to the Ohio Archæological and
Historical Society, by which it is maintained as a state park.

The Great Serpent Mound is not a burial mound. Presumably it had its origin in a religious concept, in those far-
distant days when its builders, as a part of their worship of
nature, found "sermons in stones and books in the running
brooks." The serpent has figured prominently in primitive
religion, particularly in those stages of its development in
which nature and natural phenomena were endowed with

animistic and spiritual attributes. The most striking example, perhaps, is the part played by the serpent in the Scriptural account of the Garden of Eden.

Strangely enough, the Great Serpent Mound of Ohio has been identified as the very site of the Garden of the Fall. Some readers of these pages will recall this romantic announcement, widely printed in the public press a couple of decades ago. The author of the theory was a widely known Baptist minister of Ohio. According to him, the Great Serpent was built by the hand of the Creator himself, on the site of the original Eden, to mark the "first sad event"—the deception

FIG. 149. MAP OF THE "ALLIGATOR" OR "OPOSSUM" MOUND, LICKING COUNTY, OHIO

of the woman by the serpent and man's resultant expulsion from the Garden, with all their attendant ills. The oval figure in front of the serpent's head, he believed, represents "the fruit of the tree"; the attitude of the serpent, which is about to swallow it, is significant of his deception; while the writhings of the body undulations represent the pangs of death and physical suffering. The effigy, he declared, was erected on the spot where God's work was first given to humankind that it might serve as an object lesson, expressive of the powers and wiles of Satan as manifested to Adam and Eve, and portray

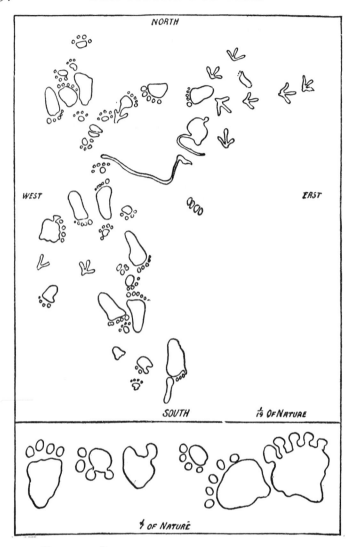

FIG. 150. ROCK PICTURES NEAR BARNESVILLE, OHIO

These petroglyphs are cut or pecked into the sandstone exposure along the margin of the Ohio River.

the pains and penalties of sin. In support of his claim he cited Job xxvi:13: "By His spirit, He hath garnished the heavens; His hand hath formed the crooked serpent."

The Great Serpent Mound, greatest of all the effigy works of the general mound area, lies entirely outside the region where such remains might be expected to occur—Wisconsin and adjacent territory.

FIG. 151.   PETROGLYPH REPRESENTING A BEAR

A single specimen of a group of many figures cut into the rock along the Ohio River near Saxon Postoffice, Meigs County, Ohio. The bear image is 4 feet in length.

OTHER EFFIGY MOUNDS

Another effigy work of the Ohio area is the so-called "Alligator Mound," located near Granville, Licking County, on Raccoon Creek (Figure 149). This interesting effigy measures approximately 250 feet in length with an original maximum height of five or six feet. It is sometimes known as the "Opossum Mound," and indeed from its form it may have been intended to represent either a mammal or a lizard. The figure is constructed from blocks and fragments of the native sandstone, interspersed with and covered by clay and soil. An elevated circular space connected with the body of the effigy by a "graded way" has been identified by early writers as an altar.

A third effigy mound, in the form of a bird with outspread

wings, is that within the great circle of the Newark works, to be described in Chapter XII. This effigy was explored by the Ohio State Museum in 1928. It contained no burials, and the evidence indicated that it was erected for ceremonial or religious purposes.

Remnants of a second serpent mound, now almost obliterated, exist a few miles south of Fort Ancient in Warren County. This is believed to have been only a little less impressive than the Adams County serpent.

ROCK PICTURES

The well-known rock pictures or petroglyphs found generally throughout the mound area are represented in Ohio by numerous examples along the Ohio River. Usually they are cut into the hard sandstone immediately adjacent to the river and tributary streams. As archæological evidence they have but little value, for although the primitive artists who made them doubtless succeeded in recording ideas intelligible to their associates, it is impossible today to interpret their meaning except in a very general way.

CHAPTER XI

THE OHIO AREA: IV, MARGINAL SUBAREAS

Western Pennsylvania—Northwestern West Virginia—Northeastern Kentucky—Eastern Indiana.

THE Ohio mound area comprises, in addition to the State of Ohio proper, the contiguous portions of Pennsylvania, West Virginia, Kentucky, and Indiana. The first two of these marginal regions present only limited areas in which important ancient remains occur, but Kentucky and Indiana possess many prehistoric monuments. None of the four, however, has received adequate attention in the way of exploration of its mounds.

WESTERN PENNSYLVANIA

Although the Keystone State is rich in evidences of prehistoric occupancy, they seldom take the form of mounds or other major works. Only in the extreme western portion of the state, contiguous to Ohio, are mounds and earthworks anything more than occasional and scattered. In the northwestern corner there is an unimportant development of mound-building, a continuation of the western New York region of the Great Lakes area.

In the valley of the Monongahela, however, and in the vicinity of the forks of the Ohio, an interesting development is noted, comprising not only mounds but earthworks and village and camp sites as well. In the vicinity of Monongahela City there are, or were, several mounds of earth and stone, one of which, explored by the Bureau of American Ethnology, yielded evidences suggesting affinity with the Ohio Hopewell culture. Another mound in the same area contained interesting stone graves or crypts. Near Belle Vernon are located a number of stone mounds, and from one of several situated near Irvine-

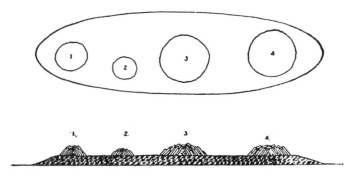

FIG. 152. FLOOR PLAN OF A MOUND WITH STONE GRAVES NEAR MONON-
GAHELA CITY, PENNSYLVANIA

Explored by Cyrus Thomas. Length of mound, 110 feet.

ton were taken numerous relics of European manufacture, indicating its historic origin. There are several small oval enclosures near Pittsfield, on Brokenstraw Creek, and a showy
tumulus is located within the city limits of Erie.

An important survey of eastern and central Pennsylvania,
which is to be extended to the western portions of the state,

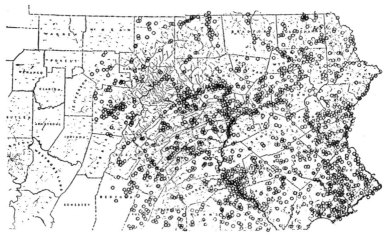

FIG. 153. ARCHÆOLOGICAL SITES IN EASTERN AND CENTRAL PENNSYL-
VANIA

Although there are but few mounds and earthworks in the Keystone State, an
archæological survey, begun in 1928, has revealed hundreds of village and camp
sites, cemeteries, and other evidences of prehistoric occupancy.

is now being carried out by the Pennsylvania Federation of Historical Societies. Hundreds of prehistoric camp and village sites, cemeteries and burial places, and occasional mounds have been located and noted on the map reproduced in Figure 153.

NORTHWESTERN WEST VIRGINIA

The principal mound development of West Virginia is that of the Kanawha valley, from the junction of the Kanawha River with the Ohio and extending up the river for a distance

FIG. 154. A STONE MOUND NEAR HOMESTEAD, PENNSYLVANIA
The venerable trees are indicative of the age of the structure.

of one hundred miles. The rest of the state, so far as known, is almost devoid of mounds. Exploitation of the archæology of the state has been backward, the only important explorations being those of the Bureau of American Ethnology under Dr. Cyrus Thomas, reported in the Twelfth Report of that institution. Although the mounds and other major remains of the Kanawha valley have certain characteristics which to some archæologists indicate a rather distinctive culture, in the main they correspond closely to the Adena culture of the Ohio area, with which for the present purpose they are classed.

By far the most interesting and important of the mounds and earthworks of West Virginia is the extensive group just below the city of Charleston. This group, which extends for a distance of five or six miles along the Kanawha valley, comprises a total of fifty or more mounds, varying in height from five to 35 feet, and some ten or twelve earthworks of the enclosure type, from one to 30 acres in area. Associated with them are found many circular storage pits, stone graves, and stone mounds or cairns. The very general occurrence of stone graves in the Kanawha valley sites strongly suggests affinity with the so-called stone-grave area of Tennessee, but the majority of the evidences point to relationship with the Adena culture. The trait of using stone graves can hardly be regarded as characteristic of any particular culture; rather it depended on the availability of stone. In this instance, however, it may well be regarded as an example of diffusion or borrowing from the area immediately to the southward.

The mounds and earthworks of the Charleston Group are situated on the terraces overlooking the river valley, well above flood level. The earthworks are of several forms—circular, oval, rectangular, and irregular. The largest and most important mound of the group was that known as the Great Smith Mound, 175 feet in diameter at the base and 35 feet in height. Its exploration disclosed a large timbered burial vault in which were several skeletons. Copper bracelets, gorgets, shell beads, mica, and other objects accompanied the burials. A mound on Cabell Creek, in the same general locality, contained an interesting burial. Two skeletons, of large size, had been buried in a sitting posture, facing each other with the legs interlocking. Their hands, extended toward one another, supported between them a crude hollow sandstone object, resembling a vessel or trough, which contained ashes and burned bones.

Other interesting mounds and earthworks are located in Putnam, Mason, and Cabell counties. Numerous petroglyphs or rock pictures formerly were to be seen along the lower course of the Kanawha.

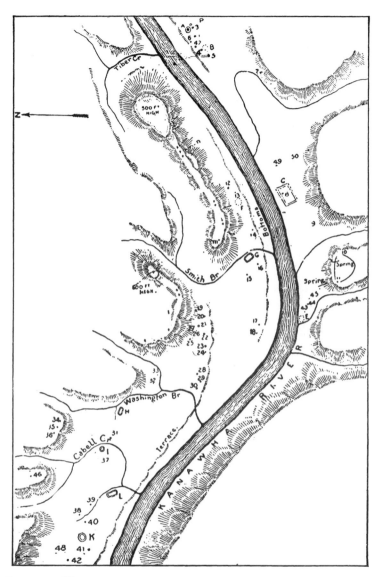

FIG. 155. MAP OF THE CHARLESTON GROUP, KANAWHA COUNTY, WEST
VIRGINIA

In Fayette County, near Mount Carbon, is an interesting enclosure, many petroglyphs, and peculiar stone mounds or cairns. These latter are situated on the high spurs about Mount Carbon, overlooking the Kanawha. The cairns are carefully made and measure up to eight or ten feet in height with diameters up to 40 feet or more. They are supplied with one or occasionally two "well holes" extending vertically from top to bottom, averaging three feet in diameter. Occasionally these

FIG. 156.   THE GRAVE CREEK MOUND

This tumulus, located at Moundsville, West Virginia, is the largest conical structure in the entire mound area, being upward of 70 feet in height. After Squier and Davis.

cairns have triangular vaults, entirely enclosed. In the "well holes" and vaults are found skeletal remains, rude pottery, and stone and flint implements.

Above Mount Carbon is an ancient stone wall, extending for one mile along the slope of the bluff, crossing its summit, and continuing for an equal distance along the opposite slope. This wall, originally five to six feet high, is now much dilapidated. The town of Clifton, Kanawha County, occupies the site of an extensive prehistoric town. Above the town, occupying a spur, is a stone wall 800 feet in length. A number of mounds are reported in the valley of Lens Creek. A small enclosure and several mounds are located near St. Albin.

The Grave Creek Mound, at Moundsville, Marshall County, has been described in an earlier chapter as the largest conical tumulus in the Ohio valley and as belonging to the Adena culture. Its exploration by tunneling is recorded by School-

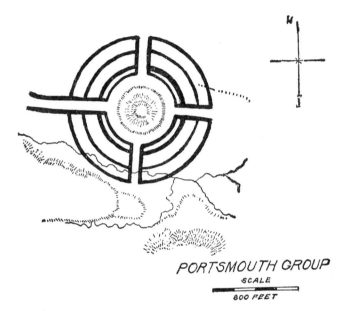

PORTSMOUTH GROUP

SCALE

800 FEET

FIG. 157. MAP OF THE KENTUCKY PORTION OF THE PORTSMOUTH WORKS

This large mound, with its enclosures in the form of concentric circles, belongs to the Hopewell culture. It is further described in the following chapter.

craft. It was found to contain two large timbered burial vaults or sepulchers, one on and below the base and a second some 35 feet below the apex. The lower vault contained two, and the upper a single skeleton burial. With these burials were found copper bracelets, ornaments of mica, and many shell beads. The partial examination shows the Grave Creek Mound to be very similar to those of the Kanawha valley, which, in turn, are analogous to the typical Adena mounds of Ohio.

FIG. 158. A BURIAL MOUND IN A CIRCULAR ENCLOSURE
Greenup County, Kentucky. After Squier and Davis.

NORTHEASTERN KENTUCKY

With the exception of the extreme northeastern portion of the state, Kentucky Mound-builder archæology is related to the area to the south, in connection with which it will receive further attention in Chapter XVIII. In the region bordering the Ohio River, however, particularly in Mason, Greenup, and Nicholas counties, there are numerous remains of the Ohio Fort Ancient culture. These consist of low burial mounds, in association with which are cemeteries and village or camp sites. The same types of burial, artifacts, and storage pits excavated in the ground as are described in connection with the Feurt mounds and village site are to be noted in this region.

The Fox Farm site, in Mason County, explored and reported by Harlan I. Smith for the American Museum of Natural History, is a replica of the typical Ohio Fort Ancient sites, while a smaller site in Greenup County, examined by Dr. William S. Webb of the University of Kentucky, appears to belong to the culture. A striking example of diffusion of traits is disclosed in the comparative study of the prehistoric

FIG. 159. THE WHITEHEAD MOUND

Situated in the Whitewater valley, southeastern Indiana; explored by F. M. Setzler for the State of Indiana in 1928 and found to belong to the Adena culture of the Ohio area.

Fort Ancient sites. Proceeding southward from the northernmost sites of the culture, located in Ross County, Ohio, it is noted that the so-called discoidal stones or game stones become of progressively more common occurrence. Beginning in the north with an occasional specimen, at the Feurt site, nearing the Ohio River, they become plentiful for the first time, while across the river in the Kentucky sites they are surprisingly abundant. Similarly, the so-called shell gorgets, almost unknown to the north, make their appearance toward the Ohio River and are in fairly common evidence in the Kentucky sites. Both these artifacts are typical of the area to the south of Kentucky, particularly in Tennessee.

EASTERN INDIANA

Indiana, rich in mounds and other major remains of the "first Hoosiers," is just beginning to receive the archæological attention it merits. Aside from the valuable records preserved in the reports of the State Geological Survey, no attempt was made until within the last few years to study or preserve the state's ancient monuments. Recently, however, through joint action of the Indiana Historical Bureau, the Division of Geology of the Department of Conservation, the Indiana Historical Society, the Indiana Academy of Science, and several public-spirited individuals, a program of preservation, exploration, and record has been launched. The first fruits of this program was the examination, in 1926 and 1927, of the Albee Mound, in Sullivan County. This project, directed by J. Arthur MacLean, then director of the John Herron Art Institute of

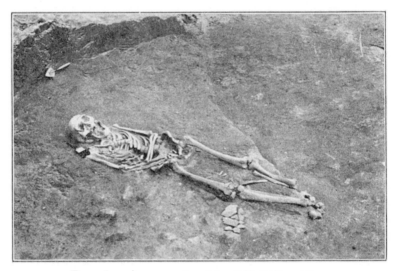

FIG. 160. A BURIAL IN THE WHITEHEAD MOUND

Indianapolis, was the first scientifically conducted exploration of an Indiana mound. Continuing the program, a preliminary survey for an archæological map, together with exploration in the Whitewater valley of southeastern Indiana, was conducted under the direction of F. M. Setzler during the summer of 1928.

Only the eastern portion of Indiana, adjacent to the Ohio border, belongs properly to the Ohio area. The extreme northern region has its affinity with the assumed Great Lakes area, while the western and southwestern portions pertain respectively to the Upper Mississippi and Tennessee-Cumberland areas, in connection with which they will be discussed in later chapters.

The official explorations of 1928 in the Whitewater valley showed definite relationship of the mounds of that region with the Ohio Adena culture, a considerable development of which is apparent in that section of Indiana.

Evidences of the trend across Indiana into Illinois and Iowa of the Ohio Hopewell culture are found in reports of earlier explorations. One of a group of large mounds in Greene County, adjacent to the town of Worthington, contained a typical burial vault of the log-tomb type, the burial being accompanied by a copper axe, mica ornaments, and human effigy ornaments, of Hopewell type. In La Porte County, twelve miles south of the town of

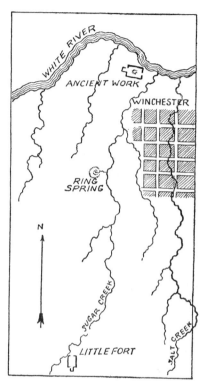

FIG. 161. ANCIENT WORKS NEAR WINCHESTER, INDIANA
Redrawn from Squier and Davis.

that name, there occurred a group of sand mounds, ranging in height from six to twenty feet. In one of these was a log structure containing a burial, with which were effigy pipes, copper axes, mica and galena, and other indications of Hopewell affinity. Two or three mounds in Rush County likewise yielded similar evidences of having been erected by the Hopewell peoples. Near Kendallville, in Steuben County, in the extreme northeastern corner of the state, is a large mound

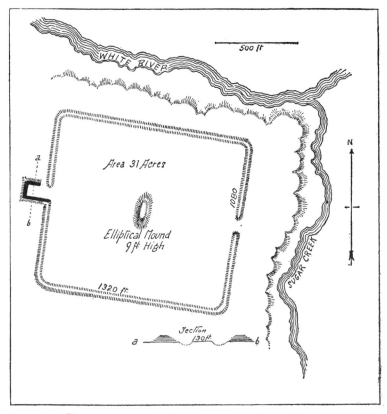

FIG. 162. ENCLOSURE AND MOUND ON WHITE RIVER, NEAR WINCHESTER, INDIANA

Redrawn from Squier and Davis.

about which cluster six smaller tumuli. These, as is true of a large oval mound a few miles south of the town, bear evidences of Hopewell origin.

Besides the definite evidences in southeastern Indiana of the Adena culture and the known and probable mounds of Hopewell origin, the eastern half of Indiana contains a number of mounds and earthworks the cultural relations of which remain to be determined. Without question certain of these will fall within the Fort Ancient culture, as the important village site at Lawrenceburg, while others will be found to pertain to the Hopewell and the Adena. Some, however, in common with minor tumuli of western Ohio, appear to be of distinct and undetermined culture.

In Dearborn County, bordering on southwestern Ohio, is what is known as the Ancient Fort, similar to though smaller than the great Fort Ancient of Ohio. A similar fort is located near Brookville, in Franklin County. This and the largest enclosure of the state, that at Winchester, in Randolph County, appear to be of the Fort Ancient type. The last-named is a parallelogram, measuring 1,080 by 1,320 feet. A circular enclosure of eleven acres near Cambridge City, in Wayne County, is analogous.

An interesting group comprising twenty mounds and some fifteen elliptical depressions, apparently house sites, is located in Henry County. The external evidences indicate a northern thrust of the Tennessee-Cumberland culture, definitely in evidence along the lower course of the Wabash River.

The noted Anderson works, a complex group of mounds and circular enclosures, is the best preserved of the ancient monuments of the state. Its culture is undetermined, but there is some suggestion of Hopewell affinity. Clark County, in the vicinity of the falls of the Ohio, abounds in mounds, fortifications, and shell heaps. The remainder of the state pertains to other archæological areas, to be considered presently.

CHAPTER XII

A TOUR OF THE OHIO MOUND AREA

The Circleville works—Chillicothe, the heart of the Mound-builder country—The Portsmouth works—The Marietta works—The Newark works—The Miami valleys—The Cincinnati works—The Miamisburg and Enon mounds.

IT IS not possible within the scope of these pages to describe all the major groups of mounds and earthworks of the Ohio area; yet their very impressiveness demands that a few of them be given some measure of attention. This is all the more desirable in view of the facility of present-day motor travel and the quickening of interest in our prehistoric fore-runners evidenced by the thousands of motor tourists who annually visit the important mounds and earthworks in the various states where they occur. For these reasons it seems very well worth while to indicate routes touching the more important remains of the several cultures in the preëminently interesting Ohio area and to furnish brief descriptions of them for the benefit of the visitor.

The logical starting point for a tour of the Ohio mound area is Columbus. After a visit to the Ohio State Museum, where the world's most extensive collections of mound relics are displayed, the tourist finds himself impatient to view the tumuli from which this wealth of material was taken, together with their accompanying earthworks. Although most of the works of major importance might be visited in a single roundabout motor tour, the more enjoyable plan is that of three separate trips out of Columbus: one directly southward through the Scioto valley to the Ohio River; another southeastward through the valley of the Muskingum to Marietta; and the third south-westward through the valleys of the two Miamis to Cincinnati and vicinity.

FIG. 163. AN EARLY MAP OF CIRCLEVILLE

This old map of the historic capital of Pickaway County, Ohio, drawn by
G. F. Wittich in 1836, affords an illustration of how white settlers frequently
came to occupy the sites of prehistoric villages and earthworks. The town was
laid out on the site of an extensive group of works, with Circle Street conforming to the enclosure, at the center of which an eight-sided courthouse was
located.

Within and in the immediate vicinity of the city of Columbus
there are several fine mounds, and a few miles up the Olen-
tangy River from the capital city is the most northerly of
the Hopewell groups. Proceeding southward from Columbus,
the tourist first finds himself on hallowed ground at Circleville, the county seat of Pickaway County.

THE CIRCLEVILLE WORKS

The Circleville works, from the circular portion of which
the town takes its name, were the first of the great groups
to be recorded. In the year 1772, the Rev. David Jones of
New Jersey, incidental to his travels among the western

Indians, recorded in his journal a plan and computation of the group. Later, in 1820, it was described by Caleb Atwater, Ohio's "first historian," and it was accorded further attention by Squier and Davis in *Ancient Monuments*. The romantic story of the founding of the town, which was laid out to conform to the great circle, with the eight-sided courthouse lo-

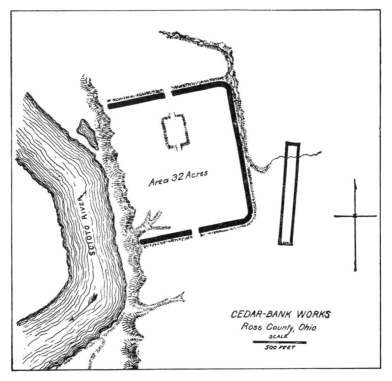

FIG. 164. MAP OF THE CEDAR BANK WORKS, ROSS COUNTY, OHIO

cated at its center, is told by Miss May Lowe in *Four Cycles: A Centennial Ode*, written for the centennial celebration of the founding of the town in 1910. A plan of the earthworks and early maps of the town are included.

The Circleville works comprised a square enclosure connected with a circular one by means of parallel walls. The circular work was unique in comprising two concentric circles,

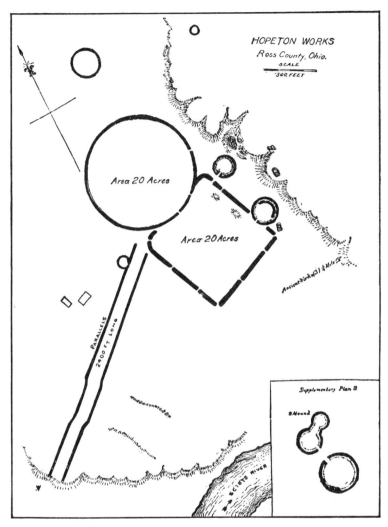

FIG. 165.   MAP OF THE HOPETON WORKS
This fine group is practically intact and is readily accessible.

separated by a moat. The diameter of the circle was 1,000 feet and the side of the square 900 feet. Although this important group is now mostly obliterated, portions of it are still pointed out to visitors, and a wealth of reminiscence may be had from old residents of the town.

CHILLICOTHE, THE HEART OF THE MOUND-BUILDER COUNTRY

Proceeding southward from Circleville to Chillicothe, a distance of twenty-two miles, the tourist penetrates the very heart of the Mound-builder country. The highway, paralleling on the east the course of the Scioto River, brings the motorist within view of several important groups and sites. First comes the old Blackwater Group, at the junction of the stream of that name with the Scioto. This group, now almost obliterated, consisted of several small circles and crescents accompanied by mounds. Next in order are the Gartner mounds and prehistoric village site of the Fort Ancient culture, from which the Ohio State Museum has secured much material. Still nearer Chillicothe, lying immediately adjacent to the highway are the Cedar Bank works, consisting of a large rectangular enclosure of 32 acres, a flat-topped pyramidal mound, and minor figures (Figure 164). The moat of the great enclosure is still sufficiently deep to hold water during a considerable portion of the year, while the embankment itself is quite bold.

At the village of Hopetown are the works of that name, close by the highway and well worth seeing. They comprise a square and a circle, conjoined, each enclosing 20 acres of land, and despite cultivation they are quite bold and impressive. Parallel walls of earth lead from the Hopetown works toward the river, across which lies the noted Mound City Group.

Historic old Chillicothe, early capital of the state, is the very heart of Mound-builder activity in the Ohio area, not alone of the Hopewell, but of the Fort Ancient and Adena cultures as well. The city itself is built upon the site of the Chillicothe Group and is surrounded within easy distance on all sides by major groups and sites. Because of its historic background and picturesque location, nestling, as it does, at the foot of Mount Logan and its accompanying chain of hills, Chillicothe affords a desirable headquarters from which to visit the adjacent remains.

At the north edge of Chillicothe is the Adena Mound and the historic estate and mansion of Governor Worthington.

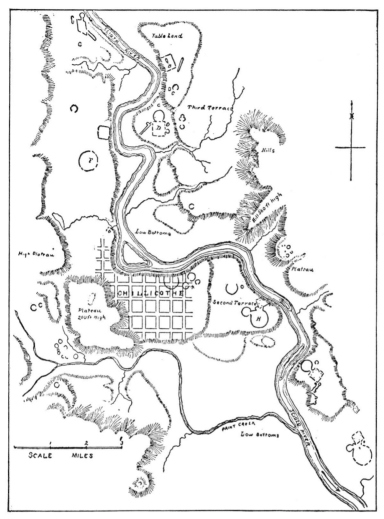

FIG. 166. MAP OF TWELVE MILES OF THE SCIOTO VALLEY ADJACENT TO
CHILLICOTHE, SHOWING FREQUENCY OF ANCIENT WORKS

This section of Ross County is the richest portion of the Ohio mound area.

Within Camp Sherman, of historic and military note, just
north of the city, is the great Mound City Group, the mecca
of many visitors. Mound City, so-called, comprises a rectangular enclosure of 13 acres in which are situated twenty-

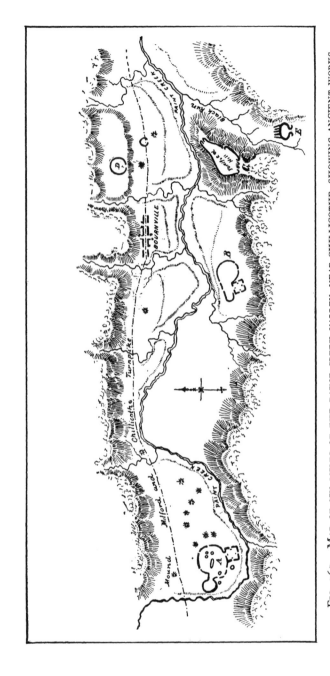

FIG. 167. MAP OF SIX MILES OF THE PAINT CREEK VALLEY, NEAR CHILLICOTHE, SHOWING ANCIENT WORKS

A, The Seip Group of mounds and earthworks; B, the Baum earthworks; C, Spruce Hill fortification; D, the Bourneville Circle; E, the Black Run fortification.

three burial mounds. It is one of the finest of the Hopewell remains. Explored by the Ohio State Museum in 1919 and 1920, as already described in Chapter IX, the mounds were restored to their original condition and the tract converted into a state park. Scenically the site is most impressive, and it is indeed a veritable city of mounds. Just north of Mound City is the site of the Dunlop works, which, however, are now almost obliterated.

A side trip of a few miles from Chillicothe, to the northwest, takes the visitor to the type group of the Hopewell culture, the famous Hopewell works, located at Anderson, on the North Fork of Paint Creek. This great group comprises a rectangular enclosure of 110 acres, a conjoined square, and a total of more than thirty mounds. Its exploration, it will be recalled from Chapter IX, was richer in results than that of any other group. Portions of the wall of the great enclosure and several of the mounds are intact.

A third short drive from Chillicothe, southwestward through the Paint Creek valley, takes the visitor to the site of the old Junction Group, located at the mouth of North Fork. This group, which closely resembles the Blackwater Group, has mostly succumbed to cultivation. Opposite the town of Bourneville is the famous Spruce Hill Fort, one of the most impressive of the hilltop fortifications of the state, as the map in Figure 145 will indicate. It is a triangular area of great extent enclosed by a heavy wall of stone; the identity of its builders is undetermined. At the foot of Spruce Hill, adjacent to the stream, is the Baum village site, of the Fort Ancient culture, and, occupying a portion of the same site, the Baum works, now obliterated, of the Hopewell culture. The village site was explored by the Ohio State Museum and yielded many relics.

Proceeding toward the village of Bainbridge, the highway passes close to numerous individual mounds and through one of the most charming bits of scenic Ohio. Seventeen miles out of Chillicothe, at the horseshoe bend of Paint Creek, is the Seip Group of mounds and earthworks, one of the largest in

Ohio. Examination of the great central mound of this group has just been completed by the Ohio State Museum, after three summers of arduous labor, with the important results described in Chapter IX. The mound itself is 250 feet in length and 30 feet in height, with a cubic content of approximately 20,000 cubic yards of earth. The Seip Group is being restored and converted into a public park with facilities for visitors and tourists.

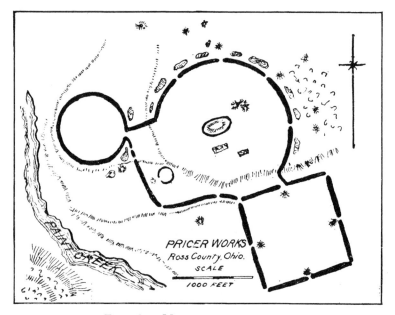

FIG. 168.   MAP OF THE SEIP GROUP

The large central mound of this group, formerly known as the Pricer works, was explored in 1926 and yielded many artifacts of its builders.

Returning to Chillicothe and proceeding southward down the Scioto valley, the tourist will glimpse two major groups before passing out of Ross County, the High Bank and the Harness works. Both are of the Hopewell culture, and although they have suffered severely from cultivation, portions of each remain in fairly good condition. The High Bank works was one of the most intricate of the state, consisting of conjoined circle and square, of 20 and 18 acres respectively, with parallel walls leading to a combination of minor circles some distance removed. Numerous smaller circular figures are associated with the principal earthworks. Proceeding southward through Pike County, passing the "Graded Way"—a peculiar natural conformation modified by prehistoric man to suit his

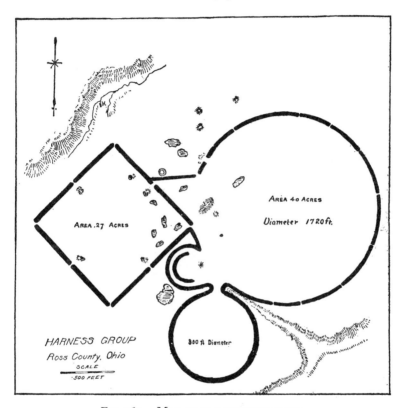

FIG. 169.   MAP OF THE HARNESS GROUP

The principal mound of this group yielded more than two hundred burials. The works were formerly known as the Liberty Group.

needs—the route leads past a modern cemetery in which is a fine group of mounds; the site of a complex group of the Hopewell culture, in Scioto Township, near the town of Jasper; the Feurt mounds and village site (Fort Ancient culture); and the Tremper Mound (Hopewell culture), the two latter being located five miles above Portsmouth.

THE PORTSMOUTH WORKS

The Portsmouth works, in addition to sharing their site with the modern city of that name, have the distinction of being the most extensive of the several great Hopewell groups; further, they are the only group dividing allegiance between two states—Ohio and Kentucky (Figure 170). The portion of the group within the city of Portsmouth, now mostly oblit-

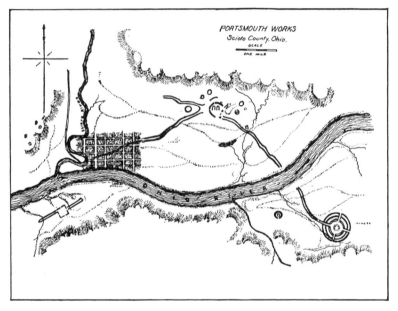

FIG. 170. MAP OF THE PORTSMOUTH WORKS

This is the only one of the Ohio Hopewell works which shares allegiance with another state, a portion of the group being in Kentucky.

erated, consisted of a series of small circles and crescents from which there extended parallel walls southeastward and southwestward to the Ohio River. Across the river, on the Kentucky side, are the Kentucky portions of the group. These latter comprise, to the eastward, a large mound lying within an enclosure consisting of concentric circles (Figure 157), and to the westward, a rectangular enclosure from two opposite sides of which extend parallel walls, closed at their outer ends.

According to Squier and Davis, who figured and described the group, the parallel walls extend for a distance of eight miles and, together with the walls of the enclosure proper, present the surprising total of upwards of twenty miles of earthen embankment.

Inspection of the Portsmouth works and their complement across the river in Kentucky completes the tour of the Scioto valley and its ancient monuments. The tourist planning to continue with the trips through the Muskingum and Miami valleys may either return to Columbus, the most convenient starting point, or may choose the alternative of proceeding either to Marietta or to Cincinnati *via* the picturesque Ohio River route.

The route from Portsmouth to Marietta traverses the rough and picturesque terrain of southern Ohio, adjacent to the river, and presents much that is of interest. The chief attraction, perhaps, is Blennerhasset Island, just west of Parkersburg, with its wealth of historic and archæological lore. Marietta itself, aside from its impressive prehistoric earthworks, holds first place in historic importance in the old Northwest Territory, of which it was the first settlement and the first capital. The region is noted also for its scenic attractions.

The Marietta Group of prehistoric earthworks doubtless is more widely known than any other in the entire mound area. From the time of arrival of the vanguard of the Ohio Company at the mouth of the Muskingum, in 1788, they have been discussed, commented on, written about, surveyed, and admired. Upon taking possession of the land where the first settlement and capital of the Northwest Territory was erected, the Ohio Company took measures for the integrity of the group and provided for its perpetual preservation. It was then that the famous Rufus Putnam map described and reproduced in Chapter I was drafted.

The Marietta works are situated on a level plain overlooking the Muskingum River from the east, about half a mile above its junction with the Ohio. They consist of two enclosures in the form of irregular squares containing respectively 50 and 27 acres. The earthen walls of these enclosures were, according to the Rev. Thaddeus M. Harris' description of 1903, from six to ten feet in height for the larger and slightly less for the smaller. Within the larger enclosure there are three "elevated squares" or truncated pyramids, measuring, respectively, 188 feet long, 132 feet wide, and 9 feet

FIG. 171.　MARIETTA MOUND AND CEMETERY

The first white settlers in the Northwest Territory, in choosing the site of the present Marietta for their capital, recognized as did the Mound-builders the desirability of the location and preëmpted the burial place of the "First Ohioans" for their cemetery. After Squier and Davis, *Ancient Monuments*. See also the early painting of the Marietta works reproduced in Figure 1.

high; 150 feet long, 120 feet wide and 8 feet high; and 108 feet long, 54 feet wide, and somewhat less in height than the first two. Each of the three is provided with two or more graded ascents or ramps leading to the level tops of the platforms. Numerous breaks in the walls of both enclosures occur, those of the smaller of the two being flanked by low mounds.

Parallel walls of earth, 230 feet apart and 360 feet in length, lead from the larger square toward the Muskingum, terminating with the terrace overhanging the flood plain. These walls, according to Mr. Harris, had provided a covered way from the enclosure to the river. Adjacent to the smaller enclosure is an impressive mound, 30 feet high and 115 feet in diameter at the base. This is surrounded by a moat 15 feet across which is flanked on its outer margin by a parapet or embankment of earth 4 feet in height. This fine mound is a most fitting adjunct to the Marietta Cemetery, in which are buried many notables of the Ohio Company and more Revolutionary soldiers than sleep in any other cemetery west of the Alleghany Mountains. Together with the elevated squares in the adjacent park, it attracts annually thousands of tourists.

THE NEWARK WORKS

From Marietta the route leads northwestward, following the valleys of the picturesque Muskingum and its tributary, Licking River, to the city of Newark, county seat of Licking County. Here are located the noted Newark works, in size, extent, and impressiveness the premier of the several great Hopewell culture groups. It is little wonder that early observers searched in vain for words and comparisons which would adequately describe this great monument to the "first Ohioans." The map in Figure 172, from a survey by Charles Whittlesey, surveyor general for the State of Ohio, as published by Squier and Davis, conveys an idea of the complex character of the group, which covers a total area of approximately two square miles. While the city of Newark has occupied and mostly obliterated many details of the group, particularly those comprising its northeasterly portion, the bolder units survive and retain much of their primitive character. This is particularly true of the great circle, approximately 1,200 feet in diameter, with its earthen walls ranging from 10 to 14 feet in height. With commendable foresight, Licking County and the city of Newark, recognizing the importance of the group as an archæological and historical asset, have included the great circle and adjacent portions of the works in the

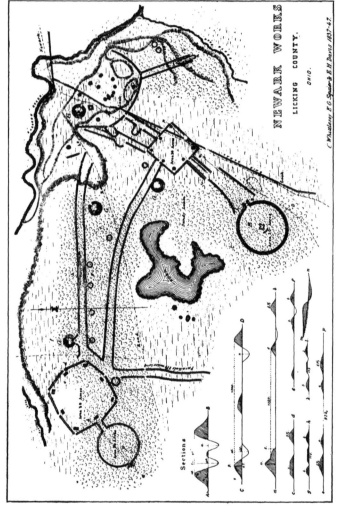

FIG 172. MAP OF THE NEWARK WORKS

The Newark works are the most extensive and complex of all the Hopewell groups of the state. The Licking County fairgrounds now occupy the large circular enclosure toward the bottom of the map, while the Newark golf links are located within the octagon. The city of Newark covers most of the square enclosure and the sites of the mounds toward the upper right-hand corner of the plan. After Squier and Davis, *Ancient Monuments*.

county fairgrounds. This tract has been converted into a delightful park, retaining the original giant forest trees and providing accommodations for tourists. The large octagonal figure and its accompanying small circle and mounds, lying to the northwest and connected with the fairground circle by parallel earthen walls, are now included in the golf grounds. The so-called Eagle Mound, situated at the center of the fairground circle, was explored by the Ohio State Museum in

FIG. 173. THE FLINT RIDGE DISTRICT

The noted Flint Ridge, one of the world's greatest prehistoric flint quarries, is easily accessible at the village of Brownsville, Ohio, on the National Pike, from either Newark or Zanesville. Innumerable quarry pits, covering hundreds of acres along a picturesque wooded ridge, bear testimony to the industry and energy of prehistoric man, who came here through many centuries to quarry flint. The multicolored flint and its accompanying brilliant quartz crystals, everywhere abundant, claim all available space in the tourist's automobile.

1928 and found to be without burials. It apparently was erected as a strictly religious or ceremonial structure.

The route from Newark to Columbus takes the tourist to Granville, where the so-called "Alligator Mound" described in Chapter X may be viewed. This effigy mound, at the eastern edge of the town, is situated on the eminence overlooking Raccoon Creek. It is supposed to represent an animal, possibly the raccoon, and measures 250 feet from head to tip of tail.

THE MIAMI VALLEYS

Starting again from Columbus, the tourist may proceed by way either of Chillicothe or of Washington Court House to Hillsboro, and thence to Fort Hill, in Highland County, and the famous Serpent Mound, in northern Adams County, the greatest of the effigy structures. Westward from Hillsboro lies Fort Ancient, in eastern Warren County. This prehistoric fortification, located on the Little Miami River, is the most important of its class in America and one of the greatest in the world. All these remains are described in Chapter X.

From Hillsboro the route leads southwestward to Cincinnati, passing the sites of the Milford and Turner groups and, at the eastern approach to the city, the great Madisonville prehistoric village site.

THE CINCINNATI WORKS

The city of Cincinnati, to which the capital of the Northwest Territory was removed from Marietta in 1790, occupies the site of a group of earthworks of the Hopewell type only slightly less impressive than the Marietta Group. The Cincinnati Group was less fortunate, however, in that no careful survey or description was recorded before it was effaced by modern improvements. Daniel Drake in his *Pictures of Cincinnati* (1815) declares that the group comprised an ellipse, 800 by 600 feet; a segment of a very large circle; two low parallel walls connected at the ends; and four mounds, one of which was 35 feet in height. In the year 1794, he recounts, this mound was cut down to a height of 27 feet, by order of General Wayne, in order that it might accommodate a sentry tower. One of the mounds of the group was situated where Third and Main streets now intersect. From it were taken relics made from jasper, rock crystal, cannel coal, mica, galena, copper, and shell. The famous Cincinnati tablet, now in the Cincinnati Art Museum, a small rectangular stone plate bearing an intricate engraved design, was found in one of the mounds of this group.

From Cincinnati a side trip of less than an hour takes the tourist to the mouth of the Great Miami, where is located the important prehistoric fortification known as Fort Miami (Figure 4) which recently has been included in the park system of the city.

THE MIAMISBURG AND ENON MOUNDS

The return trip to Columbus from Cincinnati is northward, *via* Dayton and Springfield. At Miamisburg, a few miles south of Dayton, is the Miamisburg Mound, the largest conical tumulus in Ohio, with a height of 70 feet and a basal area of nearly three acres. The Miamisburg Mound and an adjoining tract of land have been presented to the Ohio Archæological and Historical Society by Charles F. Kettering of Dayton, and at the time of writing is being converted into a free state park. At the village of Enon, midway between Dayton and Springfield, is the Enon Mound, only slightly less impressive than the great mound at Miamisburg.

Returned to Columbus, his interest stimulated, the tourist will probably wish to reinspect the collections in the State Museum, taken from the very mounds that he has visited.

CHAPTER XIII

THE GREAT LAKES AREA

Extent and characteristics of the area—The State of New York—Northern
Ohio—The State of Michigan—The Province of Ontario.

WHILE not so spectacular and important as some of
the others from the standpoint of mounds and other
major evidences, the Great Lakes area, as defined
for the present purpose, is of striking interest. This for several
reasons, not the least of which is that the region is one of
the great summer playgrounds of America, the Mecca annually of hundreds of thousands of tourists and vacationists.
Further, and this is particularly true of New York State and
increasingly so of Michigan, the marked attention accorded
the archæology of the region both now and in the past is finding its reward in a vivid reconstruction of the annals of its
aborigines. Moreover, the region presents that ideal of the
anthropologist, the combination of archæological or prehistoric
remains, a record of historic contact between aborigines and
white settlers from the earliest times, and the ethnological
distinction that descendants of the primitive inhabitants survive within the area for comparative study and observation.
With so rich a setting we need not regret too strongly that
the mounds and earthworks of the region are not so numerous
or spectacular as they are elsewhere, since even minor evidences of aboriginal occupancy are no less important and are
truly revelatory of the life of our predecessors, whether or not
they are to be classed as builders of mounds.

EXTENT AND CHARACTERISTICS OF THE AREA

The Great Lakes area comprises those portions of Canada
and the United States immediately adjacent to the Great

Lakes—specifically, southern Ontario, western New York, northern Ohio and Indiana, the lower peninsula of Michigan, and (probably) the Lake-front regions of Illinois and Wisconsin. It is not improbable that scattered mounds and other remains, not yet recorded, exist in western Ontario, northern Michigan, and the country adjacent to Lake Superior.

The justification for designating this territory as a distinct division of the general mound area is threefold. The map of mound distribution (Figure 7) reveals that to the north, east, and southeast of the Great Lakes area major tumuli of all sorts practically disappear. Between it and the Ohio area to the southward there is a perceptible gap; while to the westward the continuity is more apparent than real, since the Upper Mississippi area, with its effigy mounds, extends eastward practically to Lake Michigan, its culture interspersed with or entirely replacing the typical evidences of the Lake region. Thus the Great Lakes were clearly the topographical feature around which this division centered. In the second place, while the mounds, earthworks, and minor evidences as a whole are attributable to several distinct occupations, an overwhelming percentage of the indicia are referable to a single culture complex, the Huron-Iroquois, as the dominant feature of the area. Finally, there is the somewhat negative consideration that these more obvious phenomena are radically different from those of other and adjacent areas.

The prehistory of the area is dominated by the material and cultural evidences of the Iroquoian linguistic family or stock, which occupied the Great Lakes region and the valley of the St. Lawrence with the more expansive Algonquian family practically surrounding it when first noted by whites. Most of the walled enclosures of the area, particularly those of New York State, are attributable to the Iroquois. The mounds proper, for the most part, remain indeterminate as to origin; neither the Algonquians nor the Iroquoians are proved to have had a particular development of the mound-building trait, yet either or both may have been responsible for the tumuli. The Iroquois are known to have constructed occasional unas-

suming mounds, and the great Algonquian family, widely
spread and with varying cultural concepts, doubtless did build
mounds, under certain conditions, during some period of their
existence and in some parts of their area, as in north-central
Ohio, in Michigan, and in Iowa and adjacent territory. On the
whole, the mounds proper of the Great Lakes area seem to
have their affinities with peoples of Algonquian stock.

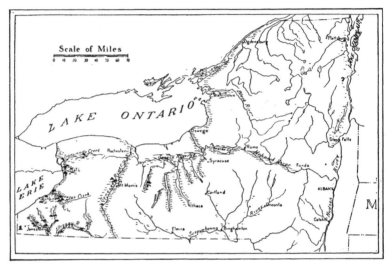

Fig. 174. Archæological map of New York State, showing location of mounds

The mounds, represented by conical symbols, occur exclusively in the western
one-third of the state. The numerous old fortifications and enclosures are not
indicated on this map. After Parker.

THE STATE OF NEW YORK

The Empire State has developed her archæological resources in a gratifying manner. Among the early writers and
investigators there appear such illustrious names as DeWitt
Clinton; E. G. Squier, the pioneer archæologist; Lewis H.
Morgan, the noted anthropologist; Dr. W. M. Beauchamp,
archæologist; Henry R. Schoolcraft, historian; and, more recently, Dr. Arthur C. Parker, formerly New York State archæologist and now director of the Rochester Municipal Museum.

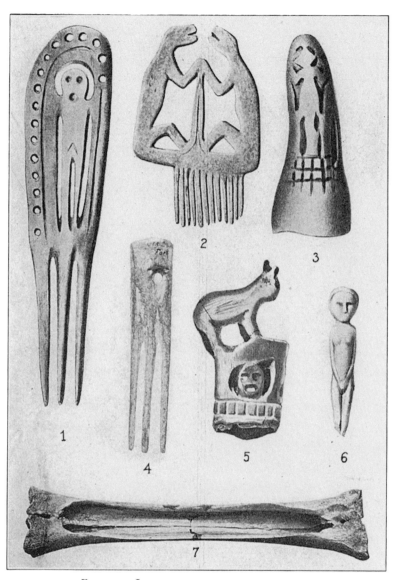

FIG. 175. IROQUOIS BONE AND ANTLER OBJECTS

1. Early Iroquois comb. 2. Seneca comb of the colonial period. 3. Antler knife-handle. 4. Prehistoric Iroquois comb. 5. Oneida knife handle. 6. Bone doll or figurine. 7. Bone beamer made from metapodial bone of elk. Scale, 2/3. From prehistoric Seneca site. Courtesy of Arthur C. Parker.

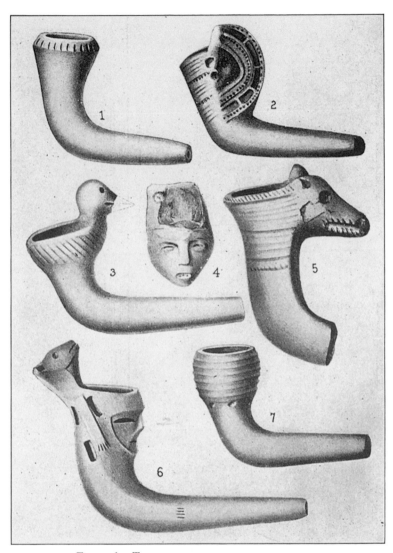

FIG. 176. TYPICAL CLAY PIPES FROM NEW YORK

1. Trumpet-shaped pipe common in the early Onondaga and Erie sites.
2. "Moon" pipe from prehistoric Onondaga site. 3. Pipe bowl with bird head
effigy, from a Seneca site. 4. Face from an Oneida pipe. 5. Effigy pipe, animal
head, Ontario County. 6. Effigy of man's head with skin robe drawn over head
and shoulders, Genesee Valley Iroquoian site. 7. Typical Seneca pipe from
western New York. Scale, 1/2. Courtesy of Arthur C. Parker.

The *Archæological History of New York State* and other contributions and explorations of Dr. Parker have made the prehistory of the state an open book for all who care to read. The *Archæological History* contains large-scale maps of the several counties of the state, on which are indicated, with descriptions, all known mounds, earthworks, and other sites and

FIG. 177. A TYPICAL IROQUOIS POTTERY VESSEL

From a rock shelter on Indian River, Jefferson County, New York. Height, 14½ inches. Courtesy of Arthur C. Parker.

evidences. It is an indispensable adjunct to travel and study in the area.

A trip through the noted Finger Lakes region of New York, through the western counties of the state, and along the Lake fronts, regions abounding in archæological interest and scenic attractions, is most worth while. Rich collections from the mounds and sites are to be seen in the State Museum at Albany and in the Rochester Municipal Museum. A visit to one or more of the Indian reservations of the state is also of interest.

The walled enclosures of the Iroquoian peoples, together with their accompanying village sites and other vestiges, are abundant throughout the western half of the state. They decrease in number toward the east, but are fairly in evidence through the Mohawk valley to the Hudson and northeastward from Lake Ontario along the St. Lawrence. The enclosures are most abundant in the extreme western counties, particularly in Chautauqua, Erie, and Cattaraugus, and in the Finger Lakes region. They occupy strategic positions on the hills and highlands overlooking the valleys; are of varying shapes conforming to the topography of the sites; often were equipped with palisades set into their low earthen walls; and vary from less than one acre in area to as much as seven or more acres. For the most part these Iroquoian enclosures are believed to be of no great antiquity, although most of them are pre-Colonial in age.

In Cattaraugus County, particularly in the valleys of the Cattaraugus, the Conewango, and the Allegheny, there are many enclosures and other remains of the Iroquois. An important enclosure is that known as Burning Spring Indian Fort, near the junction of Big Indian Creek with Cattaraugus Creek.

The principal remains of Chautauqua County are found along the Lake Erie shore, adjacent to Lake Chautauqua, and in the valley of French Creek. The Clear Creek and Conewango valleys and that of Cassadaga Creek also contain ancient remains.

In Erie County few places fail to contribute evidences of prehistoric occupancy. This is particularly true of the Cattaraugus and Tonawanda valleys. Numerous sites in this and adjacent counties are attributed to the Erie or Cat Nation, an Iroquoian people formerly inhabiting western New York, the Lake front of Pennsylvania, and northern Ohio. The cities of Buffalo, East Aurora, Hamburg, and others are built on the sites of their prehistoric towns. It is interesting to record that two thousand Indians, descendants of the original inhabitants, survive in Erie County.

Genesee County contains several impressive enclosures; Ontario County, with many remains, is noted as the former country of the Seneca; while Livingston County received them after they were dislodged from their former location. There are numerous old fortifications in Livingston County, important ones being at Avon and Dansville.

Cayuga County contains many earthworks and village sites, particularly along the Seneca River and adjacent to Cayuga Lake. An important hilltop fortification is located near Auburn.

Onondaga County is said to show more traces of prehistoric occupancy than any other in the state. This county, the home of the Onondaga people, was also the center of the great Iroquois Confederacy and the traditional home of Hiawatha. It now contains the Onondaga Reservation and the site of the national council fire of the Iroquois Confederacy.

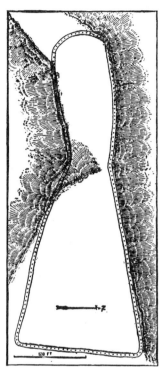

FIG. 178. ANCIENT FORT IN MADISON COUNTY, NEW YORK
After Squier and Davis.

An interesting section of the state is that comprised in Jefferson County, at the eastern end of Lake Ontario. There are numerous strongholds in the county, particularly in Rutland Hills, just east of Watertown. Several distinct occupations of the region, including the Eskimolike culture, Algonquian, and Iroquoian, are noted. The Perch Lake mounds comprise more than two hundred hut rings. A fine enclosure is located near Lockport.

The mounds proper of the state are for the most part situated in the extreme western portion, notably in Chautauqua,
Erie, and Cattaraugus counties. They occur also in the Genesee valley; in the Finger Lakes region; in Jefferson County;
and along the St. Lawrence eastward.

One of a group of three mounds near Mount Morris, in
Livingston County, yielded evidences of belonging to the Ohio
Hopewell culture. Others, judging from the results of explora-
tion, do not resemble any identified culture but appear to be

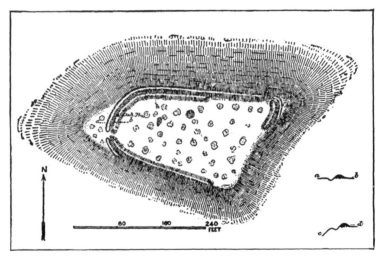

FIG. 179. A PREHISTORIC EARTHEN ENCLOSURE IN WYOMING COUNTY,
NEW YORK
After Squier and Davis.

of Algonquian origin, and are similar to some of the mounds
of north-central Ohio and the general region of the Middle
West.

The tourist may welcome this list of New York sites of
special interest: Burning Spring Fort, on the Cattaraugus
Reservation, Cattaraugus County, between Irving and Ver-
sailles; stockade enclosure with earthen embankment, near
the village of Oakfield, Genesee County; double-walled earthen
ring or enclosure with deep ditches or moats near Shelby,
Orange County; hilltop fortification at Boughton Hill, On-

tario County, and the nearby prehistoric village site (this village was visited as early as 1677 and was destroyed in 1687 by Count de Nonville); fortified hilltop near the town of Pompey, Onondaga County, believed to have been a prehistoric capital of the Onondaga Nation; Flint Mine Hill, in Greene County, where numerous old pits and quarries from which flint was taken may be seen; hilltop fortification with deep ditches or moats near Blue Stone, Wyoming County, not far from Portageville and Letchworth Park.

NORTHERN OHIO

The important Iroquoian region centering in New York State extends westward across the Lake projection of Pennsylvania and follows the south shore of Lake Erie through northern Ohio at least as far as the Maumee River. Whether or not the scattering tumuli of extreme northwestern Ohio, northern Indiana, and the Lake fronts of Illinois and Wisconsin are in any degree attributable to Iroquoian peoples remains to be determined. The sparsity of typical earthen enclosures in these regions inclines toward the probability that the mounds and other evidences observable have their affinities with Algonquian peoples.

Practically no accredited exploration has been carried out in the northern Ohio region, but the evidences of Iroquoian occupancy from the Maumee valley eastward to New York State are so obvious as to be unmistakable. Not only are the characteristic enclosures in evidence, but numerous village and camp sites have yielded typical material specimens. The explorations and reports of Dr. Parker and his associates in New York State have clearly demonstrated the character of Iroquoian archæology and thus have furnished valuable criteria for examination of the field farther west. Their observations indicate an early Algonquian occupancy for the general region, followed by the presence of an Iroquoian people, who in turn were replaced by the Erie, protohistoric representatives of the same stock. The Algonquian evidences throughout

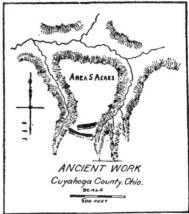

FIG. 180. MAPS OF TYPICAL MINOR EARTHWORK ENCLOSURES OF
NORTHERN OHIO

Such enclosures are found throughout northern Ohio. They are believed to be of Iroquoian origin and probably were built by the Erie, one of the native prehistoric peoples. They are shortly to be explored by the Ohio State Museum and their identity established.

northern Ohio are plain and unmistakable, and those of the successive Iroquoian occupations but little less certain. The main objective of archæological explorations to be launched immediately by the Ohio State Museum is to determine whether both these phases of Iroquoian occupancy are represented in Ohio, or whether, as has been supposed from casual evidences, the sites of the region are purely Erie.

The principal vestiges of Iroquoian occupation in northern Ohio occur in the lower valleys of the Ashtabula and Grand rivers, in Ashtabula and Lake counties; adjacent to the Cuyahoga River, in Portage, Summit, and Cuyahoga counties; along Black River, in Lorain County; on the Sandusky, in Wyandot, Seneca, and Sandusky counties; and near the mouth of the Maumee River, in Lucas County. They comprise walled enclosures, occupying elevations overlooking valleys; village sites, burials, and cemeteries; earthen mounds; and minor remains.

Of the enclosures of the region a number are similar in all essential respects to those of western New York. One of

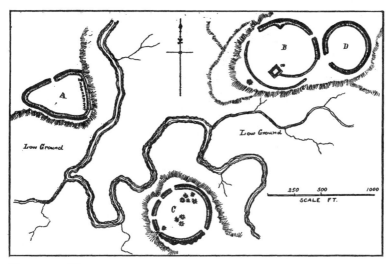

FIG. 181. MAP OF ENCLOSURES AND MOUNDS NEAR NORWALK, HURON
COUNTY, OHIO

An important example of the numerous small enclosures characteristic of
northern Ohio and probably attributable to the Erie.

these, located on Conneaut Creek, in Ashtabula County, is
oval in form and contains an area of five acres. In Cuyahoga
County, on the river of that name, are several of similar type,
and still others occur along Black River, in Lorain County.
The most important village site known is that near the town
of Willoughby, in Lake County. Many hundreds of specimens, comprising potteryware, flint and stone implements, and
effigy pipes fashioned from the crystal calcite of the region,
were taken from the site in earlier years by amateur diggers.
A portion of this material, now in the Ohio State Museum, indicates Erie origin.

A goodly number of mounds, mostly conical structures of
no great size, share the region with the remains mentioned
above. Judging from the evidences of exploration in western
New York, where similar conditions exist, they are not of
Iroquoian origin but probably pertain to certain early Algonquian peoples of rather widespread distribution. A mound of
this type formerly stood at the intersection of Ninth Street
and St. Clair Avenue in the city of Cleveland.

THE STATE OF MICHIGAN

Archæological distributions and political boundaries coincide in the Michigan section to a greater extent than in other regions, where the natural boundaries followed by state lines are less formidable than the watery barriers of Lakes Huron and Michigan. The peninsular character of Lower Michigan has affected the movements of peoples into and within the region in historic as well as in prehistoric times. In the southern part of the peninsula mounds and earthworks are found in much greater abundance than in the north, which is in agreement with the general superiority of the soil south of Saginaw Bay. Further, access to the peninsula by land could be had only from the south.

Although the present aboriginal occupants of Michigan are Algonquian, archæological evidence has established the presence in prehistoric times of at least three distinct cultures in the southern portion of the peninsula, namely, Algonquian, Hopewell, and Iroquoian, a finding which is substantiated by the first historical records except with regard to the Hopewell. This native Ohio culture is manifested at two different points in Michigan. The largest and most important center is near the city of Grand Rapids, where there were originally some forty-six mounds, with diameters of from 10 to 100 feet, in eight groups along the shores of the Grand River. Several earthen pots and other artifacts of Hopewell type taken from some of these mounds, excavated prior to 1875, indicate a very marked Hopewell influence, if not the actual presence in considerable numbers of the living exponents of that rich and complex culture. These interesting pots and some of the artifacts may be seen in the Kent Scientific Museum at Grand Rapids, and a few of the mounds themselves are still in existence. The rest of the material, including effigy pipes and a silver nugget, are in the Peabody Museum of Harvard University at Cambridge. In the report of the Smithsonian Institution for 1879 three other Hopewell mounds are described as yielding "copper hatchets and awls, large plates of

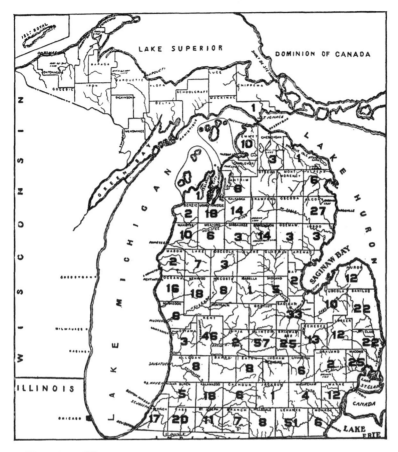

FIG. 182. MAP OF THE DISTRIBUTION OF ARCHÆOLOGICAL SITES IN
MICHIGAN

The numerals indicate the number of prehistoric remains in each county. After
Dr. W. B. Hinsdale, *Primitive Man in Michigan*.

mica, shells, pipes and pottery." The location of these mounds
appears to have been thirty or forty miles west of Grand
Rapids, near the shore of Lake Michigan.

The second manifestation of the Hopewell in Michigan is,
strangely enough, on the other side of the peninsula, about
seventy miles southwest of Detroit, at Tecumseh, Lenawee
County. Here until about 1850 there was a conjoined square
and circular enclosure on the north bank of the Raisin River.

The height of the walls was said to be about four feet. Nothing is known of this typically Hopewell geometric earthwork beyond two well-authenticated but lamentably brief records. There are also reports of circular enclosures in Macomb County with mounds opposite the entrances, but all traces of them have disappeared.

Surface finds consisting of potsherds with the characteristic Iroquois "collar" and the chevron design indicate the prehistoric presence of representatives of that powerful stock in Oakland, St. Clair, and Macomb counties, all in the vicinity of the Detroit River. Since it is believed that the Iroquois entered Lower Canada and New York from the west, it is conjectured that these rather scanty remains may have been left during their passage through Lower Michigan and across the Detroit River. A typically Iroquoian elbow pipe found near Mackinaw City probably belonged to a member of one of the Iroquois raiding parties which occasionally visited the region about the Straits in pursuit of the expatriated Hurons in early historic times.

There were formerly upwards of half a hundred enclosures in the Lower Peninsula, only ten of which, so far as is known, have survived destruction by the plow. These roughly circular earthworks, varying in diameter from 67 to 800 feet, centered in point of numbers in the southwestern portion of the peninsula, where the hardwood forest gave way to numerous prairies, some of which attain the extent of a township. All but one of the surviving ten are in the "pine barrens" north of Saginaw Bay, and the large quantities of pottery fragments found in eight of these bear the unmistakable signs of Algonquian origin—the cord, thumb-nail, punch, and other characteristic marks. Hopewell, Iroquoian, and Siouan features are entirely lacking. The remaining existing enclosure may have been an Iroquois fortification, since it is situated at the edge of a bluff, strengthening a site already well fortified by nature, some sixteen miles from the shore of Lake Huron in Alcona County. A small unnotched arrowpoint of the so-called "Iroquois war-point" type was found on the surface at one of its

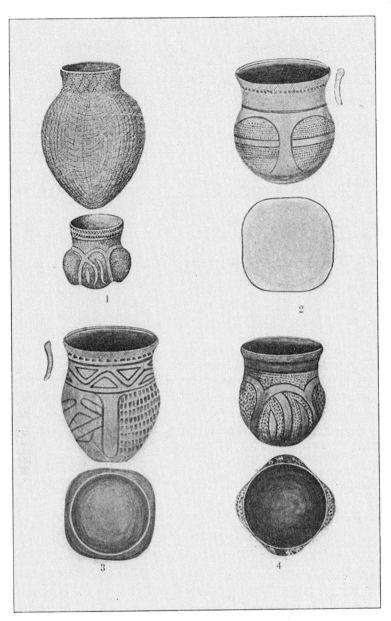

FIG. 183.   POTTERY VESSELS SHOWING HOPEWELL INFLUENCE, FROM
MOUNDS NEAR GRAND RAPIDS, MICHIGAN
After Hinsdale. Scale, 1/4.

gates. Beyond the Algonquian character of their pottery, all that is known of the builders of the enclosures is that they inhumed their dead in small mounds, used the marine shell *Busycon perversum L.,* and purposely avoided the shores of the Great Lakes as well as those of the thousands of inland lakes that abound in that region. Of this last there is small doubt, for but one of the original forty or fifty occupied a lake-shore position, at the mouth of the Clinton River on the shore of Lake St. Clair. The others, including seven of those now in existence, were located along the shores of rivers and creeks or near some more limited water supply, occasionally in groups of from two to four, and very rarely in a position for defense.

Two well-preserved enclosures, along with a considerable tract of land surrounding them, have been set aside by the Museum of Anthropology of the University of Michigan in Missaukee County, about halfway between Lakes Missaukee and Houghton. Another group of four may be seen along the Rifle River near the village of Selkirk in Ogemaw County.

Of the original five or six hundred small mounds of the peninsula, but few remain. One has been preserved in Bronson Park, Kalamazoo, and one in Fort Wayne Park, Detroit. Three mounds accompany the two enclosures in Missaukee County, and there is a fine group of seven in Montmorency County, near Lewiston on the shore of West Twin Lake. As to the identity of the builders of these mounds, the marine-shell containers and the copper implements and ornaments accompanying cremation seems to indicate Hopewell influence, while such pottery as is found is proto-Algonquian in type.

So-called "garden beds," a unique feature of American archæology, centered, in point of numbers like the enclosures, in the southwestern part of the peninsula, mainly in Berrien, Cass, Kalamazoo, and Allegan counties, occurring also in northern Indiana. Nothing now remains of these interesting earthworks, which were low ridges of earth, not more than 18 inches in height, covering areas varying in extent from one to a hundred acres and laid out in both angular and circular designs resembling formal gardens of rather bizarre appearance. Among the most intricate of the patterns were the wheel, with spokes and hub, and the checkerboard, each alternate

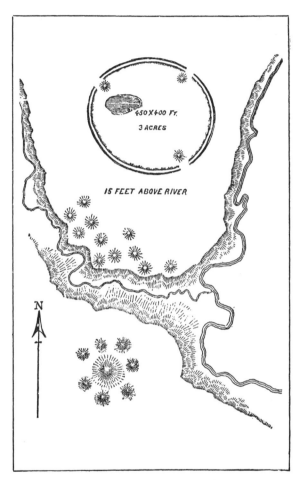

FIG. 184.   MOUNDS AND EARTHWORK ON CLINTON RIVER, MACOMB
COUNTY, MICHIGAN
After Hubbard. These remains have now disappeared.

square crossed by beds at right angles to one another. The agricultural Potawatomie, whose traditional home in Michigan was south of the Grand River, may have been the builders of the garden beds, as well as of the enclosures and some of the mounds, since these three types of earthwork are found

FIG. 185. PATTERNS OF PREHISTORIC GARDEN BEDS NEAR KALAMAZOO, MICHIGAN

After Hinsdale. Scale, 1 inch = 64 feet.

in greatest numbers in this part of the state. In connection with the garden beds it is interesting to note that this geometricity should be found so close to the Hopewell mounds at

Grand Rapids, but indications of a common origin are entirely lacking.

So far as is known, there are no mounds or enclosures north of the Straits of Mackinac, although future investigation may show an extension of some of the distinctive mound cultures of Wisconsin into the western end of the Northern Peninsula. History records the presence of the Huron about St. Ignace in the Seventeenth Century, and Hennepin's description of their stronghold on "a rising ground on a neck of land over against Michilimackinac" probably refers to a bluff near the shore in St. Ignace where very little effort is necessary to find a glass bead or other article of European manufacture held in esteem by the Indians. The open village sites of the Northern Peninsula, like those along the shores of the northern part of the Lower Peninsula, may be safely attributed to the Chippewa and the Ottawa.

Keweenaw Peninsula and Isle Royal in Lake Superior are famous for the mining pits from which the aborigines obtained the copper found in mounds and on the surface over the greater part of the eastern United States, to which reference has already been made in Chapter III. At what is known as Mc-Cargole's Cove, on Isle Royal, upwards of a square mile of the copper-bearing terrain was exhaustively worked over, as is evidenced by the numerous connecting pits left by the aboriginal miners. Numerous stone sledges and mauls, together with other implements used in the mining operations, have been found at this and adjacent sites. The fact that these ancient mines were exploited well up toward historic times is attested by the occasional finding of wooden implements and other objects made of perishable materials.

THE PROVINCE OF ONTARIO

Physical geography, rather than political, being the determining factor in the distribution of prehistoric peoples, it transpires that the International Boundary separating the United States and the Dominion of Canada is nonexistent so far as the science of archæology is concerned. That portion of the Province of Ontario which trends southward between Lakes Ontario and Erie and Lake Huron is a reversed counterpart of the Lower Peninsula of Michigan, with which, and the State of New York, it shares the same geographical latitude and becomes integrated into the Great Lakes archæological area. Historically it is a part of the Huron-Iroquois region, being the home of the Hurons and others of the Iroquoian stock whose country, sometimes called "Huronia," centered about Georgian Bay and Lake Simcoe.

The mounds, enclosures, and minor occupational evidences of the Ontario peninsula are essentially similar to those of New York State and apparently attributable to the same or related peoples. Explorations of mounds and descriptions of the numerous and interesting artifacts found in the old village sites and on the surface throughout the province have been recorded in the official Archæological Reports of Ontario, in the publications of the Canadian Institute, Toronto, and by individual writers and investigators.

The mound locations are shown on the accompanying map of mound distribution, especially prepared for this volume by Dr. W. J. Wintemberg, archæologist of the National Museum of Canada, Ottawa. A few scattering mounds occur farther east and north, in Quebec, and still others to the westward, contiguous to the Minnesota border. Further exploration doubtless will disclose additional mounds and earthworks adjacent to Lakes Huron and Superior.

A number of mounds are situated in the extreme western part of Ontario, along the International Boundary adjacent to Rainy Lake and the river of the same name. According to Winchell, in his *Aborigines of Minnesota,* and the Rev. George Bryce, in *The Mound-builders,* there are a total of twenty-one mounds extending along Rainy River, two of which are on the Minnesota side. One of the largest of the Rainy River mounds was explored by Bryce, and found to contain many implements and ornaments of copper, shell, flint, and stone. A number of other mounds exist in the same general locality, adjacent to the Lake of the Woods, and in Manitoba, all of which have their affinities with the mounds of northern Minnesota. The identity of their builders has not been determined.

Three mounds located on Pelee Island, in Lake Erie, were explored in 1899 by the Provincial Museum, Toronto, with interesting results. In that part of Ontario projecting eastward between Lakes Erie and Ontario and extending to the Niagara River there are numerous mounds, the most important

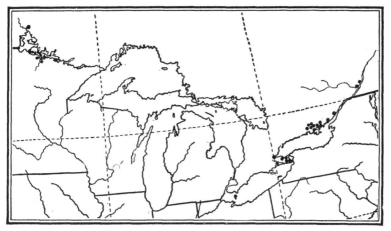

FIG. 186. MAP OF MOUND DISTRIBUTION IN SOUTHERN AND WESTERN
ONTARIO

Showing locations of mound groups adjacent to Lakes Ontario and Erie and on Rainy River. Courtesy of W. J. Wintemberg.

of which is a group of five near the village of Cayuga, Haldimand County. Others in this region are: a mound on Yellow Point, Lincoln County; two mounds formerly in the city of Hamilton; mounds on Rice Lake, Peterboro County; and others near Niagara-on-the-Lake, at Queenston, and at Niagara Falls.

The most important and extensive local area of mounds in the province is located on the north shore of Lake Ontario, mainly in Prince Edward County. A total of a hundred or more mounds are reported to have existed originally within a distance of eight miles, from Rednersville to Massassauga

Point. Not more than ten or twelve of these survive at the present time. They are low, truncated, cone-shaped tumuli, arranged mostly in pairs of approximately equal size. One of the group was found to contain skeletons and relics, the latter suggesting Iroquoian origin. Other mounds in this general locality are: mounds and burials on Presque Isle Point, near Brighton, and on the Lake shore just west of the Point; two mounds on Skull Point, in Addington County; a mound on the south side of Wolfe Island, near Kingston; and mounds on Tidd Island, in the St. Lawrence, opposite Gananoque, in Leeds County.

CHAPTER XIV

THE UPPER MISSISSIPPI AREA: I, WISCONSIN, MINNESOTA, AND THE DAKOTAS

Mound-builder cultures of Wisconsin—The effigy-mound culture—The Grand River culture—The Cahokia culture at Aztalan—The Hopewell culture in Wisconsin—Minor remains in Wisconsin—Wisconsin archæology—The State of Minnesota—The State of North Dakota—The State of South Dakota.

THE important and extensive area here designated as the Upper Mississippi corresponds to the region of the Missouri and upper Mississippi valleys and embraces the states of Wisconsin, Minnesota, North and South Dakota, northern Illinois, Iowa, and portions of Missouri, Kansas, and Nebraska. Some authorities choose to subdivide the general Mississippi area into Upper, Middle, and Lower Mississippi, while the first of these, combined with the Missouri region, is sometimes referred to as the Dakotan or Northwestern area. Such subdivision of the area is fully justified and might be carried much farther in a treatment of the subject detailed enough to call for close classification. The rather sparse evidences of the Missouri valley in mounds and earthworks might readily be classed separately, but for our purpose the classification here adopted appears to be the most practical.

None of the other divisions of the general mound area is more striking or more important than the Upper Mississippi from the standpoint either of numbers or of impressiveness of the mounds and other major works. While the effigy-mound culture of southern Wisconsin and adjacent portions of Minnesota, Iowa, and Illinois is the dominant and most obvious of the several cultures of the region, it is by no means the only one of importance. The State of Iowa and northern Illinois present distinctive cultures and important remains, and there are minor developments in the remainder of the area.

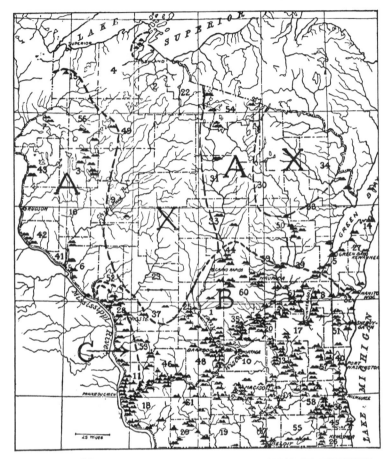

FIG. 187. MAP OF MOUND-BUILDER CULTURE AREAS IN WISCONSIN

The map proper, prepared by Charles E. Brown for the Wisconsin Archæological Society, shows the distribution rather than individual occurrences of
mounds, of which there are several thousand in the state. The culture-area outlines, indicated for the author by William C. McKern of the Milwaukee Public
Museum, are tentative and subject to revision. The areas marked *A* are characterized by unclassified conical mounds; the effigy Mound area is indicated by *B*;
the Hopewell district, overlapping the Effigy area, is indicated by *C*; while in the
regions marked *X* no mounds or earthworks have been reported. Within a small
circular area just below and to the right of the letter *B* occurs the Grand River
culture.

MOUND-BUILDER CULTURES OF WISCONSIN

Wisconsin, with its vast number of mounds—effigy, linear,
and conical, is paramount in popular interest and of pronounced scientific importance. The tumuli of all classes have

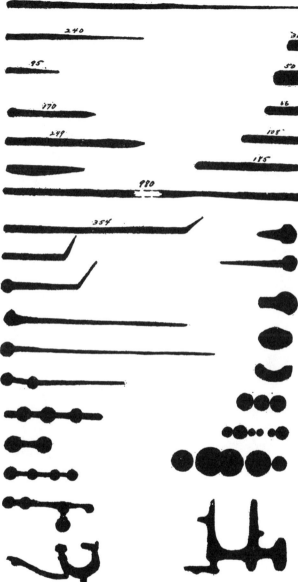

FIG. 188. VARIOUS TYPES OF WISCONSIN MOUNDS

Linear mounds, conical mounds in chains, conical and linear combinations, and composite mounds, occurring in connection with the effigy-mound groups of Wisconsin. The numbers indicate length in feet. From Lapham's *Antiquities of Wisconsin* and surveys by A. B. Stout of mounds in Sauk County and the Koshkonong area.

293

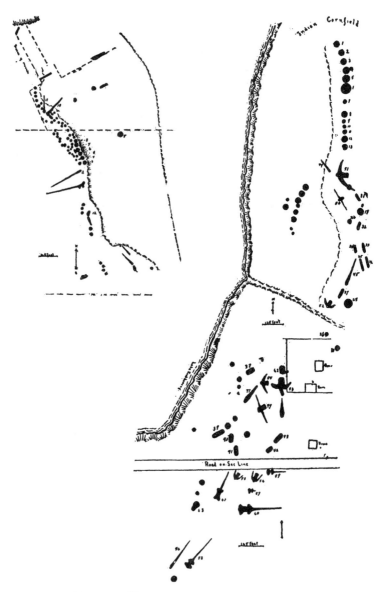

FIG. 189. TYPICAL WISCONSIN MOUND GROUPS

Two striking groups of effigy, conical, and linear mounds, located at Lake Koshkonong, Wisconsin. The works at the left are known as the Koshkonong Group, and those to the right as the Atkinson Group. From surveys by A. B. Stout and H. L. Skarlem, in the *Wisconsin Archæologist.*

been estimated to number between ten and fifteen thousand, probably more than are contained in any other equal area of the mound region. Four distinct cultures have been identified in the state, namely, the effigy-mound culture, the Grand River, the Hopewell, and, in a single important development, the great Cahokia culture of the Lower Mississippi area. The mounds of the state comprise the effigy forms, conical or semi-spherical mounds, linear or wall-like mounds, and mounds of the platform type. But few earthworks or enclosures exist, and with one or two exceptions they are not important. The approximate distribution of cultures in the state is shown on the accompanying map (Figure 187).

THE EFFIGY-MOUND CULTURE

The effigy-mound culture centers in Wisconsin, particularly in the southern half of the state, and extends into contiguous southeastern Minnesota, northeastern Iowa, and northern Illinois. The effigy mounds are constructed in the forms of animals, as bear, deer, panther, wolf, fox, buffalo, and turtle; and also in the images of birds, such as eagles, swallows, and geese. Two or three examples represent the human form; in others the intent of the builder is problematical. Most of the animal effigies are represented in profile, but a few definite forms are depicted as though viewed from above, with the legs laterally extended on either side of the body. In most instances, excepting where unusual preservative conditions existed, the effigy mounds are not so clear-cut in form as might be expected. The erosion of the centuries and the cultivation of the soil have seriously blurred their original comparatively sharp outlines, with the result that many of them are difficult definitely to identify.

The effigy mounds vary greatly in size, and they occur mainly in groups together with conical and linear mounds, the latter forms being attributable to the same builders. The conical mounds range from a foot to 25 feet in height and from 10 feet to 100 feet in diameter. Linear mounds are as a

rule of less height than the conicals but often attain lengths
of several hundred feet. Conical mounds sometimes occur in
chainlike succession, with edges overlapping, or connected by
intervening linear forms.

While the mounds of effigy forms supposedly are attributable
to ceremonial or totemic ideas, they also contain burials, in
approximately the same proportions as do the conical and the

Fig. 190. Bundle burials in a mound of the Kratz Creek group,
Wisconsin

Burials in this conical mound, explored by the Milwaukee Public Museum,
were of the bundle-burial or reburial type, which is characteristic of the effigy-
mound culture to which the group belongs. Courtesy of the Milwaukee Public
Museum.

linear mounds. These burials may be either normal interments of bodies in the flesh; bundle burials, representing the
bundled bones of from one to thirty or more individuals; or
charred skeletal remains, sometimes deposited on altarlike
platforms of stone. An interesting feature of these burials is
that they usually occupy definite places with respect to the
anatomy of the effigy—centrally within the head, midway be-

tween the shoulder and hip, in the position of the heart, or, in bird effigies, centrally between head and tail. In the conical mounds burials usually are placed at the center, but in the elongated wall-like linear mounds they may occur at any point.

The depositing of artifacts with the dead was not markedly a trait of the builders of the effigy mounds, but sufficient have been found with burials and in the adjacent sites to show the

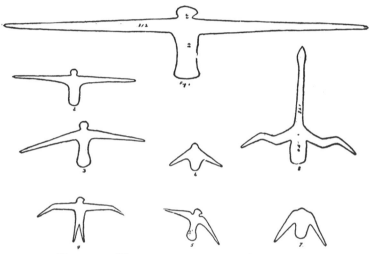

FIG. 191. WISCONSIN BIRD EFFIGY MOUNDS

No. 1 is the largest bird effigy known; it is located near Madison; 2, located in Sauk County, measures 212 feet across the wings; 3, on the grounds of the Sacred Heart Academy, Madison, has a wing spread of 218 feet; 4, with forked tail, is at Devil's Lake (from a survey by W. H. Canfield); 5, Sauk County; 6 and 7, situated at Lake Koshkonong; 8, a rare goose effigy, at Merrill Springs, near Madison.

character of their material culture. Simple forms of pottery vessels, without handles or feet and with cord-imprint decorations, occur, as do chipped stone and bone implements, occasional copper implements, stone axes and celts, and tobacco pipes of potteryware.

Fine examples of effigy mounds are found throughout the southern third of Wisconsin, particularly in Dane and adjacent counties. Several striking groups are situated within or close to Madison, the capital of the state, among them a mound representing the wild goose located on the Black Hawk Country Club grounds. At least six examples of the rare goose mounds existed adjacent to the five lakes of the locality. Other interesting mounds of the city and county are a fine group located on the University of Wisconsin grounds; a bear effigy on West Washington Street; important groups in Vilas Park, Edgewood Academy grounds, and Forest Hill Cemetery; mounds at Morris Park and at Farwell Point; and at Mendota the largest bird effigy mound in the state, with a height of six feet and a wing spread of 624 feet (Figure 191).

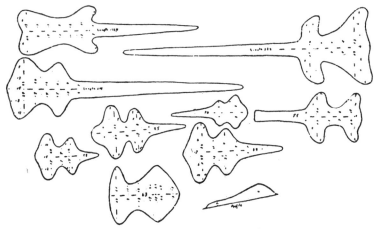

FIG. 192.   WISCONSIN "TURTLE" MOUNDS

These effigies, supposed to represent turtles, are situated at Lake Koshkonong. After A. B. Stout.

Of infrequent occurrence and decided interest are the so-called "man" mounds, one of which is preserved by the Wisconsin Archæological Society near Baraboo, Sauk County (Figure 194). A second mound in the human form originally existed near La Valle, in the same county. A fine group consisting of two bear effigies and a number of conical and linear mounds is located near Darlington, Lafayette County. One of the most prolific districts of the effigy-mound area is Waukesha County. At Pishtaka is situated one of the finest groups of the state, in which are represented the panther, the turtle, and birds. At Oconomowoc, on the Boy Scout reservation, is a striking effigy of the turtle; at Summit Center is the Pabst mound group; and at Waukesha there are groups of mounds in Cutler Park and on Carroll College campus.

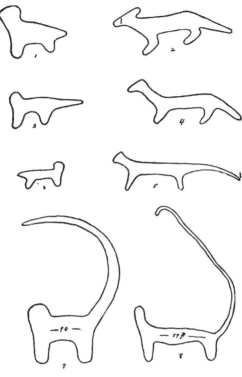

FIG. 193. WISCONSIN ANIMAL EFFIGY MOUNDS

No. 1, Devil's Lake, Sauk County, length 70 feet (from a survey by A. B. Stout) ; 2, east end of Lake Mendota, near Madison; length 166 feet (from a survey by A. B. Stout) ; 3, near Madison, length 102 feet (after A. B. Stout) ; 4, at Mayville (from Lapham's survey) ; 5, located near the city of Milwaukee (Lapham's survey) ; 6, at Baraboo, Sauk County (after A. B. Stout) ; 7, Lake Mendota, near Madison (after Stout) ; 8, Sauk County, near the Wisconsin River (from *Antiquities of Wisconsin*).

In Trempealeau County near the town of that name several mound groups are preserved, one of which is in Perrot State Park. At La Crosse, in La Crosse County, there is a group in Myrick Park; at Cassville, Grant County, a bird effigy in Riverside Park; at Devils Lake, Sauk County, a group of mounds and a bird effigy; at Lake Emily, Portage County, a group of mounds; and at Clam Lake, Waupaca County, an effigy mound. There is an interesting group on Buffalo Lake, in Marquette County, and several groups in Green Lake County, adjacent to Green Lake. At Beloit, in

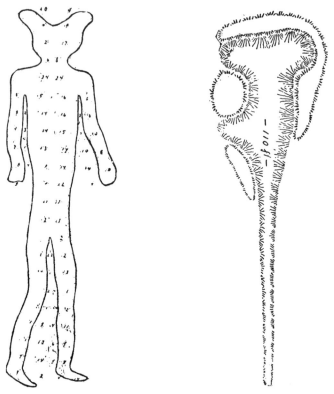

FIG. 194. RARE "MAN" AND INTAGLIO FORMS OF EFFIGY MOUNDS

Located near Baraboo, Sauk County, Wisconsin; from a survey by W. H. Canfield, 1859. The intaglio effigy is located at Fort Atkinson, Jefferson County; from a survey by C. E. Brown and A. B. Stout, 1910.

Rock County, there are interesting groups on the Beloit College campus and on the Beloit Country Club grounds. At Menasha, Winnebago County, there is a group of mounds; several groups in Sheboygan County, near Sheboygan; groups near Fox Lake and Burnett, in Dodge County; an intaglio effigy at Fort Atkinson and mound groups on Lake Kosh-

FIG. 195. A GRAND RIVER CULTURE BURIAL

A burial in a mound of the Grand River Group, Green Lake County, Wisconsin, explored by the Milwaukee Public Museum. The pottery vessel is typical of this culture. Courtesy of the Milwaukee Public Museum.

konong and Rock Lake, Jefferson County. In Milwaukee County there is a mound in Lake Park, and another in the State Fair Park at West Allis, both of which are preserved. At Racine, in Racine County, a group of mounds has given its name to the local cemetery. The Kratz Creek Group, explored and reported by Barrett and Hawkes for the Milwaukee Public Museum, and the Neale and McClaughry groups, examined by W. C. McKern for the same institution, are representative of the effigy-mound culture.

THE GRAND RIVER CULTURE

The Grand River culture is represented by a single group of mounds, located on the border between Marquette and Green Lake counties, and by scattering vestiges in the eastern counties of the state. The mounds of the culture are conical

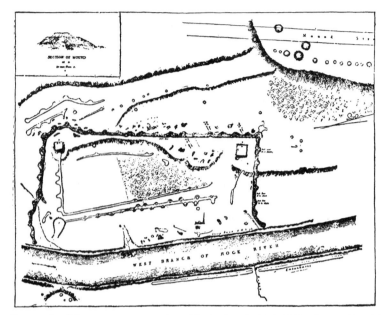

Fig. 196. Map of the Aztalan Ruins, Jefferson County, Wisconsin

A striking ruin of the Lower Mississippi Cahokia culture, the farthest northern penetration of the culture so far identified.

in type and are characterized by numerous scattered burials, often in the extended position. Pottery vessels, of globular form, either plain or decorated, occur freely with burials. An interesting feature is the occurrence of fish-shaped ornaments made of shell. Pottery of the culture has been found on camp sites in Sheboygan County and on Buffalo Lake, Marquette County.

THE CAHOKIA CULTURE AT AZTALAN

A single example of the culture represented by the great Cahokia Group of mounds at East St. Louis, Illinois, which pertains more intimately to the Lower Mississippi area, occurs in Wisconsin. What is known as the Aztalan ruins, or Aztalan Mound Park, is situated on the West Branch of the Rock River near Lake Mills, in Jefferson County. It is the most striking of the earthen walled enclosures of Wisconsin, of which there are, or have existed, some twenty examples. Aztalan, now greatly reduced through cultivation of the soil, is in the form of an irregular parallelogram, an earthen wall enclosing it on three sides and the West Branch of the Rock River constituting the fourth side. The total length of wall is approximately 2,750 feet, and the area enclosed a trifle less than 18 acres. Along the outer edge of the wall, which

FIG. 197. AN AZTALAN BURIAL

This burial was accompanied by large numbers of shell disk beads. An exhibit of the Milwaukee Public Museum.

varied from one to five feet in height, were bastionlike projections somewhat resembling conical mounds. Within the enclosure there were three flat-topped pyramidal mounds with graded approaches, one of them with terraced sides. The largest of these was originally 15 feet in height, with a level top of 53 feet square. A number of circular hut rings were a feature of the interior of the enclosure.

Aztalan has figured prominently in archæological literature

and has been minutely described by such prominent Wisconsin archæologists as Lapham, Peet, West, and others. It has recently been explored by Dr. S. A. Barrett for the Milwaukee Public Museum, whose report is pending. The Cahokia culture to which Aztalan belongs is characterized by abundant and distinctive pottery, often surfaced with a reddish slip, commonly decorated about the neck with broadly incised scrolls, and with a wide range of forms; disk-shaped shell beads and pendants made from conch shells; mussel-shell spoons; ear spools of stone and pottery, sometimes covered with copper foil; occasional copper ornaments; polished bone needles; and triangular arrowpoints. The mounds of the culture, of both the platform and the conical types, are abnormally barren of burials or other included contents. Some of the earthen enclosures accompanying the mounds are found upon examination to have been surmounted by palisades. Less important examples of Cahokia culture remains are noted throughout northern Illinois. We shall encounter typical stations of the culture in Chapter XVI.

THE HOPEWELL CULTURE IN WISCONSIN

The highly developed Hopewell culture centering in southern Ohio is surprisingly well represented in Wisconsin, as recent exploration and the renewed interest resulting therefrom have shown. In his report on the mound explorations conducted by the Bureau of American Ethnology, Dr. Cyrus Thomas described the examination of several tumuli in Crawford and Vernon counties which are now recognized as having close affinities with the typical Hopewell. One of these, known as the Flucke Group, situated near the town of Prairie du Chien, comprised twelve conical mounds, in one of which were found obsidian spears and copper ornaments of Hopewell type. In the Sou Coulee Group of eighteen fine mounds, adjacent to the Mississippi River in Crawford County, there were found copper breastplates and axes and obsidian implements; and similar objects, together with typical Hopewell

FIG. 198. A MOUND OF THE NICHOLLS GROUP, WISCONSIN

This mound, situated in Trempealeau County, near the Mississippi River, recently was examined by William C. McKern, of the Milwaukee Public Museum, and yielded evidences indicating that it belongs to the Hopewell culture. Courtesy of the Milwaukee Public Museum.

pottery, were taken from one of the twenty-two mounds comprising White's Group, in northwestern Vernon County.

Recently, in examining for the Milwaukee Public Museum what is known as the Nicholls Mound, the central tumulus of a group of several located on the bank of the Mississippi River in Trempealeau County, Professor William C. McKern has added an important contribution to the Hopewell evidence in the state. In a shallow burial pit dug into the floor of the structure, at center, there were disclosed the skeletal remains of seven individuals. With the burials were found copper celts or axe blades, copper breastplates, ear ornaments of wood covered with silver foil, chalcedony spears or knives of exceptionally large size, pearl beads, and woven fabric, the latter preserved by the copper. Above the burials in the body of the mound were found large lancepoints of obsidian, quartzite, and chert, a curved-base platform pipe, and copper beads. In smaller adjacent mounds there were found similar specimens, together with a pottery vessel of Hopewell type, copper ear spools, and perforated bear canine teeth. Evidences of Hope-

FIG. 199.   UNCOVERING A HOPEWELL BURIAL IN THE NICHOLLS MOUND
Courtesy of the Milwaukee Public Museum.

well occupancy, to be noted presently, occur also in north-eastern Iowa and western Illinois.

MINOR REMAINS IN WISCONSIN

Two other classes of prehistoric remains are found in con-nection with the effigy-mound groups of Wisconsin, the so-called "cornfields" and "garden beds" already described in Chapter III. Of decided importance but of less popular inter-est are the village sites often accompanying the mound groups. The cornfields range from patches one acre or less in extent to occasional ones of 40 or even 50 acres. They consist of series or rows of dome-shaped piles or hills of earth, a foot or more in height and three or four feet apart, the result of the continued heaping up of the soil in agriculture. In some in-stances, as in the Lake Winnebago district, the stones scattered over the surface had been carefully gathered and piled into rows and heaps to facilitate the making of the hills and the cultivation of corn and perhaps other crops. The garden beds are similar, except that the elevations are in the form of parallel ridges. They range from small patches to a length of

100 feet or more. The ridges, separated by paths, are from three to five or six feet in width. Garden beds occur principally in the eastern part of the state, between Green Bay and Racine, and mostly have been obliterated by cultivation of the land.

In the northerly districts of Wisconsin there occur many conical mounds the identity of which has not been determined. Although formerly the finding of articles of white man's manufacture in Wisconsin mounds was held to indicate comparatively recent origin, authorities on the area are now mostly inclined to believe that these are in the nature of intrusive deposits by historic Indians and that the mounds, with their original burials, are locally prehistoric. Indications point to the probability that some of the tumuli were erected by peoples of Siouan stock, but this has not been definitely proven. It is of interest to note in this connection that the Winnebago have a tradition that their ancestors possessed the trait of building mounds.

WISCONSIN ARCHÆOLOGY

The outstanding early contribution to Wisconsin archæology is the classic *The Antiquities of Wisconsin,* by the pioneer archæologist Dr. Increase A. Lapham, whose activities in prehistoric research covered the long period from 1836 until his death in 1875. This monumental work was published in 1855 as Volume VII of the Smithsonian Contributions. Other early contributors were Dr. John R. Locke, Richard and Stephen Taylor, Dr. P. R. Hoy, William H. Canfield, Moses Strong, Jr., and W. P. Clark. Following these early investigators notable contributions were made by Professor T. H. Lewis, Thomas Armstrong, Rev. Stephen D. Peet, J. D. Middleton, and Dr. Cyrus Thomas.

One of the most progressive and fruitful agencies in the entire mound area for the preservation and investigation of American archæology is the Wisconsin Archæological Society, organized in 1901. Throughout the period of its existence this organization has been indefatigable in conserving the archæological heritage of the state. In addition to the preservation and marking of archæological sites, the Society has established a number of local museums, has effected an archæological survey of the state, and has in preparation an archæological atlas. Investigations conducted by the Society have made the archæology of Wisconsin well known and have served as an inspiration to more backward states. Much of this commendable activity is due to the energy of the Society's present secretary, Charles E. Brown, who has served in this capacity for thirty years.

The more important museums of the state are the Wisconsin State Historical Museum, the Milwaukee Public Museum, the Oshkosh Public Museum, the Logan Museum, and the Green Bay Museum, in all of which may be found Wisconsin archæological material.

THE STATE OF MINNESOTA

The principal mound region of Minnesota corresponds to the southeastern corner of the state, along the lower course of the Minnesota River and adjacent to the Mississippi. A considerable development of major tumuli occurs along the Minnesota valley southwest of the twin cities of St. Paul and Minneapolis and throughout the entire eastern portion of the state from Lake Superior southward. The Lake region of the north-central portion presents interesting remains, the section lying north of Lake Superior alone of the entire state being practically devoid of major works.

Minnesota is one of the half-dozen states in the general mound area that boast pretentious volumes devoted to descriptions of their prehistoric remains. *The Aborigines of Minnesota* by N. H. Winchell, published by the Minnesota Historical Society in 1911, is a massive tome dedicated to the aborigines and aboriginal remains of the state. It is based on the extensive early collections of Jacob V. Brower and on the field surveys and notes of Alfred J. Hill and Theodore H. Lewis. More than seven hundred pages of text are occupied by descrip-

tions of the prehistoric and historic natives of Minnesota and
their mounds, earthworks, and minor relics. The surprising
abundance of prehistoric earthen remains is reflected by the
fact that the volume carries maps and drawings of more than
six hundred groups of mounds and earthworks, totaling in
the aggregate thousands of individual remains. Very little in
the way of scientific exploration has been done, however, and
hence no systematic presentation of the cultures represented in
the state is possible. Definitely recognizable, however, are the
effigy-mound culture remains of southeastern Minnesota, ad-

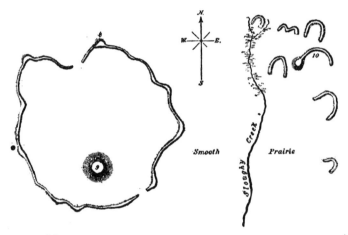

Fig. 200. Map of a group of mounds and earthworks in Pipestone
County, Minnesota

The large enclosure is more than 2,000 feet in circumference. After Thomas.

jacent to the Wisconsin region. Many of the tumuli of the
state are believed to be attributable to the Dakota and other
Siouan Indian tribes of the area.

In the southeastern counties of Minnesota, adjacent to the
Minnesota, the Mississippi, and the St. Croix rivers, there
are numerous interesting groups of the effigy-mound culture,
comprising conical, elongate, and occasional effigy forms, as
in Wisconsin. Near La Crescent, in Houston County, there
is an extensive group originally comprising upward of one
hundred mounds, mostly conical in form. A few elongate

mounds appear in this group, together with three effigy forms, two of the latter representing birds and the third being in the form of a frog. South of the La Crescent group, on Pine Creek, there is a group of twenty-two mounds, of which four are effigies of birds. What is known as the Lone Bird Effigy Mound is located near Richmond, in Winona County.

Wabasha County, bordering the Mississippi River, is one of the richest sections of the entire state in earthen remains. Numerous groups, comprising hundreds of mounds, occur in the Zumbro valley, near Lake City and in the vicinity of Wabasha. Here, as elsewhere in the effigy region, low conical mounds predominate, with elongate forms fairly in evidence, and effigies less frequent. In Goodhue County, adjoining Wabasha on the west, the so-called Prairie Island mounds comprise several large groups, totaling more than two hundred tumuli. Other groups of equal importance occur on Cannon River and Spring Creek. In one of the latter groups there are two effigy forms believed to represent serpents. In Dakota County a group formerly occupied the site of Mendota, while another group is still situated near the town. The Prior Lake Group, in Scott County, comprises four laterals and five effigies of flying birds.

Hennepin and Ramsey counties, in which respectively are located Minneapolis and St. Paul, are very rich in prehistoric remains. In the former the region surrounding Lake Minnetonka is literally dotted with mounds and groups of mounds, comprising conical, elongate, and problematical forms. No fewer than seventy-five distinct groups of Hennepin County, large and small, are mapped and described by Winchell. In Ramsey County interesting groups formerly were located in West St. Paul and in the Suburban Hills Addition to the city. A third group was located at Dayton's Bluff.

Other interesting groups of the state are those known as the Spencer Brook Group, in Isanti County; the Itasca enclosure, in Anoka County; a group of sixty-five mounds on lower Crow Wing River, in Aitkin County, comprising conical, elongate, and effigy forms; and the many groups in Mille Lacs

County, where more than eleven hundred individual mounds have been identified.

A noted archæological feature of the Minnesota region is the sacred pipestone quarry near the town of Pipestone, in Pipestone County, in the southwestern corner of the state. Here occurs the well-known deposit of pipestone, or catlinite, so highly prized by the historic Indians and their prehistoric predecessors for making tobacco pipes. The stone is grayish-red to dark red in color, and when freshly quarried it can be readily cut and drilled with stone or metal tools. Indians of the present time, particularly the Sioux, continue to quarry and use the catlinite, and the finding at the site of stone mauls and other quarrying implements shows that it was in use in prehistoric times. George Catlin, the noted traveler and painter of Indians, who first called attention to the sacred pipestone quarry and for whom the mineral was named, describes in his *North American Indians* a group of ten mounds and a circular enclosure adjacent to the quarry.

In Minnesota, as elsewhere in the mound area, many tumuli have been obliterated through cultivation. The mounds of the region as a rule are neither large nor particularly striking; but many of them are of decided interest, and the tourist will find them an added attraction to this romantic land of the Dakotahs, with its many lakes and its scenic beauties.

THE STATE OF NORTH DAKOTA

Mounds and other major evidences of prehistoric habitation are not abundant in North Dakota. The principal districts in which tumuli occur are the valley of the Souris River in the northwestern part of the state and extending across the International Boundary into Manitoba; the vicinity of Devil's Lake; and adjacent to the Red River northward to Lake Winnipeg. The Souris River mounds comprise both conical tumuli and elongate or wall-like mounds, the latter sometimes having expanded ends. They are comparatively low embankments, measuring from one to two or more feet in

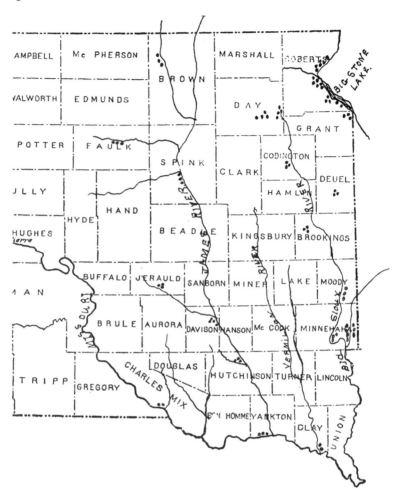

FIG. 201. MAP OF MOUND DISTRIBUTION IN EASTERN SOUTH DAKOTA
Prepared by W. H. Over.

height and from 100 to 300 feet in length. The conical mounds, mostly of small size, occur in conjunction with the elongate mounds. They are most abundant across the boundary line in Manitoba, but they occur in considerable numbers in Benson, Ramsey, and Walsh counties of North Dakota. Tubular pipes of catlinite, potteryware, flint arrowpoints and other articles, are found with the skeletal remains within the tumuli.

FIG. 202. BURIAL IN A MOUND IN YANKTON COUNTY, SOUTH DAKOTA

Showing a reburial of sixteen skeletons. Explored by W. H. Over for the University of South Dakota.

The mounds of the Red River valley are few in number and occur singly rather than in groups. In form they are conical and in size mostly small. Those explored have yielded simple burials with occasional artifacts indicating a rather low type of culture. Numerous house sites, in the form of basin-shaped depressions, together with camp and village sites, presumably of Siouan origin, occur along the Missouri River throughout the state.

THE STATE OF SOUTH DAKOTA

The mounds of South Dakota are confined to the eastern third of the state and are most in evidence along the Big Sioux River and adjacent to Big Stone Lake. Two groups, totaling more than fifty mounds, are situated in eastern Minnehaha County, above Sioux Falls. An even greater number are comprised in the group at Big Stone Lake, in Roberts County.

Exploration of the mounds of eastern South Dakota by Professor W. H. Over for the University of South Dakota has yielded numerous burials and accompanying artifacts. Two modes of burial are in evidence, burial in the flesh and bundle or reburial. In both types of burial the remains were deposited in shallow pits and the mounds erected over them. The burial pits were usually lined with bark, and often they were of a communal nature, accommodating numerous skeletons. Both types of burial also occur within the body proper of the mounds.

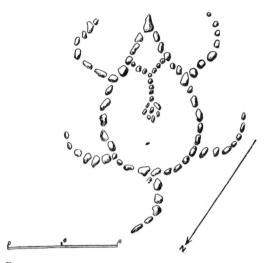

FIG. 203. BOULDER EFFIGY OF TURTLE, HUGHES COUNTY, SOUTH DAKOTA
The length of the effigy is 15 feet.

Crude potteryware, tempered with crushed or burned granite, is found in connection with the mounds. Large clay pipes and beads made from columella of marine shells and from freshwater clams are found with burials. The most characteristic implements of the region are large, rude stone axes and grooved stone mauls.

Numerous boulder circles and rings occur on the village sites and in connection with the mounds of the Sioux River district. They consist of circular or oval lines of granite boulders, partly imbedded in the soil, and are believed to represent lodge sites. A type of boulder circle or ring somewhat analogous to those of the Big Sioux district occurs along the Missouri

River in the interior of the state. These similarly are supposed to have served in connection with lodge sites, the boulders being employed as weights to hold down the skin coverings of the lodges. An interesting feature is the occurrence in connection with these of outline figures of animals, formed of boulders similar to those of the boulder circles. One of these, located at Medicine Butte, near Blunt, represents a serpent, while another, on Snake Butte, near the city of Pierre, is in the form of a turtle measuring fifteen feet in length by seven feet wide (Figure 203). Most of the boulder effigies

Fig. 204. The Hartford beach mound, Roberts County, South Dakota

Courtesy of W. H. Over.

of the region have now disappeared. They are supposed to be totemic in character or to have played a part in the religious concept of their builders.

Throughout the course of the Missouri River in both South and North Dakota there are numerous village sites, with hut rings, refuse heaps, and other evidences, supposedly attributable to the Arikara, the Mandans, and other Siouan Indian tribes. Artifacts from the mounds of South Dakota may be seen at the State University Museum at Vermilion. An archæological survey of the state is being prepared under the direction of Professor W. H. Over of the University of South Dakota.

CHAPTER XV

FEW archæological provinces of the general mound area are more interesting and important and at the same time less developed than that comprised within the State of Illinois. While the prehistoric remains of Wisconsin were accorded early attention by Lapham, those of Ohio by Squier and Davis, and the antiquities of New York State by Beauchamp and others, Illinois, with equally impressive and diversified remains, has lacked a champion of her archæological treasures.

ILLINOIS ARCHÆOLOGY

A limited amount of exploration was done in the late '70's by Dr. A. J. Patrick and Dr. J. F. Snyder, the latter publishing his observations in the Smithsonian Report for 1881. Rev. Stephen D. Peet, widely known through his interest in Wisconsin archæology, contributed casually to the literature on the Illinois region. A manuscript by W. B. Nickerson on the archæology of a portion of northwestern Illinois, which is perhaps the most exhaustive and careful study of a specific district, is in the possession of the Department of Anthropology of the University of Chicago. Until recently the most important general consideration of the region was that of Dr. Cyrus Thomas in his report on mound explorations published in the Twelfth Annual Report of the Bureau of American Ethnology. Numerous antiquities of the state were there described and figured, some of which had been subjected to examination. While these reports and descriptions leave much to be desired in the light of present-day archæological science, they are drawn on freely in this survey because of the scarcity of other sources of information.

It is gratifying to note, however, that the neglect which has characterized this important region is being replaced by archæological activity of a most satisfactory nature. Under the direction of Professor Fay-Cooper Cole, head of the Department of Anthropology of the University of Chicago, an archæological survey of the state, accompanied by systematic exploration, is being conducted, particularly in northern Illinois. In the central and southern portions of the state explorations have been carried on during the past several seasons by Professor Warren K. Moorehead for the University of Illinois, while Mr. George Langford, working independently, has examined an important site near Joliet. Professor Moorehead's work is particularly worthy of note. His report, recently off the press, deals exhaustively with the great Cahokia Group at East St. Louis and with minor groups and individual mounds of several cultures in adjacent territory.

MOUND-BUILDER CULTURES OF ILLINOIS

Upon rather incomplete archæological data, that portion of Illinois lying north of the 39th parallel is here assigned to the Upper Mississippi Mound-builder area. Although there are in the region evidences of the cultures characteristic of the area to the south, and even cultural manifestations confined wholly thereto, its affinities seem to be principally with the basic indicia of the assumed Upper Mississippi area. The remaining fourth of the state, from the latitude of the mouth of the Missouri southward, comprising the valleys of the Mississippi and the lower Wabash with their tributaries, may properly be considered as a part of the Lower Mississippi area.

No less than four, and possibly five, mound-building cultures, in addition to one or more not possessing the mound-building trait, have left their imprint in the soil of Illinois. The effigy-mound culture centering in southern Wisconsin extends southward into Illinois at least as far as Rock Island and Stark counties. Within the same belt but extending downward along the Illinois and Mississippi rivers, contiguous to a similar development in eastern Iowa, is the Hopewell culture, in evidence as far south as the mouth of the Illinois River. Bordering the Illinois River from the vicinity of Joliet to its mouth is what may be termed the Illinois culture, known locally as the "bluff" culture. The mound development along the Mississippi River in the west-central part of the state appears somewhat analogous to the Illinois culture but may prove to be distinctive and allied to that of northeastern Missouri. The district fronting on Lake Michigan presents some distinctive characteristics, and the extreme eastern section and contiguous portions of western Indiana, bordering the Wabash River, do not appear to conform entirely to any of the identified cultures of the state.

A somewhat puzzling phenomenon of certain sections of Illinois and of western Indiana is the persistence outside of the effigy-mound region proper, where it is to be expected, of tumuli in intentional lines or rows. This presumably indicates either the presence in these lateral regions of the effigy-mound culture peoples or the borrowing from them by contiguous tribesmen of this particular trait. The obviously intentional linear arrangement is to be distinguished from the persistent lines of the bluff mounds of the Illinois River, where topography was the determining factor in location.

THE EFFIGY-MOUND CULTURE IN ILLINOIS

The effigy-mound region of Illinois lies in a belt across the northern end of the state. The culture is quite salient and extensive, and although no great number of effigy tumuli occur, elongate and chain mounds and linear groups of small conical mounds are fairly abundant. Of the effigy structures, that representing a serpent, located near Galena, is interesting since the form is unusual in the effigy-mound region. Its occurrence suggests the Great Serpent Mound of Ohio and a possible affinity with the Ohio area; but since the culture responsible for the Ohio mound appears not to be present in Illinois, it seems that the Illinois serpent may be attributed to the effigy-mound culture. A few analogous forms occur in Minnesota.

One of the more interesting groups of the culture is that known as the Aiken Group, situated near the junction of Smallpox Creek and the Mississippi River in Jo Daviess County. This large group comprises twelve conical mounds, thirty-eight elongate tumuli, and an effigy representing a bird with outspread wings. The so-called Portage Group, three miles below Galena, comprises thirteen elongate mounds. Occupying the same ridge and separated from these by a ravine are twenty-six conical mounds presumably belonging to the same group, but as some evidences of the Hopewell culture were found in one of them by W. B. Nickerson in 1895, they may constitute a separate group of different origin.

THE HOPEWELL CULTURE IN ILLINOIS

An interesting development of the highly evolved Hopewell culture occurs in northern and western Illinois, adjacent to the Hopewell region of Iowa on the opposite side of the Mississippi River. Mounds of the culture were recognized in Cass and adjacent counties by Dr. J. F. Snyder as early as 1881 and were reported by him in the Smithsonian Report for that year. Recently the surveys of the University of Chicago have revealed evidences of the culture in Jo Daviess, Kane, and other counties, while the Nickerson manuscript in possession of that institution reports typical copper ear spools and potteryware from the Portage mounds near Galena.

A number of mounds definitely attributable to the Hopewell peoples were examined by the agents of the Bureau of American Ethnology and reported in the Twelfth Annual Report

(1890-91). The most important of these was the group over-looking the city of East Dubuque, in the extreme northwestern corner of the state. This group comprised a total of seventeen conical tumuli, of varying sizes, occupying the blufflike terrace overlooking the river. In the largest of the group, which meas-ured 70 feet in diameter and 12 feet in height, were found numerous burials, one of which was reported as the remains of an individual above seven feet in height. With this skeleton were found copper beads, copper gorgets or breastplates, an

FIG. 205. THE OGDEN MOUND, NEAR LEWISTOWN, ILLINOIS

This is the central and largest tumulus of a group of eleven or more mounds of the Hopewell culture. The top has been graded off to accommodate the farm-house and yard. Tunneling operations have revealed burials and remarkable structural phenomena.

exceptionally long flint ceremonial knife or spearpoint, and a necklace and armlets of bear canine teeth. In the second-largest mound of the group there was disclosed a large interior vault constructed of stones and logs, rectangular in form and measuring 13 feet by 7 feet. Within the vault were a total of eleven skeletons—six adults, four children, and an infant, the latter buried in the arms of a female, presumably its mother. The skeletons were arranged in sitting posture facing the center of the crypt, where there rested on the floor a container made from a large marine shell and several pottery vessels.

FIG. 206. SECTION OF THE WALL OF A BURIAL CHAMBER IN THE OGDEN
MOUND

Tunneling operations in the central mound of the Ogden Group, near Lewistown, Illinois, have revealed important structural phenomena so far indeterminate
in character, but apparently intended as charnel houses or burial chambers. The
walls are covered with matting rudely woven from rushes and reeds, as shown in
the illustration. Courtesy of Dickson Brothers.

The stone substructure of the vault was covered with logs,
the interstices filled with bark, reeds, and twigs and plastered
over with a mortarlike mixture of clay and ashes. Several
mounds of this group bore indications of cremation, and a
number of burials were interred in vaults of stone and timber.

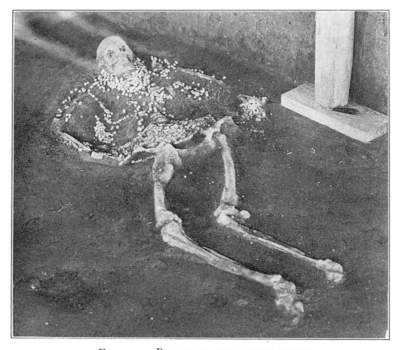

Fig. 207.   Burial in the Ogden Mound

This individual when interred wore a cloth coat or cape on which had been sewed hundreds of shell and pearl beads. Courtesy of Dickson Brothers.

A group of five mounds situated near Hardin, Calhoun County, on the peninsulalike point lying between the Illinois and Mississippi rivers, yielded artifacts of Hopewell type and revealed also a basinlike depression covered by a primary mound similar to those of the Ohio Hopewell tumuli.

The most striking development of the Hopewell culture in Illinois, however, is found in the vicinity of Havana and Lewistown, in Fulton County. Within the angle formed by the junction of the Spoon and Illinois rivers there are numerous individual mounds and several striking groups of the culture which only recently have come significantly to notice. At the invitation of Professor Warren K. Moorehead and in connection with his explorations in the vicinity for the University of Illinois, the writer recently visited and inspected the mounds of the district. One of the more important of the groups is that known as the Ogden site, near Lewistown. This consists of a large central tumulus about which are clustered some ten or more smaller ones. What appears to be a shallow moat or ditch

FIG. 208. BURIAL AND PORTION OF A CREMATORY BASIN DISCLOSED IN
THE OGDEN MOUND

Photograph by Applegate. Courtesy of Dickson Brothers.

surrounds the group, one of the few instances outside the Ohio area where enclosures are identified with Hopewell mounds.

The large mound of this group, on which a farmhouse and farmyard are located (Figure 205), has been subjected to tunneling operations by Messrs. E. and M. Dickson with the purpose of making it a public attraction. Several typical Hopewell burials with accompanying artifacts have been disclosed and left in place as found. Important structural phenomena, consisting of walls and partitions of a prestructure built of timbers and woven matting, have been partly exposed (Figure 206), but the examination possible by tunneling is insufficient to enable definite identification of the structure. Extending north and east from the Ogden site are several other groups, one at least of which appears to be of equal importance. Some fifty individual mounds of the Hopewell culture have been noted in the district.

Several mounds in the vicinity of Naples have yielded evidences of Hopewell identity or affinity. A group known as the Montezuma mounds, near the town of that name on the west bank of the Illinois River 15 miles below Naples, was examined in 1905 for the Missouri Historical Society. Typical Hopewell objects and potsherds were found along with other remains not Hopewell in character, indicating either the presence of two cultures or decided modification through contact of cultures.

Similar phenomena are encountered in mounds near the town of Havana, in Fulton County, recently examined for the University of Illinois by Moorehead and Taylor and reported in their publication of the explorations at the Cahokia Group. In this district there occur, interspersed with mounds and burials of entirely different cultures, interments unmistakably Hopewell, but showing plainly the influence of contact with associated cultures. In the same report reference is made to an early find of what to the writer are typically Hopewell objects in the Mitchell mounds, in Madison County, reported by Dr. H. R. Howland. The situation here seems to be analogous to the above, with definitely Hopewell mounds associated in the same group with mounds of another culture, possibly Cahokia.

THE ILLINOIS OR "BLUFF" CULTURE

Extending almost the entire course of the Illinois River and along some of its tributaries, such as the Sangamon and other streams of central Illinois, are the mounds and minor remains of a distinctive culture known as the Illinois or "bluff" culture. Hundreds, perhaps thousands, of small to medium-sized mounds line the bluffs overlooking the streams and valleys, and countless sites occur on which are strewn the evidences of the occupancy of their builders. Exploration of the Illinois River mounds has not been sufficient fully to disclose the culture complex of the bluff-culture peoples or the extent of their distribution. Their closest affinity appears to be with the sites immediately to the westward along the Mississippi and in northern Missouri.

In the vicinity of Lewistown, Fulton County, near where the Spoon River joins the Illinois, the mounds of the culture are strikingly in evidence. Surmounting the bluffs that overlook the valleys of the two streams are hundreds of small tumuli, plainly in sight from the highways skirting the bluffs. Five miles southeast of Lewistown is situated what is known as Dickson's Mound-builders' Tomb. It is located typically on the bluff immediately overlooking the Ogden Group, of the Hopewell culture, in the valley below.

The Dickson Mound, as it was originally called, was in the form of a crescent, the points of which were directed toward the east. It measured 550 feet in length along the curve and is said originally to have been from 30 to 35 feet in height. Although exceptional for the district in both form and size, it appears to be attributable to, and in contents quite typical of, the Illinois River or "bluff" culture.

A generation ago the greater part of the Dickson Mound was graded off to accommodate the present farmhouse. The displaced earth was filled into a deep basin within the curve of the crescent which presumably had been excavated during the erection of the mound. In the process of grading hundreds of skeletons were exhumed and hauled away in wagonloads to be reburied. Many thousands of flint, stone, and bone implements and ornaments and hundreds of pottery vessels were found, most of which found their way into various museums.

In 1926 Dr. Don F. Dickson and members of his family, present owners of the farm, conceived the idea of exploring the site, leaving the burials and artifacts in place and erecting over them a building designed to serve as a museum. Upward of two hundred skeletons have been uncovered, and apparently many more are to be disclosed. These burials, now to be seen reposing in the graves just as they were interred, were placed in various positions and at different levels, as the accompanying photograph (Figure 209) shows. Many of them are accompanied by pottery vessels, presumably food containers,

FIG. 209. GROUP OF BURIALS IN THE DICKSON MOUND, LEWISTOWN, ILLINOIS

This shows only a few of the more than two hundred burials exposed in the Dickson Mound of the Illinois culture. Courtesy of Dr. Don F. Dickson.

in which are mussel-shell spoons, the size of the vessel varying to correspond with the age of the individuals. Other relics found with the burials comprise L-shaped tobacco pipes, pendants made from the whorls of marine shells, long bone needles, bone beads, fishhooks fashioned from bone, arrowpoints of flint, axe blades of stone, and other objects. The pottery-ware of the site, including occasional effigy forms, is exceptionally highly developed.

Among the interesting interments of the Dickson Mound is a group burial comprising the skeletons of an adult male and female and between them that of an infant. Owing to the alkaline nature of the soil of the mound the skeletal remains are remarkably well preserved. A striking evidence of this is that with one of the burials there are the remains of an embryonic child, the undeveloped bones of which are practically intact.

On the terrace overlooking the Des Plaines River fifteen miles southwest of Joliet, in Will County, is the Fisher Group or site. Mr. George Langford, an engineer of Joliet who for some years past has found his avocation in local archæology, has effected a most admirable exploration of the site, with the coöperation of the Department of Anthropology of the University of Chicago. The results of his labors through the seasons of 1925 to 1927 have been published in the *American Anthropologist,* Vol. XXIX (1927).

The Fisher Group comprises two major tumuli, 60 feet in diameter and 6 feet in height, adjacent to which are seven small mounds and more than fifty "pits" or large saucer-shaped depressions, originally 3 feet deep and from 15 to 35 feet in diameter. The interesting feature of the site is that its exploration disclosed proof of successive occupancy by three distinct cultures.

The two large mounds, explored in 1925 and 1926, yielded 295 burials, all fully articulated, superimposed from five feet below the original level to five feet above it. Not only the character of the skeletal remains and the artifacts accompanying them, but the presence of lines of division and the diverse character of the earth indicated three distinct occupations and cultures. Buried in the limestone gravel below the original surface, perhaps prior to the beginning of construction of the mound, were skeletons the skulls of which were of the long- and medium-head types, interred in a crouching posture and without relics of any kind. The absence of pottery from these subsurface burials indicates that they may be comparatively ancient. Burials of the middle level of the mounds were those of short-headed individuals, accompanied by many pottery vessels and artifacts of stone, bone, and shell, indicative of the Illinois or "bluff" culture. The upper level of the tumuli contained burials of individuals of mixed head forms, the few artifacts accompanying them being distinctive from those of the lower levels.

The numerous pits or depressions adjacent to the mounds were of decided interest. The earth and gravel displaced in excavating them had been piled in high rings around their margins, and several were supplied with banks or ramps of stones leading from center to rim. In the gravelly soil below

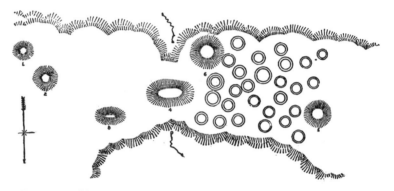

FIG. 210. MAP OF THE WELCH GROUP, BROWN COUNTY, ILLINOIS
The largest mound of the group, No. 4, is 165 feet in length. After Cyrus Thomas.

the accumulated top soil or inwash were found artifacts corresponding to those of the middle tier of burials in the mounds —the Illinois-culture level. The pits themselves appeared to be older than the objects found in them, which as a rule were taken from the numerous cache or storage pits found promiscuously within and adjacent to the large depressions.

With a single exception the smaller mounds of the site were analogous to the larger ones. In one of the smaller mounds were found skeletons of a short-headed people, extended upon the back, heads to the west. Each skeleton was accompanied by one or more trinkets of iron, brass, or silver, of European or white man's manufacture. The clay pots of the aborigine were replaced by the iron and brass vessels of the white man, and the tumulus from top to bottom was unmistakably recent or post-Columbian in origin, the product of Indians who had come into contact with white traders.

The fact that the Fisher site evidenced the presence of three distinct prehistoric occupancies and possessed in addition a mound of historic origin makes it of foremost interest and importance in the mound area, where indications of culture sequence are all too rare. The site as a whole, with exploration not yet completed, has yielded approximately five hundred burials.

Among the numerous mounds and groups apparently pertaining to this Illinois River culture is that known as the Welch Group, near Perry Springs station, in Brown County (Figure 210). The site comprises six mounds and numerous pits or depressions, like those of the Fisher site. A distinction which may mean influence through contact with the cultures of the area to the southward is that at least one of these mounds is truncated or flat-topped. Partial exploration by the Bureau of American Ethnology has revealed minor evidences of the occupants of the site, mainly similar to those of the Fisher site.

THE MISSISSIPPI RIVER MOUNDS OF ILLINOIS

Whether or not the numerous mounds and groups along the Mississippi River are to be classed as distinct from those of the Illinois River region remains undetermined. With but sporadic examinations from which to draw conclusions, they appear to have features in common as well as distinctions which may disappear on exhaustive exploration. Of the many groups along the great river the following are outstanding: an irregular line of circular or conical mounds opposite Canton, Missouri; numerous groups along the narrow ridge lying in the angle between the Mississippi and Illinois rivers, in Calhoun County, several of which were partially examined by the Bureau of American Ethnology; and many mounds along the bluffs overlooking the American Bottom in Madison County.

The remainder of the State of Illinois is attributed to the Lower Mississippi area, with which it will be described in the following chapter.

WESTERN INDIANA

As noted in an earlier chapter, the antiquities of eastern Indiana have their affinities with the Ohio area. Those of the southwestern portion of the state pertain to the Tennessee-Cumberland area, to be discussed presently, leaving only the scattering remains of western Indiana, northward from Vigo County, to be included at this point. The few mounds along the upper reaches of the Wabash and northward toward Lake Michigan presumably belong with the Illinois region, although future exploration may determine otherwise.

MOUND-BUILDER CULTURES OF IOWA

That the territory comprised within the present state of Iowa was a favorite region with the prehistoric mound-building peoples is evidenced by the surprising abundance of major and minor evidences of their occupancy scattered over the area. The total of mounds, earthworks, village sites, and other vestiges of the prehistoric inhabitants is estimated to exceed ten thousand in number. With its east and west boundaries bordering respectively the Mississippi and Missouri rivers, each with a wealth of fine tributary streams, Iowa was eminently suited to primitive human occupancy. Hardly any portion of its area fails to provide evidence of the presence of aboriginal peoples. No fewer than five distinct cultures or varieties of primitive peoples have been identified within the state by Dr. Charles R. Keyes, director of the state archæological survey being conducted by the State Historical Society of Iowa.

THE HOPEWELL CULTURE IN IOWA

An important development of the highly evolved Hopewell culture is found in Iowa, in territory comprised within the four counties of Jackson, Scott, Muscatine, and Louisa and extending in a narrow belt along the bluffs and terraces of the Mississippi from the vicinity of Dubuque southward to the mouth of the Iowa. North of Dubuque there is a gap, per- haps more apparent than real, for the Hopewell again makes its appearance in the valley of the Turkey River near Cler- mont, in Fayette County. The section is practically contiguous to the Hopewell region of west- ern Illinois, where numerous mounds and groups of the cul- ture exist.

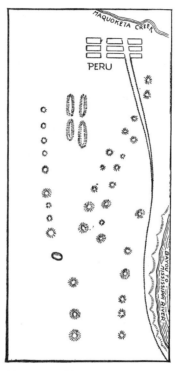

FIG. 211. MOUND GROUP NEAR PERU, IOWA
Redrawn from Thomas.

The Hopewell tumuli of Iowa are mostly small to medium in size, ranging from 3 to 10 feet in height and from 30 to 90 feet in diameter. They occur prin- cipally in groups and number approximately one hundred in- dividual mounds, many of which have been obliterated or reduced by cultivation. Unlike the tumuli of the culture in Ohio, they are unaccompanied by geometric earthworks or earthen enclosures. Burials usually are extended and often are placed in rectangular crypts of logs, as in the Ohio area.

A number of the Hopewell mounds were explored by the Davenport Academy of Sciences during the '70's and '80's of the last century. Many fine specimens now displayed in the Davenport Public Museum were derived from these examina- tions, among them being effigy tobacco pipes in the images of birds and animals; copper axes, awls, and ornaments; fresh-water pearl beads and necklaces; potteryware; and woven fabric. The largest individual mound of the culture is located on the bluff near Toolsboro in the angle formed by the junction of the Iowa and Mississippi rivers. Important groups are situated in Muscatine and Scott counties and near Bellevue in Jackson County. From a mound on Turkey River, in Fayette County, were taken platform pipes, copper beads, bear-tooth pendants, and large flint ceremonial spears. Numerous detached mounds in the region of the principal groups are believed to belong to the Hopewell culture.

THE EFFIGY-MOUND CULTURE IN IOWA

Extending westward from the center of its development in southern Wisconsin, the effigy-mound culture finds expression in some two thousand effigy, linear, and conical mounds in Allamakee, Clayton, and Dubuque counties of Iowa. These remains, comprising several exceptionally interesting groups, occupy the bluffs along the Mississippi River from the Minnesota line to near Dubuque.

One of the more imposing monuments of the entire effigy-mound region is the fine group surmounting the summit of the high bluff just above the city of Marquette, in Clayton County. This excellently preserved group comprises a stately procession of ten bear effigies, three bird images, and two linear mounds. The so-called Woman Mound, located on Turkey River in Clayton County, is constructed in the image of a human female, and measures 70 feet by 135 feet. Near the mouth of the same stream there is a group of animal mounds, supposedly representing the fox or the wolf and the lizard. Several examples of bird mounds occur in the same district, the birds being depicted both with extended and with recurved wings. Among the effigy forms the bear image predominates in relative frequency, although other animals, and birds, are often depicted.

The conical mounds are mostly small and often are connected by or included in the linear mounds. The latter are from 1 to 3 feet in height, 15 to 20 feet in width, and 60 to 200 feet in length.

Several interesting groups of mounds and earthworks situated in the effigy-mound district but probably having affinities with the Oneota, are described by Dr. Cyrus Thomas in his

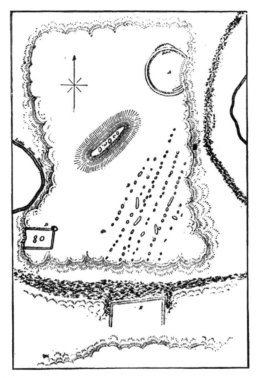

FIG. 212. MAP OF MOUNDS AND EARTHWORKS NEAR NEW ALBIN, IOWA
The rectangular enclosure, D, is 200 feet in length. After Thomas.

report of the early '90's on the mound explorations of the Bureau of American Ethnology. One of these groups, located near New Albin, Allamakee County, consists of enclosures and parallel lines of mounds (Figure 212). Several of the latter are elongate in type and thus suggest the effigy-mound culture. The circular enclosure of the group measures approximately 250 feet in diameter. The mounds, one hundred or more in number, are arranged in six parallel lines. Near the mouth of the Upper Iowa, in the same district, there is a circular enclosure 400 feet in diameter consisting of three concentric ditches or moats and two intermediate earthen walls.

Near Elkport, in Clayton County, there formerly existed an effigy mound supposed to represent the otter. This effigy, with short legs and an inordinately long tail, measured 120 feet in length. Many interesting effigies, past and present, are reported along Turkey River.

The effigy mounds of Iowa vary greatly in size, the bird images ranging from 70 to 170 feet in diameter and the animal forms from 35 by 85 feet to 60 by 140 feet. But few of the effigy and linear mounds of the state have been explored. They are known to contain burials and occasional artifacts similar to those found in the effigy mounds of the Wisconsin region to the eastward.

An interesting discovery made by the Iowa State Archæological Survey in the summer of 1928 was that of seven groups of mounds in the Des Moines valley between Fort Dodge and Boone, in which were included both conical and linear mounds. The latter forms are customarily associated with the effigy-mound culture, and their appearance outside the recognized area of the effigies is illustrative of the frequency with which the several cultures overlap or display influence or modification due to contact and borrowing of traits.

THE ONEOTA CULTURE

The interesting Oneota culture, quite widespread over Iowa, is represented by numerous large village sites, many conical burial mounds, and a few earthworks or enclosures. The most extensive village site of the state, known as the Blood Run site, covering an area of 100 acres, pertains to this culture. It occupies a fine high terrace overlooking the Big Sioux River in northwestern Lyon County. There were originally a total of 143 mounds on this site and in addition an enclosure of irregular form with an area of 15 acres.

Other sites of the culture are situated on the Little Sioux

in Clay and Dickinson counties; adjacent to the same stream in Woodbury County; on the Des Moines River in north-western Warren County; adjacent to the Hopewell group at Toolsboro, Louisa County; and along the upper Iowa River in Allamakee County. Almost without exception the sites of the culture occupy the bluffs and high terraces overlooking the waterways. In several instances small enclosures of from one to three acres are present on the sites. The type of shelter used by the Oneota peoples is unknown, but numerous boulder circles suggest house sites. Although mounds are abundant, interment was also made in cemeteries adjacent to the sites.

The burial mounds of the culture, mostly conical in form but occasionally oval, range in height from 2 to 6 feet, with diameters of 25 to 70 feet. Some five hundred mounds, immediately connected with the sites or on the adjacent hills, have been noted. Many pictographs of animals, birds, and fish have been detected on the cliffs and cave walls adjacent to the sites. Exploration of the tumuli has not been sufficient to demonstrate fully the details of the culture of their builders. From the meager data available, however, it is known that the mounds contain primary extended burials and rather characteristic artifacts. A mound of the Blood Run site, explored by Dr. Keyes, covered an extended burial placed well below the base line. With it were ear ornaments wound spirally from fine copper wire, and on the skull was a quantity of red powder or "paint." From the sites on the upper Iowa and that near Toolsboro have been taken tubular copper beads, bone awls and needles, flint arrowpoints and scrapers, and pottery vessels of distinctive character. The arrowpoints of the culture are mostly of the triangular form, and the potteryware is shell-tempered. Other artifacts are rather thick stone celts or hatchets; heavy grooved hammers and mauls; hand mullers and shallow mortars; small calumet pipes of red pipestone; and occasional disk-stem pipes and inscribed tablets of the same material. The débris of the village sites is heavy, indicating long or intensive occupancy and extensive use of bone and antler for making implements.

THE MILL CREEK CULTURE

Extending along the course of the Little Sioux River, from the town of Linn Grove, Buena Vista County, across the southeast corner of O'Brien County, and thence diagonally southwestward through Cherokee County almost to its southern border, there occur a total of twelve prehistoric village sites of a culture distinct from those previously described. These sites are relatively small, comprising from one to two acres each, and are enclosed by broad, shallow moats or ditches. Each village site contains from twelve to twenty or more earth lodge sites.

Some two hundred mounds ranging from two to four feet in height occur on the adjacent hills and ridges and apparently pertain to the culture. A single one of these, excavated by amateurs, yielded potteryware of what is known as the Mill Creek type. No mounds have been carefully explored, however, and no cemeteries have been located.

The artifacts recovered from the deep camp refuse of the sites are somewhat similar to those from the Oneota culture sites, with the addition of such types as discoidal stones and spoons and pipes of potteryware. Polished tablets of catlinite bearing incised pictographs and symbolic designs also occur. The potteryware of the Mill Creek culture is distinctive, usually dark in color, with tempering of crushed granite. The vessels generally are globular, the rims being decorated with crosshatching, rounded indentations, diagonal incised lines, and occasionally with the molded heads of birds and animals.

A single site of the culture is situated on Broken Kettle Creek, a tributary of the Big Sioux, in Plymouth County.

THE ALGONQUIAN CULTURE IN IOWA

The fifth of the several Iowa prehistoric cultures identified by Dr. Keyes is the Algonquian, which, as in Ohio and other states of the Middle West, is the most widespread and representative of the prehistoric occupations. The Algonquian evidences are found throughout practically the whole state, burial mounds attributable to the stock occurring everywhere except in the extreme northwest and in one or two counties of the southwest.

Upward of eight thousand mounds believed to owe their origin to the Algonquian peoples occupy the bluffs and stream terraces of the state. The village sites of the culture, mostly small and rather inconspicuous, are found on the numerous ter-

FIG. 213. MOUND OF FISH FARM GROUP NEAR LANSING, IOWA
The group contains thirty conical mounds. Courtesy of Charles R. Keyes.

races, in the oak groves of the lake district of north-central Iowa, and in some sixty known rock shelters of the east-central section. They retain no evidences of the houses or shelters of their occupants, nor do they display the characteristic refuse deposits and marked evidences of the use of bone which are such constant features of some others of the prehistoric cultures.

In one respect, however, the Algonquian peoples are of outstanding interest. They were the master artisans in stone and flint, and their artifacts, fashioned from these obdurate materials, occur in astonishing numbers and often are of surpassing workmanship. More than one hundred types of chipped flint implements have been noted, including ceremonial and utility forms of arrow- and spearpoints, lanceheads, knives, scrapers, and drills. The implements and ornaments of ground stone, comprising axes, celts, pestles and mortars, problematical and ceremonial forms, are not surpassed by any other region of the mound area. The pottery of the culture, its most

FIG. 214. LINEAR MOUND OF YELLOW RIVER GROUP, ALLAMAKEE COUNTY, IOWA

The group contains conical, linear, and effigy mounds. Courtesy of Charles R. Keyes.

important criterion, is distinctive, the vessels, of clay tempered with coarsely crushed granite, having bases in the form of rounded-off cones and rims and sides decorated with fabric impressions and embellished with punched, stamped, and incised designs of peculiar technique.

IOWA ARCHÆOLOGY

Although many of the finest archæological remains of Iowa are somewhat difficult of approach, those interested in the prehistoric vestiges of the state will be well repaid for the effort necessary to reach them. A few of the best preserved and more interesting are: The Jennings-Leiphart Group of ten bears, three birds, and two linears, just north of the town of Marquette, Clayton County; the fine group of ninety-five mounds, comprising three bear effigies, two birds, five linears, and eighty-five conical tumuli, on the Mississippi terrace six miles below McGregor, Clayton County; fine effigy, linear, and conical mounds on both bluffs north and south of the mouth of Turkey River, Clayton County; a bear effigy on Pike's Hill, opposite the mouth of the Wisconsin River, Clayton County; a fine compact group of thirty conical mounds four miles north of Lansing, Allamakee County. Four well-preserved conical mounds are situated in the Eldora State Park grounds, Hardin County, and five others overlook the Des Moines valley in a small park at Lehigh, Webster County. A row of nineteen conical tumuli occupy a ridge overlooking the Cedar River, near the Mt. Vernon-Iowa City highway, in Linn County, and twelve linears and an equal number of conicals are located on the Des Moines River bluff four miles east of Lehigh, Webster County.

An admirably comprehensive review of the archæology of Iowa by Dr. Charles R. Keyes appeared in the *Palimpsest* for June, 1927, published by the State Historical Society of Iowa. Maps and descriptions of important mounds and earthworks are included in the report of Dr. Cyrus Thomas in the Twelfth Annual Report of the Bureau of American Ethnology, 1890-91. Reports of explorations in the Hopewell mounds of the state may be found in the *Proceedings of the Davenport Academy of Science*, Volumes I to V; and a report of the examination of the great Boone Mound, in Boone County, by T. Van Hyning, appeared in *Records of the Past*, Volume IX (1900). A detailed bibliography compiled by Dr. Keyes is in preparation. A bibliography and summary, fairly complete up to 1892, prepared by Dr. Frederick Starr, appeared in Volume V of the *Proceedings of the Davenport Academy of Science*. Other references appear in later issues of the *Proceedings*.

Very little that is specific can be said of the marginal districts of the Upper Mississippi area in Missouri, Kansas, and Nebraska, because of the comparative scarcity of major remains and the lack of exploration. The northern portions of Missouri are known to contain numerous mounds which are similar in culture and physical character to those of adjoining portions of Iowa and Illinois. While the southern part of the state has received some attention from the archæologist, northern Missouri in the main awaits exploration. Mounds occur most abundantly along the Missouri River and the Mississippi, with impressive groups in the vicinity of Hannibal. Several tumuli formerly existed within the corporate limits of St. Louis, one or two of which, destroyed by building activities, were of large size.

A few scattering mounds have been noted in eastern Kansas, mainly along the Kansas River, and still fewer are reported from eastern Nebraska. The latter appear to be mostly low house mounds.

CHAPTER XVI

THE LOWER MISSISSIPPI AREA: I, SOUTHERN ILLINOIS, WESTERN
KENTUCKY AND TENNESSEE, SOUTHERN MISSOURI,
AND ARKANSAS

General characteristics of the Lower Mississippi area—The Cahokia culture in
Illinois—Western Kentucky and Tennessee—The stone-vault culture of
southern Missouri—Artifacts of the southern Missouri region—"Garden
mounds"—Mound distribution in Arkansas—Explorations in Arkansas of
Clarence B. Moore.

THE archæological province known as the Lower Mississippi area embraces the territory bordering on the Mississippi River from the vicinity of St. Louis southward. Within the area are included southern Illinois, western Kentucky and Tennessee, Missouri south of the Missouri River, and the states of Arkansas, Louisiana, Mississippi, and Alabama. With the exception of the stone-vault mounds of Missouri, the shell heaps of the Gulf Coast, and some minor distinctions, the homogeneity of its archæology sharply distinguishes this region from others of the general mound area.

GENERAL CHARACTERISTICS OF THE LOWER MISSISSIPPI AREA

The distinctive features of the Lower Mississippi area are flat-topped mounds, square, rectangular, and conical; enclosures, defensive and otherwise; shell mounds and flat deposits of shells, in the southern portion; and a high development of ceramic art both in the embellishment of vessels and in the variety of forms. Mounds, singly and in groups, village sites, cemeteries, and enclosures are plentiful along the Mississippi River, occurring alike on the bottom lands and on the bluffs, and this is true also of the lower valleys of all the main tributaries of the great watercourse.

Much of the area, particularly in the counties bordering the

Mississippi, is low-lying and subject to inundation, and the mounds have an important present-day use as places of refuge for stock, and occasionally for human beings, by reason of which permission to excavate is often denied. In fact, it is highly probable that the greater number, if not all, of the square and oblong flat-topped mounds were originally erected for this purpose, for considerations of drainage are paramount throughout the region whether on the bottom lands or elsewhere. In support of this hypothesis is the fact that most of the burials found in the flat-topped mounds are seldom more than two or three feet beneath the surface, having been placed after erection of the mounds as dwelling sites. Another feature often forbidding excavation of mounds is their modern use as cemeteries. Occasionally a mound is found carefully fenced in and covered with gravestones of the modern type, and probably most mounds situated in thickly populated districts contain superficial burials made during the past century.

Our knowledge of this southwestern manifestation of the Mound-builders' activities is obtained mainly from the following publications: Cyrus Thomas' report on mound explorations, published in 1890-91 by the Bureau of American Ethnology; several monumental volumes of explorations by Clarence B. Moore, published by the Academy of Natural Sciences of Philadelphia; a recent book by Calvin S. Brown entitled *The Archæology of Mississippi,* issued by the Mississippi Geological Survey; Bulletin 37 of the Bureau of American Ethnology, describing the results of Gerard Fowke's work on the stone graves of Missouri; and Squier and Davis' *Ancient Monuments of the Mississippi Valley,* issued as Volume I of the Smithsonian Contributions to Knowledge. Peter A. Brannon, state archæologist of Alabama, has done a considerable amount of work in Alabama which is yet, for the most part, unpublished.

To Clarence B. Moore we are indebted for a large part of what is known of the entire Lower Mississippi area. Between the years 1905 and 1913 he explored the navigable portions of the principal rivers of Arkansas, Louisiana, Mississippi, and Alabama, working from a flat-bottomed steamboat, with a force of men for the excavation of mounds and for handling the material recovered.

Upon the basis of ceramic features Moore suggests a subdivision of the Lower Mississippi area into two districts lying respectively north and south of the Arkansas River and a line extending eastward from its mouth through the states of Mississippi and Alabama. Although the same ceramic forms and decorative motives are found throughout the entire area, south of this line the earthenware appears to be of a superior grade. In this district the incised scrolls, circles, and conventionalized life motives characteristic of the pottery decoration of the entire area are more skillfully executed. North of the line pigment is used to a greater extent, and vessels decorated in more than one color, very rare to the south, are abundant. The main features of the northern subarea are free use of pigment in the embellishment of vessels and a great variety of effigy forms. The line between the two subareas, however, is not a sharp one. The pottery of the Arkansas River valley is intermediate, partaking of the distinctive features of both districts, sometimes in combinations found neither to the north nor to the south.

Bunched burials, or placing of the remains, frequently the skulls only, of different individuals together in one grave; ordinary inhumation, both with and without removal of the flesh from the bones; cremation; and urn burial comprise the types of interment in the Lower Mississippi area. In urn burial the bones of one or more skeletons, previously denuded of their flesh, were placed in an earthenware vessel. With the exception of urn burial, which in this area occurs almost exclusively in central and southern Alabama, there is no general correlation between burial types and the artifacts deposited with the dead.

The pottery of the Lower Mississippi area is characterized by a great variety of form, with subsidiary modifications such as bosses, rim scallops, or rectilinear indentations, and the extensive use of decoration on the outer surface. Exclusively culinary vessels, however, are usually undecorated and vary little in form, which is determined mainly by function. The characteristic shapes are the bottle, the shallow bowl, and the pot. The ware in all parts of the area is generally yellow or black, the base color on painted vessels sometimes forming part of the design. The tempering is usually sand or shell, sometimes powdered mica. Frequently vessels accompanying burials are broken or in a state of disrepair, these imperfect vessels apparently having been used as mortuary tributes in preference to usable articles of the same type, or else intentionally "killed" as a sacrificial offering. Incised or "trailed" patterns, the punch mark, the stamp, pigment, and modeling in relief are the modes used in applying design and decoration. The more ornate features of the pottery of the area have already been described and illustrated in Chapter VI.

THE CAHOKIA CULTURE IN ILLINOIS

While only the comparatively small triangular area comprised by the southern point of Illinois lies within the Lower Mississippi archæological province, it bears the distinction of possessing the largest individual mound, the greatest group of mounds, and the most extensive prehistoric village site, not only of the province, but of the entire mound area—the noted Cahokia Group. This group of mounds and its attendant village site are located in Madison County, Illinois, just east of the city of St. Louis, on what is known as "the bottoms." The city of East St. Louis, as a result of its phenomenal growth, recently has come to occupy the margins of the site and is rapidly encroaching upon the ancient Mound-builder domain.

Cahokia Mound, the great central tumulus of the group, popularly known as Monks' Mound from the fact that between the years 1808 and 1813 a colony of French Trappist monks resided on or near it, has attracted more archæological and popular attention than any other prehistoric monument north of Mexico. It is a flat-topped, truncated pyramid, approximately 1,080 feet long by 710 feet wide, with a maximum height of slightly over 100 feet. The basal area is something like 16 acres. The great pyramid rises by stages of four level platforms or terraces, an apronlike projection extending from the lower terrace northward from the structure. The assumption is that the pyramid was erected for domiciliary purposes and that a great ceremonial structure occupied the upper level while lodges and wigwams may have been accommodated on the lower terraces.

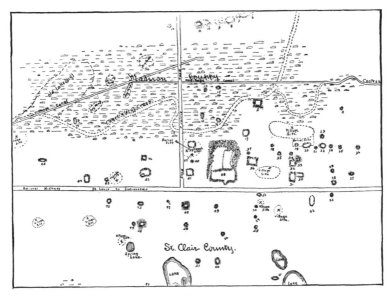

FIG. 215. MAP OF THE HEART OF THE CAHOKIA GROUP, SHOWING MONKS' MOUND AT CENTER

After Moorehead, from the Van Court Seever Survey.

Some eighty-five mounds are identifiable in the Cahokia Group, but according to Dr. W. K. Moorehead, who is best qualified to express opinion on the subject, the number originally was much greater. Within a seven-mile circle radiating from the center of the group proper he estimates that between two and three hundred tumuli of various sizes may have existed before agricultural and building operations demolished the smaller structures. Although none of the other mounds of the group approaches in magnitude the great Monks' Mound,

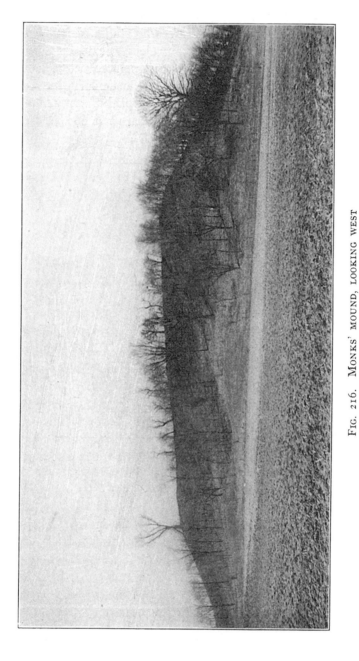

FIG. 216. MONKS' MOUND, LOOKING WEST

This great central mound of the Cahokia Group, at East St. Louis, Illinois, is the largest tumulus in the mound area. It is 100 feet in height and covers 16 acres of ground. Photograph by G. S. Severant. Courtesy of W. K. Moorehead.

a number of them, ranging in height from 30 to 60 feet, really are most impressive when compared with any other tumuli of the general mound area. Like Monks' Mound, the larger tumuli of the group are mostly flat-topped pyramids, while some of the smaller mounds, including many that have been demolished through cultivation, were more or less conical in form.

No other known prehistoric village site within the mound area, or anywhere else in the United States, approximates in size that in connection with the Cahokia Group of mounds.

FIG. 217. SOME LESSER MOUNDS OF THE CAHOKIA GROUP

In addition to the great central tumulus, the Cahokia Group comprises numerous mounds of comparatively large size. Courtesy of W. K. Moorehead.

Extending along the creek of the same name for a distance of seven or eight miles and with a mean width of perhaps one mile, the Cahokia village site has the proportions of a modern city. The soil throughout this area, in varying degrees, is littered with potsherds, bones, shells, and other débris of habitation. As a result of desultory and mostly amateur exploration during the past half-century numerous interesting specimens of the handiwork of the builders of the Cahokia mounds and the occupants of the great village have been brought to light. Most interesting of these finds, perhaps, was a deposit, discovered by William McAdams, comprising, among other things, more than one hundred pottery vessels, many of which were in the effigies of birds and animals. In his *Ancient Races of the Mississippi Valley*, published in 1877, McAdams described the find as follows:

FIG. 218. UNCOVERING THE BASE OF THE JAMES RAMEY MOUND OF THE CAHOKIA GROUP

The circle is believed to be a sun symbol. Within the two interior basins were found tobacco ash and calcined human bones. Courtesy of W. K. Moorehead.

In excavating near the base of the great temple mound of Cahokia, whose towering height of over 100 feet gave a grateful shade for our labors, we found in a crumbling tomb of earth and stone a great number of burial vases, over one hundred of which were perfect. It was a most singular collection, as if the mound-builder, with patient and skillful hand, united with artistic taste in shaping the vessels, had endeavored to make a representation of the natural history of the country in ceramics. Some of these were painted and there were also the paint-pots and dishes holding the colors, together with the little bone paddle for mixing, and other implements of the aboriginal artist.

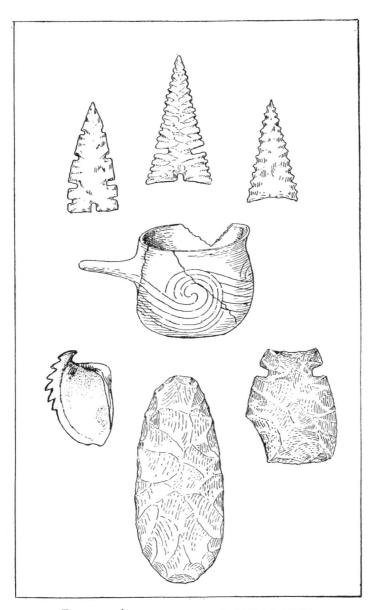

Fig. 219. Artifacts from the Cahokia Group

Above, three finely fashioned flint arrowpoints, typical of the culture; two-thirds natural size. Center, pottery vessel, 6 inches in height; lower left, spoon or ladle made from a mussel-shell; length, 5 inches. Lower center, flint spade, 11 inches long. Lower right, flint hoe, 5 inches in length. After Moorehead, redrawn by H. R. Goodwin from University of Illinois Bulletin, Vol. XXVI.

Many specimens collected from the Cahokia district by McAdams are preserved in the museum at Monticello Seminary, Godfrey, Illinois. Among these are two stone idols of exceptional interest.

The first and only scientific attention so far accorded the Cahokia Group is that sponsored by the University of Illinois under the direction of Dr. W. K. Moorehead and Jay L. B. Taylor. During the years 1922 to 1924 and in 1927 explorations were carried on under the University's program, a report of which, entitled *The Cahokia Mounds,* is recently off the press as Volume XXVI of the University of Illinois Bulletin. In this report Moorehead reviews all that is known of Cahokia and gives details of the exploration under his direction. A thorough examination of a group of such great size obviously would require years of effort and the expenditure of large sums. The partial examination comprised numerous smaller tumuli and parts of the adjacent village site. From the evidence accumulated, Moorehead finds the culture of the Cahokia builders to be basically that of the Lower Mississippi area, with local traits and variations particularly as regards pottery and some minor artifacts. Unfortunately the principal cemetery which must exist somewhere in connection with so extensive a site remains to be found. The mounds for the most part have proved to be domiciliary.

The Cahokia Group, the most important manifestation of the culture it represents, is a northernmost thrust of the great Lower Mississippi area, excluding the Aztalan ruin in Wisconsin, described in an earlier chapter, and some scattering evidences in intermediate territory. A number of models of the group, one of which is displayed at the Peabody Museum, Cambridge, Massachusetts, were made by the late David I. Bushnell of St. Louis.

The old National Pike, extending westward through Ohio and Indiana to St. Louis, passes through the Cahokia Group and within sight of the great Monks' Mound. The more important tumuli of the group have been incorporated in a state park by the State of Illinois and will be preserved for all time.

Cahokia is a Mecca for tourists and those interested in American prehistory as represented by the Mound-builders.

Certain other sites in southern Illinois are definitely attributable to the Lower Mississippi or southern culture area; they are unimportant, however, in comparison with the striking Cahokia development and may be passed by without specific comment.

WESTERN KENTUCKY AND TENNESSEE

The extreme western extensions of Kentucky and Tennessee, bordering the Mississippi River, belong to the Lower Mississippi archæological area. The fact that little or no scientific exploration of these districts has been effected, however, makes it impossible to determine just how far eastward this affiliation extends or to what degree it prevails. The triangular area comprising southwestern Indiana, lying within the angle formed by the junction of the Wabash and Ohio rivers, possibly may have its affinities with the southern culture, but lack of exploration makes this district likewise indeterminate as to its place in the general mound archæology. The probabilities are, however, that it belongs with what has been designated for this volume as the Tennessee-Cumberland area, as do the greater portions of both Kentucky and Tennessee.

Current explorations in Indiana under state direction, in Kentucky by the University of Kentucky, and in Tennessee under the historical organizations of the state promise early and definite information regarding these hitherto neglected districts. For the present, for reasons which will be apparent, they will be discussed along with other portions of these states in the chapter dealing with the Tennessee-Cumberland area.

THE STONE-VAULT CULTURE OF SOUTHERN MISSOURI

The Missouri River, traversing the state a little north of center, marks the line of the most interesting and best-known culture of the Lower Mississippi area, that of the so-called "stone-vault" burial mounds. From the mouth of the Gasconade River to Kansas City the prehistoric inhabitants buried their dead within roughly circular or rectangular walls built with varying degrees of skill of flat limestone or sandstone slabs and covered with earth to form mounds varying in size from 20 to 80 feet in diameter. The stone vaults, so-called, were not roofed over in any manner but were simply stone pens or fences enclosing areas not longer than nine or wider than six feet. The walls, a few of which attain a height of six feet, generally lean outward from the base, indicating that as each tier of stone slabs was laid down, earth was thrown up against the outside to hold the wall in place. An interesting feature of the stone vaults is a very noticeable uniformity of orientation. In the greater number the long axis lies northeast–southwest, and the doorways found in most of the vaults west of the mouth of the Osage River are usually in the south or southwest wall.

Both cremated and uncremated burials are found from top to bottom of the earth filling the vaults, but occasionally the human remains are at the bottom only, often lying scattered about in confusion on crudely made stone pavements, apparently without regard to the preservation of identities. Among the artifacts found are clay or stone "elbow" pipes, beads made from the columella of sea shells, hematite nodules which have been scraped to obtain red pigment, animal bones, flint hoes, and pottery. The whole pots taken from the stone-vault mounds during 1906 and 1907 by Gerard Fowke are described by him as "exclusively culinary," with rude, globular bodies. The principal decorative motive used was a series of incised "zigzag lines bordered by dotted indentations."

An accurate estimate of the number of individuals buried in a vault is made difficult by the badly decayed condition of most of the unburnt bones and by the fact that cremated remains are not always found in separate graves or piles, but in one vault in Howard County it was possible to count the remains of at least twenty-five individuals. That cremation was occasionally effected within the vaults is attested by the scorched and smoke-stained condition of the stones on the inner sides of some of the walls. Apparently there was no hard and fast rule among the stone-vault people as to who should be cremated and who should not. Male and female, infant and adult were disposed of in both ways, and in one instance the skull and upper bones, including those of the arms, of an adult had been cremated while the rest of the body was deposited upon the floor of the vault untouched by fire. A rare and interesting find in a mound in Osage County, near the

FIG. 220. WALL AND DOORWAY IN A STONE-VAULT BURIAL MOUND
Brenner Mound No. 2, Missouri. After Fowke, Bureau of American Ethnology.

mouth of the river of the same name, was an attempt to place the cremated fragments of one skeleton upon the analogous parts of an uncremated body which lay at full length on the floor of the vault.

Stone slabs were used in a variety of ways in nearly all of the burial mounds along the Missouri River that have been examined. Near Hartsburg, in Boone County, an extended skeleton was found on a rock floor of the same dimensions as the body, enclosed in a shallow, basinlike grave or "cist" formed by placing rock slabs on edge in an inclined position. Timbers had been placed across the tops of the inclined slabs to support a cover of flat stones, but the whole had fallen in upon the burial. This grave was but a few inches below the top of the mound, lying directly over a stone vault containing the remains of a number of cremated and uncremated individuals. In the same group of mounds, as in others in Boone

FIG. 221. EFFIGY AND PAINTED POTTERY FROM SOUTHERN MISSOURI

The upper effigy figure on the left represents a bird; the lower bears a composite effigy, with a human head and the tail of a bird. The painted vase on the right bears crosses, swastikas, and cosmic designs. Scale, 1/4. After Holmes, Bureau of American Ethnology.

and Howard counties, shallow graves covered with slabs of stone together with uncovered remains were found alike on the floors of vaults and in mounds without vaults. In one instance stone slabs were piled at the two ends of a skeleton in a shallow unlined grave with a mortar of sandstone lying on the pile at the head. From these descriptions it will be apparent that the stone vault may be regarded as simply an elaboration of the stone cist, or grave lined with inclined or vertically placed slabs and containing but a single individual, from which it was probably developed by successive stages. The vault, in which were perhaps interred the members of a group corresponding to the modern family, was a communal grave, the greater size of which necessitated a horizontal disposition of the stones upon one another and forbade a covering of any sort by which the burials might be protected from the weight of the superimposed earth.

Stone cairns, or mounds consisting entirely of stone, generally containing the remains of more than one individual, are found along the Gasconade River and at other points in Gasconade County. These represent a specialization in the use of stone in connection with the burial of the dead paralleling the stone vault with its covering of earth, and they were probably erected by the same peoples. Very likely the choice of stones instead of earth as the covering for a vault or grave was determined by their abundance in suitable form.

There is a very noticeable increase in complexity of the structural details of the stone vaults from the mouth of the Osage River westward to Clay County. Vaults without doorways are found only at the eastern end of their range, in Osage and Gasconade counties. Farther west, in Boone and Howard counties on the north side of the Missouri, the doorway is a constant feature, sometimes nicely squared and at other times left in a half-finished condition. In Boone County one entire end of a vault was left open to form the entrance. The doorways of Clay County and westward to Kansas City are flanked on the outside by wing walls extending from two to six feet at right angles to the main wall, providing a sort of ceremonial vestibule.

ARTIFACTS OF THE SOUTHERN MISSOURI REGION

The southeast corner of Missouri, between the counties of Butler, Stoddard, and Bollinger and the Mississippi River, belongs archæologically as well as topographically with the low-lying portion of northeastern Arkansas. The pottery found in the flat-topped mounds and earthen enclosures in this locality affiliates their builders with the tribes to the south and east rather than with the stone-vault peoples. The largest of the five enclosures described by Thomas measures 2,700 feet in circumference. This enclosure is in Mississippi County, in the midst of an extensive cypress swamp, on a ridge which was the only point for many miles around to emerge above the great flood of 1882. A bowl in the effigy of a human head was taken from a mound within the enclosure, and in an open village site two miles distant a variety of ceramic forms typical of the Lower Mississippi area have been found, many of which are of exceptional workmanship and beauty.

FIG. 222. ELABORATELY CARVED SHELL GORGET FROM SOUTHERN MISSOURI

The human figure design suggests Aztec influence. Scale, 1/2. After Conant, *Footprints of Vanished Races.*

The abundance of pottery both in burial mounds and on the surface in this part of Missouri indicates a very considerable aboriginal population. During the latter part of the past century broken pieces of earthen vessels were so thick in some localities that the plow made a grating sound as though cutting through gravelly soil. For two years following 1879 when the people of Charleston, Mississippi County, discovered that pottery of aboriginal make had some commercial value, a veritable mining fever broke out, and many bills were paid to Charleston merchants either by tendering whole pots as currency in kind or with the proceeds of their sale to collectors and museums.

From Perry County have come a number of remarkable shell gorgets bearing combinations of incised and openwork crosses, swastikas, human figures, and spiders. One of the finest shell gorgets in existence, from Saint Marys, bears an openwork and incised kneeling human figure apparently in the act of throwing a disk-shaped stone. On the ear of the figure is an ear plug similar in shape to those of copper and stone found in burials. From this ear ornament is suspended a series of objects terminating in strings at the elbow.

What seems to be a half-human and half-bird figure is embossed on a copper plate found some years ago in Dunklin County. The head is apparently human, with the mask of a bird; while the claws at the bottom are those of the eagle, the bill suggests the turkey.

"GARDEN MOUNDS"

Missouri possesses another class of earthworks, the so-called "garden mounds." Varying in height from six inches to five feet and with diameters ranging from 25 to 125 feet, these are found by thousands in southern Missouri, northern Arkansas, and eastern Oklahoma. In several counties in the latter region there are whole townships throughout the entire extent of which (steep hillsides and low river flood plains subject to inundation excepted) these tumuli may be found at the frequency of three to seven to the acre. While their origin has been variously attributed to erosion, earthquakes, spring and gas vents, uprooted trees, and ants, J. B. Thoburn of the Oklahoma Historical Society has identified a number of them through excavation as the caved-in ruins of timber-framed, dome-shaped, earth-covered lodges, probably built and occupied by the ancestors of the present-day Caddoan peoples. Such of the "garden mounds" as are of this type are not, therefore, true mounds, although in some cases they contain human remains.

Little is known of the archæology of the region of the Ozark foothills of Missouri, in the central and western part of the state south of the Missouri River. Thick beds of ashes intermixed with pieces of shell, bone, fragments of pottery, and implements of stone found in the numerous caves in the limestone bluffs along the Gasconade and some of its tributaries indicate a long period of occupation by Indians. Generally throughout this region village and camp sites may be found on the bottom lands where streams unite. Extensive sites are along the White and James rivers in Stone County. In Dallas and St. Francois counties mounds in groups of a hundred to a hundred and fifty are found, sometimes in parallel rows bordering the streams or on slopes with a western exposure. These are probably of the problematical type known as "garden mounds," since no sign of aboriginal occupation is found on their surfaces or in their vicinity.

Beyond the counties bordering the north shore of the Missouri River the numerous mounds, village sites, and enclosures belong archæologically with the contiguous portions of Iowa in the Upper Mississippi area.

MOUND DISTRIBUTION IN ARKANSAS

The lowlands of the extreme southeastern part of Missouri continue into Arkansas, occupying most of that portion of the state between the White River and the Mississippi. This region, including Desha and Chicot counties south of the mouth of the Arkansas River, is known as the Mississippi alluvial region of Arkansas. Most of the bottom lands are subject to inundation, and the numerous wet prairies and swamps are separated by broad, low swells of sandy land, one of which, known locally as Crowley's Ridge, runs from Greene County well into Phillips County, forming the divide between the White and St. Francis rivers.

In Greene County where the St. Francis River widens into a continuous swamp-bordered lake, the section known as the "Sunken Lands of the St. Francis," there is an interesting group of mounds nine miles east of Paragould. The largest mound of the group, 25 feet in height and 190 feet long, showed at the time of Thomas' examination a number of crevasses resulting from the earthquake of 1811 (Figure 223). In Craighead County, immediately to the south, quite a number of mounds were destroyed in the same catastrophe.

On Crowley's Ridge in Poinsett County there is a group of seventeen mounds. Although the ridge rises at this point ten or fifteen feet above the swamp, only the tops of the higher mounds, which vary from two to twelve feet in height, are out of water during the heavier overflows of the Mississippi. At the time of Thomas' survey of this region excavations were

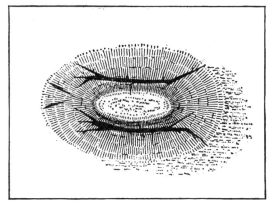

FIG. 223.   MOUND IN GREENE COUNTY, ARKANSAS, RIVEN BY THE EARTH-
QUAKE OF 1911
Bureau of American Ethnology.

being carried on by a railroad for the purpose of obtaining gravel underlying the ridge, and parts of several of the mounds had been cut away, exposing cross sections of much interest. All of the mounds thus exposed showed horizontal beds of burned clay which were the floors of dwelling structures. In one mound, 4 feet high and 90 feet in diameter, the remains of three conjoined rooms were traced in the shape of a T, each room being about twelve feet square. Charred logs and post molds indicated the position of upright timbers supporting the roof. Cane lathing closed the spaces between the posts, which were about two feet apart. Twigs and rushes were interwoven with the cane, and mud plaster was applied to both inner and outer sides. Occasionally the nests of the mud dauber are found in the remains of these wattlework houses, burned as hard as the clay which formed the walls. Sometimes when one house had burned down or was otherwise destroyed, another was built immediately above the ruins. In one case four burned clay beds in a vertical series, each

FIG. 224.   POTTERY VESSEL IN EFFIGY OF THE HUMAN HEAD FROM PECAN POINT, ARKANSAS

Height, 7½ inches. After Moore.

overlain by two or three feet of earth, indicated the successive erection of as many houses. In this manner the mound was built up to its final height. It is not improbable that we are here dealing with a "garden mound" of the type found by Thoburn in Oklahoma. Upon one of these prehistoric floors were found a number of burned clay casts of a variety of corn known in the South as "gourd seed corn."

Other groups of mounds described by Thomas are near Corning, in Clay County; the Taylor Shanty Group in the Sunken Lands region of Poinsett County; the Miller Group in Section 10 of the same county; the Webb Group of four conical mounds about ten miles southeast of Jonesboro; the Thornton Group of nine mounds, some three miles above the union of Little River with the St. Francis; and the Knapp

FIG. 225. POTTERY VESSEL WITH DEATH SYMBOLS FROM PECAN POINT, ARKANSAS

Leg bones and bones of the hand modeled in relief as decorations. Probably a funerary vessel. Height of vessel, 9 inches. After Moore.

Group in Lonoke County. The Taylor Shanty and Miller groups have yielded a considerable amount of earthenware characteristic of the region, clay pipes and disks, and many skeletons. In one of the mounds of the former group clay "pillows," slabs about a foot square and three inches thick with rounded corners, were found beneath the heads of two skeletons.

The Knapp Group, one of the finest in the country, lies about sixteen miles southeast of Little Rock, in the western edge of Lonoke County on Mound Lake, three or four miles from the Arkansas River. An earthen wall, semicircular with the open side at the edge of the lake, surrounds an area of about 85 acres. The wall is over a mile in length and five or six feet in height where it has not been reduced by cultivation. Within this enclosure are fifteen mounds, the largest

FIG. 226. CONVENTIONAL INCISED DECORATIONS ON POTTERYWARE FROM PECAN POINT, ARKANSAS
Diameter, 8 inches. After Moore.

of which, near the center of the semicircle at the open side, is 48 feet in height and 280 by 150 feet at the base. During the flood of 1844 a number of people took refuge within this enclosure, which was the only spot above water in several square miles. The mounds encircled by this wall are probably of the domiciliary type, since trial holes sunk in them failed to bring up anything of interest beside the usual refuse material found on dwelling sites.

A mound in Jefferson County, thirteen miles southeast of Pine Bluff, is of special interest because of a persistent tradition that the great Spanish explorer De Soto camped upon it for some time. It is rectangular and flat-topped, with a lower terrace at one end upon which at the time of its exam-

FIG. 227.   POTTERY VESSEL IN HUMAN EFFIGY FORM, FROM RHODES PLACE, ARKANSAS
Height of vessel, 8½ inches. After Moore.

ination by Thomas were situated two log houses and other buildings. The upper terrace measures 144 by 110 feet and is 60 feet above the level of the ground.

Effigy pipes as well as effigy vessels are abundant along the Mississippi River in Arkansas. Stone ear plugs, disks, rubbing stones and hammerstones, implements and ornaments of horn, bone, flint, and shell are also found, on the surface of the ground as well as in burial mounds. In digging a grave in a mound near Akron, in Independence County, in use as a modern cemetery, a marine shell engraved with a unique design was discovered. By its unusual proportions, 300 feet in diameter and 7 feet high, this mound is nicely adapted to use as a cemetery by the people of the nearby town.

A great many mounds in Arkansas, whether they were originally erected as places of refuge, for residence, or for purposes of interment, contain burials of both white and colored persons, and there are several instances of this use of mounds as municipal cemeteries. Professional gravediggers declare that in the course of their work they often exhume as many remains as they bury. In Desha County it is reported that in time of flood the dead had been brought in boats to a mound used as a cemetery within the limits of Arkansas City.

EXPLORATIONS IN ARKANSAS OF CLARENCE B. MOORE

Between the years 1908 and 1911 Clarence B. Moore excavated mounds on the Arkansas shore of the Mississippi River; on the Arkansas River from its mouth to a point twenty miles above Little Rock; fifty-eight miles of the Saline River; the short stretch of the Red River in Arkansas; and the Ouachita River from its junction with the Red in Louisiana to Camden, Arkansas. The Saline River region and those portions of the Red and Ouachita rivers lying in Arkansas will be treated in the discussion in the following chapter of the main centers of aboriginal culture along the two last-named watercourses in Louisiana.

The Moore expedition found one of the richest sites along the lower Mississippi at Pecan Point, in Mississippi County, Arkansas, a few miles below the town of Wilson. Here, in a field around a square mound about twelve feet high, were uncovered 349 burials and 535 earthenware vessels, the greater number of which lay near skulls. Very often a bowl and a bottle were deposited together. Only twelve vessels decorated in color were found, an unusual condition in view of the frequent use of pigment characterizing the pottery of the St. Francis valley to the west. A few pots bore incised decorations, but the execution was crude in comparison with the work of the aboriginal potters of central Louisiana. Effigy vessels predominated in the material recovered from Pecan Point, including both animal and human forms. One interesting vessel in effigy of an animal is supported by the four

FIG. 228. POTTERY VESSEL WITH MULTIPLE HANDLES FROM CRITTENDEN COUNTY, ARKANSAS

Height, 8½ inches. After Moore.

feet of the animal represented. A vessel in effigy of a human head, a rare type found only in northeastern Arkansas and southeastern Missouri, is shown in Figure 224. One of the most interesting finds at Pecan Point is a wide-mouthed water bottle with the human hand, face, and limb bones in relief on the sides (Figure 225). Other vessels of this type from Mississippi and Alabama, with similar decorations incised, will be referred to later. A strikingly beautiful bowl with a combination of deeply incised lines and figures in low relief covering almost the entire outer surface is illustrated in Figure 226.

Two vessels from Rhodes Place, Crittenden County, where in a field around a mound Moore found 65 burials and 123 vessels, are of interest. One, an effigy of a seated human figure (Figure 227), shows the arms, hands, and ribs in low relief. The other, a bowl (Figure 228), has just beneath the rim a series of eight arches or arcades, the columns of which stand out away from the body. On another bowl from the same site there are sixteen of these arches, the columns of which are pilastered against the body. This vessel, with surface decorations of lines of shallow indentations made by pressure with the end of a small stick, is of a type rarely encountered in the Lower Mississippi area.

Among the seventy-five vessels found at Avenue, Phillips County, in a series of burials on two low ridges, is a "teapot" portraying a turtle lying on its back with legs, head, and tail extended in the manner characteristic of this reptile when placed in that position. This vessel is decorated in solid red on the bottom and in lines and circles about the head and tail. The remainder of the surface, excepting the base, which shows the original yellow of the clay, is coated with a cream-colored pigment. A fine polychrome water bottle from Kent Place, in Lee County, is decorated with alternate bands of red and white with narrow strips between showing the unpainted yellow of the ware.

Another important site is at Bradley Place, in Crittenden County, on the shore of a former channel of the Mississippi River. Four mounds in a group, one of them twenty feet in height, were not excavated by Moore as they would provide places of refuge in the event of the breaking of a nearby levee; 181 burials, however, were found in the ground between them and the old channel. As is characteristic of the northern subarea, a large number of effigy vessels were found in this cemetery. Incised decoration was almost entirely absent, and among the 258 vessels recovered but nine were decorated in pigment. Two of the more interesting pieces are a wide-mouthed water bottle with a raised ropelike decoration dividing the body into ten equal parts, probably portraying the manner in which the vessel was carried; and a shallow bowl with four slightly projecting points on the rim, the two pairs of points being diametrically opposite one another. A number of copper objects also were found at Bradley Place, including bracelets and stone ear plugs covered with thin copper.

FIG. 229. TEAPOT FORM OF POTTERY VESSEL FROM OLD RIVER LANDING, ARKANSAS COUNTY, ARKANSAS
Height, 4¼ inches. After Moore.

Along the Arkansas River effigy vessels, including the "teapot," occur, but not in the abundance characterizing the territory to the north of the river. The "teapot" probably had a more or less accidental origin in the desire that all projecting parts of effigy vessels should be serviceable, as previously noted in connection with perforation from the inside of the feet of vessels in other parts of the lower Mississippi valley. In the painted "teapot" shown in Figure 229 the spout represents the tail of an animal and the knob on the opposite side is the head, originally from an æsthetic point of view the most important part of the vessel but now, through a slow process of development, nearly unrecognizable. Effigy water bottles, not often found in the southern district, are encountered along the Arkansas River. As in the northeastern part of the state, smaller vessels were often placed with the remains of children.

FIG. 230. POLYCHROME WATER BOTTLE FROM THE MENARD MOUND, ARKANSAS COUNTY, ARKANSAS

The neck and star-shaped designs are in terra-cotta color, the circular areas are orange, and the body of the vessel is buff. Height, 9½ inches. After Moore.

In a cemetery of considerable size at Greer, Jefferson County, on the north side of the Arkansas, 80 burials and 160 vessels were found, an average of two vessels for each individual. The decorations of the vessels consist mainly of varieties of the scroll incised upon the surface in broad shallow

THE LOWER MISSISSIPPI AREA

lines, many of them very intricate. The entire base of one shallow bowl is covered with an interesting modification of the swastika, a motive of frequent occurrence in the Lower Mississippi area as well as elsewhere in North America. In form alone several of the vessels found at Greer are exceptional, rivaling in simplicity and balance the best products of modern artists. In the midst of the cemetery at Greer is a mound covered with modern gravestones.

Another cemetery surrounds the Menard Mound, about four miles above the union of the Arkansas and White rivers. The site is on high ground not subject to overflow, and it was probably this consideration that determined its use by the Mound-builders. The mound is circular, truncated, 34 feet in height and 167 feet in diameter. Small rises of ground in the immediate vicinity yielded most of the burials, of which Moore removed 160, with 214 earthenware vessels. One beautiful water bottle, very graceful in outline, was the only example of decoration in two colors other than in a scroll pattern found on the lower Arkansas River. The star motive on this vessel (Figure 230) done in terra cotta on an orange background, is of rare occurrence north of the Arkansas River. A variety of pottery forms were found at the Menard site, including several bowls with the head and tail of a bird or animal modeled in the round on opposite sides of the rim, a form common to many parts of the Lower Mississippi area.

Other important sites in Arkansas are near Sawyer's Landing, in Arkansas County; near Old River Landing, in the same county about three miles above Arkansas Post; and at Douglass, in Lincoln County.

FIG. 231. POTTERY WATER BOTTLES WITH INCISED DECORATIONS FROM GLENDORA PLANTATION, LOUISIANA

The vessel on the left, referred to in the text, is 8¼ inches high; that on the right, 8 inches high. After Moore.

CHAPTER XVII

THE LOWER MISSISSIPPI AREA: II, LOUISIANA, MISSISSIPPI AND ALABAMA

The State of Louisiana—The State of Mississippi—The Moundville culture of Alabama—Other sites in Alabama.

ARCHÆOLOGICAL interest in Louisiana centers in the valley of the Ouachita River and in the narrow strip of land between the Ouachita and the Mississippi drained by the Tensas and Boeuf rivers and Bayou Bartholomew, the two latter streams, like the Ouachita, extending well into Arkansas and carrying with them the major aspects of the culture centering about the lower portions of their courses in Louisiana.

THE STATE OF LOUISIANA

Emphasizing Moore's distinction between the pottery north of the Arkansas River and that to the south, incised decoration combined with the use of pigment, generally covering the entire vessel in a solid color, reached a high degree of excellence in the Ouachita valley. On the Glendora Plantation, near the union of Bayou Bartholomew with the Ouachita, in Ouachita Parish, Louisiana, there was a center of ceramic culture where incised decorations were executed by experts. While much of the pottery found here is ordinary, as is true of all aboriginal sites, a few pieces exceed in beauty anything else of the kind in aboriginal North America. The water bottle shown at the left in Figure 231 has a beauty of form and embellishment which, if we can for the moment free ourselves of the prejudice of artistic tradition, compares favorably with anything to be found in the art stores of the present day. The swelling at the neck of this vessel, a very common feature of

371

the water bottles of Glendora, was probably derived from a compound form in which one bowl or bottle was superimposed upon another.

In the Glendora cemetery human remains were encountered by Moore at 121 different places, though it was impossible to estimate the exact number of individuals represented. The

FIG. 232. COLORED WATER BOTTLE FROM KENO PLACE, ARKANSAS

Body color is olive-green with incised lines colored brick red. Height, 7½ inches. After Moore.

greater part of the 322 earthenware vessels found on the site were with human remains in groups of from one to five. The pot, bottle, and bowl forms predominated, and many of the latter, covered from rim to base with incised designs and coated with red pigment, are of very graceful appearance.

The pottery forms from three Arkansas cemeteries bear a remarkable resemblance to those of Glendora; namely, at Keno

Place, on Bayou Bartholomew five miles north of Glendora; Haley Place in Miller County; and Battle Place in Lafayette County, the two latter on opposite sides of the Red River. One of the more unusual types of water bottle from the Keno site is superior in its proportions and in the simplicity of the colored design (Figure 232). Another unique vessel from the same site, an effigy vessel with four legs, has a rudimentary tail and a neck in place of the head of the animal and is incised with a combination of scrolls, disks, and the crosshatch pattern. A similar vessel from Glendora is shown in Figure 233.

FIG. 233. EFFIGY POTTERY VESSEL WITH INCISED DECORATION FROM
GLENDORA PLANTATION, LOUISIANA
Height, 4½ inches. After Moore.

In view of the proximity of the Keno and Glendora sites and the fact that both were occupied in early historic times, it is possible that one represents a new settlement after the other had been abandoned. Features of the Keno site not found at Glendora were water bottles with extremely long necks and eleven earthenware elbow pipes. Other objects placed with burials in these two cemeteries were chert knives, arrowpoints, chisels, and flakes; a ceremonial axe of sandstone; a small stone hatchet perforated for attachment to a handle; shell beads; plummets of hematite; stone celts; and irregular masses of galena and hematite. Traces of human remains, badly decayed like those at Glendora, were found by Moore at Keno Place in 224 places. Most of the 485 earthenware vessels were placed near the heads of skeletons, singly or in groups of from two to four.

The pottery of two other neighboring cemeteries, one at Sycamore Landing, about a mile distant from Keno Place and the other at Bray Landing, eighteen miles northward, resembles that of Keno and Glendora only remotely. Surface modelings in rather high relief on the vessels from Bray Landing and from Mound Place, a mile to the westward on the same side of the Bayou, present features noticed elsewhere in the region.

Other important burial places in the Ouachita valley of Louisiana are at Pritchard's Landing, in Catahoula Parish, where there is a group of fourteen mounds, the largest of which is 40 feet in height, flat-topped; and at Myatt's Landing, in Ouachita Parish, where thirty-eight burials and seventeen vessels were found, including several bottles of the usual type but rather crudely made.

In the Arkansas portion of the Ouachita valley both mounds and cemeteries yield pottery similar to that of the Glendora and Keno sites but for the most part of a comparatively inferior grade. At Boytt's Landing, in Union County, and at Kent, in Ouachita County, both on the south side of the river, were cemeteries around flat-topped mounds. At Keller Place, Calhoun County, in one of two flat-topped mounds Moore found traces of fifty-two skeletons and, by coincidence, the same number of vessels. A long-necked water bottle from this site, painted red, with an incised design resembling an hourglass on the body, bears at the opening the modeled representation of the ears, mouth, and nostrils of an animal of some kind. Among other articles found at Keller Place were two imitation bear teeth made of wood and coated with sheet copper.

There are mounds and cemeteries in Ashley, Bradley, and Union counties, a large number of the mounds in the latter being of the problematical type so common in Oklahoma and southern Missouri. In Bradley County on Green Lake, a former channel of the Ouachita River, there is a group of eight mounds, the largest of which, square and flat-topped, is 19 feet in height and 160 feet in basal diameter.

Along the Saline River, in Arkansas, which drains the territory between the Ouachita and Arkansas rivers, joining the former a few miles north of the Louisiana state line, human remains occur almost exclusively in mounds rather than in cemeteries. These mounds, however, are little more than irregular rises of ground varying from two to four feet above the general level with diameters up to 70 feet. While a great many of the vessels found with burials are decorated, which is to be expected in the territory south of the Arkansas River, the work is crude in comparison with the earthenware of the Ouachita valley. A deep bowl from a site in Bradley County bore on the sides a series of raised vertical and horizontal ridges incised transversely, apparently in imitation of the twist of a cord or rope, a motive occasionally encountered in other parts of the general region. In a mound near Wherry Landing, in Bradley County, Moore found thirteen out of twenty skeletons with the heads pointing toward the south, the other seven having been disturbed by subsequent placements. This is one of the few examples in the region of apparently intentional orientation of burials.

Very few artifacts were found with burials along the Red River in Louisiana. From the confluence of the Red with the Atchafalaya River near the Mississippi to the Arkansas state line mounds are fairly numerous, ranging in height from three to twenty feet. They are mostly flat-topped, and, as is the rule with flat-topped mounds in the Lower Mississippi area, burials are superficial, raising the presumption of an original domiciliary purpose. Besides the occurrence of cremation in mounds in Avoyelles, Red River, and Bossier parishes the most interesting find along the Red River in Louisiana was an earthenware pipe in effigy of a squatting human figure supporting on the knees and arms a biconical pipe of earthenware (Figure

234). A remarkable feature of this effigy pipe is a hole, inside the body of the figure, extending from the bowl to the mouth, the purpose of which was doubtless to allow the smoke to issue realistically from the mouth of the figure, which is turned in the direction of the user.

In a small mound on the Foster Place in Lafayette County, 50 feet in diameter and 4 feet high, Moore obtained 246 earthenware vessels with only eleven burials. The vessels were de-

FIG. 234. HUMAN EFFIGY PIPE OF BURNED CLAY, FROM GAHAGAN, LOUISIANA

The interior passage connecting the pipe bowl with the mouth of the image is unique and apparently was designed so that smoke might be exhaled by the effigy. Height, 5½ inches. After Moore.

posited in various manners, some vessels containing others, some covered at the top by others, inverted or upright. Shell cups covered the openings of bottles in a number of cases. Most of the vessels contained the remains of food offerings— mussel shells and bones of fish and of the gray squirrel. Others held what was probably the remains of decomposed white and green pigment, with which latter a large number of vessels had been covered. Moore says of these vessels that the coating of green was not "in connection with decoration, since the green coating was often found over vessels already decorated with pigment or otherwise, but placed as a coating as if done in fulfillment of some ceremonial rite of mourning." The vessels themselves were of a higher grade than those found elsewhere along the Red River, a number having polished surfaces. The chief designs were composed of curvilinear parallel lines with punctate instead of crosshatched interspacing, concentric circles, and the "sun pattern." A small water bottle of black ware, six inches in height, with each of the four lobes of the body incised with the "sun pattern" and accentuated in red pigment, is one of the finest specimens ever found in the Mississippi valley. Three shallow bowls from the Foster Mound were unique in having four short connected legs at the bottom of a circular base. The legs of one of these vessels are hollow and contain pellets or rattles of baked clay, strongly suggestive of the hollow-legged tripod ware of the Chiriqui district of Panama.

The list of artifacts other than pottery found at Foster Place includes small earthenware pipes; arrowheads; shell cups; slate ceremonial axes; bone pins; pendants of the columellæ of sea shells, three of which are in effigy of the lizard; a fine flint blade about 16 inches in length; shell gorgets showing openwork modifications of the swastika; and ear spools of limestone covered with copper foil.

Nothing of outstanding interest has been found in that part of Louisiana immediately to the west of the Mississippi River between the Tensas and Atchafalaya Rivers, which parallel the Mississippi. The largest mound so far recorded along the Atchafalaya is a truncated cone on Sorrel Bayou, in Iberville Parish, about 16 feet in height with a diameter of 140 feet. The pottery found along the Tensas resembles that of the Ouachita valley. Incised scrolls, circles, and the crosshatch patterns are found, and the bowl, only slightly constricted at the top, and the water bottle are the predominating forms. The mounds are of the usual type, square or circular, flat-topped, and with heights varying from 2 to 19 feet. One circular mound

4 feet high and 65 feet in diameter has been erected recently
by the present inhabitants as a place of refuge for stock.

The region about Lake Larto, in Catahoula Parish, a little
northwest of the union of the Red and Black rivers, long has
been famous locally for the abundance of artifacts upon the
surface. An interesting feature of several vessels from the
Mayes Mound, on the western shore of the lake, is the "killing"
or perforation of the bases of pots during the process of manu-

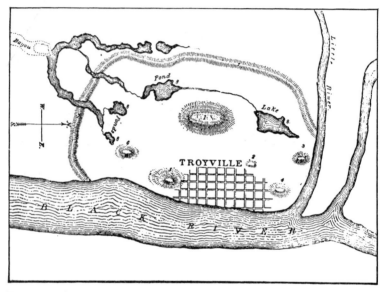

FIG. 235. MAP OF THE TROYVILLE MOUNDS AND ENCLOSURE, CATAHOULA
PARISH, LOUISIANA

Approximately 100 acres lie within the enclosure. Bureau of American Ethnology.

facture. This ceremonial perforation of vessels and the absence
of incised scroll and circle designs would indicate that the
Mayes Mound people were not in close contact with those who
conceived and made the great variety of vessels found along
the rivers to the north. Perhaps the most welcome find in the
Mayes Mound was a fine earthenware pipe in effigy of a frog,
originally coated with red pigment. Beyond doubt this effigy
pipe represents the most abundant form of "animal" life in
this low-lying, swampy region.

At Poverty Point near the town of Floyd, in West Carroll Parish, there is a group of six mounds close to the banks of Bayou Mason, the largest of which is 70 feet in height. This mound is shaped like a T, the two component parts being about 690 feet in length. The vertical portion of the T is flat-topped. Others of the mounds vary from 4 to 21 feet in height and the entire group is laid out in a rough semicircle. Although nothing was found in any of the mounds, objects from the surface of the surrounding fields are of considerable interest, offering perhaps a welcome relief from the monotony of

FIG. 236. MOUNDS OF THE TROYVILLE GROUP, CATAHOULA PARISH, LOUISIANA
Bureau of American Ethnology.

beautiful pottery forms of other portions of the state. Among the profusion of flint flakes and points, stone celts, and broken pieces of aboriginal clay hearths only a few scattered potsherds were found. Great quantities of "plummets" or pendants, ornaments, mostly of hematite, have been picked up from the surface. The Moore expedition found on this site sixty-seven peculiar objects of baked clay, of various shapes, some of them resembling the ankle bone of the deer. These earthenware objects are authoritatively regarded as "gambling cones" such as were in use during the past century by the Paiute Indians in the West. Considering the almost complete absence of potsherds and other ordinary domestic accumulations, perhaps the Poverty Point site is all that remains of an aboriginal Monte Carlo, curiously well named if prehistoric gambling led to the same financial state as in modern times. About a mile distant from Poverty Point is another mound, 51 feet in height, possibly erected by the same people.

There is little of archæological interest along the Louisiana banks of the Mississippi River. From Baton Rouge southward cultivation has been practiced for a long period of years on every available spot. Moore mentions mounds with superficial burials not more than two feet beneath the surface near Shaw Field, in Pointe Coupee Parish, and just north of Glendale Landing, in Concordia Parish. Near Transylvania, on the Mississippi, is a mound 50 feet high in a group of smaller ones.

One of the largest earthen enclosures in the lower Mississippi valley is situated in Catahoula Parish at the junction of the Tensas, Ouachita, and Little rivers, the three uniting at this point to form the Black River (Figure 235). A semicircular wall a mile in length and averaging 8 feet in height and 20 feet in width encloses on two sides the hamlet of Troyville and five mounds. The banks of two rivers close the roughly circular area, 100 acres in extent. The largest mound of the group (Figure 236), about 60 feet high and 250 feet long, was used during the Civil War as a place for rifle pits, its original shape being almost completely obliterated. In one of these mounds burials and artifacts were found by gravediggers excavating for modern burials.

THE STATE OF MISSISSIPPI

The more remunerative sites in the State of Mississippi are found in the counties bordering the Mississippi and in the valleys of the Sunflower and Yazoo rivers. In these areas mounds and earthworks of the usual type are abundant. A few shell deposits are to be found also, but these attain their greatest size along the Gulf Coast. Between Vicksburg and Greenville, however, a distance of about 124 miles by the course of the Mississippi, cemeteries in the fields surrounding mounds are completely lacking, a condition which perhaps may be attributed to long-continued cultivation of the region.

While the pottery and other artifacts found in the mounds of the State of Mississippi do not present important differences from the typical forms of the archæological province, the occurrence of artificially flattened skulls and the abundance of early historic material, such as glass beads, objects of brass, iron, and so forth, distinguishes the archæology of Mississippi, as well as that of the adjoining State of Alabama, from that of Louisiana and Arkansas. This occurrence of historic material is to be expected, since of all the states included in the Lower Mississippi area Alabama and Mississippi lie nearest to the centers of early European occupation with which the then resident Indians naturally were in contact.

In Adams County, in the vicinity of Natchez, where the Natchez Indians were first encountered by the whites in 1682, there are a number of earthworks. The chief village of the Natchez at the time they were first visited by the French was on the site of the White Apple Group of mounds, two of which are still to be seen, on the bank of Second Creek. These tumuli are conical in form, 12 to 18 feet in height with diameters of 200 and 131 feet. Part of one of the mounds has been cut away by the creek, a process which, with the deposition of silt, has obliterated a great many aboriginal sites on the banks of the Mississippi and its tributaries.

Twelve miles northeast of Natchez, near the Jefferson County line, two mounds stand upon a larger rectangular plateau with an area of some five acres. This plateau, varying from 21 to 44 feet above the level of the surrounding ground, is, in the opinion of Calvin S. Brown, State Archæologist of Mississippi, not entirely artificial. Stone pipes have been found here, and large quantities of burnt earth bearing impressions of cane indicate the use of this eminence as the site of wattle-work structures of some sort. Although Squier and Davis give the number of mounds on the plateau as eight, there are but two at the present time, at the east and west ends.

Other important mounds in Adams County are the Anna or Robson Group (Figure 237), twelve miles north of Natchez in the foothills back from the river, consisting of four pyramid mounds, the largest of which is 50 feet in height; the Quitman mounds, eight miles north of Natchez, eight in number; and the Lewis mounds, about two miles to the north. Skulls taken from the Quitman Group in 1843 showed artificial frontal flattening. This deformation of the skull is in many parts of North America an accidental result of long-continued contact with a

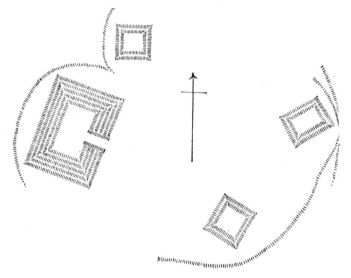

FIG. 237. MAP OF THE ANNA OR ROBSON MOUNDS, NEAR NATCHEZ,
MISSISSIPPI

Scale, 1 inch to 300 feet. After Brown, *Archæology of Mississippi.*

board designed to keep the babe "in arms" from falling out of a cradle carried on the back of its mother. Intentional deformation is practiced by primitive peoples the world over, originating very likely in some such accidental way and attaining the status of a permanent trait upon the acquisition of religious, social, or æsthetic significance. In its intentional form it is analogous to the binding of the feet by Chinese women and, nearer home, the constriction of the female torso in recent times by tight lacing. Flattened skulls are found in Mississippi in Adams and Jefferson counties and along the Yazoo River. In one of a group of seven conical mounds, the Ferguson Group, on the bluffs along the Mississippi in Jefferson County, all the skulls had been subjected to the flattening process, and a stone pipe in effigy of a human figure from the same mound has a flattened head.

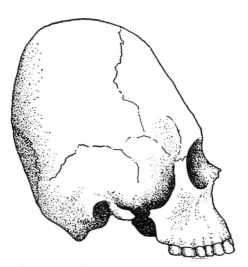

FIG. 238. SKULL SHOWING ARTIFICIAL FRONTAL FLATTENING

From the Sowell Mound, Washington County, Florida. Redrawn from Moore by H. R. Goodwin.

One of the best-preserved and largest mound groups in the state is to be found about a mile south of Winterville, in Washington County, on the Mississippi River bottom. A large central mound, square, flat-topped, and 55 feet in height, is surrounded by fourteen others with elevations varying from 4 to 30 feet.

In Union County, in the northern part of the state, is another fine group of fourteen mounds, twelve of which were originally surrounded by an earthwork, at the edge of a bluff overlooking Okanitahatche Creek. At the time it was visited by Gerard Fowke, in 1885, a small portion of the earthwork, nearly three feet in height, was still to be seen. The wall, with a ditch on the outside, was in the form of a square, each side measuring about 1,500 feet. The central and largest mound in this group is rectangular, truncated, and flat-topped, with a graded way on the east side. It was, at the time of Fowke's examination, 27 feet high and 153 by 234 feet at the base.

Of both archæological and ethnological interest is a great

mound in Winston County, ten miles southeast of the town of Noxapater, situated on a point of land formed by the junction of two rivers. It is known as "Nanih Waiya," which means in the Choctaw language, "slanting hill." Brown, in his *Archæology of Mississippi*, says of this mound that it is "identified by tradition as the place of origin or the birthplace of the Choctaws, who held it in superstitious reverence as their mother." Nanih Waiya was apparently the Choctaw Garden of Eden, since their account of the creation centers about this mound. In the words of Halbert, writing in the *Publications*

FIG. 239. THE AVONDALE GROUP OF MOUNDS, WASHINGTON COUNTY, MISSISSIPPI

Bureau of American Ethnology.

of the Mississippi Historical Society: "All the modern Choctaws living in Mississippi look upon Nanih Waiya as the birthplace and cradle of their race. . . . In the very center of the mound, they say, ages ago, the Great Spirit created the first Choctaws, and through a hole or cave, they crawled forth into the light of day. Some say that only one pair was created, but others say that many pairs were created."

Nanih Waiya is 22 feet in height, flat-topped, and rectangular, with its main axis, 218 feet in length, lying northeast and southwest. Originally this tumulus and several other small mounds nearby were surrounded on three sides by an embankment which attained in some places a height of ten feet. The translation of the Choctaw name, "Slanting Hill," aptly describes the profile of the mound. It is easily accessible by automobile and is well worth visiting. The Choctaw, greatest in the arts of husbandry among the southern Indians, numbered from fifteen to twenty thousand when first encountered by the French. A number of them are still living in Mississippi and Louisiana, and in 1904 nearly eighteen thousand were in Indian Territory on a government reservation.

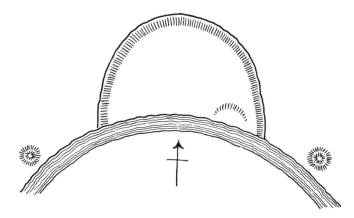

FIG. 240. MAP OF A PREHISTORIC EARTHWORK ON SUNFLOWER RIVER, SHARKEY COUNTY, MISSISSIPPI

Area within enclosure, 45 acres. After Brown, *Archæology of Mississippi.*

Aboriginal settlements were thick along the Sunflower and Yazoo rivers, particularly in Yazoo and Sharkey counties. Here, as elsewhere, flat-topped mounds are used as places of refuge for stock in time of flood, and quite recently a mound was erected for that purpose in the village of Holly Bluff.

Half a mile from the union of Lake George with the Sunflower River, in Yazoo County, is a spectacular group of mounds surrounded by an earthen wall. The central mound, square and flat-topped, is 60 feet high and covers about 1¾ acres. There are some thirty mounds within the enclosure, that next in size to the central one being 23 feet in height.

One of the mounds is the site of a farmstead, a large house and several barns. Abundant refuse material, potsherds, shells, flint chips and flakes are found on the mounds and in the vicinity.

In Sharkey County, near the union of the Sunflower and Yazoo Rivers, is an earthen enclosure with an area of 45 acres, roughly semicircular, with a ditch on the outside (Figure 240). The two ends of the semicircle terminate almost at the water's edge. This enclosure is known locally as the "Spanish Fort," but quantities of potsherds and shells found in an examination of a dwelling site within the wall point to prehistoric origin.

Two interesting groups of mounds are to be found in the valley of the Sunflower in Coahoma County, in the northern part of the state. Originally an earthen wall enclosed four mounds, one of them square and flat-topped, on the site of the present town of Clarksdale. The two ends of this deep semicircle terminated at the edge of the river bluff. The square, flat-topped mound at the edge of the bluff was probably used only as a dwelling site, but burials and earthenware vessels have been found in the others. At Oliver, on the south bank of the Sunflower, a large mound, 26 feet high and 190 by 180 feet at the base, is the central feature of a group of about twenty smaller mounds. A total of 158 burials and 68 vessels, including water bottles decorated with painted scrolls, and compound "triple" types, were found in this central mound. Judging by the strata and the distribution of burials and refuse material, it seems to have been built up as a burial mound and as a dwelling site at alternate intervals. European relics, including glass beads and brass bells and points, were found in the upper or latest level, indicating long-continued use reaching into early historic times.

Brown describes some fifty or sixty mounds along the lower portion of the Sunflower River in Sharkey, Washington, and Yazoo counties. Near Carey in Sharkey County is a group of four mounds, the largest 22 feet in height, and at St. Helena in the same county there is a rectangular, flat-topped mound 25 feet in height and 250 feet long at the base.

Skulls showing artificial deformation have been found in the Champlin mounds two miles north of Yazoo City and the same distance east of the Yazoo River. The mounds are on low ground, and Thomas records that during the flood of 1882 they were surrounded by water. The largest mound of this group is 106 feet long and 14 feet above the level of the ground at its highest point. It is made up of three smaller connecting mounds, resembling in plan three conjoined circles. Shell beads, celts, a small water bottle, and other objects were found with burials in this mound. It is interesting to note that skulls showing artificial deformation were in every case unaccompanied by artifacts. Shell heaps, from two to five feet in

Fig. 241. Incised decorations of the human head, hands, and long bones on a pottery vessel found at Walls, Mississippi

Scale, 1/2. Redrawn from Brown, *Archæology of Mississippi*.

thickness, are abundant along the Yazoo for some distance north of Silver City.

Enclosures are to be found in Panola and Tunica counties, in the extreme northern part of the state. The Batesville Group in Panola County consists of five mounds, two of which are square and flat-topped, the others being truncated cones. Near Delta a group of several mounds surrounded by a square enclosure about 20 acres in area was visited in the 1840's by Squier and Davis. In Tunica County about three miles north of Hollywood an earthen wall made up of a series of connected oval mounds surrounds a large, square, flat-topped mound 22 feet in height and seven others of lesser size.

From the point of view of the determination of culture distributions one of the most important groups in Mississippi lies in De Soto County, in the northwest corner of the state, near the village of Walls. A large number of effigy pots, including the teapot form, the short-necked water bottle, and the frequent embellishment of vessels with incised scrolls indicate contact with the tribes across the Mississippi River in eastern

Fig. 242. Earthenware bottle or vase with incised designs representing the human skull and hand, from a mound in central Mississippi

Height, 8 inches. Redrawn from Bureau of American Ethnology.

Arkansas. Compound pottery forms were also found at Walls, several of which are decorated in two colors. The representation in incised lines of skulls, leg bones, and hands on a wide-mouthed water bottle (Figure 241) is exactly the same, a little less skillfully executed perhaps, as that upon funerary vessels found at Moundville, Alabama, and at Pecan Point, Arkansas (compare Figures 225 and 247). Bowls from the vicinity of Walls representing the head and tail of birds on opposite sides of the rim recall similar forms found in the Ouachita valley and elsewhere.

Flat stone disks, occasionally notched or indented on the perimeters, are found in Mississippi and Alabama. One such disk about eight inches in diameter, taken from a mound in Issaquena County, Mississippi, in 1870, is completely covered on one side with decorations representing conventionalized rattlesnakes. This disk, which is now in possession of the Ohio Archæological and Historical Society (Figure 76), bears a remarkable resemblance to another found at Moundville, Alabama, to which further reference will be made later.

Dr. H. B. Collins of the Bureau of American Ethnology recently has carried out explorations in Mississippi and adjacent territory as a result of which the striking admixture of cultures of the region is made apparent. In eastern Mississippi and in adjacent portions of western Alabama there are numerous small sand mounds, in groups, containing at their centers masses of mixed human bones representing secondary burials or reburials. A large mound located in the eastern part of Mississippi, explored by Dr. Collins in 1925, presented a combination of unusual features indicating the handiwork of some outside influence, possibly northern. The decorated potteryware was mainly of the North Atlantic cord-marked type, with a sprinkling of South Atlantic ware. The flint projectile points were of a type unknown or rare locally, and the presence of thin flaked flint knives, struck from a nucleus by a single blow and closely resembling those of Flint Ridge material found in Ohio, gave cause for speculation.

Shell mounds or "heaps" representing in most cases the slow accumulation of refuse material from aboriginal meals are found along the Gulf Coast of Mississippi. The more notable examples are in Hancock County, near the town of Bay St. Louis; and near the city of Biloxi and in the vicinity of Delisle, in Harrison County. At the latter place there is a large bank of shells which was originally one hundred yards long and in places as high as six feet. Much of this shell bank has been removed to provide material for roads. Human remains

FIG. 243. MOUND AT KULUMI, MONTGOMERY COUNTY, ALABAMA
Where De Soto crossed the Tallapoosa River in 1540. Courtesy of P. A. Brannon.

and artifacts are occasionally found in these shell heaps, but they are in the main uninteresting. So also are the contents of the burial mounds of the region, several of which were examined by Moore in Jackson and Harrison counties.

THE MOUNDVILLE CULTURE OF ALABAMA

With the State of Alabama we reach the eastern frontier of the Lower Mississippi archæological province. Alabama might well be called the "buffer state" between the Peninsular and Georgia-Carolina districts on the one hand and the Lower Mississippi on the other, for it shares certain manifestations of cultures with all three.

The most important site in Alabama, however, and in many respects in the five states comprising the Lower Mississippi area, belongs thereto exclusively, for it shows almost no contact with other cultures of the state or with those of Florida and Georgia. Near the city of Moundville on the line between Hale and Tuscaloosa counties, on the south bank of

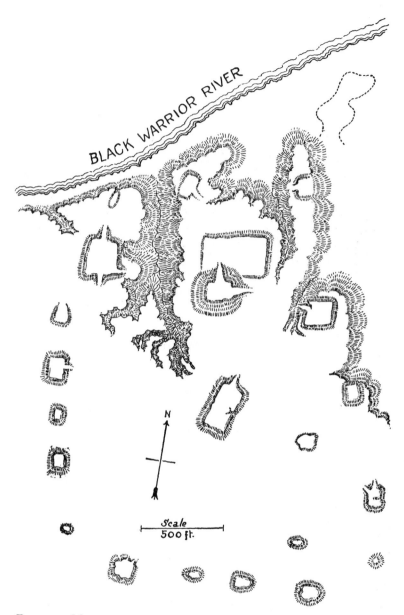

FIG. 244.   MAP OF THE MOUNDVILLE GROUP, NEAR MOUNDVILLE, ALABAMA
Redrawn from Moore.

the Black Warrior River, is one of the finest mound groups in the country. Exploration work conducted intermittently during the past twenty years, but for the most part by Clarence B. Moore in 1905 and 1906, has yielded an abundance of rich material of value to the professional student of American archæology and of fascination to those whose interests are more casual.

On a level plain extending back from the gullied bluffs of the river nineteen square and oval flat-topped mounds varying in height from 3 to 23 feet are arranged in a rough circle about two others, 22 and 57 feet high. Most of the mounds, including the two latter, have one or more graded ways connecting their summits with the level ground. The oblong mound lying nearest the center of the group covers the largest area, 195 by 351 feet, although it is less than half as high as its companion directly to the north. On the north side of this latter mound is an artificial platform about 1⅔ acres in extent. The plateau upon which the group is situated is well above the highest level reached by the waters of the Black Warrior River.

During two separate expeditions to Moundville Moore excavated some 560 individual burials. About 455 of these came from level ground around certain of the mounds, the remainder being found in the mounds themselves. A large number of earthenware vessels and other artifacts accompanied the burials, and often these objects alone were the only indications of an inhumation, so badly were the human remains disintegrated. Not a single object of European origin was met with at Moundville, and this may be regarded as conclusive evidence that the occupation of the site lay entirely within the prehistoric period.

Moundville is south of the hypothetical boundary line separating the lower Mississippi valley into two subareas, and in accord with this situation the pottery is decorated with incised patterns, painted vessels occurring in but three instances. Although a few effigy vessels were found, the representation of life forms at Moundville was limited mainly to incised fig-

ures of birds. Two stone effigy vessels, however, surpass anything else of that nature, not only from the territory to the
north of the Arkansas River, but from the entire mound region
as well.

The art of Moundville is characterized by a few basic motives admitting of relatively brief description, but the accompanying illustrations tell the story much more effectively.
Most of the designs, whether upon vessels or other artifacts,
contain these motives in various stages of conventionalization
and with differing subsidiary embellishments. These few characteristic motives are the sun pattern; the swastika; the human

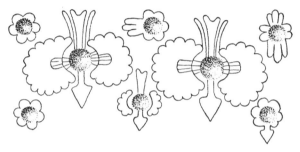

FIG. 245. SUN PATTERN DESIGNS ON A POTTERY VESSEL FROM MOUND-
VILLE, ALABAMA

The rosettes represent the sun, and the large figures the sun pierced by an
arrow. The whole concept suggests the sun as the shield of the sun-God, and the
arrow a ray or dart, analogous to the symbolism of some historic Indian tribes.
Scale, 1/4. Redrawn from Moore.

hand, eye, skull, and arm bones; the horned serpent; the eagle,
heron, and ivory-billed woodpecker, all of which birds inhabit
the region at the present time; and a design, previously met
with in Louisiana and Arkansas but which so far has been
identified with no natural object, consisting of a circle elongated into points on opposite sides with an oval, often cross-
hatched, centerpiece. These designs are incised on earthenware vessels, shell, and stone disks and pipes and excised or
embossed on copper.

The sun pattern, to which reference previously has been
made in discussion of the sites at Haley Place and Foster
Place in Arkansas, is augmented on a vessel at Moundville by

a more realistic representation of the rays, scalloped figures resembling clouds, and an arrow apparently passing through the sun (Figure 245). Moore says of this remarkable pattern, which is incised on the body of a wide-mouthed water bottle: "It would be quite in keeping to represent an arrow with the sun, the arrow representing a ray or dart of the Sun-God, and the sun representing his shield as portrayed by our Indians down to the present time."

FIG. 246. DOUBLED COMPOSITE BIRD DESIGN FROM MOUNDVILLE, ALABAMA

With the head of the heron and the tail of the ivory-billed woodpecker, while the figures within the mouth are believed to be speech symbols. Scale, 2/3. After Moore.

An appreciable number of vessels have incised on the bodies conventionalized bird and reptile forms, the heron and ivory-billed woodpecker predominating. The rattlesnake, occasionally given wings by the fancy of the artist or very likely as a result of Mexican influence, is the only serpent represented at Moundville. Often the bird design is duplicated more than once on the same vessel, and double-headed forms are abundant. This doubling of life forms by inversion of one-half the figure, very common in the art of Moundville, is suggestive of the representation of kings, queens, and jacks on modern playing cards, although it is not apparent that the prehistoric inversion served the same purpose (Figure 246). The figures issuing from the bills of certain of the double-headed woodpeckers and composite bird designs have been called speech symbols. Whatever these symbols were meant to represent, they bear an unmistakable resemblance to those suspended from the ear plug of the human figure on the shell disk from Missouri described in Chapter XVI. The resemblance is too striking to be accidental, although it affords no explanation of the real meaning of these interesting symbols.

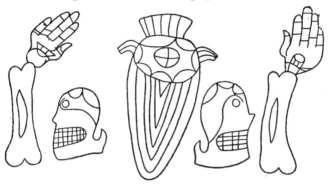

FIG. 247. SKULL, HAND, AND ARM-BONE DESIGN FROM MOUNDVILLE, ALABAMA

From a funerary vessel. The unknown figure possibly represents an earthen jar. Scale, 1/2. After Moore.

The artists of Moundville were not particular about strict maintenance of generic differences. Quite frequently the heads, tails, or wings of different birds are combined in the same figure. For example, a double-headed figure on a water bottle from a grave has the head and neck of a heron with the fanlike tail of the woodpecker, the tongue of this composite bird being extended in the manner characteristic of the ivory-billed woodpecker (Figure 246). Eagles incised on the sides of a number of vessels bear a close resemblance to eagles cut in sheet copper from the Hopewell Mound in Ross County, Ohio. With one exception these avian designs show the profile aspect. In this single instance the body with extended wings is portrayed as seen from the front, but the head is in profile. The bird represented in this particular design is the ivory-billed woodpecker.

A vessel from the adjacent ridge shows the skull, bones of the forearm, and the hand, the latter apparently as in life, with a complicated figure of unknown meaning (Figure 247). Due either to faulty observation or to the desire of the artist to emphasize a distinctive feature, the ascending ramus or articular process of the lower jaw is exaggerated and placed out beyond the corresponding process in the skull, which is a little in front of the ear opening. A somewhat similar emphasis of this element of the lower jaw has been found in certain of the Mexican codices. The slightly oval figure on the palm of one of the hands in this design may represent the human eye, since the eyes of the skulls are about of the same

FIG. 248. SKULL, HAND, AND EYE DESIGN FROM MOUNDVILLE, ALABAMA
From a pottery vessel. Scale, 1/3. After Moore.

shape and size. Much more realistic, however, are the eyes, in the same position on the palm, on another vessel from the same group (Figure 248). It is quite apparent from the shape of the orbits in the skulls that the aboriginal artist intended to distinguish between the "eye" of the death's head and that of the living being. Symbols of life and death are here portrayed side by side on the same vessel, which itself was made for no other purpose than as a tribute to the dead by the living. Perhaps the eye and hand symbolize the hope of life after death.

The human hand has been interestingly conventionalized at Moundville into several different patterns, all of which apparently retained the original significance of the hand complete. Some of the hands show the finger nails and the creases at the joints, as do those on the funerary vessel just described, while on other vessels only the fingers are shown, on a scale that would have allowed room for the palm had the fingers been drawn a trifle smaller. Four sets of three fingers arranged in a cross with diagonal arms on a water bottle from Mound-ville are possibly indicative of the four cardinal points (Fig-

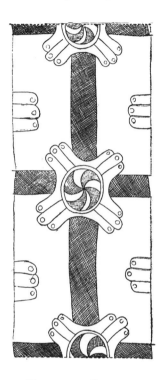

FIG. 249. CONVENTION-ALIZED HAND DESIGN FROM A POTTERY VESSEL FROM MOUNDVILLE, ALABAMA

Showing the swastika and human finger design indicat-ing the four directions. Scale, 1/3. After Moore.

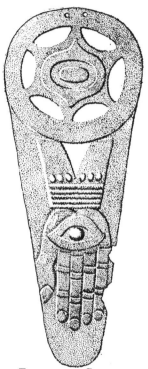

FIG. 250. CEREMONIAL ENGRAVED COPPER OBJECT FROM MOUNDVILLE, ALA-BAMA

A cosmic symbol appears above and the hand-and-eye symbol below. Scale, 3/4. After Moore.

ure 249). If this and other motives have a Mexican origin, the four sets of three fingers above and below the crosshatched band may symbolize "up" and "down," which in Mexico com-pleted the full complement of the six world quarters. This conventionalization of the hand offers a possible clue to the significance of lines on the colored cloth found adhering to a copper breastplate from the Seip Mound, of the Hopewell culture in Ohio, already described in Chapter IX.

Two water bottles from Moundville show the mysterious circle pointed at the poles. On one of these vessels the symbol is the main motive of a pattern formed by its duplication. The same symbol is found in Arkansas, at Pecan Point on the Mississippi River, and at Walls, Mississippi, either incised on

FIG. 251. ENGRAVED STONE DISK FOUND NEAR CARTHAGE, ALABAMA
Scale, 1/4. Bureau of American Ethnology.

vessels or carved on stone, as a slightly raised collar on the shoulders of water bottles or forming outlines of rims of vessels. A copper pendant from a Moundville grave has this interesting symbol in repoussé in combination with a six-pointed excised star and the hand-and-eye pattern, also in repoussé (Figure 250).

A remarkable stone disk found on the surface at Moundville during the latter part of the last century has engraved upon one side four of the motives just described. The parallel series of lines between the skulls apparently are conventionalized fingers, and the hand-and-eye pattern appears twice at the upper right of the disk. Beneath these two hands the design bearing a curious resemblance to a Roman chariot as seen from beneath is a variation of the sun pattern. The remaining figures on this disk probably are symbols whose likeness to an originally realistic form has been lost, with the exception perhaps of the series of five circles and points, which

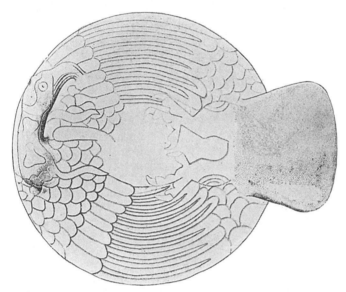

Fig. 252. Limestone effigy bowl found at Moundville, Alabama

Showing effigy of a bird engraved on sides and bottom. Length, including tail, 14 inches. After Moore.

is apparently the tail of a bird in a further stage of conventionalization than those incised on vessels. This disk is now in the Peabody Museum at Cambridge, Massachusetts. Another disk, referred to earlier in this chapter in connection with the rattlesnake disk found in Issaquena County, Mississippi, has a design of two horned rattlesnakes in a circle about the hand-and-eye pattern (Figure 251).

This extensive use of symbolic figures by the Moundville peoples may be regarded as incipient picture writing, differing only from the Maya and Egyptian hieroglyphs in their simplicity. Whereas the Maya and the Egyptian could tell a complete story by a complicated system of more or less conventionalized figures, these designs on the funerary offerings of Moundville deal with only a few fundamental concepts such as life, death, the "six world quarters," if the interpretation of the finger and swastika patterns be correct, and whatever religious or ethical ideas were identified with the serpent, bird,

FIG. 253. EFFIGY BOWL CARVED FROM DIORITE FOUND AT MOUNDVILLE, ALABAMA

The material from which this unique specimen is carved is extremely hard and its manufacture entailed great labor and skill. The effigy represents the wild duck. Height of bowl proper, 8 inches. After Moore.

and other designs not yet understood. The development of a complete and practical system of writing among the Indians of the southeastern United States was finally effected early in the nineteenth century by Sequoia, a Cherokee halfbreed, who compiled an alphabet based upon Cherokee symbols, some of which were perhaps similar to those of Moundville.

Some fine work in stone was recovered from the Moundville Group by Moore. Near one of the mounds was found a limestone bowl with the head and tail of a bird on opposite sides of the rim, a type of effigy vessel usually done in earthenware, of frequent occurrence in the Lower Mississippi region (Figure 252). The head of this bird, on an unnaturally elongated neck, is so curved that the bill returns to the side of the bowl, forming a loop handle, the tail providing a complementary handle on the opposite side. Certain features of this effigy are characteristic of the king vulture, but like many of the bird figures incised on earthenware of Moundville, it is probably a nondescript composite of a number of birds common to the region in which it was made. At the present time the habitat of the king vulture, which this effigy resembles more than any other, does not extend above southern Mexico.

FIG. 254. CEREMONIAL COPPER AXE, MOUNDVILLE, ALABAMA

A portion of the original handle is preserved in place, showing the method of hafting this type of implement. Length, 8 inches. After Moore.

One of the finest products of the art of primitive man the world over is a stone vessel from a grave in the ridge adjacent to the Moundville Group (Figure 253). This bowl, made of diorite, a very hard stone used by primitive peoples in making axes and celts, is eleven inches in diameter and of about the same height. The gracefully arched head, which the aboriginal artist probably intended as that of the drake of the wood duck, is embellished with a series of figures of unknown significance. The conventionalized tail of the bird is undecorated. The maker of this remarkable bowl exercised commendable forbearance in leaving the body unembellished except for the four well spaced and skillfully incised lines just beneath the rim. The whole exquisite simplicity of the piece rivals the best artistic productions of any age. We can be sure that whether or not the vocabulary of the Moundville people contained the word "taste," that rare quality was possessed at least by the one who, with almost unlimited patience and energy, found this "angel" in a block of diorite.

A fine monolithic stone hatchet found near one of the mounds is an interesting example of the conservation of obsolete details which in the evolution of primitive technical forms often characterizes the reproduction of an implement or orna-

FIG. 255.   EAGLE EFFIGY PIPE FOUND AT MOUNDVILLE, ALABAMA
Length, 4½ inches. After Moore.

ment in a new material. As in the specimen from the Etowah Group illustrated in the following chapter, the squared rear projection of the handle of this piece reflects the reluctance of the maker to part with an originally functional detail; the result is the monolithic reproduction of the hatchet of copper or stone which was fitted closely into a hole in a separate wooden handle which projected beyond it away from the cutting edge. In Europe, where mankind progressed gradually from the use of stone through copper and bronze to iron, there are many examples of this reproduction of functional details made unnecessary by the use of a new material.

Three hoe-shaped stone implements from Moundville, in

the opinion of Moore, are ceremonial axes, and the subsequent finding of a small shell pendant skillfully worked into the shape of one of these hoe-shaped implements hafted on a handle strengthens his contention. A number of copper axes were found at Moundville, one of which retained parts of a wooden handle (Figure 254). About one inch of the handle projected beyond the blade—possibly the very hatchet from which the monolithic piece was copied.

Cremation, copper breastplates, ear plugs, and the use of mica were known to the Moundville people. A very unusual hair ornament with a unique design, made of copper mounted upon a bone pin, may well move us to regret that the art of Moundville did not contain more objects of this kind. Among other objects taken from the graves and mounds of the site are shell drinking cups, shell gorgets, shell pins, ear plugs of wood coated with thin pounded copper, a copper fishhook, stone celts, bone awls, flint points, stone pipes, hammerstones, pitted stones, animal bones, earthenware ornaments, and a human head carved in amethyst.

OTHER SITES IN ALABAMA

Moore lists some fifty or sixty mounds along the lower Tombigbee River, varying in height from one to ten feet. The greatest diameter attained by the mounds in this locality is 220 feet, with a disproportionate height of six feet. Burials were found in the greater number of them, including the "bunched" variety, extended skeletons, flexed skeletons, and lone skulls. Objects other than earthenware included the usual flint points, knives, and drills; celts, occasionally of a volcanic stone; irregular masses of galena or lead ore; and earthenware pipes. In a mound in Marengo County on the opposite side of the river from Brown's Landing the bones of a child were accompanied, among other relics, by an earthenware elbow pipe, a mortuary offering probably unique in the annals of New World archæology and indicating that smoking, utility or ceremonial, was not confined to adults.

But two examples of artificial skull deformation were found along the lower Tombigbee, both in a mound of a group of four near Three Rivers Landing, in Washington County. An urn burial was uncovered in a mound in Clarke County, and three more near Gaine's Landing, Washington County. The pottery for the most part is uninteresting and quite different both in form and decoration from that of Moundville. The check stamp, entirely absent from the Moundville pottery, is frequently encountered along the Tombigbee. A pot with a

FIG. 256. MOUND ON TALLAPOOSA RIVER, AT PAKANA, MONTGOMERY COUNTY, ALABAMA

Courtesy of P. A. Brannon.

mortuary perforation at the base, "killed" in accord with the primitive belief that the spirit of the pot was thereby released, was taken from a mound in Clarke County.

The largest mound groups in this locality are in Marengo County. About forty mounds are at Bickley's Landing, and near Breckenridge Landing there is a group of forty or fifty in a swamp, ranging from one to six feet in height, all of them in use as places of refuge for stock in time of flood. There is still another group of thirty-one near Rembert's Landing, none of them exceeding four feet in height.

Both mounds and shell heaps are to be found along the shore of Mobile Bay. Shell deposits examined by Moore in Baldwin County contained burials, pottery disks probably used in gambling, and potsherds bearing loop handles and various designs including the crosshatch and check stamp. Frog and duck effigies in earthenware were found in a shell heap on Simpson's Island. At Blakely, in a shell deposit several acres in extent, Moore found cremated remains and a skeleton with an ornament of sheet copper, and in a sand mound near Stark's Landing, Baldwin County, containing about twenty burials, a piece of mica cut in the shape of a spearhead was

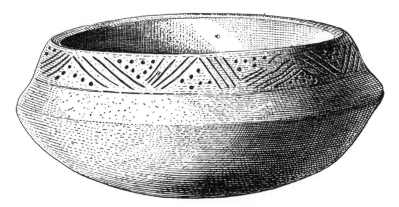

FIG. 257. POTTERY BOWL FROM MONTGOMERY COUNTY, ALABAMA
Diameter, 6½ inches.

discovered. On Bottle Creek there is a mound 46 feet in height, oblong, with basal dimensions of 300 and 250 feet.

Although there is usually little difference between the types of pottery found in the mounds and in shell heaps, the opposite is markedly noticeable in the vicinity of Seymour's Bluff. The potsherds from a group of seven mounds at the edge of the bluff were not shell-tempered, and the decoration consisted almost exclusively of the check stamp; while one mile distant potsherds in a shell bank bore incised and punctate decorations in all cases and were tempered exclusively with shell.

Moore describes some eighteen mounds on Mississippi Sound in Alabama, in groups of from four to eleven, in Mobile, Jackson, and Harrison counties. The largest of these mounds has an irregular outline and is 11 feet in height with a maxi-

FIG. 258. HUMAN EFFIGY PIPE FROM A MOUND NEAR CARNEY'S BLUFF, ALABAMA

Diameter, 4½ inches. After Moore.

mum diameter of 450 feet. It is of the domiciliary type. Nothing of importance has been found in or near these mounds.

The few shell heaps along the Alabama River are small and without artifacts or burials of special interest. The mounds, which are of the usual types, increase somewhat in size toward the north where there are fewer swamps.

Perhaps the most important site and at the same time the

most characteristic of this region is at Durand's Bend, in Dallas County, thirteen miles above Selma. Here in 1886 an aboriginal cemetery was opened up by the river when it overflowed its banks. Between that time and the excavations of the

FIG. 259.   BURIAL URN CONTAINING SKELETONS OF INFANTS

From a mound at Mathews' Landing, on the Alabama River, Alabama. Diameter of vessel, 16 inches. After Moore.

Moore expedition in 1899 a large number of relics were taken from the site by visitors. The outstanding feature of this cemetery, and of the Alabama valley as a whole, is the burial of skeletons in earthenware vessels or urns (Figure 259), usually one skeleton in a vessel but often more—the "urn burial" to which reference has previously been made. The vessel holding the remains is generally covered by one or more other vessels in an inverted position. Besides urn burials twenty-seven unenclosed skeletons were found at Durand's Bend. Urn burials were usually made in bowls of medium depth somewhat constricted at the neck. The objects found in these funeral urns include mussel shells, shell gorgets, and beads. The urns themselves occasionally have loop handles and are decorated mainly with line and punctate patterns, raised zigzag borders just beneath the rim, and rows of small knobs. One sherd bore the circle, in this case much elongated, with the points on opposite sides, as encountered in Moundville art.

CHAPTER XVIII

THE TENNESSEE-CUMBERLAND AREA

Extent and characteristics of the area—Southwestern Indiana and southeastern Illinois—The State of Kentucky—The State of Tennessee—Northern Georgia—The Etowah culture—Virginia and the Carolinas.

THE segregation of what the present writer has chosen to designate as the Tennessee-Cumberland area is perhaps less justifiable, from the standpoint both of culture and of physiography, than any other of the assumed divisions of the general mound area. Culturally it exhibits close affinities with the Lower Mississippi area, with which it obviously merges toward the west. Again, still culturally considered, it might be divided into two distinct subareas, the one comprising the region of the lower Wabash dividing the states of Indiana and Illinois and extending across Kentucky into central Tennessee, and the other corresponding to eastern Tennessee and adjacent portions of Georgia and the Carolinas. Geographically this division seems a logical one, with the rather sterile mountainous belt intervening between the two subareas. Each subarea, moreover, possesses an outstanding nucleus of development, that to the westward finding its best expression in the stone-grave mounds and cemeteries about Nashville, and the eastern region culminating in the remarkable Etowah Group near Cartersville, Georgia. However, although local differentiations are rather marked and the usual diversity of cultures is in evidence, the culture complex of the area as a whole is sufficiently homogeneous to justify its classification as a single division of the general mound area. Besides, such divisions as are assumed for this volume are intended mainly as vehicles to facilitate the reader's consideration and understanding of the mound area rather than as definitely established lines.

EXTENT AND CHARACTERISTICS OF THE AREA

The Tennessee-Cumberland area comprises the State of Kentucky with the exception of its northern and western extensions, which pertain to the Ohio and the Lower Mississippi areas; those portions of southern Indiana and Illinois bordering on the lower course of the Wabash River; Tennessee, exclusive of that portion of the state fronting on the Mississippi River; and northern and northwestern Georgia and the Carolinas.

As intimated above, the affinities of the Tennessee-Cumberland are with the Lower Mississippi area, in both material and æsthetic culture. The artistic attainment of the area approximates that of the noted Hopewell culture, but in the matter of earthen structures, such as geometric earthworks, it is not so spectacular. This is counterbalanced in great part, however, by the prevalence of the great flat-topped pyramids known as "house" or "temple" mounds. Compared with the Lower Mississippi area, the occurrence of conical mounds appears to be in greater proportion to the number of flat-topped structures, but these are not so abundant as in the Lower Mississippi area. The most persistent characteristic of the region as a whole is the frequency of boxlike stone graves, a trait which probably owes its high development to the common occurrence of stone suited to the purpose. Embankments and enclosures of both stone and earth are abundant in the region, particularly in central Kentucky and Tennessee. It is interesting to note that the general trend of these embankments and walls is northeast and southwest, perhaps in keeping with certain physiographical features. The enclosures of the region usually are roughly circular or semicircular in form, and as a rule they are situated on the bluffs and steep banks of streams, the precipitous character of which offered imposing obstacles to the approach of enemies and thus furnished a degree of protection. Enclosures almost always are accompanied by stone-grave burials, hut rings, and ditches or moats. Associated mounds usually comprise one or more centrally located flat-topped structures around which are grouped smaller conical mounds. Stone-grave burials occur both in mounds and in ordinary cemeteries. Within the flat-topped earthen tumuli are found ash beds and burned clay, indicating the former presence of domiciliary and ceremonial structures, as in the area to the south. Immediately adjacent to the pyramidal mounds a clear space devoid of other structures was maintained, presumably for ceremonial and social use.

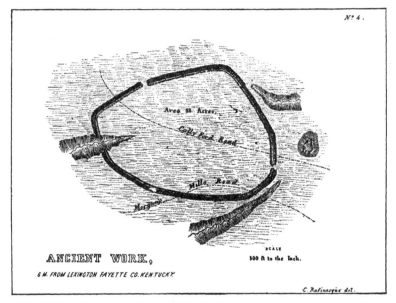

FIG. 260.   MAP OF A TYPICAL KENTUCKY EARTHWORK
After Squier and Davis, *Ancient Monuments.*

Of the minor artifacts within the area, potteryware is the most abundant and striking, indicating a high development and wide employment of the fictile art. With the possible exception of southeastern Missouri and portions of Arkansas, potteryware is more in evidence in the Tennessee-Cumberland area than in any other part of the general mound region. Other striking features are stone and terra-cotta human and animal effigies; stone idols; engraved shells and repoussé copper plates bearing intricate conventional designs; masks of the human face made from shell; large ceremonial knives, swords, and maces, chipped from flint and other silicious materials. In all instances throughout the area where the basic culture is manifest, the mound groups and their attendant phenomena represent the sites of aboriginal towns and villages.

SOUTHWESTERN INDIANA AND SOUTHEASTERN ILLINOIS

The region of the lower Wabash River on both the Illinois and Indiana sides presents what appears to be a northern extension of the assumed Tennessee-Cumberland culture area to the southward. The evidences along the west side of the river are not important as so far disclosed, but within the angle of southwestern Indiana formed by the junction of the Wabash and the Ohio numerous major remains are found. Among these is an important group partly enclosed by an earthen wall near the town of Merom, in Sullivan County. The large truncated central mound of this group is surrounded by a number of small conical tumuli, apparently domiciliary in their origin and quite similar to those of the region to the southward and those of southern Illinois and southeastern Missouri. Other groups are reported in the same county, with large truncated mounds which appear to be domiciliary. Similar mounds and groups occur in Vigo, Sullivan, Knox, Gibson, and Posey counties, bordering on the Wabash, and in Vanderburg County, on the Ohio River, most of which are accompanied by hut rings, village-site débris, and burial grounds. Although several cultures apparently occupied the area, the dominant elements pertain to the region to the southward, particularly as regards potteryware and other minor evidences.

In Vigo County more than three hundred mounds have been identified, the greater number of which are, or were, located along the bluffs of Otter Creek and in the valley of Prairie Creek.

Sullivan County has the distinction of being the scene of the first scientific exploration of prehistoric mounds within the State of Indiana. What is known as the Albee Mound, located in Fairbanks Township, was explored in 1926-27 by J. Arthur MacLean for the allied historical interests of the state, and his findings were reported in the *Indiana Historical Bulletin* for May, 1927. The Albee Mound yielded several burials of flexed skeletons with which were shell and bone beads, together with a few made of copper; notched flint arrowpoints and perforators; and implements and ornaments of bone, antler, and stone (Figure 261). The culture of the site

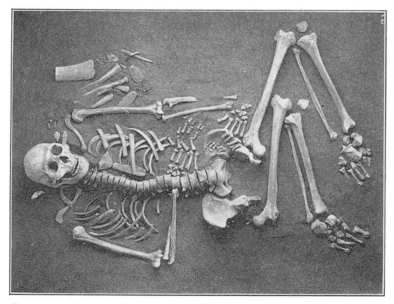

FIG. 261. BURIAL IN THE ALBEE MOUND, SULLIVAN COUNTY, INDIANA
Explored by J. Arthur MacLean in 1926-27. Courtesy of Mr. MacLean.

is unusual and as yet undetermined. In Sullivan and adjacent counties appears the interesting phenomenon of natural knolls utilized as mounds, either as they occur or by modifying and adding to their original forms. Near the town of Merom is located Fort Azatlan, an enclosure three acres in extent. An earthen wall protects one side of the roughly rectangular enclosure, while the Wabash River and deep ravines delimit the remaining sides.

Knox County, in which is located historic old Vincennes,

the scene of the consummation of George Rogers Clark's conquest of the Northwest Territory, is rich in prehistoric remains. Both along the Wabash, to the west, and adjacent to the White River, which forms the eastern and southern boundaries of the county, there are numerous mounds and sites of prehistoric occupancy. Shell mounds or shell heaps with burials contained in stone cists abound along the Wabash. Numerous

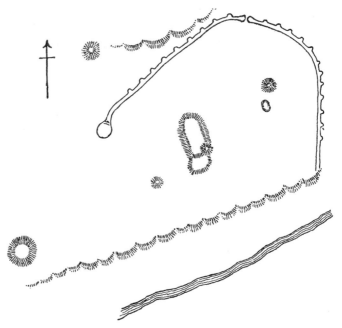

FIG. 262. MAP OF THE ANGELL MOUNDS AND EARTHWORKS, NEAR EVANSVILLE, INDIANA

Scale 1 inch to 600 feet. Redrawn after the Bureau of American Ethnology.

mounds occur in the vicinity of Vincennes, near Edwardsport and Sandborn, and on the Dixburg Hills. The mounds of a group of 52 situated six miles southeast of Purcell are arranged in lines. On the river terrace just southwest of Vincennes there are three truncated pyramidal mounds, while at the northeastern edge of the city there is a terraced mound more than 65 feet in height. In Gibson County there are mounds on Skeleton Cliff, at Dripping Springs, at Upper and Lower Hills, and near Buena Vista. In Posey County mounds are located at West Franklin, on the Ohio; at New Harmony; and near Mt. Vernon. Collections of specimens are displayed in the local museums at New Harmony and Evansville.

On a bayou of the Ohio eight miles southeast of Evansville, in Vanderburg County, is located the Angell Group, an enclosure and six mounds. The central mound of the group is 30 feet high, oblong and flat-topped, with an apronlike extension at its south end. A conical mound 20 feet in height surmounts the main platform at the southeast of the structure, which is 520 feet in length. In addition, the group comprises four smaller conical mounds and one striking flat-topped conical structure 15 feet in height. The wall of this group is crescentic, two to five feet in height and extending for a length of 2,600 feet. It has a single gateway and is featured by buttresslike earthen projections at intervals on the outside extending almost the entire length of the wall. A group of twelve small mounds, probably domiciliary, enclosed by a double earthen wall with intervening ditch, is reported in Orange County by Cyrus Thomas, to whom most of the information concerning this section of Indiana is attributable.

The most important of the mound groups reported on the Illinois side of the Wabash is one near Hutsonville, examined by the Bureau of American Ethnology. A number of the larger tumuli of the group present the unusual feature of encircling earthen rings.

THE STATE OF KENTUCKY

In justice to the writer and to the subject it should be noted that the State of Kentucky, apparently a border region in prehistoric times as it has been, in some respects, within the historic epoch, is difficult to handle archæologically. A wealth of information awaits scientific exploitation, a beginning of which has been made by the University of Kentucky under the direction of Professor William S. Webb and his associates. An archæological survey of the state together with carefully planned explorations is now under way.

As a matter of convenience, since it appears desirable to consider it in connection with certain rather well defined archæological districts, the state is apportioned to the three major divisions—the Ohio area, comprising the region adjacent to the State of Ohio; the Lower Mississippi area, embracing the extreme western extension of the commonwealth; and the Tennessee-Cumberland area, to which the greater portion of the state appears to belong.

That portion of Kentucky having its affinity with the Ohio area has been discussed in Chapter XI. The western end of the state may be disposed of in a few words, for the reason that little is known of its prehistoric evidences. The narrow Mississippi bottoms of the region are skirted by high bluffs which are cut by numerous streams; thus are formed prominent headlands with natural defensive possibilities. According to Thomas in his *Report on Mound Explorations* for the Bureau of American Ethnology, a number of these are surmounted by defensive earthworks, the most important of which is located on the point of a bluff near the town of Oakton, in Hickman County. This work, known as O'Byam's Fort, consists of a crescent earthwork within which are several mounds and numerous hut rings. The earthen wall, accompanied by a moat, is 1,800 feet in length. The largest mound in the enclosure, 23 feet high, is unusual in that, although a true flat-topped form, it is located on high ground well above flood water. Another mound of the group, originally a prehistoric burial place, is now occupied by a modern cemetery.

Further removed from the river valley and occupying the higher land of the district there occur conical mounds, built mostly of sand and containing neither burials nor other indications of use, so far as is known.

Adjacent to the Mississippi River there are numerous large shell mounds, while along the Tennessee and Cumberland rivers in the same locality the stone-grave cemeteries characteristic of Tennessee occur.

Reference to the map of mound distribution (Figure 7) shows that the greatest density of mounds in Kentucky lies within an area bounded by imaginary lines drawn from Henderson and Owensboro, on the Ohio River, southward across the state. It will be noted also that this area represents the central part of a distinctive belt of mounds, extending from the Lower Wabash region across Kentucky and central Tennessee, which, owing to the frequency of occurrence of mounds therein, appears on the map as practically isolated and as occupying the territory intermediate between the Ohio and Lower Mississippi areas. It is assumed, however, that to the

FIG. 263.   POST HOLES OUTLINING A HOUSE IN A DOMICILIARY MOUND
NEAR TRENTON, CHRISTIAN COUNTY, KENTUCKY
Kentucky Archæological Survey, 1928. Photograph by William S. Webb.

south it trends eastward through eastern Tennessee and culminates in the noted Etowah Group, the great center of prehistoric culture located near Cartersville, Georgia.

The mounds of the portion of this belt that lies within Kentucky appear to be mostly domiciliary, although exploration probably will disclose the associated conical burial mounds, cemeteries, and hut rings characteristic of the Tennessee-Cumberland area. A mound of the domiciliary type located six miles west of Trenton, in Christian County, was

FIG. 264. EXPLORING A SHELL MOUND ON GREEN RIVER, OHIO COUNTY, KENTUCKY

Kentucky Archæological Survey. Photograph by William S. Webb.

explored by Webb and his colleagues in 1928. The tumulus presented the interesting phenomenon of three different levels of occupancy, with the remains of a building on each level. The successive domiciliary structures were evidenced by the molds of posts driven or set into the surface (Figure 263); each of the buildings had been burned and the site covered with a foot or more of earth, after which a new structure was erected in its stead. This mound, in the opinion of Webb, is typical of the district above outlined. The few burials occurring in the tumuli of the region appear to be intrusive and of later date than the mounds themselves. They are of the modified stone-grave type, as identified in Tennessee in the vicinity of Chattanooga, Nashville, and elsewhere. The mounds themselves, conical in form and ranging in height from three to twelve feet, usually occur in connection with or adjacent to localities containing cemeteries of the true stone-grave peoples, although apparently not directly attributable to them. From the fact that true stone-grave potsherds were found by him on the floor levels or original surfaces of these mounds, Webb

FIG. 265. A PREHISTORIC CLIFF DWELLING IN KENTUCKY

The man in the photograph has his arm inserted in a "hominy hole," character-istic of these cliff dwellings located in Hardin, Breckenridge, Meade, and Hart counties. Photograph by William S. Webb.

concludes that they were probably erected during or after the occupancy of the stone-grave builders.

An interesting archæological feature of the Blue Grass State are the shell mounds of central western Kentucky. These occur generally on the immediate banks of Green River and often on the bottom lands, where in time of high water they represent virtual islands. The shell mounds are most abundant in Ohio, Butler, and adjacent counties. They vary in area from 3 to 17 acres, with depths of 4 to 12 feet, and consist of fresh-water shells closely packed by the agencies of time, weather, and water. Intermingled with the shell content of the mounds are animal and human bones, mostly well preserved. In the opinion of Webb, these shell mounds, which have disclosed neither potteryware nor evidences of agriculture, are among the oldest human evidences in Kentucky.

An exception to the characteristic barrenness of the shell mounds of Kentucky is that known as Indian Knoll, in Ohio County. From this mound Clarence B. Moore, who conducted explorations of the structure, obtained many striking artifacts, among which were objects resembling the so-called banner-stones, together with bone or antler "weaving hooks." The stone objects, called by Moore "net spacers," are made from several handsome varieties of stone and are remarkable for their beauty of form and finish.

In the region immediately to the west and south of the shell-mound area of Kentucky the University of Kentucky survey has disclosed an interesting culture which occupied the shelters at the bases of cliffs bordering the tributaries of Green River, particularly in Hardin, Breckenridge, Meade, and Hart counties. An outstanding trait of these peoples is the "hominy holes" found excavated in the rock adjoining their domiciles (Figure 265). In several instances the bell-shaped stone pestles have been found within the mortarlike depressions.

Throughout southern Kentucky numerous caves and shelters bear evidences of prehistoric occupants. These peoples, whom Webb regards as possibly related to the historic Cherokee, made a fair quality of potteryware, used hoes and agricultural implements of limestone, smoked pipes of burned clay, and wore shell gorgets engraved with pleasing designs. Their flexed burials, wrapped in skins and bark matting, are well preserved by the nitrates of the caves, as are their grass matting, woven bags, and moccasins.

In the general vicinity of Lexington, on the Kentucky River, there is a notable density of mounds, characterized by frequent large size and, so far as is known, by absence of burials or other evidences of use. A number of the mounds of this region attain heights of 70 feet or more and cover several acres of ground. The source of the earth for constructing them is apparent in the numerous holes and depressions in the adjacent surface. Effigy stone pipes, copper and slate ornaments, and other objects are found in the vicinity of the tumuli. The pipes usually are conoidal or are in the images of birds and animals.

The varied and interesting character of Kentucky archæological remains is evident despite the limited amount of exploration accorded the state. Thomas in his *Report of Mound
Explorations* describes the examination of one of the Lost
Creek Group, in Union County, in which the blending of various modes of burial was outstanding. The earlier or lower tier

FIG. 266. EARTHENWARE WATER BOTTLE FOUND NEAR LOUISVILLE,
KENTUCKY
Bearing the spiral "sun symbol." Scale, 1/2. Photograph by William S. Webb.

of burials in the mound were unaccompanied by stone graves
or artifacts, while later interments were covered by inclined
slabs of stone and provided with pottery vessels. The bodies
in the latter tier were buried in a circle, with heads toward
the center of the mound. In another mound in the same county
the order seemed to be reversed, in that the lower tier of
burials were laid down in a circle and accompanied by pottery

vessels and pipes, while the later interments, occupying stone graves, were without special arrangement and unaccompanied by artifacts.

In the Lindsay Mound, near Raleigh, in Union County, three modes of burial were encountered. Occupying conical pits dug into and below the base level were indiscriminate human remains; burials without prepared graves or relics lay on the original surface; while in the body of the mound were five

FIG. 267. MOUND WITH MOAT AND EMBANKMENT NEAR LEXINGTON, KENTUCKY

This interesting tumulus is 250 feet in diameter and 12 feet high. Photograph by William S. Webb.

tiers of burials, each tier arranged in two concentric circles, the bodies accompanied by earthen vessels.

Enclosures and fortifications of the types mentioned in the introductory paragraphs of this chapter are fairly in evidence throughout central Kentucky. Stone-grave cemeteries, often in connection with enclosures but occurring apart therefrom, are found alike in the valleys and on the slopes adjacent to the important rivers and their tributaries. The stone grave also is a common form of burial within the mounds of the region.

THE STATE OF TENNESSEE

American archæology would be much poorer without the rich heritage of prehistoric remains within the boundaries of the State of Tennessee. For many years the name Tennessee has been synonymous with certain spectacular phases of the pre-history of the mound area, notably the striking development

FIG. 268. BURIAL CASKET OF POTTERYWARE FROM HALE'S POINT, TENNESSEE

Length, 12 inches. After Thruston, *Antiquities of Tennessee*. Courtesy of Stewart Kidd, Cincinnati.

of stone graves in burial of the dead; the high level to which the art of pottery-making was carried; the depicting of the human head and figure and of animal and bird images in terra cotta and stone; and the perfection with which the difficult art of chipping flint was practiced.

The numerous stone graves of the state, numbering in the aggregate many thousands and occurring both in cemeteries and in mounds, are an outstanding feature. Unfortunately for the archæology of the region, these stone graves have been entirely too accessible and too attractive to the amateur explorer and the relic hunter. The fact that they frequently lie within easy reach beneath the sandy surface of the soil and that the human remains interred within them are often accom-

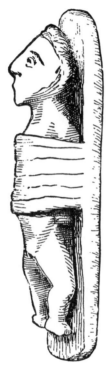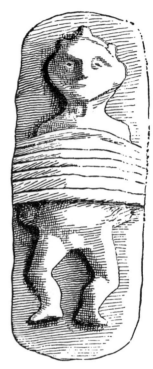

FIG. 269. IMAGE OF BURNED CLAY, FROM A STONE GRAVE NEAR NASHVILLE, TENNESSEE

This unique specimen depicts an aboriginal infant strapped to its cradle board. Note the flattened skull. Height, 9 inches. After Thruston, *Antiquities of Tennessee*. Courtesy of Stewart Kidd, Cincinnati.

panied by attractive pottery vessels and other artifacts has led to their wholesale despoliation at the hands of the curious or the commercially minded "digger."

While the stone-grave form of burial is widespread throughout the central and southern parts of the general mound area, the nucleus of occurrence is in the valleys of the Tennessee and

Cumberland rivers, in central Tennessee. The region immediately adjacent to Nashville has been the most prolific. Half
a dozen unusually large cemeteries and many smaller ones
have been located along the Cumberland and its tributaries

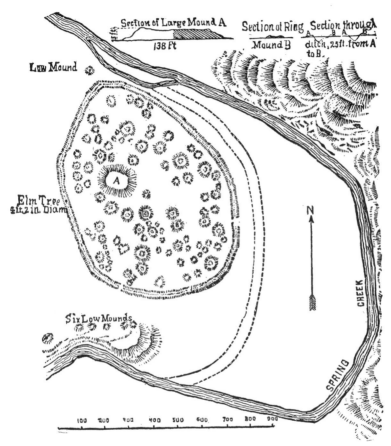

FIG. 270. LEBANON GROUP, NEAR LEBANON, TENNESSEE
After Thruston, *Antiquities of Tennessee.* Courtesy of Stewart Kidd, Cincinnati.

within a few miles of the capital of the state, and individual
graves as well as small groups of burials occur on almost every
farm. The largest of the cemeteries of this vicinity, situated
on Brown's Creek, a few miles from Nashville, is estimated
to have contained upward of four thousand burials. Not less

than six thousand graves were examined in this and adjoining districts by the late Professor Frederick W. Putnam of the Peabody Museum of Harvard University, and Dr. Joseph Jones and other earlier explorers disclosed many additional ones. A report issued in 1844 estimated that the great burial ground on the bank of the Cumberland River opposite Nashville was more than one mile in length.

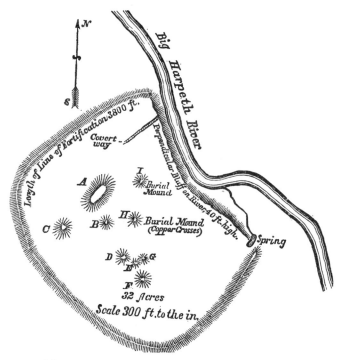

FIG. 271. MAP OF THE DE GRAFFENREID WORKS, WILLIAMSON COUNTY, TENNESSEE

After Thruston, *Antiquities of Tennessee*. Courtesy of Stewart Kidd, Cincinnati.

Within a group of five mounds situated five miles southwest of Nashville there were disclosed upward of eight hundred stone-grave burials. The graves were arranged in tiers, one above another, and in one of the five tumuli there were a total of five vertical tiers. In a mound near Brentwood, ten miles southwest of Nashville, stone graves were likewise arranged in tiers, the lowest and oldest of which were of the small square type while those above were full-length graves. A mound inside an enclosure situated near Lebanon, Wilson County, contained stone graves arranged in the form of a hollow square, while in a mound opposite Nashville, along the Cumberland River, stone graves were so arranged that the heads of their occupants were toward the center of the structure, the positions suggesting the spokes in a wheel. At the central point

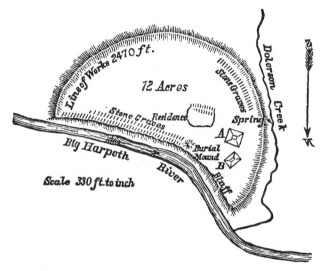

FIG. 272. MAP OF EARTHWORK AND MOUNDS NEAR OLD TOWN, WILLIAMSON COUNTY, TENNESSEE

After Thruston, *Antiquities of Tennessee*. Courtesy of Stewart Kidd, Cincinnati.

rested a large pottery vessel. A similar arrangement was noted in a mound on Harpeth River, in Williamson County.

The typical stone graves of the region are box-shaped, lined with and covered by flat slabs of native stone. As a rule these slabs are nothing more than conveniently shaped pieces gathered from the surface of the site where they occur, but occasionally individual stones have been intentionally broken, cut, or rubbed to proportions suitable to the intended purpose. The size and form of the stone graves either in cemeteries or in mounds vary greatly, although the average would be between

6 and 7 feet long, 1½ to 2 feet wide, and some 18 inches deep. The graves of children, naturally of lesser dimensions, are constructed in the sizes required. Stone graves not infrequently contain two or more individuals, particularly in cases of reburial. Occasionally in graves of this type the flat stones are entirely or in part replaced by fragments of potteryware neatly fitted to form a lining. With the burials are found

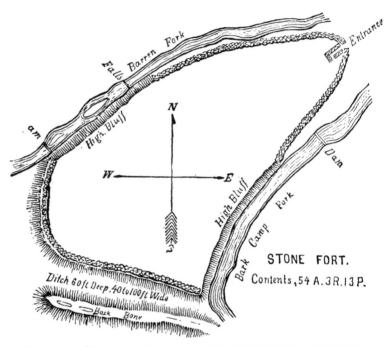

FIG. 273. MAP OF STONE FORT, NEAR MANCHESTER, TENNESSEE
After Thruston, *Antiquities of Tennessee.* Courtesy of Stewart Kidd, Cincinnati.

pottery vessels, apparently containing food when deposited, usually accompanied by shell spoons. Other implements, ornaments, and utensils likewise were placed with the dead.

Although it is believed that the authors of the numerous enclosures or fortifications of Tennessee were the builders of the stone graves, strangely enough no defensive earthworks are found in connection with the densely populated region centering about Nashville. The supposition is that the fortifications

FIG. 274.   POTTERYWARE DECORATED IN COLORS, FROM NEAR NASHVILLE,
TENNESSEE
Scale, 1/4. After Thruston, *Antiquities of Tennessee.* Courtesy of Stewart
Kidd, Cincinnati.

located in the adjoining counties of Sumner, Wilson, and
Williamson were intended to guard the frontier to the north,
east, and south and that the dearth of defensive works to the
westward indicates absence of any threat from that quarter.

Of the several enclosures and mound groups comprising
this supposed protective chain of earthworks, that located
near Saundersville, in Sumner County, is of unusual interest.
The enclosure, roughly circular in form, is 3,100 feet in circumference and surrounds an area of 14 acres. The central
mound is flat-topped and 25 feet in height. Within the enclosure a number of small conical burial mounds contain stone
graves radiating from their centers, and the usual hut rings
with the remains of fireplaces are in evidence. Many interesting implements and ornaments and fine examples of potteryware have been taken from the burial mounds of the group.
Other aboriginal remains are located at Castalian Springs in
the same county.

Near the town of Lebanon, Wilson County, on Spring Creek,
is a walled enclosure encircling some ten acres of land, with
the usual large central truncated mound and numerous hut
rings (Figure 270). Conical burial mounds of the group ex-

FIG. 275. POTTERY VESSELS FROM MOUNDS AND STONE GRAVES IN CENTRAL TENNESSEE

Showing types of artistic and effigy ware. After Thruston, *Antiquities of Tennessee*. Courtesy of Stewart Kidd, Cincinnati.

amined by Putnam yielded some of the finest examples of potteryware and art objects ever found in the mound area. Beneath the low elevations marking the sites of huts were found circular level floors of clay with central hearths or fireplaces.

One of the more striking of the Tennessee enclosures and mound groups is that known as the De Graffenreid works, located near Franklin, Williamson County, on the Big Harpeth River (Figure 271). This work, surveyed and described by Dr. Joseph Jones, is a crescentic embankment 3,800 feet in length, its ends resting on the perpendicular bluff of the river. The central mound, rectangular and flat-topped, was at the time of the survey 16 feet in height, 230 feet long, and 110 feet in width. Four other similar mounds, of smaller size, and four conical burial mounds were comprised in the group. In one of the burial mounds Jones found a carefully constructed stone grave containing a skeleton buried in a sitting posture. With it was a remarkable flint blade or sword, 22 inches in length, a pottery vessel, and large sea-shell food containers.

From other graves of this mound were taken copper designs, unique images, shell gorgets, and painted potteryware. Numerous graves in the adjacent burial ground yielded other unusual specimens, marking this as one of the richest sites examined up to that time. Similar works of somewhat less importance are located at Old Town, six miles southwest of Franklin on Big Harpeth River, and three miles distant from Old Town on the same stream, the former crescentic (Figure 272) and the latter roughly circular in form, the areas enclosed being twelve and seven acres respectively. Truncated and burial mounds and stone graves are present in each.

FIG. 276. DECORATED POTTERY VASE FOUND NEAR FRANK-LIN, TENNESSEE

Scale, 1/4. After Thruston, *Antiquities of Tennessee*. Courtesy of Stewart Kidd, Cincinnati.

In his *Aboriginal Remains* Dr. Joseph Jones reports that "fortifications several miles in extent, inclosing two systems of mounds and numerous stone graves, lie along the Big Harpeth River, about 16 miles below Old Town, at Mound Bottom and Osborne's Place. Within these extraordinary aboriginal works which inclose the sites of two ancient cities, are found three pyramidal mounds, about 50 feet in elevation, and each one exposing about one acre on its summit; and besides these are lesser mounds."

The finest example of a strictly defensive work to be found in Tennessee is the so-called Stone Fort at the forks of Duck River, near Manchester, in Coffee County (Figure 273). The fort is roughly oval in shape, conforming to the highly strategic location which it occupies. The enclosed area is approximately 54 acres.

The Savannah works, at the town of that name in Hardin County, occupy a precipitous bluff overlooking the Tennessee River. The large central mound of the group of sixteen is flat-topped, 30 feet in height and more than 300 feet in diameter. Enclosing the mound group there is a double earthen embankment, 1,350 yards in length, with bastionlike projections at regular intervals. The mounds of the group were partly explored by J. P. Stelle, and his findings, with a map of the works, were published in the Smithsonian Report for 1870. Stelle discovered in a small mound of the group peculiar passages resembling furnace flues, somewhat analogous to the phenomena disclosed by Putnam's explorations of the Turner Group, in Hamilton County, Ohio, and described in the report

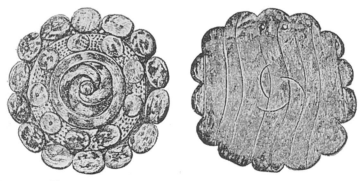

FIG. 277. ENGRAVED SHELL GORGET FROM A MOUND ON THE CUMBER-
LAND RIVER OPPOSITE NASHVILLE, TENNESSEE

Scale, 2/3. After Thruston, *Antiquities of Tennessee.* Courtesy of Stewart Kidd, Cincinnati.

thereon published by the Peabody Museum of Harvard University.

Some idea of the great size of the truncated mounds of the area and of the region to the southward may be had from the foregoing examples. The Parish Mound, in Maury County, a shapely flat-topped structure 25 feet in height, is 200 feet in diameter at the base and 150 feet at the top. The largest mound of a group on Duck River, at Indian Ridge, in Humphreys County, is reported as being 47 feet in height. An extensive system of mounds in Madison County, toward the western end of the state, has as its outstanding tumulus what is known as Mount Pinson, more than 70 feet in height and 1,000 feet in diameter at the base. Major remains of all sorts, including stone graves, are less abundant in the western portions of Tennessee, which has received less attention from the archæologist than other parts of the state. While this district undoubtedly is analogous in its archæological features with the Lower Mississippi area, the evidences are neither so numerous nor so important, so far as known, as in other adjacent regions bordering on the Mississippi.

That portion of Tennessee lying east of the Cumberland Mountains, together with adjacent portions of North Carolina and Virginia, is sometimes included in what has been termed the Appalachian archæological district. While this region presents some features not found in the district under consideration, in the main it may be classed as basically the same. The mounds and accompanying evidences are fairly abundant in eastern Tennessee, particularly along the little Tennessee River, where occasionally they are of exceptionally large size. As in the territory west of the mountains, the mound groups represent the sites of towns and villages. Basin-shaped firebeds or fireplaces one above another within the mounds, together with post holes and remains of timbers, indicate houses, circular and rectangular in form. Burial mounds are numerous, one of which, reported by Thomas, contained a total of ninety skeletal interments.

Archæological exploration in Tennessee promises to be adequate and productive in the immediate future under the direction of the state archæologist, P. E. Cox. An excellent archæological map of the state, prepared by the late W. E. Myer, recently has been published in the Forty-second Annual Report of the Bureau of American Ethnology.

NORTHERN GEORGIA

Northern Georgia, together with the western extensions of the Carolinas and Virginia, belongs to the important Tennessee-

Cumberland area and bears the distinction of possessing the noted Etowah Group of mounds and earthworks which represents the metropolis of cultural development of that outstanding division of the general mound area. The southern half of the state, in so far as is known, is rather barren of major archæological remains, and the few scattering mounds of the region may be considered for the present as belonging with the Florida peninsula.

For the limited knowledge available concerning Georgia and its archæology we are indebted to two principal sources, the Bureau of American Ethnology and Professor Warren K. Moorehead of Phillips Academy at Andover, Massachusetts. The future development of this attractive field seems assured, however, as a result of the activities of Dr. Margaret Ashley, of Phillips Academy, who recently began a detailed survey of the Georgia-Florida region with especial attention to ceramic development.

In the broad program of mound exploration carried out by the Bureau of American Ethnology under the direction of Dr. Cyrus Thomas the State of Georgia was accorded considerable attention. Actual exploration centered mainly in the Etowah Group, near Cartersville, but several other groups and individual mounds of the region evoked the interest of the survey. Aside from the Etowah Group, to be considered presently, the most important of the Georgia works to be examined was what is known as the Hollywood Mound, situated near the town of that name and some ten miles below Augusta. This tumulus, with a companion mound, was located on the low bottom land of the Savannah River, and in time of high water these were the only points in the immediate valley elevated above flood level. For this reason, as with the flat-topped mounds of the Lower Mississippi area, they have long served as places of refuge for stock in time of flood. This is true particularly of the flat-topped mound of the pair, which apparently was constructed for domiciliary purposes or as a refuge from high water. The other mound, conical in form, was 10 feet in height and 70 feet in diameter. Examination disclosed that this mound represented two distinct periods of construction, the original mound covering the contained burials having been carried to a height of seven feet, after which an additional three feet, of a different type of soil and without burials, had been added. The structure was extremely interesting in that while typical artifacts of prehistoric occupancy were found with burials, there also occurred, with interments and scattered through the mound, objects of European manufacture, showing that the tumulus had been erected, in part at least, in early historic times. Perhaps no better illustration of the survival of the mound-building trait and its practice within the historic period has come to light.

With burials of the Hollywood Mound, all of which lay within the original or primary mound, were a number of pottery vessels of interesting types. These comprised vessels with stamped patterns; a bottle resting upon a tripod of human heads; a jar incised with the plumed-serpent design; and a painted vessel bearing the sun symbol and the swastika. A number of tobacco pipes, one of which was in the effigy of a bird and two in the human form, were other objects of interest.

THE ETOWAH CULTURE

Equaling in interest and importance the noted Moundville Group of Alabama and the major Hopewell groups of Ohio, the great Etowah Group, situated on the river of that name near Cartersville, in Bartow County, represents the acme of cultural development in the Tennessee-Cumberland area. The group consists (Figure 278) of a broad ditch or moat, semi-circular in form and 1,060 yards in length, which originates at one end at the river margin and terminates at the other some distance from the bank of the stream; two large excavations from which earth was taken in constructing the tumuli; and six mounds lying within the enclosing ditch. The largest mound of the group is exceeded in cubic content only by the great Cahokia or Monks' Mound at East St. Louis. This structure, a flat-topped pyramid roughly rectangular in outline, is 66 feet

in height and covers a basal area of almost three acres. The
cubic content has been computed at 4,300,000 cubic feet. A
ramp or graded approach, constructed apronlike against the
east side of the mound, apparently was intended to facilitate ascent and descent of the main structure. Five additional

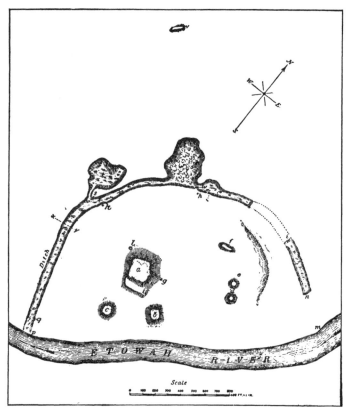

FIG. 278. MAP OF THE ETOWAH GROUP NEAR CARTERSVILLE, GEORGIA
Bureau of American Ethnology.

tumuli of varying sizes lie within the enclosure, while exter-
nally to the northwest there is a solitary mound supposed to
pertain to the works.

The earliest mention in literature of the great Etowah Mound
is believed to be that of Garsilaso de la Vega, the chronicler of
De Soto's expedition, in his record as of 1723. The first definite

description of the group is that of Rev. Elias Cornelius in 1818. Following these early descriptions came accounts and maps by Colonel C. C. Jones, Colonel Charles Whittlesey, and, later, the Bureau of American Ethnology.

The explorations of the Bureau under Dr. Cyrus Thomas were confined to the smaller mounds of the group, notably

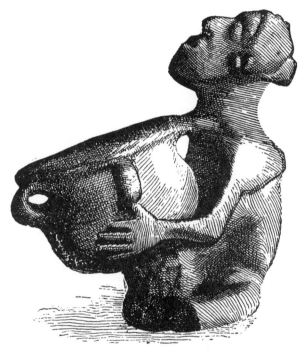

FIG. 279. STONE HUMAN EFFIGY TOBACCO PIPE FROM THE ETOWAH
GROUP

The figure is shown holding a pottery vessel. Scale, full size. Bureau of American Ethnology.

mounds B, C, D, and E. In only one of these, Mound C, were burials disclosed, the others apparently being domiciliary in purpose. In Mound C the survey discovered some ten burials, interred mostly in stone graves or cists. Numerous objects of artistic merit accompanied these burials, among them repoussé copper plates bearing designs of human figures and birds; copper maces or badges; engraved shells with conventionalized

FIG. 280. THE MOOREHEAD EXPLORATION PARTY AT WORK IN THE
ETOWAH GROUP
Courtesy of Warren K. Moorehead.

designs; human busts carved from stone; pottery vessels, and
so forth.

The most recent examination of the Etowah Group is that
of Professor Warren K. Moorehead who began the work in
1925 and continued it through several succeeding seasons. Con-
fining his work to the village site accompanying the group and
to the third largest mound, a structure 22 feet in height and
180 feet in diameter at the base, Moorehead has discovered
many interesting burials and artifacts. Among the latter is the
human image wrought from stone illustrated in Chapter VI
(Figure 68), in size that of a boy of five or six years of age.
This image, presumably an idol, was found buried in a stone-
lined grave exactly as though it were the body of a human
being; the grave with its contained burial was removed intact.
A number of rare ceremonial knives or swords, chipped from
flint, were found with burials in the mound (Figure 281). These

ceremonial blades, suggesting similar objects from the highly advanced cultures of Mexico and Central America which were used in sacrificial and ceremonial rites, appear to furnish a basis for assuming an affinity between the two widely separated areas. Among other interesting specimens are pottery vessels in color, one of which bears a double symbol representing the sun and within it a cosmic design indicating the four directions or the four winds (Figure 282); a monolithic hatchet or battle-axe, blade and handle carved from a single piece of stone (Figure 283); and several repoussé designs in copper representing human figures bearing arms, ceremonial objects and ornaments. Circular ornaments cut from shell, known archæologically as gorgets, taken from the Etowah Mound exhibit a high order of art development. One of these bears the pileated woodpecker design, repeated, a motive frequently used in the Etowah district and throughout the South on potteryware and otherwise. A second shell gorget exhibits in scroll or openwork the figure of a warrior bearing a feather robe and an antler headdress; in one hand he holds a human head and in the other a ceremonial weapon with which presumably the head has been severed. Both of these gorgets, together with other interesting specimens from the Etowah Group, are illustrated in Chapter VI.

FIG. 281. CEREMONIAL FLINT SWORDS FROM THE ETOWAH GROUP

Two of a number of extremely long and fine ceremonial knives or swords, chipped from flint, found by Moorehead. These unusual objects indicate a surprising degree of skill on the part of the ancient flint-chippers. The type is confined mostly to the Tennessee-Cumberland district of the mound area.

Moorehead finds the Etowah culture closely related to the so-called Tennessee-Cumberland and similar to, though distinct from, that at Moundville, Alabama. Specimens from the

FIG. 282. POTTERY VESSEL DECORATED IN COLORS, FROM THE ETOWAH
GROUP

This handsome vessel, in black and terra-cotta, bears the sun symbol and within it a swastikalike figure, supposed to be a cosmic symbol. Found by Moorehead. Courtesy of Phillips Academy. Scale, 1/3.

Etowah Group are displayed in the National Museum at Washington and at Phillips Academy at Andover, Massachusetts.

Historically it is interesting to note that the Cherokee Indians in their war with the Creeks are said to have fortified with pickets the summit of the central Etowah Mound as a place of refuge for their women and children.

In her program for a detailed survey of the State of Georgia Miss Ashley has already located and reported over eight hundred archæological sites, comprising mounds, village sites, burial grounds, and other occupational evidences. As is true in other sections, she finds that geographical features have a direct connection with aboriginal occupancy. The state as a whole is divided into three geographic provinces—the coastal plain, the plateau or hill country, and the mountainous terrain of the north and northwest. Mounds are found quite generally throughout the state, but their numbers vary with the adaptability of location to human occupancy. In general, however, it may be said that the tumuli occur adjacent to streams where the soil is fertile and easily cultivatable.

FIG. 283. MONOLITHIC STONE AXE FROM THE ETOWAH GROUP

This rare ceremonial specimen, found by Moorehead, is made from a single piece of stone. It illustrates the method of securing the ordinary copper axe blade, shown below, in the socketed wooden handle. Courtesy of Phillips Academy. Scale, 1/3.

In the mountainous area there occurs a variant of the true mound in the form of stone cairns, the result, apparently, of the abundance of stone and the difficulties involved in digging and carrying earth for earthen structures. Along the coast, particularly on the sea islands, shell heaps and kitchen middens are abundant and sometimes assume the forms and proportions of true mounds. As to forms of burial, the customary and widespread extended and flexed skeletal burials occur freely, especially in stone graves. Secondary burials are represented by urn burial, comprising either bones taken from the "bone house" or fragments and ash of burned bones of cremated remains.

Culturally, Miss Ashley identified in northern Georgia the influence of the Tennessee district; along the Savannah River, a strain from the coast Algonquian; along the coast and to the southward, influence from Florida; and in western Georgia, a definite connection with Alabama.

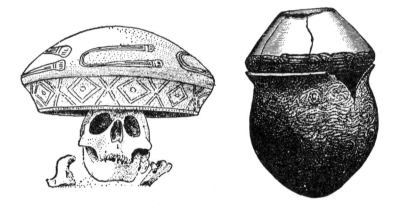

FIG. 284. GEORGIA URN BURIALS

Mortuary vessels were used both as coverings for skulls or parts of skeletons and as containers for them. Compare figure 286. After Moore.

VIRGINIA AND THE CAROLINAS

Practically nothing is known of the sparse evidences of prehistoric occupancy of the western extension of Virginia, where a few mounds and other major remains are known to exist.

As may be noted on the map of mound distribution (Figure 7), the dense occurrence of tumuli in eastern Tennessee extends well into the western extremity of North Carolina. Among the more interesting mounds examined by the Bureau of American Ethnology survey was what is known as the T. F. Nelson Mound, situated near Patterson, in Caldwell County. This interesting structure, which stood on the low bottom lands of the Yadkin River, was 38 feet in diameter and only 18 inches in

height. Prior to the erection of the mound a circular pit, of the
diameter of the tumulus and three feet deep, had been excavated in the surface and in it the human remains were deposited. The pit was then filled with earth and the slight elevation
raised above it. The bodies were deposited either extended on
the back or in the sitting posture, and over the greater number
were erected the dome-shaped coverings of stones shown in
Figure 285. A unique feature of the site is the interment of the

FIG. 285.   THE T. F. NELSON MOUND, CALDWELL COUNTY, NORTH
CAROLINA

The low mound has been removed, showing the excavated circular pit, with
burials both sitting and reclining. A number of the burials are enclosed in
dome-shaped stone cists. Bureau of American Ethnology.

central burial within the enclosing dome of stones in a standing position. Objects of cut mica, tobacco pipes, a quantity of
black pigment, and other artifacts accompanied the burials.

A phenomenon similar to the above was disclosed in what is
known as the T. F. Nelson Triangle, located on the same farm.
In this instance the excavated pit, instead of being circular,
was triangular in form, the base measuring 32 feet and the

other sides 48 feet, with a depth of three feet. Unlike the preceding structure, the earth filling the pit had not been heaped above the surrounding level. Of the fifteen skeletons disclosed, nine lay horizontally on their backs while six were interred in stone vaults, four of the latter being in the sitting posture. Within a secondary pit dug into the floor of the burial pit proper were ten or more individuals, one of whom, apparently a person of unusual importance, was accompanied by many implements and ornaments. With this individual and others of the group burial were found handsomely engraved shell gorgets; shell beads; copper beads, breastplates, and bracelets; and chisels of iron. Whether or not the presence of iron in this burial indicates contact with whites or whether the metal is of meteoric origin is not made clear. Above the several skeletons in the common burial had been heaped numerous polished stone celts or hatchet blades, discoidal or gaming stones, arrowpoints, pieces of mica, lumps of paint or pigment, and tobacco pipes.

Burial pits in every way similar to the above were located two miles east of Patterson on the Yadkin River and near the town of Lenoir on Buffalo Creek. Both were circular, and the first-named was marked by a low mound. Each contained numerous burials, interred in much the same manner as those described and accompanied by the same types of artifacts.

Other mounds examined by the Bureau survey were located near Waynesville, in Haywood County; on Cane Creek, Henderson County; and near Asheville, Buncombe County.

An ancient cemetery in central Wilkes County disclosed a triple burial presenting an unusual feature. Beneath the legs of the three skeletons reposed the skeleton of a bear.

While a number of mounds have been located in South Carolina, particularly toward the west, very little exploration has been effected and comparatively nothing is known of their contents. Two or three small tumuli explored by the Bureau of American Ethnology yielded only meager results.

CHAPTER XIX

THE PENINSULAR AREA

The archæology of Florida—Explorations of Clarence B. Moore—The north-west coast of Florida—The west coast of Florida—Mounds of northeastern Florida—The key-dweller culture of southwestern Florida—Coastal mounds of Georgia—Ancient shell mounds and shell heaps.

THE Florida peninsula was ever a land of fantasy and mirage. Its geographical location, lying in the sub-tropics and caressed by the Gulf Stream, differenti-ates it from the remainder of the general mound area. Its topography, climate, flora, and fauna are distinctive, endowing it with a charm which through the centuries has exercised an influence on its human occupants, both historic and prehis-toric. This elusive quality of land and sea and sky is evidenced by the fact that men have been too much inclined to disregard the rich material assets of this land of lure in their quest for imaginary fountains of perpetual youth and traditional stores of barbaric treasure. Within the historic period this tendency is all too evident. The potency of the spell in prehistoric days is reflected in the potteryware of bizarre forms, the strange ceremonial objects, and the grotesquely carved ornaments and implements exhumed today from the old burial mounds, the vast shell heaps, and the muck beds of the coastal and lake regions of the peninsula. Had Ponce de Leon, Hernando De Soto, and others of the early explorers directed their misspent energies toward the compiling of anthropological data, they might have given to the world a monumental contribution based on the native inhabitants of our southland of today and their prehistory. While much of interest has accrued from archæological exploration in the Florida peninsula, the unique character of the region still beckons to the explorer as strongly today as in the past.

445

THE ARCHÆOLOGY OF FLORIDA

The Florida peninsula is an ideal anthropological region, in that it combines the three elements referred to in an earlier chapter—archæology, ethnology, and history. Prehistoric remains, of both major and minor character, are abundant. The native Indian tribes, though at present much reduced through removal and admixture, have received considerable study and observation, and their contacts with Europeans are matters of historic record.

Although the wanderings of the early explorers contributed little or nothing to archæological data on the region, their records, especially those of De Soto and his chroniclers, contain valued references to the ethnology of this earliest colonized portion of the general mound area. Later the French Huguenot attempts at colonization, together with the numerous ethnological drawings by the artist Le Moine, provided sources of definite information. Subsequently the records of the Spanish governors of the colony and those of the missionaries and friars who labored among the natives were added to the literature on the region.

Strangely enough, the numerous old burial mounds and the vast shell heaps appear to have made little impression on the early explorers and colonizers, and although, as will be shown in the concluding chapter, there was a survival of the mound-building trait within Florida and the southland, little cognizance was taken of the practice.

Burial mounds of sand and earth construction occur abundantly throughout the northern portions of Florida, particularly along the northeastern coast and adjacent to the St. Johns River. Shell mounds and shell heaps, some of them of astonishing size and extent, are found along the coasts and larger streams. In addition, domiciliary mounds, covering the remains of huts or houses of open thatched construction in keeping with the mild climate, are of frequent occurrence. Numerous minor remains and artifacts are found in the mounds and shell heaps and on the surface of the ground. On the whole, the antiquity of the archæological remains of the region probably varies but little from that of similar remains in others of the southern and central states.

The cultural attainment of the Peninsular area was intermediate between the lowest and the most advanced of the mound area as a whole and bears important resemblances to the adjacent Lower Mississippi and Tennessee-Cumberland areas, with both of which it merges. Definite characteristics of the region are noted northward along the coast in Georgia and South Carolina, where Moore and others have found the typical stamped potteryware and other traits. The fictile art, as evidenced by the abundance of potteryware, was highly developed in parts of the area, as was also the utilization of shell and wood. On the other hand, the use of stone and flint in fashioning implements and ornaments was rather weak, owing to the limited occurrence of these and other suitable minerals and the consequent substitution of the more readily available materials above mentioned.

Flint implements of the usual types, fashioned from chert occurring in the limestone formations of the north-central part of the state, are fairly abundant, but the well-known stone axe and celt of other regions are largely replaced by similar implements fashioned from the heavy portions of large marine shells. Aside from clay for pottery-making, shell and wood appear to have been the two outstanding raw materials in the material economy of the ancient Floridians. From the large marine shells, such as *Fulgar perversum* and *Fasciolaria,* vessels or containers were made by removing the whorls and interior portions, and hoes and digging implements were fashioned by cutting holes through the bodies of such shells to accommodate wooden handles. From the columellæ of large shells were manufactured beads, pendants, plummets, and various ornamental and ceremonial artifacts, while from small marine and freshwater shells countless beads were manufactured. Shells both large and small, as raw material or in the form of finished products, appear to have constituted an important item of commerce with the regions to the northward. The art of the area is rather highly developed and, as intimated above, is indicative of the peculiar influence of this distinctive region on its inhabitants.

What we know of the Florida mounds and sites is attributable almost entirely to the efforts of Clarence B. Moore of Philadelphia, apart from the intensive exploration of a limited area by Frank H. Cushing for the University of Pennsylvania, to be reviewed later. Moore's explorations began in 1892 and continued for twelve or more years. During that time he examined a total of two hundred and fifty or more mounds and ancient sites and obtained quantities of specimens illustrating the habits and customs of the prehistoric inhabitants of the peninsula.

A detailed review of Moore's explorations in the area would be superfluous in view of the rather extended accounts in earlier chapters of other regions exhibiting somewhat similar features. A brief summary of the Florida explorations, however, may prove to be both interesting and instructive. Moore's labors centered in three general localities of the state, namely, along the northwest coast of the mainland, where numerous mounds were examined; along the Gulf Coast of central peninsular Florida; and adjacent to the coast and along St. Johns River in northeastern Florida.

The explorations on the northwest coast, conducted during the years 1901 and 1902, embraced the coastal territory from Perdido Bay on the west to Cedar Keys, at the mouth of the Suwanee River. A total of ninety or more mounds and sites were examined, and in them, as is true of most Florida explorations, potteryware constituted the principal finds. Prefacing his report on this district, Moore has some comments on the "relentless attack [on the mounds] by seekers for buried treasure. In no part of Florida is the pursuit of this *ignis fatuus* so intense, and persons, otherwise sane, seemingly, spend considerable portions of their time with spade and divining rod in fruitless search."

THE NORTHWEST COAST OF FLORIDA

The western extension of the coastal strip under consideration proved to be related in its culture, so far as potteryware is concerned, with the Lower Mississippi area. This was to be expected, since this portion of Florida constitutes what would have been the water-front of Alabama had the latter state extended southward to the Gulf.

FIG. 286. MODIFICATION OF URN BURIAL, FROM POINT WASHINGTON, FLORIDA

Here a funerary vessel is placed above a human skull. After Moore.

A large flat-topped mound located at Walton's Camp, on Santa Rosa Sound, was typically Lower Mississippi in form and very suggestive of that area in contents. A number of pottery vessels, one of which was in the image of a frog, were taken from this tumulus, which also yielded examples of ware with modeled bird heads as handles. Utilization of funerary vessels in burial was also in evidence. A mound near Basin

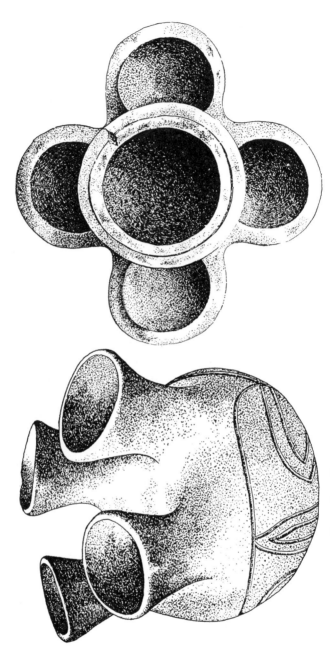

FIG. 287. FLORIDA POTTERY VESSELS WITH MULTIPLE BOWLS AND MOUTHS

Left, vessel from the Hall Mound, Wakulla County; diameter, 8 inches. Right, vessel from the Jackson Mound, Franklin County; diameter, 6½ inches. Redrawn by H. R. Goodwin after Moore.

Bayou yielded among other objects a pottery vessel in the image of a human being, while another near Joly Bay produced vessels with handles representing human heads. In a cemetery near Point Washington interesting examples of urn burial were found, one of which is illustrated in Figure 286. A wealth of potteryware was secured in the examination of this ancient burial ground.

In the second season's explorations of the northwest coast, mounds near Burnt Mill Creek and on Alligator Bayou yielded effigy vessels representing birds and the human form. Vessels with multiple bowls and mouths (Figure 287), ranging from two to five in number, were taken from mounds near West Bay Postoffice and from the Holly Mound, in Washington County. From two mounds near Hare Hammock, in Calhoun County, a remarkable series of pottery vessels was obtained, among them a vessel on which was modeled in relief a full-length human figure portrayed as though standing alongside the vessel and peering into its interior (Figure 288). Other interesting and productive mounds were the Tucker Mound, in Franklin County; a mound on Marsh Island, Wakulla County; and the Hall Mound, at Panacea Springs, Wakulla County, all of which yielded numerous pottery vessels and objects of flint, stone, and shell. From the Hall Mound and from a tumulus at what is known as Mound Field, in the same county, some of the most grotesque pottery vessels of the entire mound area were taken. Two mounds near the Warrior River in Taylor County were remarkable for the number and variety of vessels discovered. Throughout the region tobacco pipes of potteryware, usually of the elbow type, were found both in mounds and on village and burial sites.

The explorations in the mounds and cemeteries of this northwest coast region showed that its western extension, from the Alabama line eastward to Choctawhatchee Bay, may be regarded as a continuation of the Lower Mississippi culture, with evidences of influence from the northeast, namely, Georgia and South Carolina. Eastward and southward to Cedar Keys there was noted the waning influence of the Lower Mississippi culture and its replacement by that characteristic of the Florida region proper. In the westernmost portion of the northwest coast district a new form of burial, consisting of a lone skull, or a skull and a few additional bones, placed beneath a down-turned earthen vessel, was disclosed. Only a single instance of

FIG. 288. UNUSUAL POTTERY VESSEL WITH HUMAN EFFIGY ATTACHED, FROM A MOUND IN CALHOUN COUNTY, FLORIDA
Diameter at rim, 5½ inches. Redrawn by H. R. Goodwin after Moore.

the more typical urn burial, in which human remains were enclosed within a vessel and covered by an inverted bowl or dish, was encountered in this district. Incidentally, to the northward, particularly in Georgia, where this form of burial is prevalent, the covered remains invariably are cremated, but in the region under consideration cremation was not found.

As to the remaining aspects of the burial complex of the region, there may be mentioned the custom of depositing quantities of pottery vessels in mounds, apparently as tributes to the dead. These deposits occurred almost invariably in the eastern sides or margins of the tumuli and were enclosed in dark sand, almost black in color from what is supposed to be an admixture of burned flesh, possibly that of human cremation.

FIG. 289. FUNERARY VESSEL WITH PERFORATIONS INDICATING CERE-
MONIAL "KILLING" READY MADE

From a mound near Mound Field, Wakulla County, Florida. Diameter of bowl, 9 inches. Redrawn by H. R. Goodwin after Moore.

A burial trait of exceptional human interest was disclosed during Moore's exploration of the Florida northwest coast. Students of archæology, as we have seen, long had been familiar with the custom, in many parts of the general mound area, of the intentional "ceremonial killing" of pottery vessels and other artifacts at the time of interment with the dead. The idea inhering in this procedure is believed to have been something analogous to sacrifice. In punching a hole in a pottery vessel or in breaking an object of any sort, thus destroying its

utility value, it was felt apparently that the spirit of the artifact was being released so that it might the more readily take
leave of the material form and join its owner in the after-life.
While the distribution of this trait is widespread, the appearance in the mounds of the Florida northwest coast of funerary
vessels prepared in advance by making holes or perforations
in the soft clay of vessels before burning came as an interesting
surprise. These specially prepared vessels first made their appearance to the eastward of Pensacola Bay, increased in occurrence as the examination pushed eastward, and in the mounds
of St. Andrews Bay and to the east were supplemented by
special life-form vessels, of flimsy and inferior make, but bearing various geometric perforations in the body in addition to
the customary one in the base (Figure 289). In these three
stages of development we have, then, a striking example of the
evolution from a primarily strictly utility object of a specifically ceremonial artifact—pottery vessels manufactured in advance, the sacrificial or "killing" concept ready made, for the
sole purpose of depositing with the dead.

In addition to the mounds examined in the Florida northwest coast district proper Moore explored some twenty mounds
lying along the Apalachicola River, flowing southward from
the Georgia-Florida boundary and emptying into the Bay of
Apalachicola. Findings were approximately the same as in the
region just described, with increasing evidences of eastern and
northeastern influences.

THE WEST COAST OF FLORIDA

Proceeding southward in 1903, Moore examined some twenty
mounds along the Florida west coast, from the Suwanee River
to Tampa Bay. While the general culture of this region
was similar, superficially, to that of the region to the northward, it soon became apparent that the influence from the
Lower Mississippi area was almost totally lacking, particularly with regard to the fictile arts. Potteryware, though of
good quality, was much less in evidence, and life forms were

almost totally lacking. There was a noticeable absence of such traits as urn burial, depositing of offerings of potteryware in mounds, funerary vessels with ready-made perforations, and cranial flattening, all characteristic of northwest Florida.

Among the outstanding mounds examined in this region was a sand tumulus located on Crystal River, in Citrus County. At

FIG. 290. PLUMMET-SHAPED CEREMONIAL OBJECTS, FROM A MOUND
NEAR CRYSTAL RIVER, FLORIDA

Probably worn as charms or amulets. These specimens were wrought from quartz crystals. Scale, full size. After Moore.

this site, near the mouth of the stream, there is an immense shell heap, 28 feet in height, with a level, platform-like top 100 by 50 feet in size. A graded way leads from the surrounding surface to the elevated plateau. From the burial mound, which was 10 feet in height, there were taken some 225 burials, disposed variously in flexed and extended positions and including some forty so-called bunched burials. Potteryware bearing representations of the human hand and face, a number of interesting pottery vessels and pipes, and great numbers of so-called "plummets," or pendant ornaments, were found with burials and throughout the mound (Figure 290). The last-named comprise perhaps the greatest find of these interesting ornamental or ceremonial objects ever made. They are of stone, crystal quartz, shell, and copper, and range from small, almost globular forms to cylindrical or rod-like specimens upwards of ten inches in length. All are provided with encircling grooves at one or both ends for suspension by cords or thongs. It is believed that this widely distributed type was worn suspended from the neck and that it served the wearer as a talisman or charm. It is significant that a deposit of plummets or pendants comprising similar materials and forms was taken from the great Seip Mound of the Ohio Hopewell culture explored by the Ohio State Museum in 1925-28. Other objects found in the mound on Crystal River indicating relationship to or contact with the Hopewell culture were spool-shaped ear ornaments of copper, circular copper disks with symbolic excised designs (Figure 291), a copper plate rectangular in form and probably intended as a breastplate, and a copper ornament or object resembling three conjoined copper tubes. The signifi-

FIG. 291. COPPER DISK WITH SYMBOLIC EX-CISED DESIGN SUGGESTING HOPEWELL IN-FLUENCE, FROM A MOUND NEAR CRYSTAL RIVER, FLORIDA

Diameter, 3½ inches. After Moore.

cance of the remarkable resemblance between the objects found in these widely separated mounds remains to be determined.

The sand mounds, so-called, of the St. Johns River in northeastern Florida were examined by Moore and his expedition in 1894, and in the following year similar mounds in Duval County, bordering the St. Johns, from Jacksonville to the mouth of the river, were explored. More than forty mounds were included in the first season's explorations, which covered the territory adjacent to the river north and south from the town of Palatka.

The sand mounds of the St. Johns River vary greatly in size and structure. While many of them are of homogeneous sand construction, others are stratified with sand of varying shades and with shell, muck, and sand intermixed with powdered hematite. They vary in size from hardly perceptible elevations to such striking tumuli as the Tick Island Mound, 17 feet in height, and the noted Mt. Royal, which measures 555 feet in circumference. In form they are mostly truncated cones, and they appear to have served primarily for sepulture and later as house and lookout mounds. Certain of them were found to be filled with human burials, while others gave no evidence of such use. Burial customs comprised both anatomical and bundle interments, with scattered and disconnected bones and skeletons often in evidence.

The most interesting mound examined by the Moore expedition was that known as Mt. Royal, situated on the east bank of St. Johns River in Putnam County. This great mound, 555 feet in circumference and 16 feet in height, has been known historically for more than a century and a half. Examination disclosed that it contained many interments, but the human remains, owing apparently to great age, were in an advanced stage of disintegration. Numerous objects of stone, flint, copper, and clay were found in Mt. Royal, none of which evidenced contact with Europeans. The indications are, therefore, that the tumulus is purely prehistoric and of decided antiquity. Specimens of flint and stone included numerous arrow- and lanceheads, polished celts or hatchets, chisels, ornaments, and ceremonial objects. Among the last-named were several exceptionally fine ceremonial chisels and spuds, the latter having spatulate notched blades and reaching lengths of upward of one foot. Great quantities of shell beads and a few beads made from fresh-water pearls were disclosed. The mound yielded numerous examples of potteryware, usually placed with burials. The feature of Mt. Royal, however, was the numerous objects of copper, including beads, ear ornaments, plates, and problematical forms. An effigy of a serpent, in copper, is one of the few ever found in the mound region.

The great mound on Tick Island, Volusia County, was remarkable for the number of interments it contained. Aside from numerous handsomely carved piercing implements of bone, used possibly as hair ornaments, artifacts were comparatively few. This mound proved, like Mt. Royal, to be entirely prehistoric. The Thursby Mound, near Lake Beresford in Volusia County, is remarkable for the great number of "freak" effigy pottery vessels it yielded. Within a space 6 feet by 25 feet in size, just beneath the surface on the slope of the mound, there was found a unique deposit of potteryware, including pots, dishes, bowls, and effigies of animals, plants, and other objects. Practically all the pottery vessels had been perforated on the base prior to burning or firing, showing that they were intended as ceremonial funerary vessels. The animal effigies (Figure 292) comprised the fish, turtle, puma, bear, squirrel, dog, beaver, otter, and wild turkey. Among the vegetable effigies were recognized the acorn, the gourd, an ear of corn, and others. In all, more than two hundred pottery vessels and effigies were taken from the Thursby Mound. From the Raulerson mounds, also in Volusia County, a number of fine shell gorgets bearing symbolic designs were obtained. A mound on Thornhill Lake, in the same county, was unusual in that it disclosed a number of handsome stone objects commonly known as banner-stones, in form closely resembling the conventional "bow tie." These objects, of usual occurrence throughout the Mississippi and Ohio valleys, have not been found in any other mounds of Florida. Their use is unknown, but they are supposed to have served as emblems of religious or ceremonial observances. The river mounds of Duval County, extending along the twenty miles of the St. Johns between Jacksonville and the sea, were found to be, in the main, similar to Mt. Royal and other mounds of the district just described. Certain low

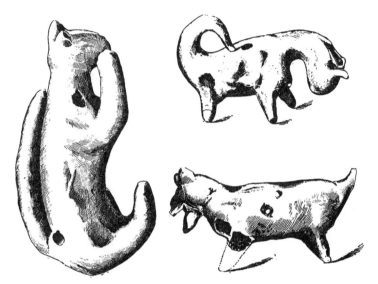

FIG. 292. MINIATURE EFFIGY POTTERYWARE FROM THE THURSBY MOUND, VOLUSIA COUNTY, FLORIDA

Left, effigy of the squirrel; others problematical. Scale, 1/2. After Moore.

regular ridges characteristic of the lower course of the river, however, differ noticeably in some respects from the mounds farther south. The occurrence of mica, of deposits of pebbles and pebble hammers, and of mussel shells buried in quantities was found to characterize the smaller mounds and ridges of the lower river district. Moreover, while but few tobacco pipes were found to the south, they were comparatively abundant in both large and small tumuli in Duval County.

The Shields Mound, near Newcastle, Duval County, is one

of the more important examined by Moore. It is a flat-topped pyramid, 200 feet long and 18 feet in height. No less than 150 burials, in advanced stages of disintegration, were exhumed from the tumulus, the remains being both anatomical and bunched interments. Large ceremonial celts or hatchets, an exceptionally large spade- or spear-shaped ceremonial implement of stone, ceremonial bannerstones and gorgets, tobacco

FIG. 293. SAND MOUND NEAR SHARPES, FLORIDA

This typical mound is 200 feet in diameter and 20 feet high. Photograph by L. A. Kolbe.

pipes of stone and of clay of the L-shaped type, and numerous flint arrow- and lanceheads were found with burials in the mound.

The Grant Mound, in the same vicinity, was exceptional in size, its height being more than 30 feet and its basal diameter 216 feet. Despite its great size, the tumulus yielded but few burials. Thirty-five earthenware vessels, several interesting pipes of stone and clay, great quantities of bone piercing implements and pins, and ornaments of sheet copper, one of them in the effigy of the human face, constituted the principal finds.

A sand mound on Murphy Island, ten miles south of Palatka in Putnam County, like the mound on Crystal River on the west coast, yielded specimens suggesting affinity or contact with the Ohio Hopewell culture. Among these objects were triple tubes of copper, a large copper crescent-shaped ornament, and shell, stone, and crystal pendants or plummets.

Sand mounds of the Ocklawaha River examined by Moore yielded many additional plummets and pendants and were otherwise quite similar to the mounds described above.

THE KEY-DWELLER CULTURE OF SOUTHEASTERN FLORIDA

Limited in scope but unique as to results were the explorations conducted under the auspices of the University of Pennsylvania by Frank H. Cushing of the Bureau of American Ethnology among the keys of southwestern Florida in 1896. Beginning on the north at Charlotte Harbor and touching successively at Pine Island Sound, Caloosa Bay, and Key Marco, ninety miles to the southward, Cushing was rewarded at the last-named place by finding deposits of perishable artifacts unparalleled in American archæology. His description of the ancient artificial shell islands, or "keys" as he terms them, published in the *Proceedings of the American Philosophical Society*, Volume XXXV, reads like a fairy tale. No less than seventy-five distinct key-dweller settlements were located, a number of which were given hurried examination and are described in his report. The vast extent of these shell islands is reflected in Cushing's reference to that located on Pine Island, of which he says: "Miles of shell road—the most beautiful in southwestern Florida—[have been constructed from it] yet still the shell material of this one old-time beginning merely, of a key, had not thereby been wholly exhausted."

We are limited here to a brief summary of the single key that was exhaustively explored, that at Key Marco, accidentally discovered by a resident who in digging garden muck from a mangrove swamp came upon specimens of remarkable character. The "Court of the Pile Dwellers," as the site was named by Cushing, is described as an artificial island built of marine shells, toward the center of which was a shell elevation, 18 feet in height, rectangular in form with a level summit. Major structural features were mounds, water courts, canals, cisterns or water holes, garden terraces, and so forth, while prehistoric wooden structures were evidenced by the finding of piles and posts and decayed thatch from the roofs and side walls of houses. The "Court" proper consisted of a rudely triangular artificial bayou, approximately 75 feet by 100 feet in size. Originally a small lake, around or over which pile dwellings had been erected, it was at the time of examination practically filled with muck and water vegetation.

The artifacts taken from the "Court" comprised, in addition to the usual objects of shell, bone, stone, and other time-resisting materials, hundreds of specimens made from wood, miraculously preserved by the muck deposit. Many of these were painted with black, white, gray-blue, and brownish-red pigments which, being partly insoluble, aided in their preservation. Unfortunately it was found impossible to preserve intact many of the objects, owing to the fact that contact with air and the evaporation of the heavy water contact resulted in warping and disintegration with consequent loss of shape and form. The many objects taken from the site, by far the greater number of which were of wood and other perishable materials, comprised, in addition to the piling and other structural items entering into house construction, a multiplicity of furniture and house furnishings; potteryware and household utensils and implements; navigating and fishing apparatus; tools and implements used in the handicrafts; weapons of warfare and the chase; objects of personal ornament and decoration; an intricate array of ceremonial, sacred, and symbolical objects; and numerous carvings, paintings, masks, and figureheads. Textile articles, as cordage, fabric, basketry, and so forth, were much in evidence and exhibited a high degree of attainment. Among the articles of wood may be mentioned artistically fashioned *atlatls* or spear-throwers; toy canoes and paddles; masks of the human face and of animals; paintings

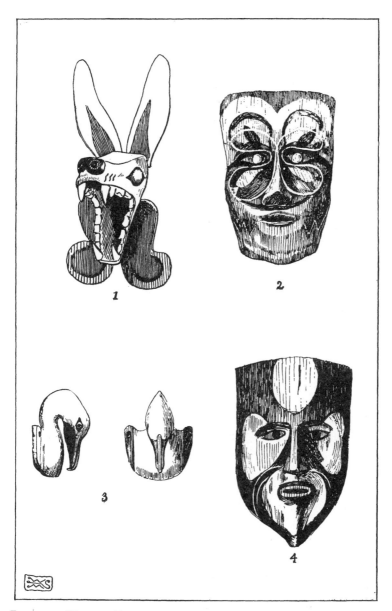

Fig. 294. Wooden Figure-heads or Masks from Key Marco, Florida

Carved from wood and painted in black, white, brown, and gray-blue. 1, wolf-head figure. 2, wolf-man mask (nine inches high). 3, pelican figure-heads. 4, pelican-man or pelican god. After Cushing.

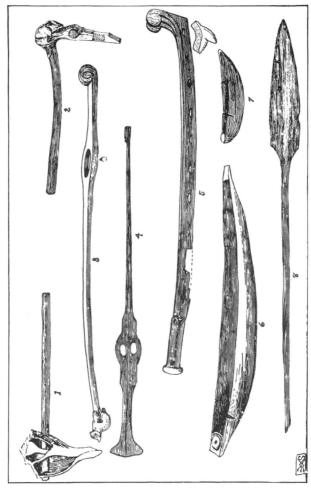

FIG. 295. WOODEN OBJECTS FROM KEY MARCO, FLORIDA

1, hoe or digging tool, conch-shell blade and buttonwood handle. 2, adze, wooden handle and antler head. 3 and 4, *atlatls* or spear-throwers of hard wood, probably ironwood. 5, sabre club of wood, set with shark's teeth. 6, 7, and 8, miniature wooden canoes and paddle, all of cypress wood. Number 3 is 19 inches long and furnishes the scale for all specimens. After Cushing.

and carvings of the human figure, birds, and alligators; and statuettes of what is considered to be the panther god.

Although the culture indicated by the relics from Key Marco is not necessarily higher than that of several other regions of the general mound area (in fact, the objects of imperishable materials taken alone indicate a lower development than do

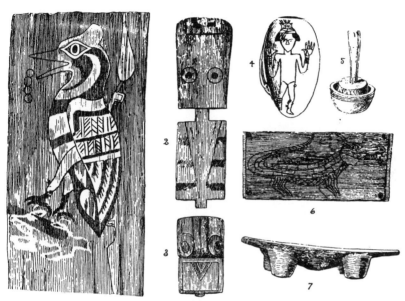

FIG. 296. WOODEN OBJECTS WITH ARTISTIC DESIGNS FROM KEY MARCO, FLORIDA

Left, wooden ceremonial tablet 16 inches long, with bird figure painted in white and gray-blue. The bird is supposed to represent the jay or the kingfisher, but might well be the pileated woodpecker of frequent occurrence in mound art farther north; note the speech symbols issuing from the mouth. 2 and 3, altar or ancestral tablets, of cypress, painted in black and white; conventionalizations of the alligator. 4, human figure painted on a shell. 5, wooden mortar and pestle. 6, lid of wooden jewel box, bearing horned alligator. 7, a wooden stool. After Cushing.

similar artifacts from the Hopewell, the Lower Mississippi, and the Tennessee-Cumberland areas) its peculiar features have led certain archæologists to believe that its origin may be attributed to the Arawaks or the Caribs of South America and the Antillean islands. Regardless of this interesting theory, the finds at Key Marco are of the utmost significance, in that they furnish a basis for determining the relative utilization of objects made from perishable materials as compared with those of time-resisting materials. From the Key Marco data it may be estimated that objects made from imperishable substances represent not more than ten per cent of the total recovered. Since the relative utilization of objects from perishable and imperishable materials presumably was approximately uniform throughout all divisions of the general mound area, it is apparent that judgment of the entire culture complex of a given region based upon the usual evidences of exploration may easily be underestimated.

COASTAL MOUNDS OF GEORGIA

Although it is customary to speak of "peninsular" and "mainland" Florida, the entire state, together with southeastern Georgia, if political boundaries may be for the moment disregarded, constitutes a peninsula; and since the primitive culture of this Georgia region appears, superficially at least, to be related to the culture complex of the main peninsula, it is here included under the heading of the Peninsular area. As we have noted with regard to some others of our divisions, however, the justification for this assignment is not conclusive; it is in part geographic and in part a matter of convenience.

Apart from the explorations in northern Georgia reviewed in the preceding chapter, no very extensive explorations of the Georgia and South Carolina mounds has been effected. Some attention is accorded them by Colonel C. C. Jones in his *Antiquities of the Southern Indians* and later by Clarence B. Moore in *Certain Aboriginal Mounds of the Georgia Coast*, published in 1897. Moore, traveling the inland water passages which parallel the entire Georgia coast, examined and reported some fifty mounds. Among the more important sites examined was a mound on Creighton Island, McIntosh County, which yielded more than 220 skeletons, most of them anatomical flexed burials. Numerous "pockets" within the mound contained calcined human bones, and in the mound and under the adjacent level surface were found urn burials containing the bones of infants. Stone hatchets, chisels, discoidal or game stones, stone hammers, and flint arrowpoints were found here in relatively greater abundance than in other portions of the coastal region. Shell gorgets, in symbolic excised and intaglio designs; shell hairpins; objects of bone; ornate tobacco pipes and burned clay; a burial urn and other pottery vessels; and a fine copper chisel were among the other finds.

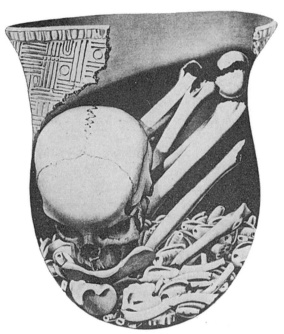

.FIG. 297. MORTUARY VESSEL WITH SKELETON OF A CHILD, FROM A MOUND ON ST. CATHERINE'S ISLAND, GEORGIA
After Moore.

The Walker Mound, in the same county, was remarkable in exhibiting a great diversity of burial customs. A total of thirty-five burials were interred anatomically, that is, as normal interments; as bunched burials; as "masses of bones"; as loose deposits of incinerated remains; and in cinerary urns.

A mound on Sapelo Island disclosed 192 skeletal burials. In addition there were eight deposits of calcined boxes, three urn burials, and three calcined interments in burial urns. Most of the skeletal burials were flexed, usually on the right side, while a few were in the extended posture. Unlike the burial illustrated in Figure 297, the skeletal parts enclosed in jars were those of adults. A few earthen vessels and a number of interesting clay pipes, effigy and symbolic, were found, together with shell objects such as cups, gorgets, beads, and agricultural implements.

Two mounds on Ossabaw Island, Bryan County, yielded upward of two hundred burials of the various types and many specimens of potteryware, implements, and ornaments. One of these mounds was unusual in that all burials, so far as could be determined, were those of women, adolescents, children, and infants. In a mound of the group there were found numerous skeletons of dogs, buried intact with the same respectful interment accorded humans.

As a result of his explorations Moore was inclined to believe that the culture of the Georgia coast differed sharply from that of Florida. This impression was based on the recognition of certain distinct traits for the Georgia region, principally as indicated by local forms of tobacco pipes and burial custom. The pipes of the region are mainly of the modified tubular, trumpet, and elbow forms, highly decorated in effigy or symbolic designs. Bunched burials were not so common as in Florida, while cremation was much more in evidence. The placing of cremated remains in cinerary urns and of uncremated remains in jars was not noted in Florida, while the ready-made perforated funerary vessels of the latter region were absent from the Georgia mounds.

ANCIENT SHELL MOUNDS AND SHELL HEAPS

Although the so-called shell mounds and the extensive shell heaps scattered along the Atlantic Coast from New England to Florida are primarily accumulations of refuse resulting from the consumption as food of various mollusks, some of them may properly be considered along with the purposefully constructed mounds and earthworks. The more striking of these

FIG. 298. SHELL MOUND NEAR PORT ORANGE, VOLUSIA COUNTY, FLORIDA
Thousands of tons of shell have been taken from this structure and utilized in road-building. Photograph by Dr. Amos W. Butler.

shell mounds are to be found in Florida, those along the coast consisting mainly of marine shells, such as oysters, clams, and conchs, while those of the interior are comprised for the most part of the shells of the fresh-water clam or mussel and other mollusks. The shell heaps were in the main merely accumulations of débris, but the shells of which they are composed came to be used rather extensively by the aborigines for the construction of mounds, sometimes for burial purposes but mostly for house and temple foundations. Shell mounds of gigantic proportions are located at Charlotte Harbor and Cedar Keys, while one deposit on Tampa Bay is thirty feet in height and covers an island of eight acres extent. A similar structure at Bluffton is spread over an area of thirty acres.

While the shell mounds and shell heaps are most in evidence in Florida, they may be found in practically all the seaboard and Gulf states, and to some extent interiorly. Shell mounds and shell deposits are abundant along the Georgia coast. The more important of these are an impressive circular enclosure on Sapèlo Island and a great shell causeway on Barbour's Island. The great shell mound at Pope's Creek, Maryland, covers an area of upwards of thirty acres.

The Port Orange Mound, in Volusia County, Florida, illustrated in Figure 298, has now been destroyed and the component shells used for road-building. Many thousands of tons of shells from the shell mounds of Florida and other states have been utilized for road-building, notably at St. Augustine, Mobile, and New Orleans. The shells are also calcined and used as fertilizer and as a source of lime.

It will be readily evident to the reader that although a considerable amount of exploration has been effected in the Peninsular area, there are not yet sufficient carefully prepared data to warrant conclusions regarding the cultural relations of the various regions, with their startling contrasts on the one hand and their close resemblances on the other. While many of the major evidences have disappeared through exploration and other causes, the area still holds great possibilities for further examination and correlation.

CHAPTER XX

SUMMARY AND CONCLUSIONS

Identity of the Mound-builders—Were the Mound-builders Indians?—Indians as builders of mounds—What became of the Mound-builders?—The native American race—Dispersal and migrations on the American continent—Conclusion.

WHO were the Mound-builders? Whence came they, and when? Why did they build mounds? What became of them? These important queries, the five "W's" of mound archæology, were proposed in the Introduction, but for reasons to be stated presently the answers to them have been withheld. The theories and speculations of early students of American prehistory have been set forth and subsequent archæological investigation reviewed, as a result of which the reader has had opportunity to form definite and unbiased personal impressions. All that remains for the author, therefore, is to summarize the evidence and to formulate the conclusions based thereon.

In the reaction following the early theories as to the Mound-builders, too often speculative and even visionary, the tendency has been decidedly toward the opposite extreme. In their zeal to correct the fanciful imaginings of pioneer writers, more recent investigators have felt themselves called upon to strip the Mound-builders of every vestige of interest and importance. Originally portrayed as a superior and separate race of people with a superior civilization, they have been relegated to the rank of mere "Indians," hardly worthy of serious attention. This reaction, it must be admitted, has been beneficial and salutary, in that it has served to curb the unbridled range of imagination and theorizing. But in the end it has come no nearer to the truth than did the early visionaries. The contrast has been too great to suit popular fancy, and although a small

471

percentage of individuals accepted the new interpretation and immediately lost interest in the subject, the greater number preferred to retain the earlier and more pleasing picture. The reactionists sought to destroy what had become a cherished tradition without offering something of value to replace it. The present writer believes that this something is ready at hand, and that the truth lies not at either extreme but in the middle ground. Reservation of answers to the basic queries for discussion in this final chapter has seemed the most practical way of revealing what he conceives this truth to be.

IDENTITY OF THE MOUND-BUILDERS

Attacking first the query "Who were the Mound-builders," it is necessary to repeat that opinion has ranged from the belief, at the one extreme, that they were a separate and distinct race, differing physically and culturally from any other known division of the human family, to the theory, at the other end of the scale, that they were nothing more nor less than "Indians," or at best the ancestors of the Indian tribesmen of historic record. In order to bring clarity into the dispute and to state conclusions intelligibly a primary requisite is the employment of descriptive words or terms of definitely fixed meaning. Unfortunately there has been until recently a dearth of anthropological terms of specific definition—nomenclature or terminology. Certain terms have been loosely employed, with consequent confusion and disagreement, for the reason that there has been no consensus of opinion as to their exact meaning. Among these offenders there stand out prominently the words "race" and "Indian," each of which has been made to cover a multitude of meanings.

It is customary popularly to speak of the "human race" as broadly inclusive of all humankind, and with equal facility to use the term "race" interchangeably with such social, political, geographical, and language designations as *tribe, nation,* and *people.* Thus we not infrequently hear the expressions, "Anglo-Saxon race,"-"Italian race," "English race," and even "American race," where *people* or *nation* clearly is intended. In between the two extremes is the familiar use of "race" long employed in the public schools for designating the supposed five great races of mankind—the white, yellow, red, black, and brown: that is, the Caucasian, Mongolian, American, Ethiopian, and Malayan. Latterly this geographical classification, determined mainly by continental divisions, has given way to what may be termed the anthropological classification, based on physical traits and comprising but three grand divisions, the Caucasian, the Mongoloid, and the Negroid, each embracing its distinctive "races" and accounting for all but a few aberrant or indeterminate physical subtypes. Under this now quite generally accepted scheme, *race* is confined in its meaning to biological or physical traits; in other words, it signifies blood relationship through descent from common ancestry, and recognizes only inherited physical attributes, as opposed to acquired ethnological traits such as manners and customs.

Under the above classification the grand division known as Mongoloid is made to include three separate races—the Mongolian, comprising Chinese, Japanese, and other less important yellow-skinned peoples of eastern Asia; the Malaysian, of the East Indies; and the great native American race, usually designated as such but sometimes referred to merely as the American Indian. Thus only a single race is recognized for what is commonly spoken of as the New World—the western continents—prior to the arrival of Europeans. This conclusion is based upon exhaustive study by the physical anthropologist of prehistoric skeletal material and living tribes and individuals. Thus it may confidently be stated that the Mound-builders did not constitute, of themselves, a separate and distinct race, but that they, together with all other aboriginal Americans, were tribes, nations, and peoples of the native American race. This race, as will be shown presently, was derived from Mongoloid immigrants from Asia, and was of Asiatic rather than American nativity; their amalgamation on the American continent, however, signalized the birth of the race proper, which may with propriety be referred to as "native."

WERE THE MOUND-BUILDERS INDIANS?

So far our discussion has concerned itself entirely with terms of race as a complex of physical attributes. Turning now from the biological or physical to the ethnological and cultural, the question as to whether or not the Mound-builders were "Indians" may be accorded brief consideration.

As with the word "race," so with "Indian": popular usage has given each a restricted meaning, while anthropologically there is a tendency to construe them in a broader sense, and to regard them, so far as aboriginal peoples of America are concerned, as almost synonymous. Everyone is familiar with the fact that Columbus, in discovering America, erroneously supposed that he had touched upon the shores of India and that in this belief he called the natives "Indians." The numerous native tribes of both North and South America with which white men have come in contact within the historic period have continued to be known as Indians. Only the Eskimo, of the far North, and the protohistoric Aztecs, Mayans, and Incas, with their impressive civilizations, have measurably escaped designation as Indians, at least in the popular conception. Whether or not all these peoples and nations of the native American race shall be classed as Indians depends, of course, on whether the term *Indian* shall apply in the broadly inclusive or in a more restricted sense.

The term *Indian,* to begin with, is admittedly a misnomer. Yet apparently it is inseparably associated with the native historic tribesmen, undesirable though it may be. However, despite the admitted racial affinity of the several peoples of the historic and the prehistoric eras in America, there would seem to be no sufficient reason for further broadening the scope and significance of so manifestly inappropriate a term. For the present purpose, then, let it be assumed that the anthropological definition of race, as set forth above, is correct; and that the more restricted use of the term Indian, as applying specifically to the historic tribesmen of the native American race, is the more desirable. If such a proposition seems somewhat inconsistent, let it be remembered that, after all, the scientific attitude toward the designation "American Indian race" for the historic tribesmen of the continent has been more receptive than affirmative.

Keeping in mind this restricted meaning of the word *Indian*, the query as to whether the Mound-builders were Indians may be transposed to read, "Were the Indians mound-builders?" The native tribesmen have been under observation throughout the four centuries that America has been known to white men. The locations of the various tribes and nations as recorded by early French and Spanish explorers, particularly throughout the southern portions of the present United States, afford in the main a good idea of the ethnological state of affairs immediately preceding the discovery of America. Although these explorers and their chroniclers frequently record the practice of erecting ceremonial and domiciliary structures on flat-topped mounds and the employment of earthen embankments, moats, and palisades as protection for towns and habitations, there is scant mention of the erection and use of mounds for burial purposes. The finding of articles of European manufacture in burial mounds is by no means rare, but the significance of such finds is not so important as once was supposed. Present-day methods of mound exploration, in which minutest care is an important factor, appear to indicate that many of the mound burials with which modern objects occur are intrusive in character, due to a natural tendency of the Indians and others to inter their dead in "high places" and in sites recognized by them as burial places. Hardly a mound of importance in much of the general mound area fails to disclose one or more intrusive burials occupying graves excavated in original structures by later Indians. Again, it has been found that some at least of the supposedly modern artifacts of metal found in mound burials are in reality prehistoric, made from native copper and meteoric iron. Further, in numerous instances hearsay and tradition are cited in the literature dealing with mounds and their contents, in which connection it should be remembered that Indian tradition has little value as historical evidence.

Nevertheless, in several instances objects of European or historic origin have been discovered in mounds under conditions indicating their construction within historic times. Both Moore and the Bureau of American Ethnology record the exploration of mounds in the Lower Mississippi and Peninsular areas in which original burials, as distinguished from intrusive interments, were accompanied by post-Columbian artifacts. A few unquestioned examples of burial mounds having their

FIG. 299. A BURIAL MOUND OF MODERN ORIGIN

Erected in 1799 by Rev. John Heckewelder, Moravian missionary, over the remains of ninety Moravian Christianized Indians, following the historic Moravian Massacre at Gnadenhütten, Ohio. Photograph by Green; courtesy of Rev. J. E. Weinland.

origin in early historic times have been recorded in the Upper Mississippi area, the most recent of which was a mound of the Fisher site, near Joliet, Illinois, described in Chapter XV. Although other mounds of the group proved to be entirely prehistoric in origin, a single tumulus contained burials which in every instance were accompanied by objects of European or historic origin. In the mound area as a whole, however, the percentage of tumuli containing recent burials is very small.

INDIANS AS BUILDERS OF MOUNDS

Referring for a moment to the dominant linguistic stocks, or language families, occupying the general mound area as of earliest record, there appear the great Algonquian stock occupying in a general way the northern half of the area and surrounding, amœbalike, the Iroquoian area adjacent to the upper St. Lawrence and Lakes Ontario and Erie; the extensive Muskhogean stock corresponding in a general way to the southern half of the area; with the important Siouan family to the westward of both. The prehistoric Algonquians have usually been regarded as non-mound-building, although recent evidences indicate that in parts of their great domain and during some period of their existence they probably developed the trait to some extent. The Iroquois proper show little evidence of the trait, although the Cherokee, a detached southern element of the stock, are supposed to have been builders of mounds. Certain of the Sioux, particularly the Winnebago of the upper Mississippi valley, are accorded the trait by some authorities, while all agree that the Muskhogean peoples were the authors of certain of the southern tumuli. Naturally, in attempting to correlate the prehistoric evidences with historic peoples, investigators have sought to identify the mounds with the several linguistic families of the same general regions. So determined, indeed, has been this effort that it has become almost a fetish. In the Middle West, for example, there has been a proneness to believe that everything prehistoric must be attributed either to the Algonquian or to the Iroquoian.

Approaching the question from the standpoint of specific historic tribes and nations, it is generally conceded that in addition to the Cherokee, most of the Muskhogean nations, as the Creek, Choctaw, and Chickasaw, and the Shawnee, of Central Algonquian stock, were at times and in certain localities builders of mounds. The theory, formerly widely held, that the Winnebago of the Siouan stock were the authors of the numerous effigy mounds of Wisconsin and adjacent territory is regarded by recent authorities as unproven.

Finally, it may be said that no very definite success has attended efforts to identify the prehistoric with the historic, as regards either the mounds or minor remains and evidences. Perhaps the nearest approach to coördinating ethnological with archæological evidence lies in the finding, in Mississippi and Alabama, of artificially deformed skulls. It is known that most tribes of Muskhogean stock practiced artificial flattening of the frontal portions of the skull to some extent, but the Choctaw, occupying central Mississippi and Alabama, had developed the trait to a marked degree. There seems to be little doubt that the owners of these deformed skulls from prehistoric sites spoke a dialect of the Muskhogean tongue.

From the evidence it is logical to deduce that the trait of mound-building as a mode of sepulture, though not obsolete at the time of discovery, was at least obsolescent. Either the outstanding trait of building mounds for interment of the dead had been in great part abandoned, or the peoples who carried the trait to its highest development had disappeared. The solution appears to derive from both possibilities. On the one hand, historic tribes, undoubtedly closely related to certain cultures of Mound-builders and presumably directly descended from them, had partially or entirely abandoned the building of mounds, contenting themselves with other modes of burial or with intrusive burial in existing mounds. On the other hand, in view of the great number of "cultures," both mound-building and non-mound-building, which must have existed through the total extent of time and space corresponding to aboriginal occupancy of the mound area, there must have been several which for one reason or another failed to survive to witness the coming of white men. Among these it may be supposed that there were some that had and some that had not affinities with known linguistic families or specific tribes and nations. The striking Hopewell peoples of Ohio and the upper Mississippi valley, for example, defy identification with any known historic stock or people. Just why so widespread and natural a trait as the building of mounds as memorials to the dead should have lost its popularity or been abandoned is a matter for speculation.

Who were the Mound-builders? To state that they were cultural groups of the native American race, along with the Indians and all other native American peoples; that in many instances they were the racial ancestors of the Indian tribes of historic times; but that as peoples, nations, and tribes, each with its distinctive cultural attainments, they were distinct and different from the historic Indians, would not be far from the truth. The Mound-builders were Indians to exactly the same extent that the Indians were mound-builders.

WHAT BECAME OF THE MOUND-BUILDERS?

The foregoing discussion answers in part the query as to who the Mound-builders were. The complete answer, and the answers to the additional queries as to whence they came and when, merge with the broader question as to the identity, place of origin, and time of arrival of the native race in America. The question as to what became of the Mound-builders, although the answer is partly obvious from the preceding pages, may be given further consideration at this point, prior to discussion of the native American race.

As intimated above, certain cultures of Mound-builders had completely disappeared from the stage of action prior to the arrival of white observers, with whom, consequently, they never came in contact. This is true in several outstanding instances, and particularly so with respect to the most highly developed of the several cultures—the Hopewell of Ohio and the upper Mississippi valley. In the case of the Hopewell peoples there is little or nothing to indicate affinity with any known tribe, nation, or linguistic stock. They simply are distinctive, unique, and peculiar to themselves, representing in certain essential respects the highest aboriginal development north of Mexico. They came into their various regions, perfected their distinctive culture, and disappeared from the scene so mysteriously as to make them one of the major puzzles of American archæology.

The downfall of human civilizations is far from being a historic rarity. With but one or two exceptions all those nations which march across the pages of ancient history have disappeared. The causes in most cases are matters of historic record —social and moral decadence; war, famine, and pestilence; conquest and subjugation with loss of identity; and so forth. Where these causes are known, they cease to be matters of interest; but because we cannot state explicitly the cause of the disappearance of the great Hopewell culture group, and some others, everybody wants to know.

There is, however, one event of historic record which probably goes a long way toward elucidating the puzzle. This event is the so-called Iroquoian invasion. It will be recalled that the Five Nations of Iroquois Indians, located in western New York State, are credited with having effected the most admirable confederacy in Indian history. Prior to 1650 they had obtained gunpowder and firearms from the Dutch of New Netherlands. Thus equipped, their ambitions turned to conquest, and, as recorded in the *Jesuit Relations,* they swept westward, driving before them, killing, or capturing all the native tribesmen from Lake Erie on the north to the Ohio River on the south, and carried their devastations almost to the Mississippi. This district includes the Hopewell region and the heart of the mound area—the great Northwest Territory. As a result, a great expanse of country was stripped of its human inhabitants, and for upwards of a century it was left a no-man's-land. Clearly, whatever mound-building peoples lived therein must have received their *coup de grâce* at the hands of the invading Iroquois.

Another theory, of decided sentimental interest but probably of little historic value, lays the blame for the disappearance of the Mound-builders on the sturdy shoulders of the American bison. It is pointed out that the buffalo made its appearance in the mound area within comparatively recent times; that its coming afforded the Mound-builder an easy source of sustenance; and that, as a result, he abandoned his laborious agriculture and sedentary life, turned nomad, and followed the buffalo into unknown parts, where he completely lost his culture and identity. Commenting on this theory, a well-known authority on the mounds facetiously remarks: "Geese saved Rome; buffaloes overthrew the Mound-builders' empire!"

THE NATIVE AMERICAN RACE

Discussion of the native American race as a whole belongs properly to the domain of the anthropologist. Certain phases of the subject, however, are inseparable from a study of the Mound-builders, since up to a certain point their story is one and the same. Only such incidents of the larger story as may have a direct bearing on the subject in hand, and these most hurriedly, will be referred to at this point. The reader will understand that few incontrovertible facts are known regarding the prehistoric life of the American race, and that many of the ideas here advanced are theoretical. They are, however, of general acceptance among anthropologists and represent a composite opinion rather than any individual view.

It is now generally conceded that the native American race belongs to the great Mongoloid division of the human family; that its progenitors came into America from Asia, in all probability by way of Bering Strait; and that the time of their arrival was subsequent to the retreat of the most recent of the several glacial invasions, which, according to geologists, was some 8,000 to 12,000 years ago.

A detailed discussion of the manner in which the physical anthropologist has determined the racial affinity of the native race with the Mongoloid stock would be aside from the purpose of this book. Suffice it to say that in all essential respects the three races comprising the stock—the Mongolian, Malaysian, and American—are basically similar, and that physical differences between them are more apparent than real, the result of greatly diversified culture traits, climatic conditions, and general environment. Of the three races the native American is believed to be physically more like the original Mongoloid stock than either of the remaining two.

Although several theories have been advanced as to the route of entry into America of the Asiatic migrants, all others, including the Polynesian islands, the mythical Atlantis, and the Aleutian Islands, have been abandoned in favor of the only logical and easy point of access—Bering Strait. At its narrowest the Strait is but sixty miles in width, with the Diomede Islands, midway of the channel, visible under favorable conditions from either shore. Human curiosity, it is pointed out, would of itself be sufficient incentive to provoke a crossing, and the migratory instinct would hardly recognize in the undertaking any serious obstacle. Moreover, it is conceivable that the Strait at that remote time may have been wholly or partly frozen over, thus affording an ice bridge. This significant migration from the Old World to the New, however, is believed not to have been an enterprise begun and completed within a comparatively short time. Continuous bands of migrants, under venturesome leaders, presumably continued to cross the Strait throughout centuries of time, as the great continents to the southward received and absorbed their first human inhabitants.

The question as to the culture status of these primitive migrants, coupled with the query as to the time of their arrival, offers an interesting exposition of the constructive reasoning by which the anthropologist may reach definite conclusions. In Europe and other parts of the Old World the existence of human life over a period of 100,000 years and more is demonstrated by the finding in certain geological relationships of skeletal remains and relics belonging to extinct types of men and to the very earliest stages of human culture. The earlier and by far the greater portion of this long space lay in what is termed the Paleolithic Period, or the Old Stone Age. From geological evidence it is known that the Paleolithic gave way to the Neolithic, or the New Stone Age, coincidently with the most recent glacial retreat, approximately, as above noted, 10,000 years ago. Had human beings lived in the Americas in preglacial or early glacial times, it is asserted, their skeletal remains and relics would inevitably be found in glacial detritus, river terraces, and caves, as in Europe. On the other hand, had their coming been much delayed beyond the glacial retreat, they would have brought with them the domesticated animals, the cultivated food plants, and the mechanical inventions known to have pertained to the Neolithic Period in the Old World. It may be noted that the imperishable human evidences found within the area traversed by the Asiatic migrants are neither earlier nor later than those pertaining to the close of the Paleolithic or the beginning of the Neolithic Period in Europe and Asia. Although alleged or supposed "finds" of great antiquity are of constant occurrence, scientific investigation up to the present time has failed to disclose a single human bone or relic antedating the epoch assigned for the beginning of human occupancy of American soil. Naturally, however, the quest for the Paleolithic is keenly pursued, since the distinction accruing to the archæologist or to the layman from a *bona fide* discovery of great geological age would be of major importance.

The arrival of the vanguard of the native race on the American threshold, as envisioned by the anthropologist, is one of the most fascinating episodes of human history. In the historic landing of the Pilgrim Fathers at Plymouth Rock nearly one hundred centuries later, the genesis of the white man's dominion of the Western World, there are to be found striking similarities and significant contrasts. Accompanied by their faithful brute friend and only domestic animal, the dog, whose earliest association with humankind is lost in the mists of antiquity, those first Americans must have felt not only the lure but the veiled hostility of the strange new country. Their culture, as nearly as may be learned from the mute imperishable relics strewn along the path of their dispersal throughout the New World and from comparisons and analogies with similar evidences in the Old World, was that of the hunter-fisher stage of human development. They simply partook of nature's bounty in so far as they were able—wild game, fish, fruits, nuts, roots, and berries—and made these natural foods suffice for sustaining life and even for increasing and multiplying life upon the earth. They possessed the simple arts of kindling fire with the primitive fire drill; of chipping flint and shaping stone and bone; of twisting cords and probably of making rude baskets. For weapons they possessed clubs, hammerstones, the harpoon, the spear, and probably the bow and arrow. Rude, untailored garments of skins and furs served as protection from wind and weather. Socially they may be conceived of as possessing the rudiments of government, centering in the family group; and a basic religious concept in which the supernatural and magic were the outstanding elements. Of their language little, of course, is known, except what may be reflected in the many tongues and dialects of the historic tribesmen. Numerous separate bands of more or less closely related peoples with varying languages or dialects are believed to have constituted the migratory movement from Asia throughout its entire course.

DISPERSAL AND MIGRATIONS ON THE AMERICAN CONTINENT

Of the subsequent dispersals and migrations of these primitive immigrants only sufficient need be recounted to indicate their connection with those interesting peoples who, centuries later and after generations of wandering, were to become the so-called Mound-builders. Dispersal from the first appears to have been both to the east and to the south. Although the rugged mountain ranges paralleling the Pacific Coast imposed a barrier to the eastward, certain bands were able to find their way across in favorable localities. From these hardy adventurers it seems plausible to trace the historic Indian stocks and nations of the Plains and the northern portions of the present United States and Canada. With these, the purpose of this volume is not much concerned, for they seem to have had but superficial connection with the mound-building peoples.

Whether or not the southerly trend of migration was numerically more important than that to the eastward, certain it is that in eventual development it was more significant. Hemmed in by mountain barriers on the left flank and enticed by the salubrious climate and never-failing food supplies of the Pacific Coast, the stream of immigrants from across

Bering Strait came after a while into Mexico and Middle America. Here, in a semitropical setting unfavorable to the more advanced planes of human civilization but eminently encouraging to the development from primitive to higher culture stages, they prospered. From wandering nomads they became sedentary agricultural peoples, able for the first time to face the future with adequate stores of food supplies against famine and pestilence; able to exist in compact populous communities and thus to develop community enterprise and specialization of labor. The magic key which unlocked the door to progress was nothing more nor less than maize or Indian corn. From a native seed-bearing grass, later known to the Aztecs as *teocentli,* these aboriginal agriculturists are believed to have developed, through conscious or accidental selection and cultivation, the world's greatest cereal, corn. With the development of agriculture—maize, beans, squash, and tobacco —came correlated inventions—spinning, weaving, and pottery-making. The high development of social institutions, religion, architecture, astronomy, and so forth, destined to make their appearance in due time within the important empires of Middle and South America, need not enter into this sketch. Nor is it concerned with the peopling from this nuclear area of the South American continent which in time materialized.

Equipped with the rudiments of agriculture and with the confidence engendered thereby, and carrying the germ of culture generated during their sojourn in the parental area in Mexico, the American aborigines again succumbed to the instinctive urge to seek new homes and to explore unknown lands. Once more groups and bands followed venturesome leaders across the visible horizon, some of them retracing, in a way, the old migration trails of the northward. To afford the reader an appreciation of the manner in which numerous highly diversified tribes and peoples, under equally diversified phases of environment, developed from a common source or stock, and to lead him, without further delay, to the objective of our inquiry, the Mound-builder area, a somewhat hypothetical but highly probable series of movements may be assumed. From the nuclear area in southern Mexico the line of migration may be followed northward, finding its first materialization in the arid region of our Southwest. Here, influenced definitely by environment, may be envisioned the development of the Pueblo culture. Taking advantage of natural shelters in the cliffs and utilizing the native clays for making sun-dried brick for the construction of communal dwellings, the Pueblo peoples develop in due time a culture complex distinctive and outstanding. This, it may be assumed, represents the first step outward from Mexican influence, and, as would be expected, it contains more elements of the parent nucleus than any other outlying region. The second stage of migration is found, not to the northward, as might be expected, but eastward in what is termed the Southeastern Woodland area, corresponding to the southern half of the general mound area. This second stage of removal from the Mexican cultural center brings us definitely into the country of the Mound-builders, and completes the hypothetical connection between the Asiatic migrants at Bering Strait and the peoples with which this volume is concerned. From this Southeastern region migration may be assumed to have extended, by still another step or stage, to the northern half of the mound area; and, ascending the Mississippi, it appears to have influenced to some slight extent the Plains area adjacent to the Southeastern Woodland, west of the Mississippi.

As might be expected, cultural links between the nuclear area and the several outlying centers are most pronounced immediately adjacent to Mexico, diminishing in inverse ratio to the distance from the parent source. In the Pueblo region the use of stone for building purposes finds expression in domiciliary structures as contrasted to its employment almost wholly for religious edifices in southern Mexico. In the southern portions of the general mound area and to a nearly equal extent farther north, stone as a structural material gave way to wood and, as evidenced in the numerous mounds, flat-topped pyramids, defensive and ceremonial earthworks, to earth. Corresponding comparisons may be made of minor artifacts, particularly those of artistic and symbolic significance. Considering only the southern portions of the general mound area, Moorehead notes the following resemblances to the Mexican cultures: truncated pyramids or temple mounds; monolithic hatchets; seated human figures; sculptured idol heads; plumed serpents as decorative or symbolic design motives; vessels with tripod feet; certain engraved shells; spool-shaped ear ornaments; and long ceremonial swords chipped from flint. The truncated pyramids or flat-topped temple mounds are particularly significant, and may be regarded as analogous to the temple pyramids of Mexico.

Although the southern portion of the general mound area, specifically the Lower Mississippi region, is assumed to be but two stages removed from the parent center, it should be noted that an intervening sterile gap of more than 1,000 miles separates the Mound-builder from the Pueblo area. Just why this great territory, reaching from the Mexican border to Alabama, should be barren of evidences resembling those of the cultures under discussion is a decided puzzle. However, its extent undoubtedly explains, in part, why resemblances to the parent culture are not more in evidence in the mound region. Additional links in the assumed chain connecting Mexico with the southern mound area doubtless will be forged when more definite explorations are conducted throughout the intervening territory and in central and northern Mexico. In the latter region investigation has concerned itself almost exclusively with architectural ruins of the Aztecs and other outstanding cultures, to the neglect of the burial tumuli, cemeteries, and habitation sites. A suggestion which may have a bearing on the existence of the "gap" separating Mexico and the mound area is that migration may have been by water rather than overland.

It is on such evidence, significant but less conclusive than might be desired, that the affinity of the mound-building peoples of the general mound area with the culture center in Middle America is predicated. Clearly, the building of mounds as a developed trait was not carried by the migrants from

Mexico; rather, the germ of that trait, originating before the assumed dispersal from the nuclear area, was destined to find expression in Mexico in the characteristic pyramids and temples, and in the mound area in the form of earthen mounds. As noted in an early chapter, the erection of mounds as monuments to the dead, as bases for domiciliary and ceremonial structures, and in the form of defensive and ceremonial earthworks, is a primary and natural human trait. The germ of the trait, brought into the area where mounds are predominant, eventually was developed to a high degree. Through diffusion it spread to other and adjacent peoples, probably including some who had taken the eastward route across the continent and had never entered Middle America.

Anticipating the possible question as to why more attention has not been accorded the non-mound-building peoples of the area discussed in this volume, it may be pointed out that, as the reader will have gathered, there is no basic cultural distinction between the builders of the tumuli and those who lacked the trait. Most of the material remains and artifacts of the non-mound-building peoples are common to the so-called Mound-builders, so that, after all, the foregoing account covers in a general way the entire prehistoric occupancy of the area. It is true that certain types of artifacts, as grooved axes, bell-shaped pestles, the so-called bannerstones, and other ceremonial and problematical objects, seldom, if ever, occur in mounds; but these, owing to their abundant occurrence and wide distribution, are quite familiar to the average person as "Indian relics."

CONCLUSION

This book has attempted to furnish the reader with what its author has been able to learn of the Mound-builders, through his own investigations and those of others. It is hoped that the resulting picture, though sketched in hurriedly and sometimes vaguely, will suffice to convey some idea of the human interest and the really great importance attaching to these native American peoples, who, although their culture was not destined to be perpetuated, nevertheless had a part in that greatest of all human experiments, the blazing of the trail from savagery toward civilization. No student of human history can afford to ignore the earlier chapters of so fascinating a subject, and human origins and cultural beginnings can be understood only through study of those early peoples who, like the Mound-builders, accepted the challenge and in the face of almost insuperable obstacles "carried on" that the world of today might enjoy the blessings of civilization.

To the student, the vacationist, and the tourist the prehistoric remains of the Mound-builder area offer opportunity for observation at first hand. In return for the privilege they should recognize a special responsibility. In each of the states where prehistoric remains are to be seen, intensive efforts are being made, through state and national agencies, for their preservation and scientific interpretation. Thoughtless destruction of mounds and graves and the carrying away of archæological material are of far too frequent occurrence. Those who have evinced sufficient interest to peruse this volume will without doubt be glad to assist in every possible way in conserving the relics which assist in telling the story of the Moundbuilders.

For the benefit of those who may wish to pursue further the study of the Mound-builders and other prehistoric peoples, a selected list of publications on anthropology, archæology, ethnology, the American Indians, and allied subjects is furnished in the appended Bibliography. Only items of primary interest and ready availability are listed; and though some of these are of limited distribution, they may be found in most public libraries. Most of these contain more extensive references and bibliographies on their respective subjects, and the reader will find before him a never-ending source of interest and information.

BIBLIOGRAPHY

Abbreviated references

Acad. Nat. Sci., Journal of the Academy of Natural Sciences of Philadelphia.
Am. Anth., The American Anthropologist.
B.A.E., Bureau of American Ethnology.
Pea. Mus., Papers, Peabody Museum of American Archæology and Ethnology.
O.S.A. & H., Ohio State Archæological and Historical Society.
Smith. Cont., Smithsonian [Institution] Contributions to Knowledge.

GENERAL ANTHROPOLOGY

BOAS, Franz.—*The Mind of Primitive Man* (Macmillan Company, 1911). Discusses the psychology of different races, the problem of race, the race problem in the United States.

COLE, Fay-Cooper.—"The Coming of Man" (*The Nature of the World and of Man*, University of Chicago Press, 1928).

FRAZER, James G.—*The Golden Bough* (Abridged Edition, Macmillan Company, 1922). An account of the primitive races of the world and their religious and magical practices.

GOLDENWEISER, A. A.—*Early Civilization; an Introduction to Anthropology* (Alfred A. Knopf, 1922).

HADDON, A. C.—*The Races of Man and Their Distribution* (Milner and Company, no date).

KEANE, A. H.—*Man, Past and Present* (Cambridge University Press, 1920). A classification of mankind, physical features, cultural characteristics and distributions.

KEITH, Arthur.—*The Antiquity of Man* (J. B. Lippincott Company, 1925). Factors in the evolution of modern man from fossil man.

KROEBER, A. L.—*Anthropology* (Harcourt, Brace & Company, 1923). An introductory textbook.

LOWIE, R. H.—*Primitive Society* (Boni & Liveright, 1920). A textbook introduction to social anthropology.

MACCURDY, G. G.—*Human Origins* (D. Appleton & Company, 1926). A manual of prehistory. Vol. I, fossil man; Vol. II, the Neolithic Period, the Bronze Age, the Iron Age.

MARETT, R. R.—*Anthropology* (Henry Holt & Company, no date). An introduction to anthropology; concise, readable, and instructive.

OSBORN, H. F.—*Men of the Old Stone Age* (Charles Scribner's Sons, 1921). Fossil man in Europe and his relation to the Glacial Period; physical characteristics and archæology.

SAPIR, Edward.—*Language* (Harcourt, Brace & Company, 1921). An introduction to the study of speech.

Wissler, Clark.—*Man and Culture* (Thomas Y. Crowell Company, 1923). A discussion of the factors in invention and diffusion of cultures.

THE AMERICAN INDIAN

Brinton, D. G.—*The American Race* (David McKay, 1901). Physical and cultural characteristics of the American Indians.

Bureau of American Ethnology.—*Handbook of American Indians* (Bulletin 30). An exhaustive encyclopædia of the native race, both historic and prehistoric.

Drake, S. G.—*Biography and History of the Indians of North America from its First Discovery* (B. B. Mussey & Company, 1851). An account of the Indians known to the first Europeans in America.

Moorehead, W. K.—*The American Indian* (The Andover Press, 1914). The number and condition of the Indians at the present time.

Schoolcraft, H. R.—*The American Indians, Their History, Condition and Prospects* (Wanzer, Foot & Company, 1851).

Shetrone, H. C.—The Indian in Ohio (O.S.A. & H., 1918).

Swanton, J. R.—*Indian Tribes of the Lower Mississippi Valley* (B.A.E., Bulletin 43, 1911).

Winsor, Justin.—*Narrative and Critical History of America*, Vol. I, (Houghton Mifflin Company, 1884-1889). Early accounts of the Indians of North America.

Wissler, Clark.—*The American Indian* (Oxford University Press, American Branch, 1922). A general summary of anthropological research in North and South America.

ARCHÆOLOGY OF THE MOUND AREA

Fowke, Gerard.—Cave Explorations in Missouri, Indiana, Illinois, Kentucky, Tennessee and Alabama, B.A.E., Bulletin 76 (1922).

Jones, C. C.—*Antiquities of the Southern Indians* (D. Appleton & Company, 1873). Archæology of portions of the southern states.

Moore, C. B.—Numerous detailed reports of archæological explorations throughout the southern part of the general mound area. Published in the *Journal of the Academy of Natural Sciences of Philadelphia*, 1894-1915, and as reprints therefrom.

Moorehead, W. K.—*The Stone Age in North America* (Houghton Mifflin & Company, 1910). An archæological encyclopedia of the prehistoric relics of North America. Copiously illustrated.

Peet, S. D.—*Prehistoric America* (*The American Antiquarian*, 1892).

Squier, E. G., and Davis, F. H.—*Ancient Monuments of the Mississippi Valley* (Smith. Cont., Vol. I, 1848). The earliest contribution covering the general mound area.

Thomas, Cyrus.—*Report on the Mound Explorations of the Bureau of Ethnology* (B.A.E., 12th Annual Report, 1890-1891). The archæology of the general mound area.

Alabama

Alabama Anthropological Society.—Publications (Montgomery).
BRANNON, P. A.—"Aboriginal Remains of the Middle Chattahoochee Valley," *Am. Anth.,* Vol. XI (1909).
MOORE, C. B.—Mound Explorations in Alabama, *Acad. Nat. Sci.,* Vols. XI and XIII.
THOMAS, Cyrus.—Alabama Mound Explorations, B.A.E., 12th Annual Report.

Arkansas

MOORE, C. B.—Mound Explorations in Arkansas, *Acad. Nat. Sci.,* Vols. XIII, XIV, and XVI.
THOMAS, Cyrus.—Arkansas Mound Explorations, B.A.E., 12th Annual Report.

Florida

CUSHING, F. H.—"Ancient Key Dwellers Remains, Florida Southwest Coast," *Proceedings of the American Philosophical Society,* 1897.
FEWKES, J. W.—"Explorations at Weedon Island," Smith. Cont., Vol. 76, No. 13.
MOORE, C. B.—Extensive Florida Explorations, *Acad. Nat. Sci.,* Vols. X, XI, and XII.

Georgia

MOORE, C. B.—Explorations of Georgia Mounds, *Acad. Nat. Sci.,* Vol. XI.
MOOREHEAD, W. K.—Explorations of the Etowah Group (in preparation).
THOMAS, Cyrus.—Exploration of Georgia Mounds, B.A.E., 12th Annual Report.

Illinois

BUSHNELL, D. I.—"The Cahokia and Surrounding Mound Groups," Pea. Mus., Vol. III (1903).
LANGFORD, George.—"The Fisher Mound Group," *Am. Anth.,* N. S., Vol. XXIX, No. 3 (1927).
MOOREHEAD, W. K.—"The Cahokia Mounds," *University of Illinois Bulletin,* Vol. XXVI, No. 4 (1929).
PEET, S. D.—*Prehistoric America (The American Antiquarian,* 1892).
THOMAS, Cyrus.—Examination of Mounds in Southern Illinois, B.A.E., 12th Annual Report.

Indiana

MACLEAN, J. A.—"Exploration of the Albee Mound," *Indiana Historical Bulletin,* May, 1927.
SETZLER, F. M.—Archæological Survey of Indiana (in preparation).

TEEL, W. R.—"Mounds near Terre Haute," *Indiana Historical Bulletin,* March, 1926.
THOMAS, Cyrus.—Mound Explorations in Southwestern Indiana, B.A.E., 12th Annual Report.

Iowa

Davenport Academy of Sciences.—Articles on mound explorations in Iowa, by Farquharson and others, Vol. I (1875).
KEYES, C. R.—Articles on Iowa archæology and the Iowa archæological survey, in *Iowa Journal of History and Politics,* Vols. XVIII (1920) and XXIII (1925).
THOMAS, Cyrus.--Iowa mound explorations, in B.A.E., 12th Annual Report.

Kentucky

MOORE, C. B.—Kentucky Mound Explorations, *Acad. Nat. Sci.,* Vol. XVI.
SMITH, H. I.—"Prehistoric Ethnology of a Kentucky Site," *Anthropological Papers, American Museum of Natural History,* Vol. VI (1911).
THOMAS, Cyrus.—Kentucky Mounds, B.A.E., 12th Annual Report.
WEBB, W. S., and FUNKHOUSER, W. D.—*Ancient Life in Kentucky* (Kentucky Geological Survey, Series VI).
—— "The Williams Site, in Christian County, Kentucky," Publications, Department of Anthropology and Archæology, University of Kentucky, Vol. I, No. 1 (July, 1929).
YOUNG, B. H.—*Prehistoric Men of Kentucky* (Filson Club, Louisville).

Louisiana

MOORE, C. B.—Mounds Explored in Louisiana, *Acad. Nat. Sci.,* Vols. XIV and XVI.
THOMAS, Cyrus.—Explorations of Louisiana Mounds, B.A.E., 12th Annual Report.

Michigan

GREENMAN, E. F.—"Michigan Mounds," *Papers of the Michigan Academy of Science, Arts and Letters,* Vol. VII (1926).
HINSDALE, W. B.—*Primitive Man in Michigan* (Michigan Handbook Series, No. 1, 1925).
HOLMES, W. H.—"Aboriginal Copper Mines of Isle Royale," *Am. Anth.,* N. S., Vol. III (1901).

Minnesota

WINCHELL, N. H.—*The Aborigines of Minnesota* (The Minnesota Historical Society, 1906-1911).

Mississippi

BROWN, C. A.—*The Archæology of Mississippi* (Mississippi Geological Survey, 1926).
MOORE, C. B.—Exploration of Mississippi Mounds, *Acad. Nat. Sci.*, Vols. XIII and XIV.
PEABODY, C.—"Exploration of Mounds in Coahoma County, Mississippi," Pea. Mus., Vol. III, No. 2 (1904).

Missouri

BUSHNELL, D. I., Jr.—"The Archæology of the Ozark Region of Missouri," *Am. Anth.*, Vol. VI (1904).
FOWKE, Gerard.—"Antiquities of Central and Southeastern Missouri," B.A.E., Bulletin 37 (1910).
MOORE, C. B.—Exploration of Mounds along the Mississippi in Missouri, *Acad. Nat. Sci.*, Vol. XVI.

New York

PARKER, A. C.—*Archæological History of New York* (New York State Museum, Bulletin Numbers 235 and 236, 1922).
SQUIER, E. G., and DAVIS, F. H.—*Aboriginal Monuments of New York* (Smith. Cont., Vol. II).

North Carolina

THOMAS, Cyrus.—Mounds Examined in North Carolina, B.A.E., 12th Annual Report.

North Dakota

THOMAS, Cyrus.—Explorations in North Dakota, B.A.E., 12th Annual Report.

Ohio

FOWKE, Gerard.—*Archæological History of Ohio* (O. S. A. & H., 1902).
MILLS, W. C.—Certain Mounds and Village Sites in Ohio (O. S. A. & H., four volumes also printed separately, 1907).
—— *Archæological Atlas of Ohio* (O. S. A. & H., 1914).
MOOREHEAD, W. K.—*Fort Ancient* (Robert Clarke & Company, 1890).
—— "The Hopewell Mound Group of Ohio," Field Museum of Natural History, Anthropological Series, Vol. VI, No. 5 (1922).
SHETRONE, H. C.—"The Culture Problem in Ohio Archæology," *Am. Anth.*, N. S., Vol. XXII, No. 2 (1920).
—— "Exploration of the Hopewell Group and others," *Certain Mounds and Village Sites in Ohio*, Vol. IV (O. S. A. & H., 1926).
WILLOUGHBY, C. C., and HOOTON, E. A.—"Indian Village Site and Cemetery near Madisonville, Ohio," Pea. Mus., Vol. VIII, No. 1 (1920).
—— "The Turner Group of Earthworks," Pea. Mus., Vol. VIII, No. 3 (1922).

Pennsylvania

THOMAS, Cyrus.—Mounds of Western Pennsylvania, B.A.E., 12th Annual Report.

South Carolina

MOORE, C. B.—Mounds along the coast of South Carolina, *Acad. Nat. Sci.*, Vol. XII.

South Dakota

OVER, W. H.—Archæological survey of South Dakota (in preparation, University of South Dakota).

THOMAS, Cyrus.—Mounds of South Dakota, B.A.E., 12th Annual Report.

Tennessee

MYER, W. E.—"Indian Trails of the Southeast," B.A.E., 42nd Annual Report (1924-).

MOORE, C. B.—Tennessee Mound Explorations, *Acad. Nat. Sci.*, Vol. XVI.

THRUSTON, G. P.—*Antiquities of Tennessee* (Robert Clark & Company, 1890).

West Virginia

THOMAS, Cyrus.—Mounds of the Kanawha Valley and Others, B.A.E., 12th Annual Report.

Wisconsin

BARRETT, S. A.—"Ancient Aztalan" (in preparation, Milwaukee Public Museum).

BROWN, C. E.—"A Record of Wisconsin Antiquities," *Wisconsin Archæologist*, Vol. V (1906), Nos. 3-4. Also numerous articles in *Wisconsin Archæologist*.

LAPHAM, I. A.—*Antiquities of Wisconsin* (Smith. Cont., Vol. VII, 1853).

MCKERN, W. C.—"The Neale and McClaughry Mound Groups," *Bulletin of the Public Museum of the City of Milwaukee*, Vol. III, No. 3 (1928).

PEET, S. D.—*Prehistoric America* (*The American Antiquarian*, 1892).

BIBLIOGRAPHIC SOURCES

Recommended sources of bibliography covering detailed American anthropology and archæology: *The American Antiquarian*, Vol. XV, under "Early Books which Treat of Mounds"; Winsor's *Narrative and Critical History of America*, Vol. I; and, particularly, the *Handbook of American Indians*, B.A.E., Bulletin 43, through references appended to alphabetical titles.

INDEX

Aboriginal Pottery of the Eastern United States, 109
Aboriginal Remains, 431
Aborigines of Minnesota, 288, 308
Academy of Natural Sciences of Philadelphia, 342
Adena culture in Ohio, 167-169, 254; characteristics, 169; in West Virginia, 239, 240, 243; in Indiana, 247-248
Adena Mound, 125, 167-169, 254
Agriculture, no modern science, 54; archæologists' method of studying, 55; products, 55-59; implements, 60-61; "garden beds," 61-62, 284-287, 306-307; Indians as agriculturists, 285, 385; development, 485
Alabama, 342, 390-408; Moundville culture, 390-403; Tombigbee River mounds, 403-404; other mounds, 406-408; urn-burial, 407-408
Alabama Anthropological Society, 96
Algonquian culture, 269-270; in New York, 276, 277; Ohio, 279; Michigan, 280-284; Iowa, 336-338; of outstanding interest, 336, 337-338; pottery, 338; Georgia, 442
Algonquian Indians, 269-270, 280, 477
Alligator Mound, 235-236, 265
Alphabet, Cherokee, 400
American Bottoms, 329, 344
American Museum of Natural History, 244
Amethyst, 403
Amulets, 147
Amusements, 182
Ancient Monuments of the Mississippi Valley, 22-24, 213, 342
Ancient Races of the Mississippi Valley, 348
Anthropomorphic figures. *See* Figures, Anthropomorphic.
Antiquities of the Southern Indians, 466
Antiquities of Wisconsin, 307

Antlers, 180, 205, 335, 439
Appalachian archæological district, 433
Arapaho Indians, 150, 159
Archæological History of New York State, 273
"Archæologists, Dean of American," 25-26
Archæology of Mississippi, 342, 384
Architecture, development, 36; primitive American, 37, 112; achievements of the Mound-builders, 37-39
Argillite, 68, 69, 73, 79
Arikara Indians, 315
Arkansas, mounds, 356, 357, 358-369; "Sunken Lands of St. Francis," 358-359; Crowley's Ridge, 359-360; Taylor Shanty, Miller, Webb, Thornton and Knapp Groups, 361-362; explorations of Moore, 364-369; Menard Mound, 369; Foster Place, 376-377
Armstrong, Thomas, 307
Arrowpoints, 207, 282, 304, 312, 326, 335, 338, 373, 377, 444, 458, 460, 467
Arrows, medicine, 150
Art, color in, 80-81, 84, 115-116; growth of interest in native, 106; significance, 109; value of study, 110-111; comprehensiveness of primitive art, 111; building arts, 112; sculpture, 112-113; plastic arts, 113-114; metallurgy, 114; textiles, 115; painting, 115-116; articles of adornment, 116-123; a criterion of culture, 123; conventional designs, 127; the "sun pattern," 377, 393-394. *See also* names of states.
Art of the Great Earthwork Builders of Ohio, 109
Artifacts, agricultural, 60-61, 76-81; ceremonial, 124, 147-151, 209, 297, 375, 488; Algonquians famous for, 337-338; unusual find in Florida, 461-462, from other states, 287, 297, 315, 322, 323, 328, 336, 355, 420,